WAKING THE TEMPESTS

ORDINARY LIFE IN THE NEW RUSSIA

Eleanor Randolph

Simon & Schuster

SIMON & SCHUSTER
Rockefeller Center
1230 Avenue of the Américas
New York, NY 10020

Manufactured in the United States of America

1   3   5   7   9   10   8   6   4   2

Library of Congress Cataloging-in-Publication Data
Randolph, Eleanor.
Waking the tempests : ordinary life in the new Russia / Eleanor
Randolph.
p.   cm.
Includes bibliographical references and index.
1. Russia (Federation)—Civilization.   2. Russia (Federation)—
Social life and customs.   3. Russia (Federation)—Social
conditions—1991–   4. Postcommunism—Russia (Federation)
5. Randolph, Eleanor—Journeys—Russia (Federation)   6. Russia
(Federation)—Description and travel.   I. Title.
DK510.762.R36   1996
947—dc20   96-144
CIP

ISBN 0-684-80912-5

To my parents
Marguerite and William Randolph

Contents

Prologue   11

1. Homes for Sale   21

2. Mother Russia   56

3. Health: Living in Soviet Ruins   107

4. Medicine: Do We Have a Future?   129

5. Alternative Medicine: From Herbs to Hocus-Pocus   165

6. Sex: Slaking the Oldest Thirst   185

7. A Stranger in the Family   215

8. Lessons for the Young   237

9. Suffering for Culture: A Ballerina   259

10. The Spiritual Bazaar   293

11. Murder: The People's Justice   331

12. The Wild East   358

Epilogue   385

Notes   391

Notes on Transliteration   411

Acknowledgments   413

Index   417

Waking the Tempests

Prologue

Oh, do not wake the sleeping tempests: beneath them
Chaos stirs.

—Fyodor Tyutchev (1803–73)[1]

T he road along the Moskva River was the long way home, but I chose it that icy November day to lift my spirits. Almost a year after the end of communism, Russia in 1992 was a society trying to create itself in midair, and freedom for many had the feel of abandonment. "We are so free we are allowed to fly even though we have no wings and no airplane," one Russian had complained to me several weeks earlier. The day's news was full of stories about people selling their government vouchers—their share of the new society—for three bottles of vodka and about suspiciously cheap meat that had been analyzed by the city's overworked inspectors. It was not cow, sheep, pig, or even pigeon going for a few cents a kilogram, the officials had announced, but dog.

That afternoon, as part of my job for *The Washington Post*, I had explored the maze of ragged kiosks across the street from Moscow's Kievsky train station. Looking for the ways that Russians were adapting to the free market, I had pushed my way through a seething crowd of small-time hucksters, the low-level speculators with their bulging plastic suitcases or feeble cardboard boxes or antiquated carts that creaked and groaned over the broken sidewalks. At a stall with frosted windows, I had seen meat that indeed looked rangy and old, but women in patched mittens and thick, woolen turbans were buying, often after sighing over expensive sausage in bright polyurethane wrappers from Denmark or Germany. The snow and mud around these small dens of commerce had created a grim new schoolyard for a cluster of street boys, urchins in blue jeans and Western sneakers who moved constantly in the cold, selling cigarettes or trading rubles at high rates for dollars. Their eyes darted from customer to customer then returned obediently to the swarthy men whose gaze was more like that of an owner than a boss. The secret transactions "on the left," as the black market had been known even a year earlier, had surfaced literally in the middle of the parks and sidewalks, and Russia's new capitalism was more like a massive street bazaar, a huge, continuous rummage sale where it seemed that any human need—from durable shoestrings to newborn children—could be satisfied for money. A few days earlier, a Russian friend had shown me an advertisement from a newspaper in Chelyabinsk as the latest example of how everything was for sale. It said: "If you've got a lot of money but don't have a child, the most important part of happy family life, we, a pair of students who are badly in need of money, suggest you exchange our nearly born child for a two- or three-bedroom apartment."[2]

Living in Russia after the end of communism was like watching an explosion in slow motion. A powerful vibrant people, controlled by tsars, then by communists, the Russians were suddenly coming unleashed in strange, exhilarating, and terrifying ways. One evening as I had been traveling this same route home, I heard a strange sound behind me on the Kutuzovsky bridge, and I turned just in time to see a young man riding a beautiful and spirited horse across the six-lane highway toward the Russian White House. As tiny cars braked and lights flashed, the dark horse and its maniacal rider galloped forward, and only when they passed one of the dim streetlights could I see that the man's head was thrown back in a joy made more exquisite by the dangerous machines screaming around him. Fool, I had thought at first. And then, I realized, why not? The idiot ecstasy of such moments only made sense in these times when everything was possible and nothing certain.

Inflation was drying up rubles like autumn leaves, and more than once I had seen aged pensioners blowing on their empty hands to illustrate how their wealth was scattering onto the ground. The few rich and the many poor were separating into two frantic societies. A small entrepreneurial class, mostly young men, old apparatchiki and new Russian *mafiya* thugs, competed for control of the untamed free market. Beneath them were the many others who were so poor and frightened that they had begun talking about drying bread, a fearsome complaint that meant the troubles were coming again, war, famine, another terror in the name of a greater good.

In grand and petty ways, Russia nourished my darkening mood that evening. The short route along the treacherous Garden Ring road would have had me near my doorway by now, despite the hazards of Russia's trucks, whose belching exhausts at high speeds left a bitter metallic taste in the mouth. The longer route would bring relief, I had hoped, giving me a moment to see the snow-covered cherry trees that lined the drive up to Moscow State University, to marvel at the huge wedding cake of a building created by Stalin as a monument to the rigid education system that was being dismantled week by week. But now, the traffic had slowed, making a long detour even longer. The workers had begun emerging from the roadside defense factory with its layers of leaking pipes along the sidewalks and its towering smokestacks that spewed unknown vapors freely into the atmosphere. I turned my head away from the factory, trying not to let its grim facade add to my depression, and as I did, Russia played its ancient trick.

Across the river was the sixteenth-century Novodevichy Convent, a cluster of sixteen onion domes set against a lake that still housed a small colony of swans. On most winter days, this serene place was lost under an ashen sky that sucked the color from the Russian landscape, the old pastel buildings, even children's faces. That evening, or at least for that moment, it was not gray and miserable, and instead I stared across the river at a spectacle that at first seemed impossible.

The Russian Orthodox crosses on top of the monastery's domes were lit, as if by firelight, and as I stared, wondering what kind of electrical power they were using to project so dramatically into the sky, I realized what was happening. The crosses had been placed so that, as the sun faded, they would catch the last rays of light, and these golden symbols were doing their ancient job that evening, adding a few precious moments of luster to this dark, depressing landscape.

When I saw them, I was so stunned by their beauty that I stopped the car and watched until the spires flickered into darkness. I was awed, not by their religious symbolism, which certainly would have sent a true believer into rapturous confirmation of his faith, but simply by the dramatic way Russia could remind a visitor not to rush into swift judgments about its people and culture. Here was beauty, ancient and durable, flawed, yes, but still a reminder of the deep foundation of Russian history and religion and society that made these present-day changes only one upheaval in many.

The day's theories began rapidly unraveling, and I started to wonder why I had been so despondent about these fierce and sturdy people. The Russians I knew had the power, above all, to survive. They were not mere victims, waiting quietly for starvation. Many were hustlers who could outmaneuver the best of them, operators like Oleg, who spent his draft time in the army absorbing (and in some cases borrowing) from the military's store of computers and electronics. His record player was made of pilfered truck parts and other contributions from the quartermaster's shop, and its triumph was not in the tone or timbre but in the fact that his odd-looking gizmo could actually produce anything approximating music at all. In the new Russia, Oleg's expertise was instantly in demand: he knew how to adapt modern computer technology to Russia's antiquated electrical systems, and by late 1992, he was not only a one-man computer consulting firm, he was a very rich man.

Around the country, there were thousands of young people who were already starting mini commodities markets, stock exchanges, businesses; they were skipping whole generations of business schools, absorbing financial concepts that outsiders thought would take decades for the Russian entrepreneur to digest, managing easily despite a childhood deprived of Monopoly and lemonade stands and junior achievement. With such Russians, how could the new country fail? As I drove the rest of the way home, I was full of enthusiasm and hope for this haphazard experiment.

I recall this evening now to give some idea of how it felt for an outsider trying to understand this wild and tumultuous era. For those of us who yearned for Russia to have some kind of democracy and fair market economy, there were swings from despair to optimism, from exhilaration to anxiety about how the Russians would cope with being thrust suddenly through the looking glass. A new decree from Yeltsin would bring hope; a notice that the press could not criticize the president would launch a shiver of distress. Word of a group of women butchers starting an uncommonly clean meatpacking operation brought a surge of optimism; news of Russian assets flooding into Swiss banks felt like desertion. It was an era when everything seemed possible in this oversize nation, even success, and it was a time when Russia's dark forces loitered along the edges, nurturing the new society's failures.

When I told a particularly wise friend, Olga Podolskaya, about my latest emotional pirouette, she had laughed quietly. "You are learning about our Russia," she had said. "The darkness around us enhances light; sadness makes better happiness. Good and bad—they depend on each other." Armed with such a power to endure and to find pain a necessary part of any progress, these people who had survived grinding communism could overcome this inhumane new capitalism. The dirt, the crime, the inequities, the confusion that we had begun to see in the early 1990s—they would all serve some durable part of the Russian soul that used suffering and disruption as tools for the better life. Moreover, the Russians had seen worse than this quiet revolution. Change, for all its problems, was better than war. Tumult was not so bad as mass starvation.[3] Or as Fyodor Poddubny, a dissident who was imprisoned in the 1970s, put it as he watched the beginning of the 1990s, "After you've faced a hurricane, a storm is no problem."[4]

I had come to Moscow during this period with my husband, Peter Pringle, who was the Moscow bureau chief of *The Independent* newspaper in London, and our five-year-old daughter, Victoria. My job for *The Washington Post* was to describe Russian *zhizn*, or life, to try to determine how ordinary Russians survived as their government, economy, and society changed virtually overnight. Instead of covering press conferences and the daily scramble over changes in laws and governments, I was able to spend hours, sometimes days, listening to people talk about their lives.

When we arrived one bright, cold afternoon in March 1991, Moscow was still a Soviet city where the government and many of its citizens viewed foreigners as potentially dangerous curiosities. We accepted the probability that some low-level KGB official was responsible for keeping us in view, and we believed our cars were followed, our phones tapped. People appeared suddenly to help us in ways that always seemed mysteriously opportune, undoubtedly both protecting us and spying on us at the same time. But we were also spared many of the hardships that we saw around us. We had access to foreign goods (which we paid for with foreign credit cards), and in a gesture that always made me feel both relief and shame, we were allowed on airplanes first to get seats ahead of the Soviet passengers. (Such Western advantages sometimes meant that the last Russian passengers had to stand in the aisles like subway commuters.) In an earlier time, we would have spent most of our energy trying to meet real Russians or see even a glimpse of the real Russia, but after Soviet leader Mikhail Gorbachev had begun his glasnost and perestroika reforms in 1985, the giant state had been steadily losing control, not only of its citizens but of its aliens from the West as well.

The real end of Soviet power came in August 1991, when the old guard made its last feeble effort to oust Gorbachev and the reformers. The putsch, it was called (or later the "good" putsch, to contrast with the disastrous conflict two years later that left at least 123 dead at the charred Russian White House).[5] Boris Yeltsin, who was still harvesting goodwill from his new title as the first democratically elected president of Russia, rallied the Russian people against the old guard and their tanks. Thousands came flooding into the streets with slogans and banners, defending the opening of their society and brazenly standing firm against the "coup plotters," as the then president George Bush liked to call them. When the old leaders backed away, some retreating to prison, others committing suicide, the U.S.S.R. was finished. The rest of the Soviet Union saw that the dreaded center could no longer hold, and independence movements, some of them still new and untested, suddenly flourished in Lithuania, Estonia, Georgia, Ukraine. The U.S.S.R. began splintering into smaller and smaller pieces, and on December 25, 1991, in a quiet, anticlimactic moment, Mikhail Gorbachev announced that the state created by Lenin, hardened into a terrorist nation by Stalin, and controlled by the Kremlin communist leaders for seventy years had formally disintegrated.

Russia seemed ready to join the twentieth century, ready to fulfill its vast possibilities as a free-market economy. What the world talked about was Russia's freedom, focusing on such events as Dzerzhinski's statue tumbling from its pedestal across from the KGB's headquarters or the Russian eagles replacing the red stars or the talk of market forces and free prices. What those of us who lived there saw was chaos.

Outside the government, change began slowly. Without instructions from above, people simply continued doing whatever they had been doing in the past. Then, one weekend in February 1992, I saw the first line of people selling goods that they had been storing for years in their apartments. "The gauntlet," some called it, because walking through the two rows of people, most of whom were standing all day in the snow, meant weathering the frightened looks from those who were selling their emergency supplies.

In earlier years, the smart Soviet customer routinely bought whatever was on the shelves—often two or three each of a set of tea glasses or toothpaste with real mint flavor. After they bought, they traded the extras, and along the walls of the Taganskaya metro near my apartment in 1991 were hundreds of typed notices of this elaborate barter economy. A family would list what they had on one side of the notice and what they needed on the other. ("Size 8 boots. I have three new pairs," said one of the signs I noted in early 1991. "I need a baby carriage, aspirin, and linoleum floor tiles.")

By the late winter of 1992, grandmothers and teenagers alike were on the streets unloading their inventory, evolving week by week into middle-men and -women, low-level *spekulyanty* (speculators) whose role in society had been illegal and immoral only a year earlier. For the old, there was despair and melancholy as they were forced into this degrading new marketplace where many sold plastic bags for a few cents a day. For many of the young, the opportunities seem to sprout from the muddy ground where they stood, and there was a rush of un-Russian optimism that selling cigarette packets on the streets would be a quick, easy route to owning a tobacco company.

While individuals I knew converted overnight to the new order, the giant enterprises—the farms, industries, institutes, and government agencies—all moved awkwardly in the upturned society. After years of pleasing one grumbling old customer in the Kremlin, they now had to compete in a world where they were three to four decades out of date.

Some closed; many lingered, waiting for help from Moscow. These anti-quated industries served for many as job placement centers; they remained officially open, allowing workers to come and go, drink tea, and pretend to produce while they looked for real jobs outside on the streets, in the new businesses, in their small apartments.

Some of the larger industries also adapted. Their directors took over the company, privatizing the assets, selling stock to bewildered employees, and making their first real decisions about what to produce and what to sell. The flexible had more chance of survival, and there were many stories of the ingenious ways that Russians made do. Space was at a premium, for example, but the quick found rooms. A number of private industries rented bomb shelters from Moscow's civil defense agency where they set up gyms and bars, garages and small stores. The rent was cheap, and the only hitch was that rental agreements included a clause that tenants must be prepared to move on six hours' notice.[6] As industries ran out of rubles, they began to pay in goods, which meant that an immediate class of traders had to appear to translate the goods into money. One of the most bizarre was in Arkhangel'sk, where the lumberjacks in the summer of 1993 were paid in cases of tampons.[7]

In this turmoil, the losers were those who could not grab assets or adapt quickly. Often they were the old and the very young, the sick and the slow. Women found an increasingly hostile workplace, especially if they had children. The cultured lost clout and state support. The intellectuals found that their poetry bought little in a scrabbling new marketplace. It was a grasping time, when delicate natures were shoved onto the sidelines, and the survivors were the ones who grabbed at the possibilities, as though this period was not so much an evolution toward a new order as a short feast, a brief interim when gluttony and greed would be allowed. Some of those who stripped the people's resources for themselves were the old apparatchiki, the old communist guard whose hands were closest to the state's treasures. Others were simply mobsters who gained clout and control in man's most brutal ways. And many were young, bright, well-educated Soviets who were energetic enough to ride the untamed market animal that suddenly ap-peared before them.

Many Russians tried to explain how they felt when their economy and society turned from communism into capitalism, virtually overnight. "We are living in Absurdistan," one writer decided as he looked around the globe for a comparison.[8] Another young Russian told us that he was trying to have his brain reprogrammed to switch all notions of good and evil. The jokes about stagnation in the 1970s and early 1980s now turned to the unpredictable 1990s. One recurring favorite: Gorbachev brought us to the abyss. After that, we took a step forward.

Like their forebears earlier in the century who were caught in the Bolshevik Revolution of 1917, the Russians we met had grown up mastering a code for survival that was instantly out of date. The difference in the 1990s was that instead of learning a new set of rules, there were no rules. For the first time, Russians had no leader, no authority to tell them what to do. When communism was declared dead, the new capitalism was not ready to take over, and the word on the streets for what was happening was chaos. Pronounced with a guttural *h* like *hah-os,* it sounded in Russian like a curse, as if people were whispering about some secret plague that had invaded their land.

As the Soviet grip loosened and then gave way, the increasing turmoil meant that Russians suddenly welcomed foreigners, hoping we would serve as guides to this new *diky kapitalizm,* or wild capitalism, that had invaded their society and their economy. But in some ways, the place that had once been the Soviet Union was now foreign territory to all of us—Americans, Germans, Australians, and Russians alike. The confusion created a rare time when people felt free to talk recklessly to outsiders, not to fill the air with words as some had learned to do artfully in the Soviet years, but to tell about their lives, their fears, and their feelings. In earlier times, such conversations could be difficult and dangerous, especially to anyone caught with an American journalist, and by 1995, many Russians were asking again for anonymity, fearing retaliation from the *mafiya* or some government official who had suddenly decided to enforce one of the country's many feeble laws. The early 1990s provided an opportunity for the outside world to peer into a closed society and watch the many shades of Russian character—its spiritual and its profane, its criminal and its bravely honest, its strange and its ordinary.

Although I lived in Moscow and many of those who are described here were Muscovites, the new freedoms also allowed correspondents to travel in an unsupervised way that would have been impossible only a few years earlier. As a result, I could see a hospital in Khabarovsk and talk to young people in Arkhangel'sk near the Arctic Circle. I was free to spend time not only in the cities, but in the countryside, and when I wanted to see a midsized town that had been virtually untouched by the West, I visited Chapayevsk, where the school principal asked my colleague Kathy Lally of the *Baltimore Sun* and me to talk to their high school civics class in late 1992. He introduced us as "former enemies," and for these young people, we were the first Americans they had talked with in their lives. (The young children in the school—who were still wearing their red star pins with their photos of baby Lenin—stared and giggled, as if we had come from another solar system.)

What I have seen and tried to document on a personal level was the way many Russians coped with freedom. These are small sketches compared to the great complications of this enormous country, with its eleven time zones and its 148 million people. But perhaps they provide one of the few ways to gauge the enormity of what happened in Russia in the last few years—by looking at the life rather than analyzing the system. For most of us, such massive change is impossible to understand abstractly; we must circle it, examining bits and pieces so that we can digest it more easily, by studying the parts and allowing greater minds to analyze the whole.

To put it more directly, this is not the work of a scholar or a historian. In each field, I have consulted experts, but I do not approach medicine, ballet, religion, law, or the other areas of life described here as an authority. I am a journalist, an observer who was fortunate enough to be in an extraordinary country at an extraordinary time.

1

Homes for Sale

If you have it, you can keep it. If you don't have it, you'll never get it.
—Proverb, Brezhnev era

Everything's for sale, even what isn't yours.
—Proverb, Yeltsin era

Every day in the winter of 1991, more cracks appeared—not only in the Soviet government and in its obedient society but also in the streets and windows, in walls and buildings and bridges. Communism was disintegrating and the country was disintegrating, and people seemed to be falling into a black hole, trying to latch on to whatever edges of capitalism the Soviet Union's last days would allow. On one particular spring day, when a group of energetic young deputies at the Kremlin were trying to make the free market sound like a commercial paradise where everyone would wear a business suit and use a car phone, I saw my first homeless person in Moscow. A large woman with frightened eyes, she had assembled her cardboard shanty on a tiny triangle of land near Moscow's Taganka Square.

By the end of 1992, the *bezdomniye,* or homeless, had arrived in the cities—as if the worst of Western individualism had made it to Russia long

before the benefits of the new capitalist experiment. One summer afternoon, I saw a small boy crawl out of a bush near Moscow's Kievsky train
station. He was completely naked and covered with dirt. His mother,
equally dirty but wearing a tattered dress, hurried over to shoo him back
into the bush, which I could see had been turned into a makeshift home.
A few weeks before the parliamentary elections of December 1993,
supporters of Boris Yeltsin sent word that on cold nights, homeless people
would no longer be allowed to roam the streets but would be swept up
and locked in shelters. On the first cold night of November, a cluster of
shivering, hungry people stood outside the shelter door, waiting to be
"arrested."[1]

Such sights were troubling enough to me, but I had seen them in New
York and other Western cities. To ordinary Russians, these *nishchiye* or
beggars—were a new source of pain and embarrassment. The first homeless Russians of the 1990s served as a stark reminder that the Soviet state,
for all its obvious flaws, had not allowed Russians to freeze to death, as they
had earlier this century outside the tsars' Winter Palace. Some of the
Soviet homes—the *obshchezhitiya* (dormitories), or even the communal
apartments—were inhumane places, where people lived like hamsters,
sometimes five families to a bathroom, twenty to a toilet. When the state
was handing out living quarters, apartments were bought with clout,
barter, and bribes, but almost everybody had something.

With the new Russia came a new system. In its simplest form, people
were allowed to own, or "privatize," what they already had—to keep it,
lease it, or sell it. The apartment was a Russian's major asset, and almost
overnight a swarm of mostly young men appeared in the cities to deal with
the new markets for *nedvizhimost,* which the dictionary translates as "immovable property," including houses. Real estate had come to Russia.

From outside the stained cement-block building on Prospect Mira , it was
hard to imagine that somewhere inside was one of Moscow's most dynamic
new corporations. The door was hanging on one hinge, the walkway
littered with twisted cigarette packets and curling bits of metal. Lights
along the stairs, in Soviet fashion, had long ago been stolen or destroyed,
and in the late November afternoon in 1993, it was so dark that my friend
Natalia Alexandrova and I had to slide our feet over the steps like blind

people. We bumped toward the light and a polished brass sign bearing the name of Transtrade Trading House, a company that trafficked in some of Russia's richest commodities, including houses. As we arrived, blinking into the well-lit waiting room, a young woman rushed out, took our business cards, and quickly escorted us to the real estate department.

Transtrade's real estate section was confined to a large spare room furnished with three metal desks, a rickety-looking cupboard, and a set of Soviet telephones like one I accidentally dropped a few months earlier, rendering it into a mound of bolts, wires, and shards of thin black plastic. Three young men were sitting against the lime-colored walls of the room, and if they were riding a building boom to new riches, they hid it well. I had been told that in Moscow's elegant new restaurants and casinos, these same brokers had been seen in expensive suits and gleaming European shoes. On that day, any wealth was camouflaged behind lumpy Soviet clothes and the flat gray boots that had been the standard uniform of millions of Russian workers for decades.

Almost as soon as we sat in our thin metal chairs, Andrei Zastavenko, the lawyer in the group, began his pitch. A boyish-looking man who frowned and glowered, trying to look more authoritative than his twenty-nine years, Andrei said his job was to focus on the convolutions in Russian property law. As we talked, he would occasionally lecture us about his role in the new-market experiment, often sounding more like an old party apparatchik trumpeting the gains of the people than a fledgling real estate broker creating rules and instant new-market maxims as he went along.

"Real estate is not only in the United States," he began, stretching his long legs before him in the manner of one who would not quickly tire of sitting. "Russia used to be developed too. Russian landowners lived on estates. Now there is again a possibility, a chance to build. It really started earlier, in Gorbachev's time. We have been here two years. In 1991, the number of European-style houses—you could count on your fingers. Now they number in the hundreds or more. Active construction is going on around the city—although of course now in winter it is stopped because of the weather."

Andrei, even in his Soviet disguise, was a man of the new Russia, and he was like thousands, maybe millions, of young people who suddenly realized the power of artful hokum. He was a Russian version of the American drummer earlier this century, the snake-oil salesmen in the wild West. There were no manuals to tell them what to do, so the smart ones like Andrei created an elaborate, enticing artifice that they then sold for bank transfers, goods, and even cash. It was a skill as old as human society, and in spite of years of propaganda about the evils of salesmanship, the selling gene had resurfaced in Russia with a wild vengeance in the likes of Andrei.

In this case, the item up for sale was a *kottedzh,* or cottage, and when Andrei began talking about communities of new cottages around Moscow, it sounded like suburbia, the first Russian Levittown. The hope, of course, was that this new economy would revive a Russian middle class, one of the primary needs for any future democracy. I was dreaming of such a place, some minuscule percentage of the great space of Russia carved into little rectangles with houses, backyards, barbecues, and individual garden plots, when Andrei reached up to a cabinet and brought down a model to illustrate his point. If this was a cottage, it was made for Marie Antoinette. The model, if built to size, looked as though it would be a large brick house with reddish shingles on the roof, fortresslike windows, and a kind of tower at one corner. The house would have been around seven thousand square feet, complete with a small swimming pool at a subterranean level that was not yet called a basement. The house also had a two-car garage, clearly a necessity in the new Russian suburb. Natalia and I stared at the little jewel of a model, as out of reach for all but a handful of Russians as a spread of well-cut diamonds from Yakutsk.

"How much?" I pointed to the miniature as we turned it to peer inside the tower like children.

"Three hundred thousand dollars," said Andrei.

"Dollars?" I said, the model freezing in midair.

He smiled. "Of course."

Asking $300,000 for a house would not be astonishing in a Western city the size of Moscow, but at this point in Russia's climb to world-level prices, salaries for most people were low, and bank mortgages were still a distant fantasy. The full price would be paid before the house was completed. More startling was that Transtrade's clients had to pay a fee to these agents of 2 to 20 percent before the first stake was hammered into the ground. The average wage was about $53 a month; inflation had turned most savings accounts into dust; and the society was dividing into two dangerous layers—a few new rich who could afford such luxuries and the many poor.

"They have got enough money, most people who buy this, and the source of the money is not questioned," Andrei continued, anticipating the next question.

"Who exactly are they?" I pressed, guessing that the answer would be nebulous. After some whispered consultation with another member of the group, who never spoke to me and did not give his name, Andrei continued. "There is a new class of Russian businessman," he said. It was indeed vague, but we all knew who they were. These were the entrepreneurs, or *spekulyanty*, who had suddenly become dollar millionaires, often in a few months, usually by selling the leftovers of the old empire to the West or trading Western castoffs here in Russia. They undoubtedly bribed officials or paid off the *mafiya* along the way. Or maybe they were the officials. Or the *mafiya*.

"Others were already part of the power culture," Andrei said, meaning the old apparatchiki who ran the government, the party, the institutes and industries. "Those who possess the possibilities to sell state resources at exorbitant prices," he added pointedly. Russia was for sale, and anyone who could claim control over an asset could try to sell it. From icons to oil, timber, and antiques, the laws were weak and contradictory; the officials who enforced them could be bought. And the nation's leaders were bureaucratic layers away from the workaday world where newly formed businessmen and -women were often forced to carry out their infant profession with a certain degree of banditry—a Russian-style corruption that was conducted under a blanket of legal-looking documents.

"They pay in cash, bank transfers, currency transfers, hard currency, and even rubles," broke in Amiran Kobakhidze, a dark and handsome Georgian who was the department manager at age twenty-eight. "Anything for us is acceptable. We can convert any currency."

Out of curiosity I wanted to know what $300,000 in cash looked like. Amiran laughed and made a shape with his hands about the size of a child's lunchbox. "If you use thousand-dollar bills, three hundred is not so bulky," he explained. If you used rubles, however, it would take a wheelbarrow. The ruble that day was about twelve hundred to $1. Using ten-thousand-ruble notes (which were not that easy to find) would still take thirty-six thousand pieces of paper.

"Cash is usually the rare case." Amiran corrected my imaginary transaction. "In fact, the sums usually come in transfers. About half of the customers use a combined method, with some rubles."

Banks would not give credit for a whole year. For six months, Amiran estimated, most banks asked for 240 percent interest. "That adds substantially to the price," he noted, laughing quietly. Amiran was the kind of person that most Western companies yearn to have on their middle-management sales team. He appeared candid and funny, and his easy manner gave off the air that simply by meeting him you had entered some elite club of cognoscenti, in this case a group whose superiority came from knowing the arcane secrets of the Russian land and banking market.

"High interest rates." He shrugged and smiled, ready to pronounce another insider's truth: "But on the other hand, if you deposit money now, you can get one hundred sixty percent after three months.

"Money is very hot in Russia now," said Amiran, smiling. "It is possible to invest and get a lot of income very quickly."

By the spring of Russia's second year away from the Soviet family, the cities had sprouted banks. Every corner had something called an income bank, and their operations were so complicated and erratic that only a few could keep pace with what was happening as money flooded in and out of these places. Muscovites told stories of investing $1,000 in a bank and getting it back with 40 percent interest in one month. Others admitted handing a bank a packet of dollars one month and coming back to find an empty building the next. People whispered about ways to make money like novice gamblers trying to pick the right horse at the track. The free-for-all that made banks an insecure place for money also made the business safe for a new, rough breed of criminals, and during 1993, thirty leading bankers were killed in Moscow. Money was transferred from one institution to another through an army of bodyguards carrying Uzis and Kalashnikov rifles. At a money exchange near where I stayed in Moscow in 1995, a hand-lettered sign on the door said GUNS, DAGGERS, GAS PISTOLS in big letters. Underneath, where I expected to read "prohibited," it said in smaller letters, "must be registered with security." "Security" was a bored young man standing inside the door and lazily fingering a twelve-gauge shotgun. Money was indeed very hot in Russia.

The free-market economy was also free in a way that Americans had not seen since the days of unregulated capitalism in the last century. Russia in the 1990s was witnessing its own corporate fat cats beginning to carve up the national loot. I suggested this theory months later to an American executive doing business in Russia, and he nodded. "Russia today is America in the 1880s." Then he added, "plus nuclear weapons."

The real estate business was still so raw in Russia that it was hard to imagine anyone brave enough to hand over so much money to these young men. When I asked how they worked, Andrei and Amiran said their entire operation was built on trust. Most of that trust, it appeared, came from the buyer, who paid 30–50 percent of the cost on signing the contract.

By the time it was constructed, the home was paid for, Andrei said. The real estate broker's fee of 2 percent to 20 percent was charged, apparently, from whoever would pay. This particular part of their business was a long and elaborate process that undoubtedly tested the bargaining skills of buyer, seller, and agent. Usually it was the buyer who paid most of the fee, but sometimes the seller paid as well. Most settled on 4 percent to 5 percent, he said. Translated, that meant $12,000 to $15,000 per deal—not a bad cut in the West. In Russia, it was better than a year's salary for most top government officials.

If the buyer paid some of the fee and the seller some, which one did the brokers represent? I asked. Amiran and Andrei consulted quietly, deciding again that there was no harm in telling the truth.

"We represent them both," said Amiran.

"We take both hands together," said Andrei, mimicking two hands not wanting to meet and then, finally, being forced together with a tug.

Amiran laughed. "We try not to leave them [the buyer and the seller] to themselves, because they always get into an argument. What we do always takes translating from Russian into Russian."

As we talked about the problems peculiar to Russian real estate, it became clear that these two were not interested in expanding their business beyond the rich. Was it possible that these houses would be for more than one family? Duplexes, I was thinking, something for the still-unformed middle class.

Andrei sniffed at the idea. "Communal living—we've had enough of that."

What about other, less expensive houses?

Andrei shook his head; he saw where I was going. "Polarization is very severe, and we do not see these people here in this office. Our prices grow too quickly . . . the prestige places have already grown fourteen times what they were two years ago," he said, launching what sounded like another lecture. Then he stopped and answered more directly.

"No," he concluded, "in Russia, we do not see a formation of the middle class."

As we made our way out of this place, Natalia and I reacted almost involuntarily as perfect representatives of our different societies. As an American, I saw these brokers as part of a necessary but still forming trade. Customers, however, would eventually demand that they represent seller or buyer, not both. Fees would become stable, and the whole concept of private property, if it were encouraged by the government, could restore pride in the nation's land and property, I imagined. Swamp peddlers were not such a distant part of the American real estate business, and perhaps it would not be long before Russian matrons, like the socialites in today's America, would be describing themselves proudly as Realtors—capitalize the *R*, please.

Natalia, educated since childhood to believe that such people were unproductive parasites, had shuddered as the Transtrade door shut behind us. She had been trying to shake off a residual horror about people who did not work, in the traditional sense, people who made money by being in the middle. These were the types that had been the easy villains of communism, and suddenly they were thriving in the very society that had mocked them for years. Natalia had been to the West and knew many Westerners, but the echoes of her childhood would never quite leave her, and in the case of the Transtraders, she was perhaps more correct in her assessment than I was. We laughed at my tolerance and her upbringing, and later I heard her deliver the fatal blow on the new Russian realtor: "If they make so much money," she giggled to a group of us that evening, "then why don't they wash their hair?"

A few days later, Natalia and I drove out of Moscow to look for one of the houses being built by Transtrade. We bumped along roads best negotiated in a Land Rover, past a barking dog whose energetic warnings roused no one, and into something that looked like a suburban tract being built along the bank of the snow-covered Pakhra River. At one end of the road was a replica of the model from Transtrade—this one frozen at three-quarters completion for the rest of the winter. In real life, it was about the size of a standard American three-bedroom, two-story duplex. The tower looked strangely small and unnecessary, and the bricks were a yellowish beige that did not seem to be the shade we remembered from the model.

We walked around to the back of the structure, where we found part of the roof resting under a bank of snow. It was a huge triangle of reddish metal, molded into the shape of roofing tiles. For $300,000, were these people getting real roofing tiles or a metal replica? What about the bricks? The structure? As I stood staring at somebody's future home, I remembered what the Transtrade people had said about their guarantee. "We have a standard reference paragraph," Andrei had said. "We are responsible [for the construction of the house] for one year." A year seemed a safe bet for Transtrade. Barely.

Overnight, it seemed, Russians had remembered the concept of private property, and by the time President Yeltsin said, in October 1992, that "we need millions of property owners," it had already begun to happen. The Yeltsin government gave each citizen a voucher worth 10,000 rubles (about $50) in 1992 as their share of Russia's wealth. By the time the system had ended officially in June 1994, the voucher's value was about 40,800 rubles (less than $20), and an estimated 80 percent of those eligible had used them. Some bought stock in companies with their government vouchers, pooling the family allotment to make a larger purchase; others sold their share of Russia for a pair of new winter boots.

Apartment dwellers also became apartment owners—slowly in 1992 and in a rush by 1993 as residents stood in long lines and endured difficult bureaucratic challenges to get the necessary documents. By the end of 1994, about 10,923,000 apartments had been privatized under this system.[2] Like most other Americans, I had come to believe that private ownership could be the key to restoring some of Russia's old beauty. By that, I did not mean that the country should be returned to the rich landlords who had dominated the countryside before the Russian Revolution earlier this century. What would work, I believed, was for ordinary individuals to control a plot of land, their own apartment, their own country house—to own it and therefore take care of it. I felt this every day when I walked into our apartment near Taganka Square, where we stayed during the last year of Soviet rule.

In the winter of 1991, Moscow was like a huge dirty beast, and the apartment complex where I lived with my husband and daughter was one of its shabby, unnurtured offspring. The towering wall of flats, constructed above a cavernous and often empty Soviet grocery store, curved around a communal space that was shared more or less equally by a children's playground and a mountainous garbage dump. The wooden swings and tiny cottages that had looked storybook quaint in photos sent in advance of our arrival turned out to be treacherous things, full of splinters and shards of glass. Broken vodka bottles littered the sandbox, and in spite of old women with their twig besoms who cleaned twice a day, the wind scattered garbage into the small plot for the children of over one hundred families.

In my first months there, I never saw an ordinary person pick up a piece of trash, never saw any mother or grandmother lean down to clear away the glass. They warned their children about debris, but they did nothing to get rid of it. I had asked Yuri Sigov, a writer for *Argumenty i Fakty* magazine, why our little park was so dirty, and he had laughed at me. "What's mine is mine. What's yours is yours, and what's ours is nobody's," he had said, giving me one of the favorite saws of street communism.

The communal society, after seven decades, had wiped out the community spirit. Although their apartments were often tidy and organized, people were wary of cleaning up the apartment hallways, fixing up a shared playground, doing anything that made their shared space, as Westerners called such areas, better than the others. Equal had come to mean equally shabby, and the Western experts in those days were saying that it would take a generation before Russia could regain any sense of pride in workmanship and community.

The first time I felt these experts were wrong was in May of 1991, when our family went to Zelenogradskaya, where my husband had rented a dacha, one of the small country houses that surrounded most Russian cities and places that were far more like cottages than a Transtrade *kottedzh*. At the time, such rentals were technically against Soviet laws that made it illegal for a Russian to earn foreign money, and our weekend retreats outside our compound were deemed not only adventurous but downright stupid by some of our Western colleagues. (A few months later, with a shift in government, many Westerners began searching frantically for weekend dachas to rent from dollar-hungry Muscovites.)

Zelenogradskaya was a tiny community only an hour outside Moscow, but when our gray Volvo first lumbered through the streets—past the ragged children's home and a decaying apartment building—the Russians stared at us silently, wary of the first aliens they had seen in their community in years, perhaps decades.

As we drove from the town to the dacha area, we were stopped at train tracks behind a puffing Lada, its five seats filled with large adults, spindly children, sacks, cartons, garden equipment, and a small cat weaving through the smoky interior. Outside stood the guardian of the railroad crossing, and to see her was to know that her mission was as vital as that of any mere deputy of the congress. She marched to her post, swinging her club vigorously to let us know that any transgression meant certain disfigurement or, perhaps worse, her disapproval. A small, spidery woman, she worked a lever that brought the heavy wooden arms over the road protectively, and we sat fifteen minutes wondering whether there was a train coming or whether this woman, knowing we were foreigners whose presence was still officially forbidden, was at that moment calling the KGB. As we chattered quietly about the possibilities, a train whizzed past with maybe twenty passenger cars—ranging from overloaded with five faces to a window in the "hard car," to luxurious and virtually empty in the "soft car." The destination announced on the side of the cars was Arkhangel'sk on the Arctic Circle, a place that was virtually off-limits to foreigners. (A year later we would be on that same train, speeding on our way north to see the white nights of summer, and we would mark our passing of

Zelenogradskaya by peering out the window and waving vigorously at the cars and the tiny speck of a crossing guard.)

With the train gone and silence returned, the Russians restarted their engines, and the gate mistress proudly returned to the wooden arms, lifting each one with obvious effort and allowing the cars to bounce over the old tracks. As we crossed the railroad tracks, past the gatekeeper, who peered into our car sternly, we moved from the tattered remains of the Soviet empire into a small Russian wonderland.

Set in an intricate network of dirt roads was a dacha community built for members of the Academy of Sciences of the U.S.S.R., and it was much like other clusters of country houses for state-approved writers, artists, ballet and opera stars, scientists, teachers, and politicians. These wooden houses were attached to garden plots that Russian citizens had cultivated as their own, some of them remaining in the same families for several decades.

There was a pecking order to the dacha that may have been beyond a Westerner's comprehension, but for many Russians it was as clear as military rank. Some dachas were as small as a shed, large enough only for a cot and the tools to work the garden plot that surrounded it. Others were little cottages, Hansel-and-Gretel structures that were divided into sleeping chambers and a living area—the washing and outhouses at least thirty feet away. The communities of Peredelkino and Nikolina Gora outside Moscow were for the privileged, where each home was at least the size of an average American three-bedroom house with top-of-the-line Soviet luxuries— electricity and plumbing. A year later we would rent a dacha constructed and given to a Nobel Prize–winning scientist, Nikolai Nikolayevich Semenov, and even though it was modest by Western standards, it was a Soviet showplace. It had a second floor, an indoor toilet, and an outdoor *banya*, or bathhouse.

The village of Zelenogradskaya was for the upper-middle-level scientists, and as we turned down a bumpy road that first day, the rows of Russian country houses looked as if they had been built by architects whose heads were filled with old fairy tales. Baba Yaga, Russia's wicked witch, could have perched contentedly on the intricately carved eaves. The colors were from Russian legends, it seemed—the bright blue of a prince's secret cloak, the dark greens of a magical forest, the blood reds of a firebird.

As enchanting as these colors were, however, what stunned those of us who had come from Moscow was the care being taken of these gardens and homes. The earth had been turned in meticulous rows, and people were painting their windows, not with the moplike brushes used by Moscow's painters (who were called daubers) but carefully, like artisans turning a sill or a fence into a lovely summer treasure. (A year later I saw one of the most original of these dacha art houses. This cottage, a strong robin's-egg blue, was in a large garden full of raspberry bushes and cherry trees, and it was owned by the family of a Soviet artist, whose talented offspring had covered the walls around the house with sprays of hand-painted summer daisies. As we left Moscow in 1993, I asked the daughter about the daisies and she shook her head as if I had just mentioned the dead. The family had torn down the old dacha to build a "real house" out of cement block.)

We drove along the dirt roads that day, gawking at the fresh new gardens and the hand-hewn water towers in the same manner that the people from the railroad crossing had stared at us moments before. Weaving through Lenin's Way, down Akademicheskaya Lane, we arrived at number 8. As the owner of this dacha opened the gate, we stood silently in the first blades of spring grass and surveyed the compound. To someone fresh off a Western plane, it may have looked like a part of Appalachia, but to those of us who knew, it was an estate, a reward for a family that had contributed extensively to the Soviet empire as some of its top physicists, geologists, and teachers.

The main house, which had electricity but no running water, was a wooden structure held up by cement blocks and sheer Russian willpower. There were three bedrooms, a living room, a kitchen, and two lovely porches that drooped slightly away from the front and side doorways. The bedrooms were lined with books and "thick journals," the magazines of the Soviet intellectuals, and a stove in the central living room was covered with paintings of flowers and folk dancers. The front porch was made of glass panels, some of them chipped or broken, and the steps leading out into a garden that was once a glorious spread of perennials were slippery with rot.

Water came from a well next door and had to be boiled, even to wash the dishes. An outhouse made nightly excursions treacherous, and when our landlord decided to build us a shower, it was an outdoor unit, a hodgepodge of wood and tile that was scavenged from stores, underground markets, and friends. A thin plastic sheet had been adapted as a shower curtain, and the rainwater was drawn from a misshapen water tank overhead. Most disturbing was the hot water system. An electric extension cord traveled from a small dacha at the back of the compound and was attached to a large version of the curled water boilers that many travelers take with them to make tea. The bather, gambling that the joy of a hot shower would not end in electrocution, usually withstood the operation for only a few harrowing minutes.

Still, our dacha gave us an opportunity to see how Russians could live a good life—a pleasant existence that could not be imagined from inside the foreigners' compounds, where we were kept during the week. We shared our dacha with the owner's daughter, whose name was Marina, and her six-year-old daughter, Masha. Marina, a thin woman with a face that appeared to be settling early into a permanent look of sadness, taught me about the hardship of Soviet life in the 1980s and early 1990s and how a Russian woman had to be, first and foremost, a magician. An artist who found work restoring icons, Marina was an ingenious cook—she could make oatmeal, the only certain foodstuff in 1991, into a small gourmet feast. Her father brought her milk one afternoon later that summer, and when she opened the four cartons, they were all sour. Without a sigh or sign of distress, Marina lit the stove, poured the milk into a huge pot, and made a delicious soft cheese, which we ate with bread, fresh dill, and cucumbers.

Nothing was thrown away, and we learned to rinse out our plastic bags and hang them on the line for a second or third use. (Our trash in Moscow, leftovers from the exotic imports that we could buy at Westerners' groceries, was alluring to kids and later to the homeless, who foraged through the metal Dumpster bins in Western compounds, racing to get there before someone, possibly the cleaning women, set the trash on fire. Youngsters rooted through the debris for colorful boxes that still held the intoxicating smell of chocolates and empty beer cans that could be sold to Russian collectors in the markets. Later, in 1993, old people could be seen rummaging more urgently for leftovers in yogurt packets or sour fruit juices, and I once found a woman going through garbage that I had left temporarily outside my apartment door. She looked at me in embarrassment, then shrugged and continued foraging in the black plastic sack. Yearning to help her, I couldn't figure out how to do it. I quietly shut the door and left her in peace.)

The first of two summers in Zelenogradskaya, we tried a garden. It was erratic but satisfying, and the owner came in to help us one sunny weekend, planting potatoes for us and then sharing our lunch of bread, wine, sausage, and cucumbers in the sun to celebrate our communal efforts. Each weekend we stopped at the roadside stands that sold seeds rolled into a triangle of newspaper or plants grown in tin cans or waxed cardboard milk cartons. What we planted never fared as well as the perennials—the lupines, calla lilies, roses, phlox, and columbines that came up automatically each week in memory of the owner's parents, who had planted them years earlier in the rich, spongy lawn.

At the end of the season, we went back to get our harvest, and as we drove onto the dacha grounds that day, past grasses that were as high as the door handles of the car, my husband gasped when he saw the garden. In strategic spots, there were holes: our potato plants had been stolen. It was a stark reminder that for Westerners, watching the vegetables grow was a hobby. Our neighbors, who spent good days hoeing and carrying water from the community well, were not puttering in their country gardens; they were preparing for winter. Their dachas had grounds that looked like something in an American seed catalogue. Every mound of dirt was treasured. The beans curled upward on elaborate string trellises, the squash trailed along the pathways. Potatoes, carrots, and root vegetables were kept in rows (and guarded day and night). Each day's ripened tomatoes were carefully carried inside. Raspberry bushes lined the fences, and herbs, like dill and cilantro grew in pots and spare corners around the yard.

One particular garden a few hundred yards from us was so enticing that we stood peeking through the fence one afternoon on our way to visit a neighbor's goats. As we stared, an old woman stepped out of her house and stood, her face threatening us to not even salivate over her spread of vegetables. "Hello," we said in our strange Russian. She nodded. That was all. We were outsiders, and any hopes of being invited in for tea were quickly forgotten. Her house, like others in that area, was on sacred ground: it had been in her family for almost sixty years. This was as close as any Russian came before the end of the Soviet state to true ownership, and these homes were treated not merely with respect but with reverence.

The dacha community at Zelenogradskaya and places like it I would later see all over Russia would stand as small but exquisite refutations of experts who said Russians were not ready for private property.

In some ways, the most revolutionary of all the reforms of the post-Soviet era would be the shift of property from the state to commercial or individual control.

It was not merely a dry process of governmental decrees and bureaucratic documents. These transactions brought forth an emotional upheaval for buyer and seller alike, and they often went against all the moral codes ingrained during a Soviet childhood—that property could not be owned by an individual and that it could not be sold for profit. Earlier in the century, such ventures could easily attract revenge from the neighbors. A private farm would suddenly go up in flames, as surrounding peasants "let the red rooster fly," the old Russian term for torching one's betters. A tamer version of the same tendency had reappeared in the 1990s. One Russian woman I knew found that after she purchased her apartment in the outskirts of Moscow, her mailbox was routinely turned into a tiny stove, with letters from friends and family often nothing more than a pile of cinders by the time she got home from work. Her newspaper was routinely stolen, and once, when she caught an old man tucking it under his arm, she demanded that he hand it over. "What?" he asked in a voice heavy with indignation about her good fortune. "You have your own apartment and you want your own newspaper as well?"

The sales and transfers of apartments, dachas, and homes were part of the revolution, and these transactions were ahead of the law, which was slow and confused, as lawmakers fought among themselves in various political arenas. "You have to look at legal questions in Russia on two levels. One is the formal doctrine; second is the actual practice," Alex Papachristou, an American attorney well known for interpreting Russian property law for Westerners, explained in early 1994. After seventy-four years of communism and centuries of tsars, the law was always viewed as negotiable, something to push against until the authorities pushed back.

By late 1993, Yeltsin had issued a decree saying land could be privately owned, at least by Russians, and the constitution, approved in December 1993, had reaffirmed this right in principle. But the concept of private property was still in dispute as late as 1995 when the current prime minister Viktor Chernomyrdin was pushing for legislation and a national referendum on the issue while the powerful communist and agrarian parties were predicting catastrophe if the nation's land could be as easily bought and sold as everything else in the Russian marketplace. Ownership, or *sobstvennost*, was still a shaky legal concept, and by the mid-1990s Russian property owners still faced layers of law and reality that seldom seemed to intersect.

Before the Soviet Union disintegrated, of course, the law had been far simpler. The state owned the nation; the government was the landlord. Apartment dwellers received their papers from the local government, never an easy or uncomplicated process, and these documents could determine who lived in the apartment and who could remain in it once a couple divorced or the official tenant died. Over the last thirty years, the cooperative had also become an acceptable method of inhabiting an apartment, even though any transfer required not only approval of the local bureaucrats but also the co-op itself.

The government's authoritarian grip on property loosened somewhat in the countryside where dachas—country homes or plots of land sometimes given as rewards for service—remained in some families for decades. But the nation's rich farmland, minus a small percentage of acreage allotted to individuals, was controlled by the people's bureaucrats.

In the cities, the lease arrangement in apartments had made it almost impossible to move. Moving meant swapping apartments, and such transactions were arcane and elaborate events that would try the patience of anyone except the peculiar Soviet house hunter who had time, patience, and the desperate yearning for a new apartment. Two small flats for a larger one was a normal exchange, but Papachristou recalled a couple who spent a year organizing a swap that involved thirteen different trades in order to get the apartment they wanted, a spacious cluster of rooms across the river from Gorky Park.

"These were highly successful professionals who anywhere else in the world would have been able to buy such an apartment for themselves," he said, "and it almost broke down at the end because one of the people was in the hospital, and in fact, they had to bribe the notary to go to the hospital and everybody else too, to sign all the papers at the bedside."

Although money sometimes helped grease these complicated transactions, money alone would not work. Real estate was not a commodity that could be turned into cash, and people would hoard apartments, just as they stored everything else for the emergency that always seems imminent in Russian life. If two apartment owners married, they would live in one and rent the other. (By the early 1990s, however, renting was risky: the renter might prefer the apartment to the friendship and refuse to leave. "I heard countless stories of people with empty apartments simply waiting for the right to sell them or the chance to lease them, and of course that contributed to housing shortages and the typically stupid and inefficient situation that we saw there," Papachristou said.)

Within a year and a half after the end of the Soviet state, such transactions had changed dramatically. People bought and sold apartments with an ease that made Westerners shudder. Technically, whoever owned the building did not own the land beneath it—a fact that often made the sale of land or home even more complicated than the old swapping of apartments. There were no title insurance and no title searches, but there were legitimate documents and a working legal system that could give them the state's stamp of approval. Sort of.

"It's just that the laws are not crystal clear and the way they are enforced is not reliable," Papachristou said. "While you can get a piece of paper and it probably means what it says, you can't be sure that somebody else doesn't have it as well."

A whole nation educated to abhor the idea of private property was suddenly coping with the foreign idea of owning your own home. Privatization (in Russian *privatizatsiya*) became the way of the future, and nervous customers suddenly found themselves plowing through a legal swamp peopled with bureaucratic slugs who had to be bribed into action or fast-talking leeches who were handing out bills of sale to anyone who had bags, literally, of money. It did not take much foresight to see that control of property would be a source of friction—in the courts, in the backstreets, or in the battlefields of the former Soviet Union—for many years to come.

The conflicts over territory had already begun along the borders of Russia—in Chechnya, Georgia, Armenia, and Azerbaijan. On a smaller scale, plots of land and apartment buildings, even individual apartments, were up for grabs, and the questions were strong and deadly: Did anyone who owned land before communism have any rights? (The Baltics said yes, in some cases. Russia in late 1993 decided against any claims prior to the Soviet years.) Did the renter or the manager own the apartment? The city or the country? The community government or the communal farm?

By late 1993, the ones who worked on the land or lived in the apartment, so it seemed, would have the first right of ownership. After that, the market would intervene, and in its first stages, the trade in homes seemed like all the other markets in the new Russia—a bazaar where rules changed from area to area and from week to week. Real estate became a walk on the high wire, a performance many people felt was necessary whether they were adept or clumsy at such transactions, in order to stake a permanent claim on their nests before it was too late.

In late 1992 and 1993, people invaded apartments being built for someone else, the first post-Soviet squatters. They were, as always in Russia, ingenious. They made their flats look only marginally livable, conjured up elaborate stories about how the authorities still had some small touches to finish, and then "rented" them to those who were desperate to have a place to live in the city. How the confrontations were solved was how differences in many areas of life were settled in the new Russia—an effort to appeal to law, an attempt to call forth moral principles, tears, threats, bribes, muscle, and in many cases, violence.

Workers for a Western company that had leased a spacious office in downtown Moscow arrived one morning in March 1992 to find the Pappe family spread out in their conference room. An electric samovar was bubbling near the company's Xerox machine. A large cot had been spread out near the office supplies, and cabbage soup was stewing on the small office stove. When the businessman shouted to his agency about the problem, the family shouted to their agency. Both groups had official papers saying that they could live in the same space.[3] A few weeks later, after a series of negotiations that included numerous threats and posturings for the Moscow newspapers, the family was moved to another space.

Those who actually privatized their apartments sometimes found fat tax or electric bills to go with their new status as property owners. One Russian man explained how electric meters could be "adapted" to the new system. He had crafted a small pincer-like device that grabbed the wheels inside the meters that registered electricity and slowed them down to a crawl. The levers could be removed instantly if a meter reader arrived at the door.

Electric bills seemed erratic at best. Some remained low, as in the Soviet years, when workers estimated their utility bills at several dollars a year; others could be several hundred dollars. (A British couple once told me the story of the time they had a Soviet visitor who left on the gas burner on the stove to light his cigarettes, with no understanding of what it would do to the host's gas bill.) The utility bill—like everything else in the new Russia—was negotiable.

There were worse hazards to ownership than the electric company, however. By late 1993, government officials were warning about real estate brokers who preyed on the elderly, promising big bonuses in return for their apartments. "Guaranteed lifetime support of single elderly residents," said one such ad. The loophole was that many pensioners' lives ended shortly after they had signed all the documents.[4] Tatyana Kuznetsova, who headed a department in Moscow investigating apartment-related crimes beginning in 1993, said criminals paid about $450 to petty functionaries for lists of people who lived alone—i.e., potential targets. By 1995, when even the smallest apartments were going for $40,000 each, there were about five cases a week of apartment owners disappearing after they had agreed to sign over the documents to privatize their flats.[5]

As the laws changed, people began yearning to own something—to have a place that did not depend on the death of relatives or the bureaucrats who decided who could live where. Smart young couples saw the inflation rate as an indication that they should buy something immediately, while the savings in their parents' cupboard were still worth something. Katya and Pavel[6] were part of this stampede, and from the time they began looking for an apartment in early 1992, they took elaborate notes. After almost a year, Pavel presented me with a five-page document that outlined a byzantine method for buying a tiny two-room apartment in the outskirts of Moscow for $17,500. It was a success story, really—since these two were bright and energetic enough to overcome the bureaucratic hurdles and they had relatives and friends willing to loan them money (in dollars) when inflation changed the price almost overnight.

Still, nothing was easy. Every time they stalled or wondered whether they were doing the right thing, they could hear the invisible army of other young couples ready to take their place. They had suffered one bad experience a year earlier, when the market was a lot less predictable. Katya and Pavel had been sharing an apartment with Katya's parents, an exercise in communal family living that ignited daily storms in the parents' marriage as well as their own. To get out, or get their parents out, the family agreed to pay about $10,000 for another apartment assigned to a man planning to leave the country. A few months after he "sold" them his apartment, the émigré changed his mind and moved back into his old place—declaring the deal canceled by "life's circumstances" before the new owners had moved in.

Fortunately, Katya and Pavel retrieved most of the $10,000—some of it already transferred out of the country. Now they intended to bargain hard and fast, complete the deal, and move swiftly into the apartment so that they could fight from a position of strength—i.e., squatters' rights. The idea of throwing people out of an apartment in this period was considered an impossibility, too inhumane even for the new Russia. It was part of the country's past—Stalin had been known to wrest people from their beds and truck them to Siberia, making way for others who found the hearth still warm and the pantry stocked for winter. And it could be part of the future—the worst of a soulless capitalism that loomed as a possibility, when new landlords could throw out poor people to make room for the rich. But in 1992, there was still some safety in having keys to the front door.

Pavel talked about the search for an apartment in 1992 as one of the most depressing aspects of his life in the new Russia. People were asking thousands of dollars for "stinking little rooms," as he put it, in buildings downwind from the city's industrial smokestacks. The good ones often had been sold by the time they got there. To get the flat they bought, they had to pay a company called Babylon $1,000 for services (introducing the buyer and the seller, mainly), and even though they were not happy with the flat, the price, or the location, "we were desperate because of months of fruitless search and growing prices," as Pavel wrote in his diary. Six months later, the same apartment would have cost $25,000.

"Usually the sellers want the whole sum at once in cash or, more often, to be transferred to a bank outside the country, since the flats are mostly sold by those who are leaving Russia for good. In our case, they wanted to get half of the money to their bank account in Austria and receive the rest in cash in Moscow," Pavel wrote.

"The deal was not to be completed until the money arrived in Austria, which was extremely unpleasant for us," he said. "They could have said that the money never arrived and they could keep both the money and the flat—there was no way to check it. Luckily the people were decent, and shortly after the money arrived in Austria, the transaction was completed by a notary public provided by Babylon."

The deed for the transaction said that the flat was sold for ten thousand rubles ($100), because it was illegal to sell for dollars and because neither party wanted to explain where the dollars came from to the state or *mafiya* (the various gangs of thugs who patrolled Russia during this period looking for people to rob). Then the papers had to be registered in the local technical inventory bureaus, which kept records of all the property transactions in the district. It took a day of standing in line to hand over the documents and pay the necessary fifteen rubles. The couple then had to wait two weeks to return and stand in another line for over an hour to get back the same documents with a stamp on them.

"The last step to become a property owner was to validate the papers in the Moscow local council. Luckily, we spent only two days there, which was amazingly fast work," Pavel wrote. "All this took place in winter, and most of the queues stood right on the street. All the offices work two or three days a week and usually are open for two or three hours a day, never on Sundays or Saturdays. Everything takes much longer than it may seem on paper, and you practically have to give up your job because of it."

Finally the day came when the paper was stamped and the money had changed hands. This was in late April 1992. Katya and Pavel were thinking about wallpaper and celebrating their good fortune—liberation, really, from her parents. And then they made a mistake. The apartment had a telephone, and they wanted to change it into their name. Pavel said later he would never forget the woman who took the request. She had the look of someone who thought privatization was a form of piracy, and he knew instantly that the kind of bureaucratic gnarl that the Russian government has cultivated for centuries was about to engulf him.

"We thought the red tape was over," Pavel said. "In principle, we should have applied for a *propiska* [a residence pass] for the new area, but since there were no laws whatsoever about private flats, and we thought it was absurd to ask for permission to live in our own flat, we decided to skip it."

The *propiska* was a particularly irritating leftover from the Soviet years, when anyone without a proper pass—say, to live in Moscow—was not allowed to work, to receive health care, to participate in any of the benefits of society. In early 1991, I was interviewing people in Zagorsk (now called Sergiev Posad) when I began talking to a young man who told me his name and age, but not where he was from. Finally, when I asked a third time, he said, "I am homeless," and his friend standing beside him explained, "He lives with me, but he doesn't have a *propiska*." It was a way of controlling people's movement, to limit the population in cities like Leningrad or Odessa. Once the controllers of the masses stepped down, however, the new government kept the *propiska* system going. (The Soviet Union was not the only country to require passes to live in certain cities. European cities have long had such requirements. In Switzerland, for example, one needs a *permis de séjour*.)

"We were wrong about not needing the *propiska*s," Pavel said. "In a month, we were told that without them we did not have a right to have a telephone line, according to the regulations issued a half century ago. The telephone company warned us that they would cut the line if we didn't get the *propiska* in a month's time. The only concession made to the new market was that we could keep the line if we paid a commercial price, of almost one hundred thousand rubles [about $800 at the time], which was preposterous because we did not need a new line (we already had one) and changing the name of the user of a phone costs about thirty rubles—not to mention the fact that one hundred thousand rubles was an annual salary of an average Muscovite, and we already had nothing but debts. We had no other choice than to get the *propiska*."

Pavel checked with a man in charge of the internal passport regime about what he needed. Two papers from his former place, two from the housing office of his new place, he said. Then they went to see the militiaman, feeling they had some clout since they were talking to one of the head people.

He shook his head over their pile of papers. "Didn't I tell you that you need the marriage certificate and a copy of it?" he said.

Back for marriage documents, they returned a week later. This time the official peered through their documents and decided that their internal passports were not valid. After the age of twenty-five, a new photo should be pasted into the documents, and their pictures were clearly from their teenage years. Katya and Pavel got new photos and rushed to the office where they dealt with new passport photos. At the new passport office, they were told that gluing new photos in passports took two weeks, which would have meant that by then the telephone would be dead. At that point Pavel learned that the woman in charge was a neighbor of his grandmother. The grandmother was called; the neighbor got out her glue pot, and the passports were fixed in a few minutes.

"Proud and happy, we brought the heap of documents together with our passports back to the militiaman, and having examined them carefully, he started to write something that seemed terribly important and complicated, because he was sweating and had to tear several papers to pieces and start all over again each time. When, fifteen minutes later, the task was completed, he handed the slip of paper to us solemnly and said that now we had to go to the main city passport department. The paper he gave us read: 'It is beyond my competence to allow a *propiska* for a private flat.' "

As they stood reading the paper, Katya tried to hold back tears. Three months they had been working on the apartment, almost a month had been spent trying to get the phone, and this stupidity meant that they had to start again. They had both stretched the goodwill of their employers to what they believed were the limits, and they had traveled around the city, pulling strings, nudging, coaxing, and pleading as they tried to buy their apartment and change the phone according to the rules.

Disillusioned, they went on their carefully planned holiday, telling friends that only on their return would they be strong enough to face the wall of bureaucrats and a life without a home phone. When they returned, the phone was still working, however, and it was only after a few days—when they had relaxed and figured that somehow the huge document monsters had missed them—that the telephone suddenly went dead in midring.

"It took a cream cake to make it work again," Pavel said. Katya carried the cake carefully to the telephone station and gave it to the chief of telephones. "We knew it was a woman, the kind with a huge, lacquered pouf of hair on the top of her head [the 'Soviet power bun' I had called this hairdo, since virtually every top woman official wore her hair that way], otherwise it would have been a bottle of cognac," Pavel said. They bought the best cake at an ordinary bread store, not a Western store, and together they made up a story about how they were a young family struggling to better themselves, trying to hold on to food and clothes and jobs as the world dissolved around them. "This story could squeeze a tear out of a rock," Pavel said later.

Indeed, the tear was shed and the dial tone restored. Touched by their story, the telephone mistress knocked down the price to human level—about $40. Pavel rushed to the telephone company the next day, and after he paid the money, the clerk told him that he was just in time. The orders were filtering that very day through the system to cut his phone line permanently. As he walked out into the September sunshine, Pavel figured out how much time he had spent preserving his telephone—more than five months had passed since he had tried to change the name. If he had left it alone and passed the number around, it probably would have been there for decades.

"As a responsible citizen, I made another attempt to follow the legal routine [to get a *propiska*], but I was ultimately horrified by the huge line of people and even a bigger list of documents that we had to produce there," he said. When he handed me his letter in December 1992, Pavel noted that so far the telephone continued to work, but that without *propiski* there was a constant fear that the authorities would find out and cut off the lights.

The lights, the phone, the cut rates for what could be stolen tiles and wallpaper—everybody had some secret scam making them worry about what would happen "if the authorities found out" and they were forced, not to go to prison, but to stand in the long lines at dark offices where bureaucrats were still in charge of making life miserable.

In late 1993, I drove out in southeast Moscow for my first visit to Katya and Pavel's new flat. The newspapers that morning had carried a story about how a block of apartments being sold in one of the seediest parts of the city had been bought instantly for prices that had surprised even the auctioneers. The apartments, the same size as or smaller than Katya and Pavel's—in a rougher, industrial neighborhood—went for an average of $14,406.

As in many Russian apartment buildings, the shabby entrance led to a grimy elevator. The hall gave no evidence that anything decent could lie behind the padded steel door. But the apartment was clean and bright, a tiny ship with everything carefully stored in its place. Young and modern, they had forsaken what I called the *uyutny* or cozy, look, the warm Russian womb surrounded by keepsakes saved through several generations. There is a special color to these places—a warm amber that can make any Russian, especially one who has left for the better life outside, ache with nostalgia over the idea of home.

Katya and Pavel, who said they planned to live in Russia forever, had none of this émigré sentimentality toward clutter. They cultivated the spare look, making their apartment seem European, Scandinavian, or even Italian. And they were like owners of real estate everywhere. They feared the tax man. They worried about the elevator. They wanted to oust the neighbors—"drunkards," Katya had whispered—people who were renting, *renting*, next door.

Katya and Pavel were part of a trend in 1992. By the end of the year, authorities reported that 1,807,000 Moscow apartments[7] had been privatized—mostly in decent buildings or better sections of the city. One Russian family paid the equivalent of $28 in fees to the various departments of government to privatize a relatively large prerevolutionary apartment in mid-Moscow. A construction expert looked at it while I was visiting one afternoon in 1993 and shook his head in awe. "It is worth maybe $150,000, or maybe $250,000 now. If it is fixed up, maybe more." For the friend who owned it, the hope was that he would not have to pay taxes on that possibility, only that he could find someone to rent until he was ready to sell. There was something heady about the knowledge that this man, a pauper several years ago, was worth as much as one quarter of a million dollars. I mentioned it once, to congratulate him. "Don't say that," he whispered frantically, spitting over his shoulder to ward off the bad luck that is supposed to arrive with any moment of self-satisfaction. "They will come and take it all away."

While the cities turned into property bazaars, the countryside was undergoing a different sort of revolution. In essence, Russia was making another try at land reform—a treacherous business that had always unearthed dangerous and ancient conflicts for people with such a powerful, even mystical, attachment to the land. As Mikhail Gorbachev, then Boris Yeltsin tried to change the patterns of ownership toward the end of the twentieth century, they studied similar attempts at the beginning of the century. It became very much the vogue to look back at the prerevolutionary reforms of Pyotr Arkadievich Stolypin as evidence that land reform was working when it was interrupted by the Bolsheviks. (Stolypin was credited with creating a farming community that increased productivity of crops by 14 percent in Russia, 25 percent in Siberia between 1906 and 1915.)[8] But Stolypin, for all his efforts to create an independent farmer, does not provide a particularly comforting example. While he was attempting reform in one area, he was also trying to subdue Russia's growing revolutionary movement with so many hangings that the noose became known as "Stolypin's necktie" and "Stolypin's wagon" was the word for railroad cars that carried his enemies to Siberia. When he was assassinated at the opera in Kiev in 1911 by a young anarchist, Stolypin was not only out of favor with many in the public and the government, he was also on the outs with the royal family. Tsarina Alexandra later told Stolypin's successor: "I am convinced that Stolypin died to yield his post to you, and that this is for Russia's good."[9]

In Stolypin's day, land was owned by the tsar and the landed gentry. Peasants generally lived in communes—a society that they had known since the beginning of recorded history[10]—and beginning with the serfs' emancipation in 1861, there were efforts in the nineteenth and early twentieth centuries to parcel out land for individuals or families.

Stolypin, a giant bear of a man whose role in the prerevolutionary era was as complex as any in recent Russian history, was forty-four when he became chairman of the Council of Ministers in 1906. His reforms, the most radical of which were started when the parliament of the time was not sitting, allowed peasants to claim their share of the land and thus become independent of the commune, or *mir*. Later, by lifting the regulations that in effect kept the peasant tied to his commune, Stolypin gave the peasants their first real freedom to move. The reform resulted in about 3 million people moving to Siberia (with 547,000 giving up and later returning).[11] By 1915, there were more than seven million households with peasants as proprietors. When the Bolsheviks took over, land owned by the Stolypin farmers was among the first property seized.[12] As a result, Stolypin's purpose and success have been matters of vigorous dispute among historians—with Soviet historians calling his efforts "the Stolypin reaction" and others suggesting that he began what might have been an earlier evolution toward a bourgeois, parliamentary state. Whatever the reasons for Stolypin's efforts to break up the communes, his reforms apparently troubled Lenin, who felt his enemy would be a new middle class. Lenin was worried that Stolypin's reforms, if continued, could make the farmlands "completely bourgeois," and he felt that it was "a race with time between Stolypin's reforms and the next upheaval."[13]

Despite the similarities between the beginning of the century and the end, however, it would be hard for Russia to simply pick up reforms where the Bolsheviks destroyed them. The large farms, for example, were communal in many ways in 1992, but they were no longer communes in the nineteenth-century sense, and their workers no longer tied forever to the land. These were large industrial farms, and the people who labored there were employees, not serfs. Some undoubtedly would move into the cities and become mechanics or factory workers or kiosk owners. The most industrious could help convert the state farms into new business or even start their own smaller operations. But as the agricultural system shifted in the early 1990s, many of the old state farms were dying at a time when there seemed to be little ready to replace them.[14]

The kolkhoz, or collective farm, was adapted from the old Russian communal farm by Lenin, honed into a merciless system by Stalin, and maintained at such a low level that Russia, once a grain exporter in prerevolutionary days, had become a major importer by the Brezhnev era. (There are some analysts who believe that the death of the Soviet Union was caused in large part by the slow deterioration of these large industrial farms, whose output became so obviously inadequate when the United States cut off supplies of grain because of the Afghan war.)

Lenin, in a time of economic disaster in Russia, backed away from the totally communal agricultural system in 1921 and tried the New Economic Policy, which allowed some privately owned land for those who produced. But those who did well caught the eye of the *Vozhd*, the spiritual leader, as Stalin wanted his followers to call him, and in 1929, Stalin ended the NEP and starved, shot, or evacuated to Siberia those working on their own. Using the remnants of a communal culture that had long been a part of peasant life in Russia, Stalin's men easily incited the ancient jealousies that make people mistrust anyone who succeeds. Individual prosperity became a form of treason, and people were killed for having more chickens than the neighbors or being too proud of owning a gizmo on the front door that rang inside to announce a visitor. (One Russian scientist told me the story of a committee that came to such a home in the 1930s, ripped off the doorbell, and notified the owner that he could not have such luxuries until everyone else did. In the meantime, a fist knocking on the wood was sufficient, he was informed.)

When the countryside opened to allow journalists and other Westerners beyond the model farms that Soviets had allowed them to see in the past, we found places like the Progress kolkhoz, a large communal farm about two hundred miles south of Moscow. By late summer 1994, Progress had become an agricultural ghost town, a shabby collection of barns and untended fields. In earlier years, the farm had been a large dairy operation with over twelve hundred cows tended by almost half as many humans. Running on cheap fuel and electricity, Progress farm made its quotas even though workers became increasingly disenchanted with their lives. Waste, inefficiency, and drunkenness began to plague the big farm community, and by the mid-1990s, with fewer than three hundred people still working in the three small towns around the farm, the Progress kolkhoz was near extinction.

"We are simply dying," Viktor Ralo told the Muscovite who came to see him in the late summer of 1994.[15] "All the villagers are trying to get away, while the people coming in are nothing but bad news—one month and they turn into alcoholics."

The farm had dwindled to 160 cows by then, and the usual herd of calves was down to seventy, villagers reported. Many calves died when they were born, drowning in the manure around their mothers, the townspeople said. Others were simply stolen by the villagers, who acknowledged openly that they were slowly setting up their own farms, pirating feed or spare parts or whatever they desperately needed from the kolkhoz operation.

Progress kolkhoz helped to explain why gross production of such staples as milk, meat, and corn had been dropping in Russia. Corn slipped from 104 million tons in 1990 to 99 million in 1993, and other crops were dropping at a similar rate. With each decline, the fear grew that Russians would face hunger in future winters.

Despite the inefficiencies of these collectivized farms, experts like Professor David A. J. Macey at Middlebury College were warning against using Stolypin as the guide for turning Russia into a nation of middle class farmers. Seventy-four years of communism had made the country dependent on these big farms, which employed 20 million people and produced all but a small percentage of the nation's food supply.[16] These larger-scale farms, or *krupniye khozyaistva,* could be privatized, but the Russia that stretched from Europe to the Bering Sea could never be carved up into millions of mom-and-pop operations. How the government would solve these problems was still a subject of emotional debate in the early 1990s when I visited the farm of Oleg Stekolnikov a few hours' drive south of Moscow.

Oleg Stekolnikov was known by his tractor. In the early autumn of 1991, along the dirt roads of his small rural community about forty-five miles south of Moscow, man and machine could be seen lurching through the dust like some large failing monster. His vehicle, the faint memory of a tractor, had been patched and wired together so disjointedly that the whole apparatus seemed to defy the laws of earthly auto dynamics. Its dented and rusted red front was held aloft by a circle of thick baling wire. Bits of rubber and cloth and metal spewed from its innards, and the tires glittered in the sunlight after years of overuse. Bouncing along on top was one of the rarest and bravest of Soviet creatures—Oleg, the private farmer.

Such farmers, who would make up a mere 3.9 percent of the farming community by late 1993,[17] were the front line in the battle to reform the Russian economy, and Oleg, who had broken away early from his neighboring kolkhoz, seemed to defy cultural history and the laws of survival to control his own dairy farm.

In his slow rural Russian, he explained one day about how he had faced a system that was against him. The community fought his request for land when he first proposed it, soon after Gorbachev announced that private farmers would be encouraged to start their own businesses. The same community was still trying to make him fail when I visited his family almost five years later. Yet, when people talked about hope for change in the countryside, about reforming the old communal farms, where workers produced just enough to keep the country alive, they were talking about Oleg and his few brave and even brazen compatriots.

Oleg's biggest problem as a dairy farmer was not the feed or the weather or the water supply. It was the Soviet farm next door, where his energy and success made him a dangerous man. This basic envy of anyone doing better, a human failing that the Soviets nurtured over the years in the name of equality, would remain in the psyche for a long time, and even though Gorbachev and Yeltsin worked on agricultural land reform, the powerful communal-farm establishment resisted on virtually every level. For Oleg, that level was in the town of Domodedovo, where he went to ask his local kolkhoz to share some of its land, most of which had been lying fallow for years. The state farm had eighty-nine hundred acres; Oleg asked for five.

"They told him he must have just come from the moon, because he asked for so much. All they would say was, 'Give it to us in writing.' Orally, they refused to consider it. 'Write your application, and we will consider it,' they said, but they were all laughing," Valya, Oleg's fresh-faced wife, said a few months later.[18]

Oleg carefully wrote his application to organize a private farm so that he could request more land. He received this response:

> To comrade Stekolnikov:
> Having considered your application on a question of organizing a privately owned farm in the village of Churilkovo, I inform you that, according to the fact that a piece of land suggested for personal auxiliary farming is 0.25 hectares and considering the resolution of this small council of the Moscow district council of peoples deputies as of December 16, 1992, the decision "On the limits of sizes of land pieces offered to Moscow district resident" according to which the minimum size of the land piece for farming is 2 hectares, it is impossible to decide this question positively.
>
> L. P. Kovalevsky

What Mr. Kovalevsky was saying was that Oleg did not have enough land to qualify as a farmer. He could not get land because he did not already own land. The absurdity of this became clear to anyone who watched how hard

Oleg and his family worked, their seven cows yielding twenty to thirty liters of milk per cow per day. The kolkhoz next door, with its seven hundred workers tending two thousand cows, produced twelve liters of milk a day per animal. Instead of state support for salaries, tractors, and seeds, all in the name of feeding the Russian people, Oleg was paying his own way and working twenty-five *sotki* of leased land, a little more than half an acre.

A former train conductor who met his wife on the job and who now had one daughter, Oleg talked about what pushed him to work seventeen hours a day, tending the cows, foraging for feed, and finally bringing his *tvorog* (a creamy cottage cheese) to the market. "I love animals, cows, and of course, I would like to live in my own house and to live in decent conditions. That's what makes a person move forward. I want to bring my *tvorog* to the market and have people say, 'Thank you.' I want to share the results of my efforts with people. I like working and to see the fruits of my labor."[19]

(The kolkhoz worker was supposed to be on the job eight hours a day, six days a week, and dairy farmers often were required to work such hours to keep cows milked regularly. The farms across the countryside that could be seen in the summer months growing cabbages by the mile and corn that seemed to stretch to the horizon generated intense activity only on planting and harvesting days. In between, life was relatively easy. My own trip to a kolkhoz in eastern Russia was a perfect cliché of the communal farmer's existence. It was early afternoon, and the man who was supposed to be guarding the place was sleeping on a battered sofa. College students who had to go to such farms to work in the fall as part of their education usually learned to stay away from the farmhands, especially after lunch. "We did all the work," said one woman, who remembered her teenage autumns picking potatoes.)

"If you work at the kolkhoz, you're not distinguished from anyone else, and it doesn't mean much," Oleg continued. "It's a low salary; it's useless."

A thick-set man , Oleg had large, gentle-looking hands that seemed lost without work; and he was anxious to end conversations so that he could move to the next task. But he was also patient and polite with these foreigners, and when he smiled or broke into a quiet laugh, his round cheeks seemed to engulf his eyes and make him look like a large weathered cherub.

"I have a truck, a tractor, a car, and a house going up." He beamed. "It's a pleasure. All my troubles are pleasant."[20] But more land would have been more pleasant, he acknowledged. Pigs and hens, a vegetable patch—he yearned for such luxuries. With this huge agrarian country, it was hard to imagine how a man like Oleg would have trouble finding five acres.

In late 1993, when I visited Oleg's family, they had moved into his new house. It was brick, two stories, with a lovely wooden staircase—a mansion in Russian terms. But they did not have a phone, and we had descended like a dollop of snow on the head, as the saying went. Oleg's wife sat us in the living room, where Zorro galloped across the television, and she scurried into the kitchen to fix us something to eat, even though we had arrived in midafternoon, hoping to spare her such problems. Full of apologies and still wearing her bathrobe, Valya brought us to her kitchen table. She smiled, a true Russian beauty with her dark hair and blue eyes and skin a rosy blush that comes from a diet of milk and cheeses. Oleg had gone to the market, she apologized as she swept her hand over the well-laid kitchen table, outfitted in the best china and undoubtedly most of the food in the house. If we had come the next day, she protested, the table would have been heavy with the delicacies he always brought with him from the market.

Then she served us tea like the queen she had undoubtedly become in this community. With it came *tvorog* topped with *smetana,* or sour cream, all dusted with about two tablespoons of sugar per serving. I could hear my arteries groaning as I finished, only to find Valya spooning seconds onto my plate.

They now had five cows and three calves, she said, and they had received an unusual but useful form of foreign aid—after my husband and Australian journalist Robert Haupt had written stories about Oleg. When Peter's article appeared in *The Independent* of London, a group of British pensioners sent ten pounds. When Haupt's story appeared in the *Sydney Morning Herald,* an Australian Rotary Club bought Oleg a small tractor. The day I saw his house, the new machine was in the backyard, with a tiny Australian flag in the window. The other tractor was still there, and it still worked.

"More land?" we asked hopefully. Valya shook her head. It belonged to the people it had belonged to for sixty years, and there seemed to be every indication that no matter what the government did, those who controlled the land would continue to control it. That same week Russian president Boris Yeltsin declared it legal for individuals to own farmland. The decree was seen as a big boost to Russia's 265,000 private farmers, and the country's 20 million farmers were supposed to get a chance to privatize the land they had worked for years. But many farmers either did not want the burden of owning their own land or, like Oleg, feared that they would never be able to actually wrest it away from the commune.

At a meeting with reporters a few days earlier, Aleksei Bespakhotny, the beefy director of the Yermolino dairy farm near Moscow, had been giving his predictions about what would happen to Russia without the large industrial farms created by the Soviet state. "If they get rid of the collective and state farms, the people will starve," trumpeted Bespakhotny[21] (whose name means "without plowed land"). Bespakhotny's operation owned 750 cows, which yielded about 26 percent less in 1993 than they had four years earlier. Nevertheless, he saw the private farmers as a greedy and lackluster group, whose main aim was to charge more for milk that could be watered down or worse.

Private farmers, he pontificated, are people who "scrabble around in the dirt and never manage anything. Most of them live in old trailers." Mr. Bespakhotny had not met Oleg Stekolnikov.

To discuss Russian property, both in the city and countryside, is not to say anything about the Russian home, which is something that will undoubtedly be warm and noisy whether it is a room in a communal apartment or a palatial four-room flat in downtown St. Petersburg. When a Russian invites you into his—or, more important, her—home, it is like being enveloped in a loving family for as many hours as you would like to stay. The guest is some higher order of being for a Russian family, and even the poorest host would quickly thaw out the last remaining sliver of meat for a visitor, especially from far away. I tried always to come at teatime—midmorning or midafternoon—not to be unsociable but because a visit near the meal hour depleted most people's supplies of food and drink. Even when you brought gifts, the host and hostess simply added them to the spread of family treasures from the icebox or the frozen corners of the balcony.

Perhaps because they had not been allowed to concentrate on decorations and elaborate furnishings, their homes focused on comfort, on making a visitor feel at ease. One of my favorite traditions was the one that asked guests or visitors to shed their shoes at the door, to be replaced by *tapochki,* or bedroom slippers, kept in a variety of sizes under the overcoats and boots and umbrellas. As the feet relaxed, so did the guest.

For examples of hospitality, none will ever match for me the time I first met Boris and Masha Ryzhak. The Ryzhaks had invited us, as friends of friends, to their dacha for Easter weekend 1991. They were wintering in a summer house, borrowing a dacha from a friend because they had rented their apartment in Moscow to a foreigner. It was cold that weekend, as the wind swept easily through the plastic attached to windows and past the rugs nailed against the walls. The wooden house, filled with goods and papers, was kept warm as much by the crowd of friends as by the small creaking heaters placed strategically in the coldest rooms.

My daughter was not feeling well, and before the adults celebrated Russian Easter with a three-hour midnight service followed by a traditional feast on *kulich* (a tall, rich cake) and vodka , Masha told us to sleep in a side bedroom on a small double bed. As the night ended, I woke to a chorus of snores from the newly blessed revelers and then tiptoed into the main room, where I learned for the first time the luxury of our sleeping arrangements. Entwined on a narrow cot were Masha, who is a large woman, her husband, who is a very tall man, and their squirming baby. As I stared at the figures, their feet and arms spilling over the sides of the bed, Masha opened one eye and smiled sleepily. She could not move without dislodging the other two, and I could do nothing but wave and slip back guiltily to my tiny daughter. Because my child and I had spread out on a double bed, three people had spent the night trying to balance on a cot for one. When I told the story to a Russian, she did not understand what was unusual. "Of course, they gave the bed to you. You were the guest."

2

Mother Russia

"We are not stepping on a road but on a stream. Everything is moving underneath us."

—Zoya Krylova, editor of *Rabotnitsa* magazine, 1992[1]

"We used to have rights on paper. Now we don't even have that."

—Yelena Yershova, prominent Russian feminist, 1993[2]

Taganka Square is at the center of a workers' neighborhood that, despite its few elegant prerevolutionary structures, a famous theater, and one huge Stalinist sand castle of an apartment building, teemed with crowds of "engineers," who really guarded the metro escalators or made automobile tires or swept the city's sidewalks with handmade twig besoms. It was here, in the last year of the Soviet Union and my first days in Russia, that I often stood watching my new neighbors on their way to factories and homes that were still secret and mysterious to most outsiders like me. It was here also that I first focused on what a young Russian woman would later call "the invisible ones"—the powerful army of old women in oversized winter turbans and dark woolen coats that, after years in the rain and snow, had taken on the bulbous shape of their owners. These old ones moved faster; they stood more patiently in the lines; and most important, they seemed to be the city's most efficient distribution system, carting necessities in used plastic bags and cardboard boxes tied with perilously thin bits of string.

Taganka Square, in short, offered my introduction to babushka, the grandmother, who became for me an important gauge of the way Russia's new society was treating its people, especially its women. And although I had wanted to write about women and how their lives changed as the society shifted from one form to another, my friend Olga Podolskaya kept telling me that the place to start was not with the young women—who were like the young everywhere—but with the old ones. "The babushkas know everything," she had said at one point in these early days. "They know our real secrets."

Indeed, I suffered from the ignorance that afflicts most Westerners on this subject. I had come to Russia believing that the babushka was a kind of all-purpose nag—the irritable last stage of Soviet womanhood. She was the logical conclusion of a difficult adult life that began as a young woman, often a beauty said to be mercilessly on the make, absorbed in herself and her slim moment of happiness. After a Soviet woman found a husband and produced a child, a worker for the state, she began the rapid descent into old age. The drudge at home, the underling at work, the shopper, the cook, the organizer, the worrier, the matriarch—before long the young girl would slide into the legion of old women, the experts had said. Once that happened, she would feel that she had earned the right not merely to impart her wisdom but to thrust it noisily on anyone in her path. These self-appointed scolds will rush at you like harpies, my American colleagues had predicted before we came to Moscow. They will screech at you for trying to enter the exit doors. They will shout from a bus stop if you are not wearing a hat. Forget your child's mittens on a cold day, and woe be unto you; and what is worse, my American friends had predicted, is their belief that only they know all the codes of survival in their native Russia. The same babushka who has scolded a woman for sitting on a cold stone, an act that can insure sterility, can be seen in late November forcing her two-year-old grandson to endure a barbaric rite of winter: in an effort to harden the young one against the cold months ahead, she will dip the completely naked child for an instant in a lake or pond that is a few days away from freezing.

Months later I would realize that Russia's meddling babushka felt her mission was nothing less grand than preserving the society, the lore, and the next generation. But during my first weeks in Russia, before I had succumbed to the full enchantment of these old women, they filled me with a schoolgirl's terror as they squinted critically from under their brown woolen scarves. I saw only their fierce exteriors as they waited in lines at the Taganka grocery store, an echoing warehouse as big as a Western supermarket.

The Taganka was my introduction to the idea of Soviet shopping, and the facility's main purpose, as far as I could tell at that point, was to occupy pensioners, who milled through its emptiness constantly like creatures trolling for food. If the idea was to have a variety of shops under one roof, the Taganka fell far short of its goal in those last Soviet days by being almost perpetually out of everything but children's cereal, bread, and cartons of sour-smelling milk. The sausage section, the fish section, the wine section, and the egg section—they were all shut down so often that I believed at first that they were Potemkin markets, fake stalls set up to give the store a pretense of variety. On rare occasions, however, the word would go out through some mysterious network that a truck had arrived, and the store would fill suddenly, and you could ask, as I often did, "What are they giving out today?" "Giving out" was the operative phrase, since it was considered a gift of the Super Distributor, the Soviet State. "Toothpaste," they would say. Or sour cream. Or purplish Soviet sausage. The old women in the lines would know and they would wait, sometimes for hours, until the day's treasure was gone, and once again the store would feel empty.

Once, when the cavernous Taganka store was full of buyers, the line stretching almost half a block, I forced my way to the front to see what had attracted so many customers. The activity was near the fish market, and I wanted to see if it was true that the traditional Soviet catch was frozen into huge blocks and then sold in random chunks so that, like a cruel lottery, some purchasers got filet and others received an inedible tail fin. That day the stall, with its elaborate stained-glass fish overhead, was selling real fish. Live. For about twenty cents, each customer received three luminescent carp, which were stuffed, still gulping for air, into a plastic bag. Those who had succeeded in buying the fish then wrestled them into knapsacks, and as one old woman with her wiggling trophy passed those still waiting, she took on a queenly look of triumph and superiority.

(Much later, after the Soviet system had disappeared and there was plenty of food at unbearable prices, I unwittingly asked the old question "What are they giving out?" to a woman in a line. She turned on me angrily and said, "Nothing. They are *giving out* nothing," which by then was absolutely true. By late 1993, Taganka was filled with stalls that sold such luxuries as Italian leather coats for about $450 each, and on one nostalgic visit, a Russian friend pulled me toward one of the doors to witness something he thought a Westerner should see. A young woman was droning through a memorized routine, a laconic barker trying to sell a golden chain for $20, which would provide you with another golden chain and a matching bracelet, a free camera, and a roll of film. In spite of her lack of enthusiasm, she drew a crowd.)

If the Taganka was the depressing center of commerce in the neighborhood, it had its antidote across the square. Under a ragged sign that said "Bulochnaya" was a simple bread shop, operating behind a fog of windows that always beckoned on a cold Moscow morning. Bread—heavy white or delicious lemony black bread or sometimes egg bread twisted into golden braids—cost about sixty kopecks (less than a dime) in the spring of 1991. When it had cooled enough for the women in their starched white coats to sell, the shop filled immediately with customers who knew the appointed hour for buying the freshest loaves of the day.

On one particularly cold morning in March 1991, I stepped inside the bakery, as much to feel the warmth and smell the sweet, fresh aroma as to do my company's bidding—to interview people about an early change in bread prices, the first signs of an inflation that later would virtually wipe out most families' security and savings. As always, Russia seemed to lead me away from my mission and into something far more intriguing, long after the original purpose had dimmed in my memory. Olga Podolskaya, who went with me that morning, and I would talk for years about the three women we met there that day.

The troika, as we called them, stood as almost-perfect representatives of the babushkas that Olga had wanted me to meet, and when I would try to call them the "extraordinary ones," Olga would contradict me gently. They were extraordinary only for me, she would remind. For Russia, they were very normal, her country's backbone, its real historians, its trusted folk doctors, its believable priests, the entire support staff for many a Russian family.

In the bakery that day, the line for fresh bread had curled through the shop, and the women stood silently like farm animals, shifting from boot to boot, waiting to be handed their allotment of food. Our three women stood with what seemed to be an uncommon elegance, and as a newcomer I felt a surge of anger that such people spent their days fighting lines and standing on aching feet. Why didn't they rebel? I asked myself in the manner of all Westerners unaccustomed to Moscow. As someone who had protested when an elevator stopped at almost every floor in a low-level building in Washington, I had come to a place where people waited with such excruciating patience. I felt in those early days that Moscow was a city about to explode, and it took some time to realize that I was the one seething about the way they were being ignored. They did not have the freedom yet to be truly angry. That would come later.

When we approached one woman in a steel blue coat and a thick fluffy turban made of swan feathers, she squinted at me suspiciously and refused to give her name. In a voice full of gloom, she said that the time waiting in lines was not so terrible as what would come, if the people were not careful. "We have seen worse," she said. "We have seen war. We have seen terrible times." Beside her, Elizaveta Morozova and Lidiya Shadrova, both ancient-looking sixty-eight-year-olds, nodded in agreement, but they laughed as they did. Their sudden laughter brought silence around them as other customers, ever mindful of their place in line, managed nevertheless to crowd around us and savor the distraction. The nameless one felt too much of the dreariness around her, Lidiya and Elizaveta said. They hinted that she was one of the old Russian women who are full of warnings and cautionary tales. The KGB, now supposedly defanged and overrun by public relations men, would lurk for years in her stories, whispered to defenseless young ones at bedtime. But her friends, who had seen the same war, the same deprivations, the same daily routine for survival, welcomed change—not for themselves but for the grandchildren they stood in the lines to help feed every day. They talked about how prices were changing and money was like the autumn leaves. Lidiya blew on a weathered palm and pretended to watch the invisible stack of rubles scattering in the air—a gesture that I would see over and over in the next few years. They talked about how long it would take for Russia to be "rich like America" once the market arrived. Capitalism would finally offer the big bonanza, the era of plenty that communism had promised but never delivered. It would happen overnight. Instantly, they would all be not simply capitalists, but rich capitalists. The nameless one did not believe in such promises, she said as she began shaking her head in way that sent tendrils of swan feathers quivering like a halo around her weathered face. To change quickly would require "too much blood."

Elizaveta and Lidiya tsked the thought in unison, and Lidiya pretended to spit three times over her shoulder at the specter of more Russian troubles. They were optimists, Lidiya said. It was a term I heard often in Russia, and I learned that being an optimist was not a choice but a necessity for survival, especially for a woman. If you tend to be depressive, dreary, melancholic, or simply negative, Russia would easily accommodate. "We are not afraid of change," said Elizaveta, grinning proudly. "We are not afraid of anything. We have seen everything there is to see. It will work out better, you will see."

When Olga and I walked out of the bread shop, we felt vastly better about the future of Russia than when we entered. These three old women had boosted our spirits. Their generation had become the masters at fanning hope and cheer in the face of something worse than mere adversity—the unknown. But even as they had cheered us like young children that day, it would become clear in the next few months that if capitalism made some people very rich, these old women would be its first victims. A proud legion hoping for capitalism's bonanzas, they became almost an instant poor as the market arrived.

A few days after our visit to the bakery, I told the story to two Russian guests, emphasizing in the telling that it was inhumane to have old people waiting for hours in line. They should be sitting in the sun, playing shuffleboard, enjoying their retirement, I argued loftily.

"Pfff," one of the visitors, Yuri Sigov, exhaled in disgust. "Your old people, they are sent off to Florida to rot."

Sigov, then a journalist for *Argumenty i Fakty*, was a frequent visitor to our apartment during the early days of our tour in Russia. He taught us many of the street sayings about Soviet life, and he was full of maxims and stories, truths and yarns. On that day Yuri began a long lecture on how important the grandmother was to Russian life. He told about his mother-in-law, who left their apartment at 6 A.M. and returned at 8 P.M., doing her work for the family. She had spent one whole day fighting her way through the lines at Detsky Mir, Moscow's gigantic children's store, to buy a bicycle for her grandson. She carried the bike—a bulky and heavy frame in a huge, frail cardboard box—on the metro and the bus, then up the stairs to the apartment.

"When she got there, she was the hero," Sigov said.

" 'I did it,' she said to us. 'I helped you.' She was so happy; she wasn't angry about all the trouble in the day."

In the West, the old are not allowed to participate in family life, he continued; they are put out to nursing pastures, where they slowly deteriorate from lack of use. We were about to launch into a heated discussion comparing the American and Russian way of treating the old when I asked his mother-in-law's age. She was fifty-six, he said. I tried to hide the look of dismay on my forty-nine-year-old face. Yuri had been talking about a woman bravely sacrificing the last years of her life. I was still planning projects like a college graduate.

Most workers retired at age sixty (fifty-five for women), but within a few months after the end of the Soviet state, it became clear that pensions and benefits would not keep up with inflation. When I arrived in Moscow in early 1991, bread was sixty kopecks a loaf. By late 1993, it was 240 rubles. Inflation was so steep and so sudden that many people were paupers overnight. Some Russians would ask an American to imagine waking one morning to find that a new automobile cost $10 million and a lifetime savings of $10,000 would not buy a pair of tennis shoes.[3] Pensions increased from 70 rubles a month ($15) in 1991 to about 3000 in late 1993 to 150,000 ($30) in early 1995. As one couple in their mid-seventies explained in late 1994, as they struggled to buy fruit or even milk, "Freedom is wonderful, but you can't eat words."[4] Such complaints have always been a strange art form in Russia, where it can be unseemly and unlucky to boast about one's personal good fortune. But with the new society, even the pretense that the nation's 37 million pensioners[5] were being given their due from the state had evaporated. They had little wealth to hide and many woes worthy of complaint to anyone with the time to listen.

Many of the women who before had stood in lines at state stores were now the new street peddlers. They sold plastic sacks to customers going into markets or grocery stores. They stood in snowbanks outside metro stations or near bus stops to hawk cheap plastic toys or Chinese-made kitchen utensils.

The system changed, but the grandmothers were still standing in the snow for hours. They were no longer waiting to buy. Now they were waiting to sell.

Olga, who went to the bakery with me that day in early 1991, had a sacrificial mother—an energetic woman who took care of Olga's teenage daughter. She was the true babushka who shopped, cooked, and cleaned while Olga worked or, occasionally, went out for the evening. By early 1992, however, Olga's mother, called Babushka, was growing frail, and the doctors were telling her not to tax herself lugging groceries or clothes home from the stores and street markets. Olga began to take on some of the shopping, often simply buying what she needed at the new stores that sold goods quickly and at a premium. This new method did not sit well with her mother, however, and every so often the elder woman would hear about a bargain somewhere in the city and she would slip out the door to get it before Olga got home.

One day in the summer of 1992, Babushka learned about a place that was unloading sugar at half the price of the marketeers, and she dressed, took her shopping sacks, fought the crowds, and bought several heavy bags to help sweeten the long winter. When Olga got home that day, her mother was struggling for breath, suffering from a massive heart attack that ended her life a short while later. "I begged her not to go out," Olga said, daubing her tears as she told the story a few weeks later. "Of course, she would not listen."

An optimist, even in the face of such devastating news, Olga looked at one bright moment in her ordeal. The funeral had been "uplifting," Olga said. Her mother's friends had come, many of them wearing World War II medals, all of them full of memories about the cruelty of Stalin and easier times under Brezhnev. "They had suffered through the terrors of our history, like our three graces," Olga had said that day, referring to the three women we had seen in the bakery a year and a half earlier. "But they were still so alive, so much more alive than my own generation."

A few days after Olga and I talked about her mother and her mother's generation, I went back to the bread shop near Taganka. There was no line this time. The price of bread was almost sixty times what it had been on my last visit, a price that was closer to what it actually cost the baker to make it and no longer so cheap that farmers fed loaves to their animals instead of raw grain. The shop looked brighter; the windows had been cleaned and someone had fixed the sign. Instead of two kinds of bread, there were six, and in one corner a clerk was selling coffee beans, pretzels, and jars of honey.

Outside, a few steps away, there was another difference. An old woman was begging to passersby for *meloch,* or small change. Even though it was warm, she wore a thick hat, a heavy raincoat, and dirty gloves, and when she saw me, a foreigner, she grabbed my arm and whispered what may have been her story or what may have been simply a street beggar's tale. I would never know. "I am a veteran. I was in the camps. Stalin sent me. I have nothing to eat. There are grandchildren at home I am supposed to feed. I feed them first. You are very rich. You help me." Her breath smelled of cheap vodka and she swayed gently as we stood in the cloud of automobile exhaust wafting over the sidewalk from cars circling Taganka Square. There were no old women *nishchiye,* or panhandlers, when I came to Moscow in the waning days of communism, when such public displays of neediness were seen as an affront to the state system. They seemed to be everywhere when I left two years later. The babushka, symbol of the power of Russian womanhood, had become a beggar.

In many ways, the new freedom did not serve women of any age. The Soviet society had given lip service to women's rights. Now, even that hollow promise of equality had disappeared, and most women found that the pressures on them had multiplied. As in the Soviet days, the woman had to take care of the home, the family, and the husband, if there was one. Now, however, she had to try to keep a job, if she could meet the demands of the new businesses run for profit, not for the good of the state. As some women said at the time, "We must work like Russian women at home and labor ten hours a day like Western women at work."

Still, they were not equals at the office anymore. Men routinely talked about how women belonged at home, how they weren't up to work—physically or intellectually. Lesser beings, they noted, many without qualification. Even the government, once the ally of women demanding their share of the jobs, had hardened against them. At one point in 1994, Russia labor minister Anatoly Melikyan was trying to explain why the unemployment rate was so high among women. "Women get fired first," he said, "and this is quite normal because women are less competitive. . . . Men are better workers and they are more reliable as a rule."[6]

For support, of course, there were a few women's societies—from the small gatherings of women around the countryside, who seldom actually referred to themselves as feminists, to interest groups like cat clubs or dancing societies to religious gatherings organized to offer more relief than resolutions. A few cities had hot lines that had been started to hear complaints about problems ranging from simple despair to rape to sexual harassment. But many women considered anything that smacked of Western feminism as un-Russian, and they trusted only their friends or family to help them combat the forces trying to send them back to the traditional roles of either wife and mother or seductress and whore.

As I listened to the talk about how Russian women were losing ground, however, it was hard to imagine the powerful women I knew submitting to second-class status. The U.S.S.R. had forged its young girls into tough and durable creatures, and it was hard to believe that this Sovietized female could wither into the background in such a few short years. I began looking for women who could make the new order work. One was Olga Romashko, formerly an esteemed Soviet doctor, scientist, and researcher, who by early 1992 had become the manufacturer, producer, and distributor of "the best face cream in all of Russia."

The Southwestern Conference Center, a collection of heavy square buildings that had the unfinished look of most late-Soviet architecture, stood on the outskirts of Moscow like a monument to the grand and outdated concept of "the People." As I passed through the front doors one day in the autumn of 1992 and waited for my eyes to adjust to the dim light cast by a chandelier as big as a tractor, I wondered whether this conference promoting business and capitalism would be like dozens of others being held during the first year after communism. Grandly entitled the International Conference on Women and the Free Market, this one was designed to help hundreds of elegantly dressed Russian females (undoubtedly wearing their best and only such outfits) to make the transformation into "small businesswomen," as one brochure described the wave of the future. It would take more than speeches, I thought sourly as I eased into a plush auditorium seat. The pronouncements from the distant podium were full of inspiration and encouragement, all of it slightly tainted with recent reports that women were losing ground in the new society. The latest data showed that 70 percent of the unemployed were women, only a few of them by choice. A Westerner explained how businesses were started in the West, a recipe that could not have been that helpful, and after several women tried to show how the same kinds of things were possible in Russia, a large Soviet-looking woman stood to excoriate the government. It was now full of men who threatened to limit a woman's working hours by law and to give husbands more control over their wives' decisions to work and to have children.[7]

Exasperated by the endless theory, a commodity never in short supply in Russia, I sought relief outside, where a few small-time merchants were said to be selling real products and making real profits. I slipped through the auditorium's thick padded doors and walked into a large marble alcove. One one side of the alcove stood a single table, a kind of spindly TV tray that was being used to support a pyramid of small, apple green jars. Beside the jars, each with a tasteful silver-and-black label that said "OLGA", was a hand-lettered cardboard sign in English and Russian that said DIOR? ESTÉE LAUDER? NOW, YOU HAVE OLGA.

As I stood staring at the sign and wondering what odd concoction was in the jars, a tall handsome woman appeared and smiled at me like a store clerk in the best shops in London or New York. "May I help you?" she said in a soft, heavily accented English. I was not accustomed to such a question after living in the new Russia of 1992, which retained so much leftover rudeness from the Soviet years. The Soviet clerk, knowing that there were always shortages of goods, had clearly enjoyed belittling the buyer, as though purchasing some product were a great privilege granted not only by the state but by the salesgirl. By late 1992, prices went up, more goods appeared, and consumers were more careful about what they bought, but only a few smart salesmen and -women like Olga had begun to realize that the buyer could be something other than a nuisance.

"This is my skin cream. I have introduced it," she said, switching to a soft Russian that came in short, rapid-fire bursts. "There is nothing quite like it—in the world."

The pitch, which drew a small crowd of others escaping the conference, was my introduction to someone who would become for me a symbol of the possibilities for women in this tumultuous era. Her full name was Olga Olegovna Romashko, and it did not take long before I believed firmly that if any woman could survive in the new *diky kapitalizm*, Olga would be among them. Physically, she was commanding. Almost six feet tall, she wore her short black hair swept away from her face to accentuate her clear brown eyes and high, Slavic cheekbones. Her large, expressive hands moved constantly as she talked, and she quickly enticed the women around her to sample a product she could make sound both medicinal and magical at the same time. Once her new customers had bought most of her stack of creams, at fifty rubles (about twenty-five cents) a jar, we moved to a bench under the stairs to talk.

"I am a professor of medicine," she began matter-of-factly. "I am a specialist in human cells. I was at the Moscow Institute of Biophysics of the U.S.S.R. Health Ministry; it was the best. But soon, we had no money for research. There were no chemicals for the laboratories, no reagents. We had to scramble for everything, for paper even, and I began to understand that in this period it was useless to try to continue research. To do what we wanted, we needed hard currency, and I could see that it was going to be more and more difficult for us to get it."[8]

Olga decided against adapting her lab's research. Instead, she used her medical knowledge and her babushka's magic.

"I was sitting in my lab one day, and everybody, all these top scientists and researchers, we were discussing the problem of financing our research. The state"—she sighed—"well, as you know, we are not given the same kinds of subsidies now. Everything was so sad. I realized there was not much hope for financing. We could wait forever.

"So I began to think about what I could do in this situation. How could

I live? I knew the secret recipe my grandmother in St. Petersburg had told me for Catherine's face creme."

Catherine, the Great?

Olga nodded. "My grandmother had passed it on to her daughter, my mother, who passed it on to me. I had made it before, but never with the idea of using it as a commercial product. Then, when it became clear that nobody was going to help us and that we had to start doing something ourselves, I started a 'family private business,' or entrepreneurship, in early 1991. In August 1991, when I went to register my new business, there were tanks in the streets [from the aborted coup by communist leaders]. It was very complicated in the beginning, but no more did we have the feeling of hopelessness," she said.

"Then in March [1992] I decided to leave my institute and go into business. Our bureaucratic system is very hard and it needs a lot of force to overcome. It's terrible; I don't want to even talk about it," she said of trips to offices to get stamps and documents and the long list of approvals that came, most people said, with pushing, threatening, begging, and bribing the line of people who demanded their part of any business deal.

Even more difficult than coping with the bureaucracy was the prospect of leaving the institute. It meant giving up her pride in being a professor while reviving the skills of the previous generation, when her family, the men at least, were all entrepreneurs. Eventually she decided that leaving the intellectual world was more honorable than lingering at the sad dying establishments where people sat around "drinking weaker and weaker tea with less and less jam." We both knew many other people in Moscow whose positions suddenly required little more than an occasional appearance at the office, often to use the phone to try to find other jobs. People drifted away from some of the nation's once-prestigious centers, sometimes keeping one foot in the old institute while working full time somewhere in the new market.

Olga's story sounded unreal, the palaver that any good saleswoman must spin out to gain the confidence of a new buyer. But as she talked that day, Irina Akimushkina, a university researcher who had been trying to promote women's studies in the new Russia, joined us. When Olga leaped to her feet at one point to sell her face cream to a wayward conferee, Irina quietly filled in the background. Olga was quite well known among university graduates as the 1992 president of the newly formed Russian Association of University Women, an organization of educated women trying to push for women's issues after the end of the Soviet Union. She was also a respected medical researcher who had published more than sixty works on the influence of radiation on blood and the workings of the cell in human skin.

Something in Irina's manner made me sense that there was more to this story. Was there some jealousy among Olga's academic colleagues now that she was going into business? Did they think she was belittling her talent? I asked. Irina shrugged, as if to say, it is not important. Only later would I learn that among the hardships Olga faced as she tried to enter a new world was a resentment from the old one. There were those, one friend of Olga's told me later, who said that she was abusing her title and her education and her expertise. She was too personally ambitious, they huffed indignantly. It was not yet a compliment in the communal Russian society, if it ever would be.

Before I could ask Irina more, Olga returned, triumphant from her latest sale. As if nothing had interrupted her, she continued talking, now about biology and its relationship to beauty. "I knew from my research what cells need to help them look well and be beautiful," she said. She had helped create creams for people who had been living near the Chernobyl plant, for those with eczema or psoriasis. Her long-range plans were to recreate these creams for ordinary citizens—a one-woman contribution to the nation's widely advertised military conversion from tanks to armored cars, from missiles to samovars, and now from Soviet ointments to Olga's skin balms.

She grabbed my hand as I left. "I will always be part of the women's movement," she said firmly, as if making a blood promise. It may have been calculated, since women would be the ones to buy her product, but it was clearly more than that. "I will use something of what I make to help other Russian women."

Such a statement was rare, even from an educated woman like Olga. Any thought of a Western-style women's movement made many Russian women shudder. Feminists were not real women, one Russian writer told me. They were caricature lesbians, antimale, antifamily, she said. As I had listened to her that day, I thought that she would not like it if I told her she was parroting the old Soviet propaganda about feminism. The Soviet line was that feminism was a hollow, decadent movement in a hollow, decadent West and that it was unnecessary in the U.S.S.R., where women were supposed to be equal. Feminists, who suggested that Soviet women were really paid less or promoted less often or lived a harder life, were widely criticized and even persecuted. In 1979, Maria, a group of women in St. Petersburg (then Leningrad), put out a book called *The Almanac: Women and Russia,* which gave modest advice about how to cope with the era's hardships. Four of the group were charged with anti-Soviet propaganda and forced into exile for two years. Their very public punishment had served as a fierce warning for almost a decade.[9]

Even as glasnost allowed Russian women the freedom to complain about how society was treating its hardworking sisters in the late 1980s, feminism still had such a bad name that those who pushed for women's rights routinely called it something else. Irina Yurna, editor of the journal published by the Foreign Political Association, wrote that in the early 1990s—when the term "feminism" was still loaded with Soviet images of women who hated men—"our women's movement can be described only in the context of its 'Russian specific character.' "[10] That character, basically, meant that Russian women wanted to be able to work at decent jobs but also to be viewed as extremely feminine and attractive to men. Many even yearned for men to take care of them, Cinderella style. The ideal Soviet woman too often wore sturdy clothes, had arms bulging with muscles, and generally looked as if she could plow a field by hand. Women did not want any new ism that said it was wrong to want bright nail polish and slinky dresses and an easy life.

What women actually needed, however, was support in a world that was beginning to abuse them at home and at work. An old maxim began to appear with increasing frequency in the graffiti of the day: *Kuritsa ne ptitsa, baba ne chelovek*—a chicken isn't a bird and a woman isn't a person.

Women's pay dropped in relation to that of men. Fewer women had the more lucrative jobs in private business.[11] And more women lost jobs in the new marketplace. Tatyana Ivanova, president of a nongovernmental organization in Moscow called the Women's Alliance, said that by late 1993, almost 90 percent of the unemployed were women (an increase from 70 percent a year earlier). Ivanova, calling for an end to what she called "kitchenization," said that women had begun feeling like "grains of sand in a sea of male indifference."[12]

Working women with children were among the ones facing the most severe problems, as Russian law required extra benefits for these women, and new employers simply fired them rather than pay.[13] Benefits for children under the age of six had dropped precipitously from 14 percent of the average wage in May 1992 to 6 percent in May 1995.[14] Many proprietors of the new businesses also did not want women with children because they often had to take off time when their young were sick or had problems at school. A woman's place at work became fragile and temporary, especially at establishments like the Moscow Women's Bank—a name that apparently meant the women were there more for adornment than as managers or customers. The bank's head man, Yaroslav Angelyuk, explained in early 1994 that he had no trouble with married women employees wanting time off for sick children or demanding husbands. As he explained, without apologies: "If a woman working for me gets married, I fire her."[15]

The authorities sympathized with the employer. Valerii Yanvariov, vice minister for social problems at the Ministry of Labor, told one interviewer, "I think when employers review the issue of reducing the number of workers in an enterprise and have the choice as to whom to keep, he has practical reasons for firing women."[16]

Women also faced growing problems with health care and contraception. Abortions, the accepted form of contraception, were often done without anesthetics, and estimates on the number of women who used birth control pills or IUD's was around 22 percent—an official figure that many believed was high. Some stories in the Russian media suggested the Russian woman had four to five abortions during her lifetime; but doctors I interviewed said they had known women who had suffered more than twenty such procedures during their childbearing years. The official figure given to the media on abortions in 1993 was about 3 million, but women's health advocates said the figure for secret abortions made the figure far higher—perhaps as high as 8 million a year, maybe even 18 million. While the abortions could cause infection and sterility, giving birth was even more dangerous. Although some women's groups in 1993 had estimated that almost ten times as many Russian women died in childbirth as in most industrialized nations,[17] a top Russian health official said at about the same time that the rate of maternal mortality in childbirth was two and a half times higher in Russia than in Europe.[18] Whichever was correct, the number of Russian women dying in childbirth was abysmally high.

Sexual harassment, never very secret in the old Soviet society, began to surface in simple and open ways. For some women, the work contract could be a direct exchange of sexual favors for a job.[19] Rape was a problem, not for the male but for the female, who was often seen as the guilty one, provoking the male to his violent arousal. The number of rapes was estimated at thirteen thousand, but most experts suggested that the figure was extremely low, since women were often too timid or ashamed to go to the authorities. Spousal abuse, often a drunken man coming home to release his anger on his wife, was viewed as a woman's fault—she had chosen the wrong husband.

For all the discussion of crime sweeping the Russian landscape, only a few fledgling women's groups had begun to focus on the ways the men had abused their women. They found that almost half of the murders in Russia in 1993 were committed by men who killed their wives or girlfriends. In 1993, according to data from the Interior Ministry, 14,000 women were killed by their mates (of 29,213 murders that year).[20] Another 54,000 women were seriously injured by their angry husbands, even though one report (in *Komsomolskaya Pravda*) estimated that only 7 percent of domestic violence victims filed claims to police.[21]

"Police won't take reports. If you report it, the police say, 'Go home and sleep it off,'" said Martina Vandenberg, an American who has helped organize Russia's first rape-crisis hot lines including one in Moscow called Sisters.

"It's like giving the entire country permission to beat their wives," she said.

"Most women who are beaten don't consider themselves to be victims—they just think they made an unlucky match," said Maria Gaidash, a member of the Russian parliament who was trying to draft a new law on domestic violence in early 1995.[22]

In short, there was plenty for women intellectuals like Olga to do, and some of them tried to solicit the help of international women's rights movements to combat the slide in women's status in their new society. In some ways, they were like Bolshevik revolutionaries eighty or ninety years earlier, never using the word "feminist" except with foreigners who understood the need for it at this stage in Russia's political upheaval.

As a result, women's networks began forming to help those who wanted better status in the workplace and more safety in the streets and at home. Vandenberg estimated that by 1995 there were "literally thousands of small, grass-roots, nongovernmental women's organizations" around the country, little clusters of women trying to bring one another relief. For all the grim news about women's issues, this fact was enough for many women to hope for something better.

Olga's dedication to women's issues, while certainly helpful to her in her business, also made sense on a deeper level. For all the problems of their lives as Soviet citizens, many educated Russians feared losing a kind of moral superiority they felt in the communist years. Whether they were ardent communists, passive believers, or underground dissidents, many felt that no matter how they suffered in the old U.S.S.R., their values were superior to those of the moneygrubbing West. They read books; they devoured ballet and opera; they were educated better than most people in the rest of the world; and they were spared such diversions as advertising, pornography, and soap operas. Once you became a capitalist, the spirit had to be fed from somewhere else. Some found religion as church membership soared. Some did nothing but complain of an emptiness or loss of purpose. Some began to worship the gods of hard currency and easy profits. Olga dedicated part of her proceeds—a tithe of 10 percent, as she put it—to promoting women's issues.

She also established a joint Russo-American venture with a small cosmetic company in Wisconsin called Beehive Botanicals. The venture faded for reasons that Olga would not explain in 1992, but in 1995 she would say only that it failed because Beehive was "only interested in using me as a distributor to sell their products here." In the earlier days, however, her American partner had provided her with packing machines, allowing Olga to shed the packers who demanded 50 percent of what she earned. But the rest of the process was still so laborious that the hundred thousand jars of cream produced each year were, for all practical purposes, handmade. "It is very, very tiresome work," Olga had said. "Like in the Stone Age."

Throughout 1992, OLGA was selling at a rate of ten thousand jars a month—"as many as I can make," as she put it during one phone call to her home late in the year. She told of hauling sheets of apple green plastic to the boxing factory and of her husband delivering boxes of creams to TSUM, the rambling department store behind Moscow's Bolshoi Theatre, and of scrambling through the bureaucracies to get the right documents for selling cosmetics. "You know it is like all of Russian family life," she explained with a favorite maxim. "Before you can do something, you have to wear out three pairs of boots."

Although nobody talked about profit in this era, because at some point there would be not only tax but legitimate tax collectors in this new society, Olga Romashko seemed to be among those thriving in this fast new world. By spring 1993, the Russian parliament estimated that about 6 percent of the new entrepreneurs were women. Olga's was a very rare success story.

(When one of Moscow's women's groups made an appeal for the rest of the nation's women, who were slipping rapidly into poverty, especially single working mothers, the response from parliament and the press was not very comforting. *Izvestia* called it "another in a series of ladies' chats."[23])

I had asked repeatedly to see Olga's "factory," and she promised that it would be possible but that, like all factory owners, she wanted to have the place ready for visitors. We arranged the tour, but my car broke down on a Moscow freeway and I was left guarding it until a friend came to fix it. The excuse seemed to irritate Olga, who undoubtedly had many more difficulties than those of a rich Westerner whose private automobile had failed, and although we talked on the phone several times, her life was full of deliveries and arguments with shops and family matters. For all the pleasantries, underneath it all there seemed a kind of Soviet professor's tone of finality: I'd had my chance and I had failed. Finally, after I'd moved back to New York and returned for a visit in late 1993, she agreed to see me.

Olga's factory was in her family's apartment in one of the large academic sections of Moscow. When I had first arrived in 1991, there were still guard posts along the avenues where police had once been instructed to keep out all but a select group of scientists and their families. The area had been a secret compound housing the physicists and engineers who built Russia's atomic bomb. In those days, nuclear scientists were among the most privileged and pampered of Soviet comrades, and they lived in spacious and elegant apartments built by German prisoners of war. By late 1993, the once-prestigious complex was simply another decaying sector of Moscow, in this case, the large untended apartment blocks full of Russian intellectuals who had suddenly been forced to scramble for a living like everyone else.

Olga's apartment was on the second floor, and as the heavily padded steel door opened slowly, a soft smell of roses spilled out into the hallway. Olga, her face brightly made up, her hair longer and swept away from her forehead with a jeweled comb, led me into the hall to deposit bags, coat, and boots. Then she directed me to the living room/office/bedroom. She apologized for not serving tea. During the day, she had to use a neighbor's kitchen for food, she explained. Her own kitchen was used exclusively as the factory.

In contrast to a year and a half earlier at the women's conference, Olga was now slightly dispirited. The government did not seem to be coming to the aid of people like her who needed support for short-term bank loans (the going rate was about 40 percent interest over a three-month period). Her start-up money, the family's considerable savings of five hundred thousand rubles, was being whittled away as the price of ingredients soared and the stores delayed paying her what they owed, riding the waves of inflation, as she put it. The big merchants were also wary of anything that wasn't Western, even though the waxy rose-scented cream, which I had used for months in Russia, was as good as or better than many of the low-budget Western brands being sold in the big city stores. She was still selling ten thousand jars a month, the same number as a year earlier (and by 1995, the same system would generate only a little more—about fifteen thousand per month).

She needed more room, Olga said. She had tried renting from the state but it was impossible. The going rate was about fourteen thousand rubles (then $14) per square meter per month, while for her, a businesswoman, the charge would be fifty thousand ($50) to two hundred thousand ($200) per square meter. Her efforts to set up a new production line, so that she could begin selling elsewhere in Russia, were also stalled. First, there were too many bribes to be paid—both to the bureaucrats and to the *mafiyas*, gangs that extorted money from virtually all businesses. As Olga put it, "There were people standing in a long line with their pockets open." Second, a group of chemists who wanted to invest in her product and expand its production also wanted to change the name to Dianor, which sounded more Western. Olga had no plans to give out her secret recipe to anyone who wasn't going to call her concoction OLGA.

In fact, although she was ready to show me her factory, she would not give any clues to either the process or the ingredients. I could guess some of them. Beeswax? Rose hips? Lard? Olga simply smiled demurely. She had a difficult time keeping OLGA a secret and, in 1994, a group of young entrepreneurs—undoubtedly the same group that had been copying Lancôme and Estée Lauder to sell in Russian kiosks—had already tried to market fake OLGA cream.

"Come, let me show you the place where OLGA is made." She stood and escorted me a few feet away to her kitchen factory. As she opened the door, with a fanfare that would have suited any marketing specialist in the world, she presented a spotless Russian kitchen, large by Soviet standards but about the size of a standard walk-in closet in America. The cabinets were white-and-brown, the walls done in a beige-and-brown wallpaper, and the floors standard-issue flowered brown linoleum. Somewhere in Russia, there was a factory that created this committee-inspired linoleum with its muddy-colored flowers and yellow borders. They were everywhere in Russia, these floors, and in future years, the sight of one tile for anyone who lived in this era would undoubtedly bring back a rush of memories of Soviet kitchens with their lackluster food and endless conversation.

What was unusual about Olga's kitchen/factory, even two years after the end of the Soviet state, was that it had two refrigerators. One was for the family, Olga explained. The other was for OLGA, the secret ingredients.

As we stood in the doorway, a woman in a white technician's coat moved a handheld electric mixer around a large plastic bowl, whipping a lemon-colored cream to the right consistency. She looked up, clicked off the mixer, and smiled timidly at Olga.

"This is Lena," Olga said. "She was a lab technician before at the institute [Olga's medical institute] and now she works for me."

When I asked how much she earned, Lena quickly announced that it was now one hundred thousand rubles a month (about $100)—compared to eight thousand rubles a month at the institute. "You can feel the difference," beamed Lena.

Olga's other employees included a publisher and a law professor—both working for her part time. Her husband, a cinematic director, helped deliver the product in the family's battered Zhiguli car. Her two grandchildren came by to help with the packing. But by far her most significant staff member was her homegrown model and, as Olga put it, "the best advertisement I have for my products." She called to another room, and within moments, Olga introduced a tall woman whose gray hair and soft-looking skin made her look like a Russian émigré in Paris or New York. In Moscow, every year made its notch on a woman's face, and people were old in their fifties. I had no idea of this stately woman's age. Maybe sixty-five, probably younger, I guessed.

"Meet Momma, Tatyana, who is a specialist in gastroenterology," Olga said as she slipped her arm around her mother's shoulders and hugged her proudly.

"She is seventy-two."

Tatyana smiled as I tried to take in this statement. A seventy-two-year-old woman in Russia was usually weather-beaten and shriveled like some storybook crone. There were no face-lifts in the U.S.S.R., and this woman had not been out of the country. I must have been staring, or perhaps I emitted a soft "nyet."

"We use her for advertising," Olga said, laughing at my reaction.

She explained that Tatyana had been using the original face cream formula for years—Catherine the Great's wrinkle cream, the secret pre-revolutionary recipe brought by Olga's grandmother from St. Petersburg. Tatyana made one slight change in the story of the origins of OLGA. It had not been passed along from Catherine to the Romashko family exactly. Babushka, Olga's grandmother, had learned the basic recipe in a cosmetology course in St. Petersburg. Olga smiled at her mother and shrugged at such detail.

"She made the cream secretly for us," Olga said, meaning her grandmother. "I remember this magic. I remember that when Babushka prepared it, she would recite poetry."

Olga inherited the recipe and kept mixing the cream, adding a few things here or there from her knowledge of human cells, she said.

"After all the research, we tested the samples on me," Tatyana said, her smile bringing only a few wrinkles to her eyes and forehead. "I was the guinea pig."

After a few more minutes, we walked across the hall to the apartment of her friend the law professor so that she could serve me tea from a kitchen that was not being used as a factory. As we talked about the changes in the new Russia and what they meant to her class of academics and to women in general, Olga's light brown eyes narrowed in anger at those who lamented the loss of old order and tried to destroy the new one. She was one of the new privileged class, yes, but she had worked harder than she had ever worked in her life. Now she was doing a little better than the others because she had been a gambler who had figured the odds were against those who sat and waited. There were a few others—she told about a woman whose husband was always drunk and who started making little toys with bits of fur and material. She had been selling them well enough to support the family, including the husband. But many of her old friends had been struggling to replace their barely adequate existence with some method for long-term survival. I mentioned the criticism of Olga for being a self-promoter among some of those in the university community as I thought about how such ambition would have prompted an interrogation by the workers' committee a decade earlier. She paused for a moment, checking some comment that would certainly be part of the analysis of our visit after I had gone. "My close friends, they think what I'm doing is terrific," she said pointedly. The others, she implied, would have to go their own way in the new, individualistic Russia.

By 1995, Olga's apartment and factory looked the same, but she had expanded to new areas around Moscow, added three employees, had plans for adding new creams. She had invested in a bank run by a woman friend and had become a member of the board. It helped getting credit, she explained with a sudden laugh. (The documents she proudly displayed said she had bought fifty thousand shares at one hundred rubles each in July 1994. That was 5 million rubles, which at the time was worth about $2,500). A few days after I saw her, talking about the "addiction" of the marketplace ("It resembles a drug; it's like gambling a lot") and promoting her latest favorite book, *Going For It: How to Succeed as an Entrepreneur* by Victor Kiam (New York: William Morrow, 1986), I met with a colleague who was related to Estée Lauder. In the 1940s and early 1950s, Estée and her husband worked in the basement of an apartment building on New York's Upper West Side. They mixed creams and cosmetics in vats the size of lobster pots with a tap on the bottom to pour it into the bottles.[24]

Such stories made me realize that if Olga could make it, so could the women who had taken over a small state beauty shop in Moscow, shedding the obligatory male partners by the end of 1992 because they were "too weak." The woman I talked with about being an entrepreneur, who was basically a one-person commodities exchange working out of her apartment, would be the next decade's grand dame. There were possibilities for the women who were taking over the knickknack shops and the bread stores; the new female farmers; the women's bread cooperatives; the women's meat store that was as clean as the best Western butcher shops. On some level, women had given Russia its hope, its barest threads of optimism, and these entrepreneurial pioneers were trying out a new form of survival.

I met many women like Olga and her mother who bore Russia proudly on their backs and who led me to the conclusion that the Russian female would keep the society from bitter failure, if anyone could. Most were from the cities, not only Moscow and St. Petersburg, but Arkhangel'sk in the north and Khabarovsk in the east. But many women from the villages also had the powers to enchant—their pure physical strength bolstered by a confidence of spirit that seemed undaunted by the political revolutions in Moscow. My favorite of these was Irina, a farmer's wife from western Siberia, who declined to give her last name to the first American she had ever met, but who gossiped and philosophized and joked about Russian life during an all-night train ride in August 1991.

It was the time of the "good putsch," as it was called later. Boris Yeltsin had stood at the White House and defended the first buds of democracy against the old communist guard, and by late August the Soviet Union was crumbling week by week, republic by republic. I had been sent to Lithuania, where the parliament had declared its independence and the Soviet KGB colonels were burning their files in panic. I had missed the "soft" train, which left in the evening and, after allowing a reasonable night's sleep, arrived in the early morning; and I had barely made it to the next train, which left Moscow late every night and arrived in Vilnius seventeen hours later. I boarded the late train to find my compartment, wandering past the stench of an overused toilet and a cluster of leering Russian soldiers with their rough cigarettes and tea-colored vodka. Baring silver teeth and raising their olive hats in mock salute, they waved sluggishly at something they seemed to recognize as a woman. Seventeen hours, I thought heavily as I bumped along the corridor to find my place.

The compartment was small, but it had been reserved, somehow, for women. There were four narrow bunk beds covered in red leatherlike plastic, the higher ones about two feet from the ceiling so that passengers could sit comfortably on the lower ones. A small table stretched into the center aisle, and the three women who were already there shifted so that I could put my bags under one of the lower bunks. I smiled wanly at the group. They stared back, unsmiling. A thin woman and her daughter left, visiting family elsewhere in the car, perhaps to spread news of the stranger. I was left alone with a woman who had a face of stone and hands so large and muscular that I thought at first she could be a man. She wore a light nylon dress with a plastic belt around her middle and brown plastic sandals. A small triangular scarf was tied around hair that had been treated with the only Soviet hair dye available. When diluted, as it obviously had been in this woman's case, it turned the hair a bright plum color.

As I looked for a spot to sit, she nodded to the place near the window, but her lips were caught in her teeth as she stared at me in what I took to be obvious disapproval. I looked out the window at the seething underworld that had begun to take over the Belorussky train station, an ornate blue-green complex of buildings that was becoming one of the most treacherous bazaars in Moscow. The train lurched, pulling away from the city for what I presumed would be a long, merciless trip spent trying to sleep despite the screaming wheels of a Soviet passenger car, a privy from hell, drunken Russian soldiers, and a room full of sour babushkas. I felt a tap on my left hand and jumped slightly. Across the compartment, the stone-faced woman was now smiling, her features transformed into a warm Slavic face, bright gray eyes, high cheekbones, and a set of teeth that were rotting away one by one. Her hand was stretched toward me, and in it was a kind of

Russian scone that she had brought with her from her home village in Siberia. The bread was soft, sweet, and delicious, an appetizer for one of the best nights I spent in Russia. Ira (she asked me to use the diminutive of her name even though I could not know the rest of it) and I spent most of our waking hours chatting about her children and how she worried about their addiction to things Western and how, although she was not religious, she believed that the young were tapping into a whole new dimension of immorality. She spoke at great length about her fear of Russian dentists, who seldom had such luxuries as Novocain, and marveled at my extensive dental work, a lifelong investment for a child of the prefluoride age. Her parting words were advice: I must enjoy myself with what is there, not what isn't. If that seemed too lofty, she added with a mischievous grin that I must appreciate "every day and every hour" how lucky I was not to live with aching teeth.

Each time I met a woman like Ira who could overwhelm her audience with wisdom or laughter in the face of difficulties that would demolish all but animal instinct in most of us, I realized that Mother Russia was no whimsical bit of émigré nostalgia. Russia's women were the survivors in a nation besieged by civil war, world war, communism, and now capitalism. Like survivors everywhere, they were not delicate flowers; they could be cold and ugly to strangers or outsiders, people who were alien or simply different. But the best of them kept the ancient stories alive, evoked the old images from Russian folklore, taught their children to love irony, taught them that sadness makes better happiness, that whatever was superficial and obvious was only one meager layer, and that if what you could see around you was too dismal for the human spirit, as it often was, inside the head were far better fantasies and enchantments.

I saw it almost every time I went into a home or talked to a group of officials. Often the woman would not be in charge, at least not officially, but she would be the one who had the most energy left to talk about what was wrong and what should be done to change it. The men, long ago, had given up and accepted their serflike existence under the Soviet state. Unlike her husband, if there was one, or her boss, the woman still had light in her eyes.

Like many people who had been given a chance to glimpse the Russians in the Soviet era, I became convinced that this powerful female had evolved out of necessity, because of the history of her country and the weakness of her mate. I knew Russian men who were smart, energetic, and decent, but there were too many more who, for all their physical beauty, made my skin crawl in sympathy for my female Russian friends. Their husbands and boyfriends were babies, they told me. They were beasts. They were objects of ridicule. They were docile on one level, waiting to be told what to do, waiting at home to be served, resting after a long day at a slow job. On another level they were snarling at the world, driving automobiles and making love like angry hornets looking for a place to release their venom.

It was not their fault, many Russian women clucked as they lamented the state of the Soviet male. The twentieth century had taken its toll on their men and forced the female in the old U.S.S.R. to take roles that had traditionally gone to the male, they said. War stories about women—later magnified into war myths by the Soviet propaganda machines—were the tales of girls cutting their braids to go into battle on the front lines, using pneumatic drills deep in the mines, digging tank trenches. They were also the ones left behind to scramble for shelter and forage for food, to raise the children, to take care of the elderly. The stories, like those in parts of Europe during the Great War, told of people learning to eat paste made for wallpaper, burning books for warmth.[25]

Even decades afterward, the Soviet Union had the look of a nation that had just emerged from the war, and Soviet propaganda tried to keep alive the camaraderie and self-sacrifice of those earlier years. In the 1970s, when an outsider commented on the shabbiness of apartments or the worn look of the streets, a good citizen would note that their country had lost too many men during the Second World War. The working estimate used by the Soviets was 20 million dead. By the early 1990s, historians were giving an even higher figure, suggesting that with Stalin's terror Russia had lost as many as 27 million people in the war years. Even thirty years after the end of World War II, women outnumbered men by 20 million in a total population of 250 million.[26]

The male also suffered from an educational and industrial system that punished many of those who showed initiative. If trying to make life better only made life worse, what else might the Soviet worker become other than a stereotype: a lackluster drunk whose product was as shoddy as his life?

But if the women grew in the late 1970s to blame the system, the system blamed the women. Some Soviet writers were suggesting that Russian women had emasculated their mates, an idea that appeared at about the same time that the Kremlin decided that not enough babies (i.e., future workers) were being born in European Russia. Women needed to consider their traditional roles, the government began saying, leaving the factory work to their husbands and concentrating on their "true" work, at home. One of the best known appeals to the Russian woman's "feminine" nature came in 1984, the year before Gorbachev began his revolutionary glasnost and perestroika. An article in *Pravda,* designed to rally the Soviet woman to return to her "nature," described a Russian wife coming home from work to find her husband washing dishes.

"I saw him wearing an apron, red in the face, sweating, and my heart broke. I went up to him. I wanted to spare him, caress him. And he, poor thing, answered me with a wet hand on my hair, and said, weakly, 'It's going slowly. I'm tired.' I saw how my husband had changed—even his voice. . . . 'Take off your apron,' I said to him. 'In the future, there'll be neither the kitchen nor the washing up for you. Be a man!'"[27]

By 1992, this movement to end the "tyranny of equality" for women had been emphasized for more than a decade by the media, state officials, and even by intelligent women I knew. Of course, some of these women yearned for the luxury of staying at home—not only rearing kids but also enjoying what they perceived as Western luxuries such as electric dishwashers and glittering clothes and rich, indulgent husbands. When the job market shifted, however, the business world began to push women into frivolous, decorative jobs or to send them back to the kitchen sink. It did not seem to matter that many of these women—10 million was a generally agreed upon estimate—were single mothers with almost no source of income except themselves.

The society had begun to force women back into their more traditional roles: girl, wife, mother, housekeeper, grandmother. It was a long way from the female coworker marching hand in hand with her male colleagues to build the communist state, and it set the stage for dramatic changes in the way families operated. If the woman stayed home to take care of the children, what happened to the grandmother, who had been filling that role for the last seven decades or more? If the ideal woman was no longer a strong coworker but a good little housewife, schoolgirls and young women had to spend less time preparing for work and more effort figuring out how to find men who could take care of them.

Thus, the new Russian woman was supposed to be a creature who was beautiful, educated, feminine, and antifeminist. As such, for some businessmen, she became part of the Russia that was up for sale. Like the missiles, raw materials, icons, and art, women, especially the young ones, began to put themselves on the block. Some went for the easy money—servicing Westerners at city hotels, making enough in one night as prostitutes to get them through a Russian month. But many wanted more.

When Russian women realized that their beauty and mysterious Slavic sensuality were marketable, they found plenty of customers. A latent sexism seemed to explode into the free marketplace, where such concerns as equal rights or sexual harassment were still a distant Western luxury. In the past, there had always been grasping apparatchiki and powerful officials who would trade goods for a girl's service. Now the businessmen were in charge, and they were people who often felt little state pressure or personal obligation to keep women on the payroll if they became pregnant, distracted by family, or merely unkempt and overweight. Many of those who stayed at work or maneuvered themselves into new jobs felt that their figure and face were their fortune and that they were only as secure as their youth.

The least secure were those working the streets, and their numbers increased visibly in this period. Kristina, a nineteen-year-old who worked in a bar in the same building as the Russian press center where the government gave out its daily notices, talked to a television crew one evening in late 1994. She wore a black silk pants suit, no shirt underneath, and her hair was short, layered with hair gel so that it broke into fashionable strands over her face as she talked.

"This is part work, part pleasure," she said nervously, her eyes darting into the camera and then suddenly moving around the room, as if looking for approval.

"A man I like offers me money. If we make a deal, then I just go away with him." She smiled. It was a big smile, undoubtedly one she used for work and now for television.

She ran away from home at age fifteen, she said. There was little work, but she was pretty—large black eyes, soft fleshy lips, now painted a luminescent scarlet—so night jobs became available.

"I had no choice. My only choice was to survive or not to survive," she said. She looked down and away when she shed her seductive poses, and when she was asked about the life, she struggled to keep her chin up, blowing smoke suggestively to the camera. "Yes, this is a tough situation. You can imagine what it looks like." Imagining it herself through the interviewer's untrained eyes, she smiled almost sheepishly, looking for the first time like a young girl and not an experienced hooker. "Psychologically and physically, it is a difficult job."

Behind her in the dark room, where the lights play against the walls to the low bass of the music, were her friends. She waved to them.

"My future?" She repeated the interviewer's question. "I don't know. I live in the here-and-now. My future is . . . quite vague." Then, the interview mercifully finished, Kristina strutted back to her friends looking like a young girl pretending to be brave and brazen, which I suspected was exactly what she was.[28] Some women, including women like Kristina, began to fantasize openly about a savior arriving on the next plane from Germany or Italy or, preferably, America. Whether he was handsome and funny or fat and slow, he would nevertheless be a man who would whisk them away to the land of bright lights and credit cards, decent food, and painless medicine. Men engaged in this sort of mythmaking as well—like the young man in a blue jeans jacket and spiked hair who once bayed at me in English as I walked past his car.

"Hullo, do you have passport?"

I nodded in surprise.

"Okay. Will you marry me?"

The young man and I both laughed that day, since he had clearly been memorizing a phrase book and decided to practice on the first American woman he met, even one thirty years his senior. But marrying an outsider was a serious business for many people, and the marriage brokers seemed to sprout like corner kiosks in the early 1990s. I went to two in Moscow to find out why hundreds of women were joining these agencies, to learn how these proud, even haughty, females could endure a system that asked them to present themselves like produce in an international marriage bazaar.

When I arrived in Russia at the end of the Soviet years, Moscow's main shopping avenue was called Gorky Street after Soviet writer Maxim Gorky, and when I left, the name had been changed back to Tverskaya Street, meaning the street that leads to the town of Tver. In many ways, it was the street to watch as it shed its shabby communist shops one by one and became a stretch of elegant international boutiques, where clothes and shoes and cosmetics were as exorbitantly expensive as in London or Tokyo or New York. In 1992, the dusty windows from the Soviet days that always made stores look empty and forlorn were steadily being replaced with Western-looking fineries like those at Yves Rocher. Rocher was a clean and brightly lit store that shone in comparison to its neighbors. Its apple green paint beckoned any young woman with money to have a real Western haircut or buy a sparkling array of cosmetics that promised to repair any flaw in hair, face, or skin. In front of the Soviet communications building a short distance away, a kiosk painted like a can of Coca-Cola had appeared, and the Intourist Hotel, once a place where midlevel foreign visitors suffered through their time in Moscow, had begun to tart itself up for the invasions of midlevel Western businessmen. Inside the hotel, there were fur markets and expensive gift shops, a café that served Western beer, and a small "pharmacy," a glass counter, really, where Western aspirin and mag-nifying glasses were for sale at premium prices. Outside, spilling onto the sidewalk and sometimes the street, were men offering taxis or long-legged Russian women who stood sullenly in the background waiting to supple-ment their meager salaries as clerks or factory workers with a nightcap of hard currency.

I had come to the area in the summer of 1992 to find what was advertised as Russia's first and foremost bridal agency. "Alliance," I told the cluster of taxi drivers in front of the hotel, "I am looking for a place called Alliance." They pointed listlessly to a modest prerevolutionary building next door that, in all my trips up and down Tverskaya, I had never noticed. The woman answering the phone at Alliance had said to look for a silver heart, so I had been looking for a garish sign that would stand out among the new lights and Western distractions that this neighborhood had introduced to the city. Instead, the silver heart was about a foot tall, its lettering a modest script, and its position such that only someone who knew it was there would be able to find it easily. Still, during the late 1980s and early 1990s, it had been enough to draw hundreds of people inside, where the first hurdle to any romantic idea of love and marriage was a scowling guard trained in the simple task of picking out those allowed to enter. Westerners of any sex passed easily. Russian women could enter if they were young, heavily layered in makeup, and outfitted in the kind of finery that would have labeled them prostitutes by their parents' generation. (Some hid their finery under Soviet-drab overcoats along the streets to Alliance, protection against the trawling men from the Intourist Hotel next door, who pursued any girl ripe enough for mating.)

Once past the males outside and the guard inside, these women climbed the stairs to face interviewers who analyzed their ability to lure Western husbands a little like poultry graders judging how the product will move in the butcher shop. They were breasts and thighs and pretty faces first, then "personalities," which meant sweetness, gentleness, and passivity. Unlike the growing army of part-time Russian whores, these women came looking not to be rented for an evening but to be bought for good. Or at least for the few years it usually took to gain foreign citizenship. Unlike the contestants for the new explosion of beauty contests or model competitions, where women paraded for up to seven hours for a swarm of official and unofficial judges, these women were not planning to strip down to G-string bikinis so that the newly rich mafiosi could pick off "Miss Bust" or "Miss Legs" for a weekend in the West or a Moscow night in a Western-style hotel.[29] They were more like the mail-order brides who helped fill up the American wild West, women who were not exactly puritans but who were not prostitutes. In the United States, these women would be teachers or nurses, stewardesses or secretaries. They would be hunting for a nice husband or a better job, often both. These women no longer believed they could find either in the new Russia.

While I toured this world of bridal agencies in mid-1992, I watched young hopes colliding with real odds, fantasies about American males crashing against the realization that the knight galloping to their rescue probably lived in a small industrial town in middle America where the center of culture was the household TV.

When I walked into the small, crowded Alliance office that day, three women looked up from their gray metal desks. One, who had been talking on the phone, quickly replaced the receiver without giving notice, it seemed, to the party at the other end. She walked toward me menacingly and asked what I wanted. Clearly I was not looking for a Western husband. I was already Western, and I was wearing a wedding ring. I wanted to talk to Russian mail-order brides, I said. The woman, who would not give her name, looked nervously at her colleagues and said she would have to call the director, Tamara Shkunova. She dialed a number and talked with her hand cupped over the receiver. Tamara would come, she said, but I must wait outside. The other women in the room protested that this seemed unfriendly, and she shrugged, giving me a chair that had been sitting against the wall.

An American man came into the room where I sat and told the woman that he had heard about Alliance and wanted to know how they worked. He spoke very slowly in a Midwestern accent, and when he feared being misunderstood, he shouted, thinking as people often do that if he increased the volume, he would somehow be more understandable to someone who doesn't speak the language. About age fifty, his hair cropped short on top, he had the kind of beard along his chin that men wear if they are members of a religious order, such as some Mennonites or Mormons. He did not look at me, and after he talked in a corner to one of the women, he was given a desk and a scrapbook of sorts, which he flipped through looking at pictures and descriptions of women who were available. I had the strange feeling that this man had slipped away from a group of missionaries in town to convert communists and that his mind was more firmly rooted in the possibilities of sin that afternoon than holy matrimony. My reveries were interrupted by the buzz of the phone, and after a short conversation, the woman handed over the receiver to me. Tamara introduced herself and said she was not in the city. If I could come back later, she would be happy to see me.

A few days later Tamara was waiting in the room with the three desks. The woman who had greeted me so frostily was gone, and Tamara invited me down the hall to a fancier office that she said had been redecorated for a business that had not yet moved into the building. "I borrowed the key." She smiled coyly as she sat me in a comfortable chair on one side of a long wooden conference table. The room still smelled of paint, and the wallpaper was garish and new—red, flock roses of the kind that were popular in the 1960s in the American South. A long golden mirror at one end lent the idea of elegance, even if it was really a tawdry copy of the gilded mirrors of the past.

As I looked at Tamara across the table, I saw a middle-aged woman straining against time and the ravages of Russian life to look like one of her young clients. Her hair was an overly bright maroon color, and it was swept back with an oversize purple bow that dangled about eight inches on each side of her head. Her neck, wrists, ears, and fingers were laden with silver-and-garnet jewelry, and her blouse was cut low so that her breasts heaved as she chuckled about how she ended up as a Russian matchmaker. She had been a journalist, she said, writing for the women's section of a well-known Moscow magazine, but writing what she called critical journalism, which she explained was a regular feature of the Soviet media designed to chastise the worker or bureaucrat who was stepping out of line. She criticized the populace for not keeping the workplace clean, for not being polite, for not keeping up the libraries, and, at one point, for the sad state of Soviet marriage agencies, matchmaking services that most young people viewed as laughable outposts used only by the most desperate. This last series of articles drew hundreds of letters from heartbroken Russian women, she said, so when Mikhail Gorbachev declared that the cooperative movement had begun, she decided in 1987 to create what she called "the ideal bridal agency."

"I had to use my underground connections, and I knew how to use them," she explained, giving a little smile that had to suffice for the gaps in her story that she was unwilling to fill. "When our catalogue was almost printed, the Moscow censor called and told me not to print it."

Women were posing in photographs, not in the nude or even décolletage, but in ways that hinted at the unmentionable idea of sex. Five years later, in 1992, the photographs I saw were still modest to the point of seeming old-fashioned. One packet for an applicant from another agency, called Nakhodka (which means a windfall), showed a twenty-four-year-old typist, Tanya Vlasova, in poses that looked like a professional model's portfolio from the 1950s—including one shot in a gingham dress, with bows in her hair like a dark-haired Donna Reed. Tanya's friend Natasha Zhurakovskaya showed me her own sultriest shot, which featured the thirty-year-old blonde secretary pouting over her shoulder. She was wearing a black evening gown with spaghetti straps. The earlier photos had not been too different, and the censors, after failing to get Alliance's photos outlawed on grounds of pornography, used another tactic. They simply said that such pictures would lure people to Moscow who did not have a *propiska*, the document that allowed them to live there.

"But the chief censor was a friend from my journalist days. I spent one half hour in his office in 1988 crying, and he signed the paper that let us publish it."

Her matchmaking statistics were impressive, if not quite believable. More than three thousand had applied in the five years since she started. More women than men, but for every one hundred women, she had sixty men—all Russians, in the early years. By the time I met her, she had been trying to tap into the huge market of Russian women looking for a way West, and she was spending most of her time trying to match hordes of Russian girls with non-Russian husbands.

"My dream is that someday I want to link a worldwide organization of marriage brokers to a headquarters here in Russia, where we will export beautiful white women all over the world," she said, waving a silver-laden arm to signify the sweeping possibilities. "It would not damage the interests of Russia, I can tell you that. My point of view is shared by some of those in the government."

The West needed her brides, she said. These women had not yet been ruined by Americanization, as she called the desire for equality at home, sharing of household duties, and equal rights on the job.

"If you asked me, if I were a man, I would marry a Russian woman. I have a very high opinion of American women, but for the last two hundred years, American women have carried on their shoulders the whole civilization. They have formed a new type of woman, an independent woman, with some masculine features."

The women that Tamara advertised had already made the transition to this perfectly feminized female, she boasted. "I hear a lot of Americans complain about their tough American wives. Women there begin to look like cowboys, and soon, the men say, 'I am not satisfied with them. Now, they are no longer tender.' These men want mothers, sisters, wives. That is why they are attracted to our Russian women."

A few weeks later, Tamara invited me to a meeting between American men and eighteen prospective Russian brides in the room with the red flock wallpaper. The table was set with the kind of spread Russians put on to show respect, and it must have been expensive for Tamara and her colleagues. There was juice in large pitchers. The plates were loaded with carefully layered slices of sausage and cheese, pickles, and dark bread. Bowls of paper-covered candies seemed to be at measured distances—one every twelve inches precisely.

When I arrived, the women were arranged just as carefully around the table, all sitting up very straight with their hands crossed demurely in their laps. As the door opened, they turned in unison and smiled. When they saw only women, the smiles faded instantly and they settled back in their chairs or shook their shoulders to relieve the tension. There were four empty spaces for the men, and the best food was within easy reach from these central positions. The women, girls really, wore bright makeup and they had built their hair into elaborate edifices—mimicking Western looks that were at least a decade out of date in all but a few places in America. Their heels were high, their blouses cut low, and they smiled without showing their teeth, most of them. As we sat waiting for what seemed like half an hour, the girls began whispering and giggling until a knock on the door brought instant silence to the room. Three young men entered. One was tall and thin. He had the look of an engineer, a computer technician maybe. Another was very attractive, young and handsome, a natural leader who described himself as an American businessman and who did the talking. The third seemed embarrassed to be there. He looked tired, perhaps hung over, and he was wearing jeans and a T-shirt that were not stylishly ratty but simply old and worn, as if he had come from working in his garage. This guy—the frat man, I called him silently as I watched—was not looking for a wife. It was hard to tell about the others.

The next few minutes were excruciatingly painful. Each girl gave her name and a little biography. Some spoke in Russian, which had to be translated. Some spoke in English, which also had to be translated. Two spoke in very good English, and even though other girls were more beautiful, these two would eventually win over at least one of the Americans for at least the rest of the afternoon. The process, which Tamara described as only a beginning, would never be easy.

At the other agency, Nakhodka, the Americans came in prearranged tours. The girls were paraded before the "groom tourists" at large banquets, and there were sometimes as many as fifteen women per male. When a man chose a prospective bride, Nakhodka offered apartments, drivers, translators, and choices of other girls in case the first one didn't work out. Only if the man actually decided to marry one did he have to pay $3,000 extra. ("What is this?" Tamara had hissed when I asked her about it. "Isn't this prostitution when you have to pay additional money only if you take a bride? Who will want to marry them at that price?") Needless to say, the Nakhodka agency, both in Moscow and in America, was run by men. The American Nakhodka representative, Ron Rollband, who had the healthy, perpetually self-improved look of a Californian, was fifty-six the day I met him at a downtown Moscow café in late 1992. He was not angry or even surprised when I asked him about whether he was running a variation of the oldest profession in the world.

"If a man wants a prostitute, it would be cheaper to stay home and hire hookers," he said in a voice that sounded as though he had answered this question dozens of times before. "I know that some of those who come, their intentions are definitely not honorable, and the competition here is very keen—these women will do almost anything to snag a man. But to the best of my knowledge, nobody has come here simply on a sex trip," he told me when I met him in a Moscow café with his own bride-to-be.

As Rollband had talked, trying to explain why he never asked the potential grooms their intentions or even whether they were married, I stole looks at his mail-order bride, a Russian girl he introduced only as Lidiya. Lidiya was indeed beautiful. Blond and thin, she was a twenty-five-year-old whose look was carefully un-Russian. Hair, makeup, clothes, nails, jewelry—it was all unnaturally subdued for a place where women desperately loved to celebrate in bright colors and any available glitter. When she looked at Rollband, she smiled adoringly. The smile dropped instantly when she turned to hiss orders or comments in Russian to a girlfriend who had pulled up a chair beside her. I felt that there was nothing soft about this woman, and Rollband, who had been divorced three times, was not going to have an easy time with the fourth. My musing was interrupted by Rollband, who saw me looking at Lidiya.

"She sings like an angel. She is trained as a doctor. She even sews her own clothes," he said as his hand reached out to pat Lidiya's arm. "She is like somebody who fell off a Christmas card," he cooed as she smiled up at him and then blinked in what may have been shyness or more probably embarrassment. I found the phrase embarrassing too, not because she wasn't beautiful, but because it was such an asinine thing to say about a Russian woman who was undoubtedly anything but two-dimensional. I hoped that she would get what she wanted out of this Western connection.

At Alliance, Tamara talked more about brides and weddings. She still swooned at the idea of romance, even if she knew the odds were minuscule that the rare matches she made would result in anything so lofty as true love. Somehow, Tamara made it all seem more wholesome than it was, and the business side of her operation was tempered by her own girlish fantasies. She also inadvertently arranged an introduction for me to a group of women who explained what may be the most difficult part of Russian life for any outsider to understand: how Russians find joy in what often seems like a bleak and desperate existence. I called them the cat women, and Valentina Krymova was one of their leaders.

It began during my last visit with Tamara, when I asked if she had age limits for her brides. She frowned at such an unfriendly thought. Love comes at many ages, she huffed, and then she began to tell me about her "old clients." I was thinking about seventy-year-olds when she handed me a slip of paper with Valentina's phone number and address written in the elegant manner that is virtually universal among those educated in Soviet schools. "Valentina is forty-six years old," Tamara said, "the age when a woman is not needed by anybody."

Valentina Krymova lived in one of the newer high-rise apartments that stand like barren cement dominoes on the outskirts of Moscow, without trees or green lawns or relief from the hazy summer sky. I had come that day to talk about mail-order brides, but the conversation about Alliance was little more than a brief detour from the important issues in Valentina's life—her sadness about the humans around her contrasted with the pleasure that came from her animals.

The day I met Valentina, her well-pedigreed Persian cat was nursing six kittens, and when the door to her apartment swung open, our hostess waved a hand at the kitchen and apologized for the smell. Cat lovers in Russia were forced to cope without litter or backyards or canned cat food, she explained. What was deposited in the corners or sprayed on upholstery by cats who turn up their noses at a box of dirt from the parking lot had to be cleaned up with weak Russian disinfectant. The acrid smell of cat urine mingled in her tiny foyer with the odor of fish being stewed for dinner. The plumbing was also backing up that day, she explained, and the *remont*ers, or renovators, were fixing the kitchen, exposing her apartment to drafts from the garbage areas outside. Valentina sat me down in her sitting/ sleeping room, put the tea kettle on, and returned spraying a musky Russian perfume, which added to rather than subtracted from the cloud that hung over the tiny apartment.

After apologizing a third time for the state of her home, Valentina suddenly stopped, waved her hand as if to say enough, it did not matter, and began laughing at herself for fluttering like a teenager over her foreign guest. Nobody ever died from the smell of cats, she said giggling infectiously, and within a few minutes, Valentina had begun to cast her spell. My young friend Slava Zelenin, a handsome twenty-five-year-old Russian who had come to help me as an interpreter, began to take on the look of the lovelorn as she talked and served us steaming Russian tea. Valentina had the gift that some Russian women possess of making people around her feel good in spite of everything. Undoubtedly it was a charm that could come and go, but on that day we felt the full blast of this vibrant woman's girlish optimism. When she talked, she laughed almost constantly, with one of those giddy contagious laughs that make everything in life seem tolerable, even funny. At the end of the afternoon, I realized that as this masterful storyteller had spun out the terrible details of her life as a Russian woman, we had laughed through every sad chapter.

"I am an economist by trade," she had begun, offering cookies as she settled gently into a brittle wooden chair. "I graduated from a trade institute, and for a long time, I have worked in a small state enterprise as a bookkeeper. Two years ago, I got a divorce."

I had already been told about the divorce by Tamara. There had been another woman, maybe many other women. Tamara said he had left her. Valentina's version was that she had decided he was more trouble than her children and, since he wasn't one, she had kicked him out.

"I realized that I needed to have a normal life," she said, rolling her eyes and laughing at the absurdity of such an idea. "But, really, I had three children—two young ones and my husband. And my husband was the most difficult one of all."

She described her day—which did not change much after her husband was gone. She worked at her job in an electronics factory from 9 A.M. to 5 P.M., sometimes later. Before work, during lunch, and after work she waited in the shopping lines. At home, she cleaned and cooked. She cared for the children, washed them, nudged them toward their homework, put them to bed. Her husband had been an academic, which meant that he read or wrote while she worked. "He was an intellectual," she said, clucking at the loftiness of such a life. "I supported him for sixteen years while he worked on his dissertation on gas dynamics." Valentina shook her head and sighed. "Sixteen years I supported him. It was enough."

I had heard other Russian women talk about men as the major inconvenience associated with marriage and reproduction. Some of it was empty talk. With estimates that 10 percent of the children born in Russia were illegitimate and with poverty rates soaring for single mothers, any help would seem to be better than none.

"Our Soviet society created a new Russian man," Valentina continued that day. "Many of them are not responsible, infantile. I can understand when you need a good rest, when you've been responsible and worked hard, but not this way, just coming home after school and sitting on the couch. After the divorce was when I had a lot of time to think about him, what were the reasons for this Russian man. One thing, the genes are degenerating. The best of our people were killed for many years. Many good people left. Our society was such that for many years, the most industrious men were deprived of their initiative. Then their initiative was killed altogether.

"I see it in my own son. The education of the boys is done so that they end up without initiative. He didn't see what I call good ambition in his father, so why should the son have it? He is a brilliant boy; he is at an aviation institute, but he lacks what I want to see in a man. He has latent ambition, but no real initiative. That was one of the things that made it difficult to live with my husband. He was exactly the opposite of me," she said. "I had all the initiative."

Valentina, once she had begun, talked like many Russians—in an endless rapid fire, so that to interrupt means leaping into the fray midsentence instead of waiting for her to take the next breath. The soliloquy would not end until late in the afternoon. Slava and I were behind schedule. Our families would be irritated. Still, we sat there, transfixed by this woman and her story.

"Probably it was my fault as well. I didn't care for him myself. We never really had a vacation together. I went to work when the youngest was four months old. I took him to the *detsky sad*, the state kindergarten. As any mother here, I had to pull myself together and drop him off. I was always late for my job. I would leave him on the merry-go-round at eight A.M. At six, I would come back and he would be at the same place waiting for me. They said he did not eat well; he did not cry. He just waited in that terrible place, where there were twenty-five kids, and when it's cold, they dress them up one by one for a walk, and when the last is dressed, the first is sweating, and soon half are sick and they don't care. The less children for them, the better it was at that horrible place. But I had to leave him there and see his face all day in my mind, and in this state, I went to work. How can you work?"

She stopped, drank tea, shook her head as if to send the memories away. Just as I began to think she would burst into tears, one of her cats stepped into the room, almost on cue. A large, fluffy calico with green eyes, this animal walked like a tsarina entering a rather small palace, and with each elegant step she let out a sharp little meow as if protesting that the visitors had disrupted some vital part of her day. Valentina swept the cat into her arms and continued talking, now fortified with the noisy purr of her favorite Persian.

As she talked it was hard to imagine how anyone, even someone who loved cats, could breed them in a one-room Moscow apartment. The small flat was better than the communal apartments, which were among the most squalid of the Russian housing available in the Soviet years, but it was still cramped for three people. The living room, which converted to a bedroom at night, was warm and comfortable. She and her daughter, then age nineteen, slept on the couch, she said. Her son, who was twenty-three but who still lived at home, slept on the bed. The six kittens and two grown cats were kept in the kitchen, mostly.

The cats, Valentina explained, were also a business. The kittens of fine Persian parents went for the equivalent of $40, and although they were cheap by Western standards, it was one of the ways a Russian could make good money at home. Valentina said she agonized each time she sold a kitten. "I love them," she said at one point during our afternoon, as she handed a ball of hair with tiny green eyes and a little hairy toothpick of a tail to me as a potential customer. I handed the kitten back, explaining that I had two parakeets.

Valentina fluffed her hair, cut short in a 1960s American bubble, as she talked about her "little friends." The wisps of gray around her face blended with strands of blond and brunette—a tricolor picking up the shades in the calico on her lap. As we left that day, Valentina made two promises: she would call us after her second meeting with a prospective German husband, and she would invite us to Moscow's premier cat club. The German, a lawyer in his sixties, had taken her to dinner, given her flowers, and now promised to bring her to Germany for a visit. They had gotten along well, she said—the same politics, the same ideas about religion and children and literature.

"Did you ask him whether he likes cats?" I asked.

Valentina looked at me and did not smile. "No. I didn't," she said softly. "How can anyone not like cats?"

I did not hear from Valentina for several months, and finally Slava called to find out about her two promises. Valentina did not want to talk about marriage—the German had turned out to be a dry old man who ate vegetables and drank only one beer a week. "He had no blood. He was brittle," she said. *Kuznechik* was the word she used—a grasshopper. No, she wanted to talk about "the nice things, the cats." We were to meet her a few days later to attend a regular meeting of the Fauna Club, the oldest club of cat enthusiasts in Moscow.

A few weeks, not days, later, Slava and I drove northwest of Moscow to an area that would have been off-limits to both of us a year earlier. As we wandered through the streets that evening, Slava tried to read the battered street signs and match them to my old Soviet map of the city. Street names had changed, and many streets were simply not on the public maps. At one point Slava stared at a sign, checked the empty section of the map, and said softly, "I don't believe this."

"It's not on the map?" I asked.

He laughed. "No, the name of the street is Secret."

"So, we can't know the name of the street?" I asked.

"No, we *can* know the name. It's called Secret Street."

I drove along laughing, talking about the strangeness of Russia, all made more unreal by the snow now falling so heavily that it was beginning to cover the rusted pipes and dilapidated road signs along our route. "It's magical," I had whispered, using one of my favorite Russian words. Slava snorted and shook his head. As long as you're looking at the snow from inside a nice warm car, it's paradise, he said.

Valentina met us near a metro stop, leaped eagerly into the car, and then directed us past a wall of apartments to a one-story, cement-block community center inside. This communal center, like those in virtually every Soviet apartment complex built in the last few decades, was architecturally utilitarian. A cluster of rooms, each with a few windows, was built around an indoor toilet and one large meeting area. The hallway had been painted a dark blue, a peculiar Soviet color that was intended to brighten but in fact did just the opposite.

As we made our way through the hall, we heard the unmistakable sounds of a cat club—women laughing and arguing, mixed with a chorus of meows, from the soft cries of terrified kittens to the growling of a large, unhappy tom.

Club Fauna met twice a week here, on evenings when the room was not being used by one of Moscow's best dog clubs, Valentina explained. The room, where I would soon watch women swooning at the sight of an Angora or turning up their noses at a Persian with a slightly bent tail, had the faint smell of a veterinarian's office. And even though it was a shared space—dogs and cats supposedly given equal treatment—the decorations favored the dog owners: a skeleton of a hunter pointing at its prey and a series of anatomical photos of what looked like German shepherds. One picture showed the young Tsar Nicholas II with two hunting dogs. Valentina explained that the Russian hound—exterminated during the Soviet years as a symbol of nobility—was now being imported back into Russia.

As I made my way to the front of the room, a young girl pulled a ball of fur out of her basket and set it down in front of Lidiya Mikhailovna Nasedkina, the club president. Lidiya Mikhailovna's job that evening was to assess the status of newly documented cats. Although she had a nice, round face and a maternal smile, the cat owners approached her with obvious anxiety about the judgment at hand. The girl's cat now stretching and unfolding before Lidiya Mikhailovna was a soft, alabaster color. Its hair was long and silky, and the eyes, suddenly open wide as she was being examined from tooth to genitalia, were a bright, clear green. Throughout the room, there was a murmur of approval. This was a chinchilla Persian, they whispered. Beautiful.

Lidiya wrote her assessment in a slow longhand, applied the stamp, without which Russian transactions would never be complete, and handed the animal to its owner. Tamara Tarasova, a seventeen-year-old student whose family had eight cats in their three-room apartment, beamed as she saw the document. The cat had received the top ranking: excellent. A female chinchilla could go for forty-five to fifty thousand rubles, Valentina whispered. That was $145 to $160, but if it seemed cheap to a Westerner, the clients were not yet from Europe or Japan. They were Russians, and in the autumn of 1992, this was an astronomical amount of money. This Persian was not simply a pet, but a product. These people loved cats, yes, but they loved them more when they made money.

The second petitioner pulled three furry kittens out of a gym bag. They were also Persians, but the murmurs throughout the room were low and disapproving, as if someone had marched brazenly into their midst and asked for papers on a litter of alley cats. "Weak," one older woman whispered and shook her head. The three kittens were the product of a good merger, Valentina explained. The owner of the female had three kittens out of the mating, but the owner of the male cat had also come to the club meeting that evening. It was her right to choose one kitten produced by the union.

The room grew quiet as the owner of the male cat peered at the furry cluster. "That one," she said, pointing to a little white fur ball, now sitting down to take in the bewildering scene.

"No," hissed the woman with the kittens. "You cannot have the female. This is not fair."

The hand reached down swiftly and snatched the female kitten away. The owner of the two remaining males began to cry softly into her woolen scarf.

"It is not fair, not right," she sniffed to Lidiya, who had begun filling out the kittens' documents. "I only had her male for a day. That's not long enough, you know that, to have a large litter of kittens."

Lidiya shook her head in sympathy but judged the two males weak. The woman rolled up the papers, tucked the kittens back into the bag, and stormed out of the room.

Fauna's members waited uncomfortably for the moment to pass and then returned to the subject that brought them there. With a foreigner in their midst and the documentation out of the way, the cat lovers began to talk about their passionate business. As they sat in the steaming room, most of them still wearing their fur hats, they agreed that the smartest cats are plucked "from the lids of the dustbins" and the dumbest are overbred Persians, who "can sit around like an old hat on the chair, if you are not careful."

Valentina, with other members nodding and commenting, walked us through the details of cat breeding in Russia. If cats have defects, broken tails at birth or crossed eyes, it is up to the owner to decide whether they should be taken out to the countryside and drowned. "I usually give them away to people for symbolic pay," Valentina said. "Many people love cats but cannot afford fifty thousand rubles. "If I sell it for four thousand, I know it will be loved. I would be very sorry to kill it. But sometimes when they are weak. . . ." Her voice trailed off. The others shook their heads at this side of the animal business. At Moscow's pet market, I had seen a man selling rabbits. When I asked the price, he asked how I planned to use it— as a pet, a dinner, or an article of clothing? Cats and dogs had been converted into collars and fur *shapki*, or hats. There was no SPCA in Russia.

The talk continued that evening, but what was most memorable was the joy of this business. In a place where "Have a nice day" would sound like a cruel joke, these women—there were eight thousand cat club members in Moscow alone—were enjoying themselves immensely. They were there to talk about their cats, their families, their problems, in that order. They would be there for another two hours, gossiping, laughing, drinking tea and telling stories about the angora sold to a Japanese family for $200 or a fine cat stolen by a woman's ex-husband. If Russia's women were being shortchanged, many of them had a powerful source of strength—other Russian women.

One of the cat women had the look of the lost old people on the streets. Lena Zolina, who gave her age as sixty, wore a ragged brown fur hat and whistled through broken dentures as she talked. "I have eighteen, maybe twenty-five cats living with me," she said. "I live in two rooms, but I don't let them in the corridor or the kitchen."

I could not imagine the smell or the noise in an apartment with twenty-five cats. None of them were neutered, since they were being bred in this tiny space, and that meant that when they were in heat, they sprayed and howled in search of mates.

But the stink? I protested. Lena shrugged. Not a big problem, she said. The noise? "They are quiet, and they shout only when they have meat. So I don't give them too much meat. They eat a lot of oatmeal."

Lena's cats made her happy, she said, because she liked cats and because they kept her alive in the new Russia. She had sold two kittens in the last six months—one for $200 and another one for $150. It was more than two years' salary at her regular job.

Before my family left Russia, Valentina telephoned to say she was going to California to try another potential husband. In a few months, the Californian was deemed inadequate as well, but a year later, she tried a third foreign mate. None of us knew by then whether Valentina was looking for a husband or a plane ticket. We began to figure that this would go on for years—a wily Russian woman husband shopping the world—but in early 1994, I found her in California again, and this time she was married, although I suspected not for better. When I called, her new husband got on the phone and almost kept me from talking with her. "She is fine," he kept saying, making me more nervous about her each time he said it. Finally, when I insisted, Valentina grabbed the receiver. There were no giggles, and she whispered that she could not talk. "An argument?" I asked, begging her to speak Russian, which her new husband did not understand. "Yes," she said, in English. "That's correct." Then she took my address and promised to write, but for a year I did not hear from her. Her friends in Russia said she was trying to make a wedding bed out of nettles, meaning that this marriage might not last even long enough for Valentina to get her papers.

But in late 1994, Valentina called me from California. She refused to speak in Russian; it was important for her to speak English, she said in a strange Russo-Californian accent. Her husband was "kind, but I live not a very easy life." He had problems with his family, and she was trying to help, she said. Her daughter was with her, also beginning life as a Californian, and her son had decided to stay in Moscow.

"I will stay with him, because he is not a bad person," Valentina said finally. "But it is not an easy life. I feel that we are hunters in our life," she concluded. I did not understand what she meant until finally I realized that for her, it was impossible to sit and enjoy. She had learned in Russia that the woman must always be searching, scavenging—for food, for comfort, for work—and that did not change, even in California. The dream about a Western husband was simply fantasy.

Somehow I felt that Valentina had been happier in Russia, but she had decided that she could grow old in California, where she would not ever be a Russian babushka. "I will be an American," she had said, "no matter what."

In many ways the push west—either to buy gear or find work abroad or catch a foreign husband—had been a powerful force in Russia since the late 1970s. By 1995, the glamour of the world outside the borders had begun to fade for many, and Russians were trying to figure out, not how Russia could become more like the Western countries, but how or whether foreign ways should be adapted to their old welfare state.

Some women had decided that for all the flaws of the old system, it had been better for them, for their children, for their aging grandparents. I met one such woman when an American friend asked me to deliver a book to her husband. Her name was Natasha Zvonareva, and when I asked her if she could talk to me about how the new Russia treated its women, she had laughed quietly and then invited me to come to her apartment for coffee and details.

The "sleeping area" outside Moscow where Natasha lived with her two-year-old son, husband, Andrei, and mother-in-law was a startling reminder that only the cities had driven themselves into a fever of commerce and Westernism by the mid-nineties. The community of Bibirevo, on the outer edge of Moscow, still had the deadened look of a Soviet city with its massive apartment towers, their outside shells slowly deteriorating into the sad little parks around them. Somehow the aging of an old building is not so depressing to look at as the deterioration of a new one, and in the starkest sense, this apartment complex, probably constructed sometime in the previous twenty years, already looked like an American slum. Doors to buildings were warped and dirty. Trash blew aimlessly through the communal spaces. Cars in various stages of repair sat on the sidewalks. The hallways were dark, the banisters grimy. The elevator had the rank odors left from the last rider and his undisciplined dog.

The Zvonarev apartment, behind a padded steel door that had become more than a luxury in recent years, was bright and clean, a vision in red and scarlet, mauve and dark rose. Red apparently was the favorite color of Andrei's mother, who owned the apartment and who had allowed the young couple to live there with their two-year-old son. Later in our afternoon together, Natasha would tell me that it was not convenient, this living arrangement. Three rooms, and Mother-in-law had the big one. They had a small one with a balcony (a genuine luxury), and the baby had a playroom. The size of the apartment was grand by Russian standards, and the reason was that Mother-in-law was a personnel manager at a nearby factory. In the Soviet days this was a powerful position, giving her this spacious apartment as part of her status. She still did well enough to support Andrei, a teacher, and his family, and although she was not present, I suspected that she was the dominant woman, whose demands had the effect of law in her small household. Mother's room—the living room, where we sat—was meticulously decorated in a way that reminded me of small motels in the South forty years ago. Red-and-white filigree wallpaper blended into pinkish red curtains. The floor was a mock Oriental carpet, mauve its dominant color, and the couch and chairs were covered with a red velvet fabric, clearly a touch that was added only for visitors. An orange-red Soviet phone sat on a nearby cabinet. The only contrast was a large Toshiba television set that dominated one corner of the room.

Natasha looked young and fragile as she sat among all this plush velour and heavy Soviet furniture. At twenty-five, with the first strands of gray beginning to appear, she was still thin, her light brown eyes still bright. Natasha's hair was tied back in a Soviet-style hairdo, a little pouf in the front, a tight bun in the back, but she wore Western jeans and an overly large men's shirt—a combination of styles, a little Russian and a little American. As she talked about her career and her view of this new Russia, she spoke so quietly at first that I could barely hear her. Her voice grew louder, however, as she began to describe what had happened since the end of the U.S.S.R. She was a teacher who was earning an extra degree in psychology, she said, and, "These changes, they are terrible." She shook her head like a schoolmarm watching a group of children misbehave.

The lack of stability was perhaps the worst, she said. Before, she could have depended on a decent salary as a teacher. Now, she had to ask the principal whether she would make enough money to live. The very idea of asking about her salary made her wrap her arms around herself in distress. Before, the institution took care of everything—extra food, medical care, even vacations.

"But even that is not the worst. The worst part is the attitude toward children. I think they are the most important part of our life. I think they are our future. Now, nobody thinks about them. Nobody is interested in them. We have one lost generation [the graduates from the last ten years, who were not trained well enough as Soviet citizens and not taught how to succeed in the new society], and now we are about to lose another one."

Outside the apartment she had heard the children playing in the sand a few days earlier, she said. They were playing for dollars. They were screeching about who had the most money; instead of cowboys and Indians, it was cops and robbers. The robbers were the good guys. "Feh," she said, shaking her head in disapproval.

"My son's friend gives him something, a toy, and he says, 'Be careful. This toy costs three thousand rubles, so don't break it.' " She sighed. "It is a terrible thing to tell a child. Before, all toys were very cheap. All pioneer camps were cheap, and everything was made for children."

Nothing was cheap anymore, she said. Her degree, once free for anyone who qualified (or had the right connections, I wanted to add), now cost money—$500 tuition now, even though she had managed to receive a scholarship.

If the young were forgotten, so were the old, Natasha continued. And "old" did not mean ancient; it meant anyone over thirty. Part of the reason for problems among the older generation was their attitude, she admitted. But part of their attitude was also due to the way they were being treated. Her father, for example, was miserable. He had been a plumber in a factory. "He has golden hands." She sighed again. Before, he worked and made a decent salary, and "he was able to buy not only what he needed but to buy for others as well. Now he cannot, and he thinks all the world is against him."

Natasha's father had roamed around the commercial structures, where young men, mostly, rejected him with the flick of a hand. He had just turned fifty, an age that would have made employment difficult anywhere in the West as well. But his problem was that he was over thirty, they told him. You are too old to be one of us, they said. Try to find a job hauling, heavy labor, maybe. Natasha sighed again at the ugliness of these new entrepreneurs.

Natasha, who served coffee and nudged me into drinking it when it seemed in danger of growing cold, found a new attitude among her friends as well. She was so lucky, she said, to have a child and a husband. Her girlfriends now did not want children, she said. "They think about their career now. Later, they will have children."

She smiled at the thought of them. "Most of them will have a child without a husband, I think." She laughed gently. "To take care of a child is quite enough, they say. To take care of a husband is too much."

These friends were the professionals—the ones who wanted to teach or work in the new enterprises while they still could. In this way, for the young woman, there was a great possibility for what Natasha and her friends called self-realization. Unlike in the old days, when the state found jobs for graduates, a young woman now could look for her own position. The opportunities were there—in business, in private schools, even in some of the government-supported enterprises like the public schools.

Some had opted for marrying rich, she added. Their idea was to be housewives, and their status was worthy of a sociological study at some point, she suggested.

"They look wonderful, and they take care of the house, and they go to the shops," she said. "But usually, they don't take care of the children. We see it often at the school. The father is in business. The mother is a housewife, and the children are neglected."

In a long discussion about Russian life, Natasha had come full circle. Each discussion of the society came back to a description of the treatment of Russia's children.

"Basically," she concluded, "I think that the [Soviet] society was more humanistic. The attitude toward women who had children was better." Society will be judged by the way it treats its children, she said, and Natasha Zvonareva judged this one harshly.

On the highway back into central Moscow, watching the old Soviet suburbs changing into a city that had become an oasis of commerce and wealth, I began to wonder if the growing number of Russians who yearned for the old method would bring it back upon themselves. Russia thrives on its discontent, an ancient tendency that would make it easier on the politicians who wanted to oust any establishment. What Westerners like me feared was that there would come a government that refused, once again, to be voted out of office or to tolerate further complaints about its leaders and their methods. When I listened to Natasha and others like her, I wondered if our fear was their secret wish—to have a dictator to tell them what to do. In the old days, even though they were not equal, women enjoyed the myth of equality and the idea that men were supposed to respect them as mothers and grandmothers, coworkers and comrades. Now, even the myth was gone, and the view that women were inferior had surfaced, spoken by journalists, men on the streets, and people of culture and renown.

Rabotnitsa, a magazine for women workers, still one of the most popular in the country, even with *Cosmo* and *Good Housekeeping* available in the cities, conducted an interview with Nikita Mikhalkov, whose film *Burnt by the Sun* appeared to international acclaim in 1995. Mikhalkov at one point said: "In my soul, I am Asiatic and consider woman to be a lesser being." The comment provoked no public reaction, from either the magazine editors or its millions of readers.

3

Health:
Living in Soviet Ruins

I don't think being healthy is the most important thing for a human being. Donkeys are healthy.
— Russian heart attack victim, 1992[1]

Russian booksellers, who hawked their wares in the streets and underground in the subways, offered an excellent way to recognize the new interests of ordinary Russians after communism. As makeshift publishers began to specialize in what an extraordinarily literate people wanted, instead of what the government thought they should want, the rickety tables were overloaded with books on sex, pets, art, crime, and how to learn Japanese or English (preferably American). Seldom in the early 1990s was there anything on exercise, diet, or health, except for a few tracts on home remedies or herb gardens, and the reason was easy to understand: to focus on health in Russia meant concentrating on depressing and frightening forces beyond the ordinary person's control.

In a place where pollution pours into the air from industrial pipes that look to Westerners like leftovers from another century, jogging made little sense. In towns where water was so tainted that typhoid had begun to reappear and raw sewage had been known to overflow in the city streets, drinking less vodka seemed a waste of self-control. In a country where DDT was used long after the rest of the world banned it and where its residues left at least 25 million farm acres poisoned,[2] eating fruits and vegetables was not the easy answer to a healthy, happy life.

For all the lusting after an American lifestyle, Russia was years away from importing the self-improvement neurosis that afflicted most Americans in the 1980s and 1990s. A few women in the cities began taking aerobics classes, a form of which also began to appear on television. The square Soviet matron began to test Herbalife, a concoction that promised the lean look of Europe's most fashionable women. But in general, anxiety about life's risks seemed much lower than in the West, even though the risks were far higher. Only the foreigners on Aeroflot shuddered openly as planes getting ready to take off from Domodedovo taxied past the wreck of another airliner, a brutal reminder that if something happens to an airplane, there is nothing under it but air. Only newcomers stopped and stared on a freezing winter day as truckers defrosted their machines by sticking a fiery rag under the oil sump. Food was stored on balconies, where it froze and thawed and refroze many times before it was finally eaten. (This tendency bothered me, and I argued gently with several women that it was unsafe. No, they explained, they had been eating this rethawed food for decades, giving it to their children. Besides, there was nothing else, they often concluded, ending the argument.) Milk traveled from farm to city in tankers so rusted and filthy that they barely seemed suitable for toxic wastes.

The hazards to health were everywhere. Some, like pollution, were the legacy of Soviet industrialism. Some risks the Russians invited—smoking, drinking, and driving in ways that toyed with disaster. The rate of traffic deaths in cities, for example, lent credibility to the feeling that Russia's streets and highways were a war zone.[3] The urge to end this carnage seemed strangely minimal, and Western concerns for safety had a way of sounding limp and cowardly to a Russian driver. When I got into a cab front seat in Yalta and automatically began looking for the seat belt, the driver looked insulted. "There aren't any seat belts," he said, pointing to the place where they had been severed some time ago. Then, recognizing that I came from a different world, he smiled and took a hand off the wheel to point at his large chest. "You don't need a seat belt when I am driving," he said proudly.

In some ways it seemed an insane way to live, jousting constantly with the fates. But I often wondered which was healthier—living with danger by ignoring it, as Russians had been forced to do, or frantically trying to obliterate every newly identified hazard in the manner of the average health-obsessed American. From a slower Russian world, where people sat around smoking in their tiny apartments and talking about the perils of freedom or whether good needs the balance of evil, I returned to America with my family to find people picking at their food for fear of not getting enough antioxidants and, worse, talking about it endlessly. A few days after we returned to New York, we turned on the evening news just in time to see a woman wearing a gas mask as she looked through the lush green vegetables at her grocery store. She was part of a new movement in California to ban perfume in public places.

The Russian health problem, by contrast, was real and deserved all the human energy and intelligence that could be applied to it. In the late 1980s and early 1990s, after Gorbachev began to allow more freedom to talk about the society's problems, the former Soviet people had begun to learn the extent of the damage to their country and its people. Each time new data was released, often from files kept secret in the Soviet days, it brought bad news. Life expectancy, a way of determining a nation's overall health, dropped steadily, and by 1995, the figures were alarming, especially for men. From 65.5 years in 1991 the figure for Russian males dropped to 57.3 three years later (compared to 72 years for American men). Russian women did slightly better, with a life expectancy of 71 years, compared to 79 years for American women. The reasons for such a precipitous drop were baffling, but experts listed many of Russia's woes as possible causes: among them were deteriorating medical care, high infant mortality, high accident rates at work, at home, and on the highways, and, finally, the environment. The Soviets had left a wasteland, a poisonous heritage of bad food, bad water, bad air.[4]

One early report from Aleksei Yablokov, President Yeltsin's advisor on ecology, asked readers, "What are we breathing?"[5] then laid out latest details of air laden with toxic gases. Viktor Danilov-Danilyan, Russia's environmental protection and natural resources minister, declared that almost half of the nation's tap water was unfit to drink. Virtually all rivers and major streams were polluted, he said. One in four children was deemed healthy by Russian standards—one in five if international standards were applied.[6]

Day after day new horror stories emerged about how the Soviets had used the country as a dump. Clumsy industrial giants without any check from consumers, media, or government—no EPA, no Greenpeace, no CNN, no militant army of local mothers—let toxins of all varieties seep, evaporate, or spill onto the landscape. A small lake outside Chelyabinsk in Southern Russia served as a harrowing but typical example. From 1951 until sometime in the 1960s, Soviet officials dumped nuclear waste into Lake Karachay, a one-hundred-acre body of water that stewed like an open Chernobyl, its deadly liquids seeping into the ground water for neighboring towns. In 1990, scientists estimated that radiation was so severe that an unprotected human being standing on the shoreline would receive a lethal dose in an hour.[7]

The most depressing Western analysis of health, medicine, and ecology in the Soviet Union, Ecocide in the USSR; Health and Nature Under Siege by Murray Feshbach and Alfred Friendly, Jr., was published while I lived in Moscow. The authors wrote the best summation of the problem that I had seen: "No other great industrial civilization so systematically and so long poisoned its land, air, water, and people. None so loudly proclaiming its efforts to improve public health and protect nature so degraded both."[8]

Some Russians had started asking publicly the questions that could have been asked only in a whisper to a trusted family member a few decades earlier: Why did a people's government care so little for the people's health? Why wasn't the new government doing any better? For answers, I went to the industrial zone along the Volga to a chemical factory town of Chapayevsk. It was an ordinary Russian industrial town that had been abused by governments in the past and had little hope for anything better from Moscow in the future.

Chapayevsk had suffered many indignities over the years, including the fact that it was situated on a tributary of the Volga that was once called the Mocha River. Mocha in Russian means urine, and perhaps that was why, even in the tsarist days, it was viewed as a wasted area, not to be preserved for lovers of the rural countryside. Originally named after a tsarist general, the Soviets renamed the city after a Russian civil war hero, Vasily Ivanovich Chapayev. In the thirties, Stalin's moviemakers produced a classic film called *Chapayev,* which was supposed to show young people the ideal Soviet hero, a Russian warrior who would do anything for the good of his country. But in the 1960s and 1970s, Chapayev and his two sidekicks, Pietka and Anka, became the characters in hundreds of jokes that generally made the three of them into stooges whose stupidity mocked the old Stalinist creed. The very name Chapayev could make most Russians laugh.

The real town of Chapayevsk, however, did not inspire much laughter. In December 1992, when my friend Kathy Lally and I became the first American journalists allowed to visit, it was a city of eighty-two thousand people whose apartments, rooms, or small wooden dachas were completely surrounded by fifteen factories. The wind from each direction brought a different acrid smell.

The community began its industrial career as a center for making potassium chlorate as detonators used during World War I, and it went on to make ammunition, dynamite, herbicides, fertilizers, and even poison gas in the 1940s. Vladimir Kruchin, a seventy-seven-year-old Chapayevsk pensioner in a worn woolen coat and an ancient sable hat, remembered the men from the Central Asian republics who came by the trainloads to make the gases. The pay was excellent, and the work was advertised as easy. "They were illiterate, and nobody could help them," Kruchin said, shaking his head. "They didn't listen to us; they couldn't understand us when we warned them that the gas was deadly." Kruchin had invited us into the yard of one of the old wooden houses that still stand in the center of this city. Once ornately decorated in the style of Russian country dachas, the structure was now a dilapidated house and barn where the old man kept a cow and a cat; the cat for the mice, the cow to give milk and meat. "They got their pay and put it in those pointed caps they wore," Kruchin continued as he showed us the place where he slaughtered a calf recently to earn a little extra for his family. The blood and bits of meat had frozen a clear ruby red color in the snow. "After the Asians died, people rushed to find the money under their hats," he said. In many ways, this folly was also the story of Kruchin's town, his neighbors, and his family.

A Soviet guidebook for Chapayevsk, like all such official propaganda, told about how terrible conditions were in the tsarist days before the Soviets took over. In 1916, it said, 596 were born and 607 died. In 1991, as the Soviet Union disintegrated, 337 were born and more than 500 died. And of those 337 surviving newborns, 33 percent had defects, a rate three times higher than in the rest of Russia.[9] Those born with problems often grew more frail and sickly if their mothers nursed, and many of the youngest children we saw in school, all still wearing their tiny red plastic stars with a picture of baby Lenin in the center, had pale, almost translucent, skin, even though winter was just beginning.

"In breast milk, we have found dioxin, biphenyls, hexachlorbenzol, and benzene," Dr. Alla Shumilina told us one dark winter afternoon as we sat around the mayor's conference table to talk about how people survived. "Ninety-six percent of the children here are sick, and their children will be sick. We have just studied them; we have not really treated them.

"We call them the dioxin children," she said.

For adults, there were increases in bronchitis, asthma, tuberculosis, kidney trouble, heart attacks in men, diseases of the stomach and nervous system. Average life expectancy in Chapayevsk was seven years less than in the rest of the country and fourteen years less than in the United States.[10] Cancer was higher than in most of Russia, and lung cancer, Dr. Shumilina told us, was a third higher in Chapayevsk than in the rest of the region, which was already higher than in the rest of Russia as a whole.

For most of a day, we sat in the office of chief administrator for the city, a pleasant forty-three-year-old man named Yuri Lipchenko, and listened to officials talking about their problems. Some were angry; some were afraid. Others, like Lipchenko, talked more about how to solve the problems, weighing the possibilities in sensible and political ways. To me he looked like the state legislators I had interviewed in Illinois, the mayors from midsized American towns, the perfect all-purpose official in his dark suit, white shirt, and tie. He was full of ready sympathy for his fellow citizens, but he was also cautious about just "picking up an ax and carving away at the factories," as he put it.

"I can say that in general the system we had was not designed to help human beings. They exploited human beings and threw them away like wastes," he fumed about the Soviets. But, what could be done now, we asked, especially about the tons of dioxin stored outside the massive herbicide factory on the river? Lipchenko looked uncomfortable. It was always easier to talk about past abuses.

"The director of the factory must say what we should do," Lipchenko said. It was not a very promising answer. "The city gets a lot of taxes from these industries. Since last year, those who converted [from defense to commercial] are deeply in debt. If we now demand that they change their methods, it could lead to shutting down the factory. The best form of social protection is if the job is guaranteed. If one has no job, we have no resources to help them anymore."

The director of the largest factory in Chapayevsk was like the owner of the mill in any small town in the world. His power was far greater than the mayor's, and he virtually owned his workers, who feared losing their jobs far more than eroding their health. While we were in Chapayevsk, the director of this largest factory, the one with the uncovered dump sitting by the river, was out. He would not be in, we were told, until after we left. It did not seem to be a coincidence.

Our guide, Igor Muzurov, chief of ecology for the city, had promised that he would show us the factory and the dump from a field directly across the river. But first, we had to pass a kind of mysterious test, it seemed, that involved listening to his experts and his gentle lectures in order to get the proper bearings on his city. Muzurov, who had the look of a truck driver, a large face, huge hands, had been quiet when he first met us, overtaken perhaps by a kind of shyness about meeting Americans for the first time. He kept his face frozen in the way Soviets had learned out of self-protection over the years. The Soviet shell, however, often gave little clue to the person inside, and Muzurov turned out to be one of those Russians who make their country so interesting and mysterious to outsiders. Simple yet deep, ordinary yet complicated, in many ways he was as much a character out of Russian literature as he was a midlevel city bureaucrat. He had rejected Soviet communism but not socialist ideals, and to go through the city with him was like taking a philosophical tour of a small Russian town as much as a physical one.

Muzurov understood the real basis of communal living in Russia—not as a philosophical idea enforced from above but as a deep and traditional code of morality. "For you everything is freedom," he said as we sat over lunch one day. "For us, it is different. Only collective freedom works, not just freedom for a few. It is part of the tradition of Russian life. Many were peasants; they had communities and worked within the community. Our tradition is much more collective. How we lived under communism was collectivism taken to the absurd, but it was based on a real phenomenon."

As we toured the city in his van, he talked about what these new freedoms had brought to replace the old goals of working for a better world, of bringing everyone up together like the incoming tide. In the Soviet days, many workers felt that even though they were struggling, it was for a good and decent cause. It would enrich the many, not just the few as in the West. The schools drummed it into them that they were good people working for a great cause. Even the young often believed somewhere deep inside that they were somehow more moral and righteous than the greedy West.

"People have no goals, nothing to work for now," Muzurov had said. "We are still empty. Religion is not enough. I supported Yeltsin but now I have some doubts. I don't see the goals to work for. . . . I love Russia, and maybe that's saying a lot. I'm interested in Russian history, and we've so denigrated our history after the revolution and it was so bad in the last years that one can think we have nothing to lose if we're so bad. Dostoyevsky said you have to have a core in your soul, like a stone. This part of the soul is taught in childhood. If afterwards you say, as we have to the young person, 'All we taught you is not true,' it is not a very strong stone."

He took this job with the city government because his children were often sick and he wanted to do something for them, but his way of protecting them was not to leave, like the others. Instead, he wanted to stay and change his Russia. He wanted to stay in Chapayevsk.

Muzurov did not rave about the inequities, the abuse in the Soviet years. He left that to his friend Piotr Mikhailovich Vasyukhin, who also accompanied us on our tours of the city. A fifty-four-year-old former chemistry specialist who had been leading the fight against dioxin in the Chapayevsk area, Vasyukhin lost his job because of it. Without daily work, he lived to fight the chemical factories. His briefcase was full of details, chemical analyses, anything he could find to build his case. He reminded me of the people I had met in factory towns in America, the person who carried the battle with him every day, everywhere he went. In yesterday's Russia, he might have been put in a straitjacket or in prison. In the new democracy, he had been allowed to surface—a new breed, the community activist. We invited him to our sitting room one day to lay out the problem for us. He talked, uninterrupted, for almost three and a half hours.

At one point Vasyukhin fumed, not about what the Soviets had done to his town, but about how the present economic conditions brought little hope for something better: "Now, we are a society of slaves, which are not known by other societies. We don't speak about the rapacious overexploitation, because we are slaves of poverty. Poverty is the background for slavery. Poverty is worse than any sort of repression. Physical repression provokes resistance, but poverty leads to submission." He took a breath and then made his point: "The people at the factory, they know now that some of what they do is harmful, but they keep quiet. They need their jobs."

Driving through the town to the factory of chemical fertilizers was like touring a war-ravaged slum, and it was hard to imagine how people believed in a system that had forced so many of them to live in such unrelieved poverty. The buildings where people lived, shopped, and worked had the look of places long ago abandoned. As we stood outside a communal house where some of the four thousand workers from the "big factory" lived, a young woman in elegant clothes and freshly applied makeup came out of the door. She looked like someone who had just been to the hairdresser, but as we stepped inside we knew that she performed what some women would later call "our daily miracle." Her home was like a huge flophouse motel. The corridor stretched to six doors on each side. Some were painted, but most were grimy with fingerprints around the doorknob and a layer of mud along the bottom. In the middle of the hall were the communal facilities. An old woman stood in the kitchen, which was gray and black from the damp mold and the mud. Next to the kitchen was a narrow chamber with one toilet minus the seat (each family brought its own). With only a small window, opened even in the cold, it was putrid. I scrawled the word on my notebook, as if I would ever forget.

When city officials talked about the number one complaint among the people who lived in Chapayevsk, it was housing. These apartments and others we saw with the bathrooms and toilets across a short walk outside (barnlike outhouses) were what bothered most people, Lipchenko said. Only later did they mention the pollution and health of their children.

Muzurov had shown us the housing to explain why the town's politicians talked about the issue so often. In the Soviet days, some of the occupants could at least feel that they were sacrificing for a larger cause. Now, with word of Western riches making its way even to this heartland, it was simply a slum, almost as bad as the industrial slums in England and America at the turn of the century. As our van traveled around Chapayevsk, Kathy Lally reminded me about a visit she had made to a small town in the east a few months earlier. She had met a little boy who stared at her in awe as the first real American he had ever met. Then he looked at her with pleading eyes and asked: "Tell me, are we poor?"

It was a question none of us could bear to answer.

After the tour of the housing, Muzurov's next stop was the dioxin dump that had brought us to Chapayevsk. The van traveled around the factory and then bounced across the back roads, its wheels whirring as it pulled us up the snowy hills. Sometimes we rode our machine like a scooter, getting a running start and then shooting over a hill to the makeshift path below. Finally we could see the back side of the factory, where four thousand people worked to make herbicides and pesticides. As we peered through the cattails on the riverbank at the mound of snow-covered dioxin on the other side, we saw a narrow fence around the lumpy patch that had been the major dumping ground for dioxin-tainted waste for over a decade. From the 1960s until 1987, Chapayevsk's factories had been producing chlorinated substances—for farms and for the defense industry. Nobody knew exactly how many tons of waste, which become more toxic as they age, were under the snowbank. The records had been secret. They had been badly kept. Probably no one would know. One famous Russian physicist had analyzed Chapayevsk as part of tests for Russia's industrial dumping grounds. The dioxin levels ranged from 18 parts per billion to 186 parts per billion. In 1983, the United States government evacuated the town of Times Beach, Missouri, because dirt was found in the area with 100 parts dioxin per billion.

Perhaps the problem for Chapayevsk's new ecologists was that the mound of dioxin did not look dangerous. There was no smell, and with its white covering it could have been any patch of land, a dump or a garden. As Muzurov was describing how the winds sometimes blew clouds of the tainted dirt into the water, a small motorcycle roared past. It was a pensioner with his grandson, the boy bouncing along in a sidecar, a vehicle that was one of the most popular and dangerous forms of transportation outside the cities. They made a sharp turn near us, the boy rising happily into the air with the sidecar and then bouncing back onto the path. On one side of the motorcycle were fishing rods. They stopped at a spit in the river almost directly opposite the bank from the dioxin and beneath a small, rusting sign that said, "Danger. No Fishing."

"We have tried to tell them," sighed Muzurov. "There are these signs. Nobody listens. They are probably fishing for pike. Will they eat it? Of course. People are seduced here by sports. Others believe it is simply a good way to get cheap fish, and they don't care. When you ask them about these fish, they say, 'It's okay. I don't eat the heads.' But, of course, it's not okay."

On the way back we stopped at a store to see what people were eating with these tainted fish. Bread, subsidized by the city, was four cents a loaf, sugar thirty cents a kilo, cake almost fifty cents. The line was longer than in Moscow but the food was far cheaper. In many ways, this was still a Soviet city, a year after the end of the Soviet Union. The women standing patiently in line looked sourly at us and one, who said she was sixty-three but would not give her name, was so angry either that we were asking questions about her life or with the life itself that she fairly spit out her views, shaking her head after each comment to emphasize the unfairness of it all. "We are poor, I am ashamed to say, and only the entrepreneurs out there selling things have a good life. The honest people are poor." Entrepreneurs, she was saying by implication, are dishonest. Capitalists were thieves whether they were in America or on the street corner.

As always, a crowd gathered quickly, and suddenly we were at the center of a vigorous debate on who was to blame for the state of their lives. A lively sixty-five-year-old named Klara Gladkova took the floor and declared that her family together had worked a total of ninety-four years at the factory and then after all that loyalty, the worst had happened. Her daughter was sacked. "Now she can do nothing but hang herself," said Gladkova, waving a free arm at the audience of nodding shoppers around her. "And if I die, I am not sure I will have a coffin to rot in. There are lines for coffins." She paused to gulp air, to adjust her packages. "And now, the water is polluted. The air is polluted. Everything we grow in the garden is tainted. Before Gorbachev it was a good life. Under Brezhnev, it was better," she said, drawing nods and murmurs from those around her.

The woman who would not give her name protested in a frail voice that strained to be heard over the echoing din. "No, no. That is not true. It was not Gorbachev; it was all the leaders. They took from us. They robbed us. We gave them everything, and they took everything."

She turned to the Americans and frowned in such a stern way that the others in line grew quiet. "Why are you here? This is a secret place," she said, referring to the fact that four of the factories made chemicals or ammunition used by the military.

"No more," I said. "We were invited to come here by your city leaders," my colleague Kathy added. The woman shook her head. All the old truths had disappeared. Even the old enemy was right there in her grocery store.

"Did you work in the factory?" I asked.

Tiredly, she nodded her head, tied in a brown woolen scarf. "I was chief librarian for eighteen years. Then I was forced to go work in the factory because I couldn't feed my family on that pay. My husband is sick now. He participated in Novaya Zemlya (one of the test sites for nuclear explosions) in 1953. Now he is dying of lung cancer. I had to leave the library and go work in the factory to feed my children." She had begun to cry, and in a moment she turned away from us, careful not to lose her place in line or her remaining dignity.

As we returned that night to the place where we were staying, we passed a small city market of four makeshift stalls. That morning, there had been potatoes, onions, and beets at one stall. At another, guarded by a fierce-looking woman with gold teeth, were two lemons for one hundred rubles each (about twenty-five cents). At the end of the day, the potatoes were finished, the onions and beets picked down to the last bruised leftovers; but the lemons were still there, and they were still one hundred rubles each. The market had not yet arrived in Chapayevsk.

It was such a dreary life that a Western visitor's eye yearned for color to break up the gray landscape, just as, after so many complaints and so much despair, the ear longed for the sound of laughter. As if in response, one night we saw a party leaving the town restaurant as we were trying to enter.

It was about 8:30 P.M., and the sign on the door said they were open until 9 P.M. As we passed the doorway and stood downstairs outside the foul-smelling bathrooms, a small woman who looked capable of lifting each of us physically out of her way cantered down the stairs and hissed that the restaurant was closed. "Perhaps just a bottle of mineral water?" we begged, looking toward a long night without food or drink since there was no public restaurant at the *profilaktory*, or health center, where we were staying. She looked at us with a fury that came from dealing for twelve hours with parties like the one we had just passed outdoors. "No water, no food. Nothing," she said, shoving us out the door and slamming it noisily.

Outside, the young people who just left the restaurant were swaying in the snow and asking, "Where can we go now?"—the universal question for anyone trying to extend an evening's merriment in a place without bars or cafés or movie houses open after 9 P.M., the factory worker's bedtime. The air reeked of sour beer and their Russian had become incomprehensible, even to our friend Andrei Mironov, a chemist who came with us from Moscow to help translate the technological terms into English for us. Two women were apparently arguing about whether to fight over a man who was no longer there. They shouted and crouched, one circling the other, taunting, screeching in anger. The remaining men were busy in the shadows, smoking and watching with amusement. One began pissing noisily into the snow. In a few minutes, the women lost interest in a fight and one began to weep, drawing the other easily into her dark mood. One woman was carried home, but the other and a male friend later sat under our window at the *profilaktory*, singing, drinking, and playing the guitar late into the clear, cold night.

It was a typical Russian scene, and not just in Chapayevsk. I would witness it across the country and in any season, the desperate efforts by the young to shake off today's burdens, no matter what it did to tomorrow's. There were few joys. Music, sex, humor healed many, but for others the small joys of a cigarette and an evening of vodka were the greatest sources of relief.

The only people I met in Russia who did not smoke were either religious or asthmatic, and the official estimates that 70 percent of adult Russians smoked seemed low. Heart patients smoked. Doctors smoked. Virtually everybody indulged, at least occasionally; a smoke-filled room nurtured ideas, one Russian woman insisted one day when I was arguing about the perils of tobacco. As Russia began courting Western companies, one of the first to leap into the marketplace was the tobacco industry. R. J. Reynolds and Philip Morris began building factories in Moscow and St. Petersburg in 1992. Cigarettes from the West flooded the street kiosks. Marlboro, long the most popular cigarette in Russia and once used by Westerners as a kind of currency for hailing taxicabs or tipping waitresses, was facing competition from a variety of old Western favorites and new brands, like one featuring an American flag, which appeared to be made somewhere outside St. Petersburg. For these companies that had been so harassed in America, Russia was a glorious new market full of customers who were not obsessively concerned about their hearts and lungs. When several Westerners tried to make an issue of how Western tobacco industries were taking advantage of innocent new Russian consumers, the advertising manager for a Moscow television station undoubtedly spoke for many of his fellow citizens when he said, "In the conditions we live under, smoking does not look like such a big deal."[11]

The Russian attitude to vodka (the word means "little water") is far more complex. In a very Russian way, vodka is both solution and problem—a force for good and evil enclosed in one simple bottle. Vodka has created how many poems, how many marriages, how many murders? It is medicine—a dab of it on cotton is the cure for children's earaches. It is comfort—a quick hot draught that burns its way down the throat can soothe the pains left behind after a long day on the street selling a not-so-new pair of shoes. It is death—when Russians count the number of people frozen to death or killed in accidents, murdered, or abused—alcohol deserves a large share of the blame.

Vodka and its place in Russian society is a subject for essayists, philosophers, historians, and doctors, and this is not the place to look at its full impact on the Russian life. Alcohol's role in the deteriorating health of the Russians was another matter, and what I saw in Chapayevsk was evident elsewhere. The information on alcoholism coming out of the old Soviet Union was still full of conflicting data. One figure widely used was that there were 4.6 million Soviets diagnosed with alcoholism and alcoholic psychosis in 1989, three times more than in 1970.[12] Privately the experts at the time estimated that the real number was four to six times higher.[13]

Some estimates claimed that only fourteen of every one thousand people were serious alcoholics, and others said that up to two-thirds of the workforce suffered from alcoholism.[14]

Whatever the real number, and many statistics were still haphazardly collected in this era, there were times of day and seasons of the year when drunks seemed to be everywhere—late at night on the Moscow metro, in winter in the small rural towns, littered across the background of any rite of passage like a wedding, a departure, a funeral. Any holiday could bring out the toasts; a summer weekend was a reason to celebrate. On Women's Day in March 1991, I remember watching a group of men who had been vigorously celebrating the day in their wives' honor. They were stumbling along the sidewalk, their women behind shepherding them like children in case they strayed into the traffic a few feet away.

As the society began to talk openly about itself and its leaders, word spread about how Khrushchev and Brezhnev gulped cognac from huge tea glasses. Russian president Boris Yeltsin, whose staff has been known to shoo away television cameras because his gait was unsteady, his nose a bulbous red, suffered little public censure from such lapses. Ordinary people seemed to trust Yeltsin, who overindulged occasionally, more than Mikhail Gorbachev, who tried unsuccessfully to limit Russian access to their national drink. The effort to end "drunk shovels," or shoddy products put out by inebriated workers, faded as the government lost revenue; and, worse, people began brewing more of homemade booze, often tainted and blindingly poisonous concoctions made from cologne, paint, and even the emetic drugs used for cattle.

By 1988, Gorbachev, who would have done better to study his Bolshevik history before attempting to do away with vodka, had backed away from the reform. Lenin had spoken against state production of vodka and approved of the prohibition that had been put in effect as Russia prepared for World War I. But legal vodka returned in 1925 because brewing had simply moved from state factories to people's homes and, as Stalin rationalized two years later, "Giving up vodka means giving up that profit, while there are no grounds for assuming that alcoholism will decrease, since the peasant will start producing his own vodka, poisoning himself with moonshine."[15]

Perhaps that was Stalin's reason, but anyone who spends time in Russia knows there are deeper and less practical ones. One of the best descriptions from an outsider came in a 1985 editorial from the *Guardian* in England: "In Russia one does not have a drink; one opens a bottle. Once it is open, it seems a matter of honor, of domestic tidiness and/or machismo to empty it. It usually contains vodka or some other spirit, and the purpose of the exercise seems to be to attain oblivion as quickly as possible."[16]

I found drinking vodka in Russia to be a hazardous pastime, and after one particular session, I began to take advantage of the opportunity most Russian men afforded a woman to refuse the tiny glasses of a drink prized more for the power of its afterburn than for its taste. Sipping is not allowed, and the first time I fully understood that fact was at the start of a long lunch in Minsk. The lunch began when the host poured a round of vodka, raised his glass, and said, "May whatever is left after you drink be the sign of your evil intentions." Not wanting to offend, I remember little else that day.

Of all the stories about vodka and the Russians, the one that seemed to show the most reckless attachment to the drink came after the opening of the country to the West. The head of Russia's Atomic Energy Ministry, Dr. Sergei Maltsev, told a conference on alcoholism in Moscow in late 1992 that the workers dealing with atomic energy routinely drink because "they believe that radiation acts less on the body when you drink a low dosage of spirits. It's sort of legend. Supposedly alcohol saved people's lives during some accident, while the ones who didn't drink died of radiation poisoning."[17]

The legend grew after a nuclear engineer named Georgy Kaurov met his first covey of Western reporters in late 1992 and told them that his favorite tipple in the late 1950s and early 1960s was a vodka stirred vigorously on the nuclear testing grounds of Novaya Zemlya. Kaurov was an engineer during the underground atomic tests at the Arctic island, and before each bomb was detonated, workers would place a glass of vodka on the earth above ground zero. The first one to reach the vodka earned the right to drink it. Now sixty and still in relatively good health, Kaurov said he downed "many, many" irradiated vodkas over the years. "It wasn't dangerous," he boasted. "Radioactivity is a natural phenomenon."[18]

Chapayevsk undoubtedly had its own vodka lore, but it also had its own system for dealing with the fallout from alcoholism. As we were standing on a country road one afternoon, an olive-drab-colored truck that looked like a relic from World War I rumbled past us and then screeched to a slow stop. A young man leaned out of the window and asked why we were outside, staring at an oily film covering a bend in the river. Muzurov laughed, waving him on his way. It was his friend who operated the drunk truck, he explained. By night they picked up people who could freeze to death in the snow. By day, they sometimes cruised around looking for people so badly hung over that they were acting peculiar. Staring at the river on an icy day was considered strange behavior, he suggested.

The dumping rooms for these drunks were among the most gut-wrenching places in the country. They were large jail cells with cots, rooms that became foul from vomit and human waste as the evening wore on, places where people howled and screamed at one another in drunken fury. Children were routinely warned that if they misbehaved or didn't eat their dinner, they would be thrown in with the stinking madmen and -women for a night of unspeakable horror.[19]

At factories, alcoholics were sometimes forced into a prisonlike regimen in which they worked during the day for little or no pay, and at night they were confined in treatment wards. This was during the Soviet era. When capitalism arrived, companies tried less to save the drinkers from their problems. The drunks, in most cases, were simply fired.[20]

For those who wanted to move out of the sad world of Russian alcoholism, some doctors began offering more rigorous treatments, including an antialcohol medicine called the torpedo. The torpedo, which was advertised in newspaper columns as the most successful way to end drinking, cost about three thousand rubles, or about $10. The practitioner lanced the arm or thigh and then sewed several tablets of the drug under the skin. The drug, which American experts described as a form of Antabuse, or disulfiram, reacts with alcohol and makes people vomit, producing what some patients have described as an "advanced stage of panic."[21]

No one knew how many of the nation's estimated serious alcoholics were actually using the torpedo, and it was not until early 1993 that the public began to realize that the drug could do more than make people avoid alcohol. If the drinker suddenly weakens and goes on a binge, he can slip into unconsciousness and die. But the reaction from some of those dealing with Russian drunks was anything but sympathetic. Used to treating alcoholics like demented children, they placed the blame not with the drug but with the drinker. Aleksandr Sergeyev, deputy chief of Moscow's main narcological Hospital No. 17, said of the torpedo deaths, "If a patient dies, then it is because of alcohol misuse, of course, not the drugs we give them."[22]

I gained a different, more sympathetic picture of how ordinary people felt about drunks when I saw Russians dealing with them in the streets and the subways. Early one evening in the spring of 1992, a man, clearly drunk, tumbled backward down a long escalator in Moscow's Taganka subway stop. The people behind him quickly recognized what was happening and caught this man, whose smell and inarticulate rage at his rescuers made him anything but a lovable victim. They carried him up the escalator and laid him carefully on the marble floor, most of them looking more sad than disgusted at his pitiful state. When I explained the scene to a Russian colleague, she said that Russians don't hate drunks "like Americans," as she put it; they understand them. Their pleasures are brief and few, like the young people in Chapayevsk whose boozy late-night singing never drew the howls of protest or the police, who would have cut short their performance in America.

The morning after we'd seen the young revelers, we had asked for breakfast at the *profilaktory* where the mayor let us stay. A kind of in-town spa, the Chapayevsk *profilaktory* was a pleasant facility, with clean rooms and an array of carefully tended house plants. It was supposed to offer a kind of rest home for people from the factories, mostly the upper-level employees. When we were there, it was silent, except for the sounds of an old television in the early evenings in the common room, where a few middle-aged women in bathrobes waited for bedtime.

The tables in the breakfast room that morning were mostly empty, and a waitress with an unusually sunny manner told us to sit down, that she had plenty of food, no problem. Breakfast was a syrupy juice, fatty sausage, a sweet roll, and a thick glutinous mass, much like grits, that was topped with butter. When data appeared that said 50 percent of the calories in a Russian's diet came from fat, compared to 37 percent for an American, which is also high, I always thought it was in part because it was impossible to do otherwise. But in this place, nothing was spared for the clientele. This was a meal designed to make people healthier.

As we sat worrying about the Russians' arteries, we learned that the supervisor of the *profilaktory* was outraged that we had eaten a meal in the patients' dining room. The problem was that we had not been through a medical exam. Now she had to sterilize everything because we were Americans. Why because we are Americans? we asked. Because we might have AIDS, came the answer. It was a strange moment. We were worried about the state of their health. They were terrified about the state of ours.

Muzurov had promised us that we would meet the chief expert on health in Chapayevsk, and finally we were taken to see Dr. Valentina Lukyanova, head doctor at the Medical Sanitary Department for the chemical factory. The front door of her clinic was so filthy that it took nerve to touch it, and the stairs were so littered with dust and cigarette butts that by the time we reached her office, I expected very little from the medical professional inside. I was surprised and wrong. Dr. Lukyanova was a bright, warm woman, full of life and anger about what was happening around her. "There was a system of hiding the illnesses. We have archives marked 'Top Secret' from 1935, and workers were not allowed to know anything about 'professional diseases.' Only the chief doctors knew how bad it was."

While her staff looked for the files, two patients were brought in to talk with us. One was Elena Mishina. The other was Aleksandr Sorokin. Elena, who wore a beige wool hat and down coat during the hour we talked, was forty-three-years old but looked like a woman in her late fifties. She said that she had worked twenty-nine years in the factory, starting as a helper while she was still in school. Her face was red and her voice had a rasping sound that prompted me to ask if she smoked. No, never, she said. "But I did work in the hazardous area for ten years, from 1976 to '86," she said. "I was alone with my child, and I needed to buy food. The pay was fifty percent more in the hazardous section. I had no choice." Her son was fine, she said, healthy as a bull. But she was suffering from a classic problem caused by dioxin. It was chloracne, a form of acne that looks a little like blackheads, and she had scrubbed her face forcefully before meeting the foreigners. Chloracne did not mean for certain that

Elena would face other problems from dioxin such as cancer, but it was an ugly, visible sign that she had been contaminated.[23]

"We were told we had professional dermatitis. They never used the term 'chloracne,'" said Elena. "Even though it has been six years since I have touched the chemicals, I have severe problems with my joints, pain in my joints when I try to sleep. I have chloracne now all the time. On my face, on my back. They are like blackheads, but if you wash them or pick them, suddenly you can smell the hexachlorabenzene."

Aleksandr Sorokin, in contrast to Elena, looked much younger than his age. At sixty-one, his hair was still dark, and his eyes were bright. He had worked in plant maintenance. "I cleaned up," he said. "It was the worst job of all.

"We had such a good chief doctor," he said, his voice full of sarcasm. "He hid the documents on us. He never told the truth to us. This problem was a secret problem. In fact, at one point, after they treated the large sores with balm, they came back to me and they put the stuff we were working with in the factory right on my skin to see if there was any reaction. We were like experimental animals. Rats."

Aleksandr's sickness, Dr. Lukyanova told us, was one of the classic reactions to the byproducts of Chapayevsk's industries. He had heart trouble; probably he had been suffering for years. Other patients had been luckier. Sometimes the problems went away if the patient left the city and lived somewhere with cleaner air and water.

An assistant brought in a huge pile of folders, bound with old twine. Dr. Lukyanova opened one to 1971. It was marked "secret" and full of thin, yellowing papers. She studied a few of them and read out the diagnoses never shared with the patients: "Chemical hepatitis, gastritis, professional dermatitis. Nobody calculated how many have died. It was a secret. They always wrote another reason.

"The main bulk of our problems was in the mid-sixties, when they produced chlorinated substances. If we had problems, we doctors tried to put it in the documents. If I mentioned one thousand cases, they removed a zero at the regional level. When the region sent the report to Moscow, they removed another zero."

"Some people knew what was wrong even then," interrupted Aleksandr. "Drivers came from the kolkhozes [communal farms] and they would tell us, 'Take the document, say we paid, but then throw this stuff somewhere else. Say you loaded it, then don't.' Even they knew it was harmful."

After talking with school children and citizens and top officials, it seemed clearer why President Boris Yeltsin's problems reforming Russia were so massive. Nikolai Sergeyevich Maltsev, the peoples' deputy from Chapayevsk, had been trying to get the Kremlin to show some interest in his city's problems. Finally he had gotten through to someone in the administration who promised to study it. It was not very encouraging, but at least this official had agreed to listen. Then, even that encouragement disappeared when the official was swept out of office along with a number of reformers in Yeltsin's entourage.

"What we have now is stacks of documents signed by officials no longer in power," said Maltsev (who had voted against those very officials a week earlier in Moscow).

"The government practically led to the collapse of the industrial and governmental complex. To my mind, we cannot survive now without state-owned companies, factories, and farms. We can evolve into private owner-ship, but so quickly . . . we cannot reform the country."

Maltsev, who was elected first secretary of the Communist Party in this area in 1988, had only barely adapted to any reforms. At heart, he may have been like the people in Chapayevsk who believed that life was better in the old Soviet days, even if most people did not know how bad it really was. Truth was not always a welcome change, and some people began to believe that those who revealed the problems were responsible for them.

When we left Chapayevsk, Muzurov seemed to feel our departure like a personal loss. We promised to tell people in Moscow about the dioxin, to tell people everywhere, to write about it. But as we drove through the countryside toward the nearest airport, I could feel the vastness of the ecology problem, as the Russians called it. A farm operated under a factory's smokestacks. Mounds of trash, including rusting barrels spilling their mysterious compounds, marred the landscape. I knew that citizens' groups had begun to protest in some regions, but they were few. Most people had so much trouble worrying about the week's supply of food that they had no time for something that could kill them in twenty years.

As the van sped past the clusters of smokestacks toward the airport, we talked about how the U.S.S.R.'s leaders had felt free to loot their own rich territory. Their country had been a massive pristine continent that could be mined; the people were an army of slaves to be worked; the fields and waters were a vast dumping ground for the nation's toxic refuse. I had seen industrialists in the West using small towns for chemical dumps, but by 1970, Americans were beginning to concentrate on the problems and consider pollution a priority. Here, with the communist past and the new capitalists in their present, Russia was a poisoned nation. Most people who looked at the extent of the damage felt that it would be years before anything could be done.

In March 1992, *Izvestia* reported that for the first time since World War II, the death rate was higher than the birth rate in Russia. Infant mortality was higher by 9 percent, and the largest declines were in the cities and what the Russian Statistics Agency called "ecologically unsafe areas." A few months later, over a roundup of the lastest health statistics, the *Moscow News* ran this headline: "Is Russia Dying?"[24]

It did not seem like a reasonable question until one looked at a town like Chapayevsk and saw the weak young, the clouded air, the polluted water, and then realized this important fact: in 1992 Russia compiled a list of the areas that were the most polluted and most in need of immediate help cleaning up their environment and adapting their industries. Chapayevsk was not on it.[25]

4

Medicine:
Do We Have a Future?

The forty years of existence of Soviet public health, with its great accomplishments and perspectives, leave no doubt that in its achievements it has exceeded everything which has been done in this respect by mankind in a thousand years.
        —G. S. Pondoev's *Notes of a Soviet Doctor,*
        1959[1]

The state of medicine here is nothing short of catastrophic.
        —Dr. Zakhar Mikhailovich Simchovich,
        head doctor, Clinic No. 7,
        Moscow, October 1, 1991[2]

The waning of the U.S.S.R. and its propaganda machines destroyed the last shred of pretense that Soviet medicine was the best in the world. Glasnost in the 1980s had allowed the first truly skeptical press reports, and as the borders opened, doctors, medical experts, and even Western journalists were allowed to see how this superpower had treated ordinary people. The world came to know how the Soviet-approved picture of contented patients lying in their crisp clean sheets, smiling up at the authoritative and learned doctor, was a state-approved myth, a sad lie. Instead, the hospitals in Russia had become decaying contradictions of this unreal Soviet dream. With elaborate mosaics at the front doors or towering bronze statues in the entrance halls, they were designed to build confidence in a system that promised decent health care for the masses. In reality, like most other health care systems in the world, it provided well only for the few. Medical care for the average citizen was too often haphazard, impersonal, and dangerous.

Most Westerners who went to Russia knew the perils of the medical system there, and we were told in 1990 not to let a Russian doctor touch us "even to pull a tooth," as one Polish friend warned before we arrived. Diplomats, journalists, businessmen and -women—we had our own doctors and emergency airplanes for such problems as appendicitis or a broken leg. As a result, my real understanding of the Soviet medical system did not begin until late one afternoon when a Russian woman I knew announced she was going into the hospital the next day. She cried quietly as she told us her news and gently touched my daughter's cheek, as if to say good-bye forever. I thought she had terminal cancer, and I was terrified for her as she left, hiding her eyes and her fear under a fur-lined hat. It was not until a few hours later that I learned from a mutual friend that what was really bothering her was a gynecological infection, a condition that would have been very difficult for her to explain, out of shyness or Soviet prudery, even to another woman. When I learned it was probably an infection caused by an abortion, possibly done without properly sterilized instruments, I was deeply relieved and felt that as painful as it was, the worst had passed. A round of pills would make her instantly well, I presumed. As with virtually everything else in Russia, the problem turned out to be far more complicated than I could imagine.

Because I had a car, I helped take her things to the hospital, said to be one of the better gynecological centers in Moscow. As I drove up the badly tarred road and pulled into a parking place, I wondered whether this could possibly be the right address. It had the look of an ordinary Soviet apartment building, dilapidated and decaying, with a small flower bed outside representing someone's effort to make it a little less inhumane. Inside, the wide corridors and high ceilings had all the heaviness of an official government building. The smell of a sour strawberry-scented disinfectant hung over the waiting area. I held flowers, an odd number for good luck in the

Russian fashion, and a colleague who had come with me to help carried a plastic bag stuffed with tea, cookies, and extra pajamas. People grew quiet as they recognized by our clothes, our shoes, and our strange faces that we were not Russian and did not belong. The nurses looked at us warily, like people whose very presence would make trouble.

I went to a small caged window to ask about my ailing friend. We were barred from the wards, a woman told us, but after some kind of consultation with officials, who peered at us occasionally from behind the window of an administrative door, our friend shuffled out to see us. She seemed slightly embarrassed to have us there, and I only hoped the attention would help her, not make things even worse with the medical personnel, who were known to demand extra money from someone who had access to foreigners. Dressed in a drab bathrobe and slippers, she moved so slowly that I thought she must be in terrible pain. She repeatedly assured us, however, that she was perfectly fine. Later one of her friends explained this transformation from a bright, confident professional into a woman whose posture was hunched in apology and fear. "In a hospital, you are a prisoner," she said. "You walk along the walls. You try to make yourself invisible." My friend may have been in pain, as well, both physical and psychological. A different doctor had examined her on each medical shift, and there was no agreement about what was wrong with her. Doctors, who often specialized so much that they could speak only about the endocrine system or the respiratory system or the nervous system, were also taught that they should see at least six patients an hour. One doctor estimated that because of paperwork and other duties, she actually spent one minute and fifty-four seconds with each patient.[3] This rotation system meant that people were often misdiagnosed or never given a concrete reason why they were sick.

Shortly after our visit, the doctors had begun suggesting a hysterectomy, and when the patient finally confessed this to her friend, who then told me about the doctors' proposal, we decided she needed Western medicine. My husband helped arrange for her to go to England, where a physician gave her Western antibiotics that worked virtually overnight. But the English doctor was also alarmed at the results of her Russian treatment. After a week in the Russian hospital, her entire buttocks and hips were bruised from three shots a day of the weak Soviet antibiotics, drugs she had bought with a handful of rubles in hopes that her medical care would be better than the average.

I became so alarmed that this could happen to an ordinary educated person—a person whose illness was so minor and whose income level in America would have been solidly middle class—that I began trying to find people who would talk to me about the medical system in what was then the U.S.S.R. and soon to become the new Russia. By then there was less pretense about having the best medical care in the world, but some hospital officials were still reluctant for an American reporter to see exactly what kind of care it was.

In the next year, I visited hospitals and clinics around Russia and I interviewed people who told terrifying stories about their escape from the jaws of their local medical facility. My tour through the Russian medical system also took me to places that were sickeningly dirty and pitifully underequipped. Some doctors were clearly on the make, and the way patients looked at them, in fear and barely disguised anger, made me wince at the thought of having them aim a hypodermic needle or scalpel at a human subject. But roaming the dark halls of Russia's medical system also brought me in touch with some of the most intelligent and dedicated people I have ever met. After the initial shock of seeing facilities that most Americans would reject for their veterinary clinics, I became convinced that for all the problems, there were still some doctors who treated patients better than could be expected, given their weak medicines, home remedies, old-fashioned skills, and outdated equipment. The challenge for the Russian was always to find the doctor who could make the impossible work.

How Russia treated its sick in this era provided a concise and frightening example of what was happening to the country's welfare structure as the Soviet Union died and a new Russia struggled to be born. In this crucial period of 1991–92, the currency required for decent medical care changed dramatically. Before the end of the Soviet Union in 1991, one bought access to the best care with clout, or *blat*, and modest bribes, or "gifts," the same way one aquired a new apartment or better job. Once settled in the hospital and connected to a doctor (who might have an established private fee for each service), the patient passed the staff a few rubles or a nice box of chocolates for "extras," like having the sheets changed or getting a hospital bed in a room instead of the corridor. But connections, not money, often made the difference between a good doctor at a decent hospital and a place where the staff was drunk and the doctor untrained. As one seasoned Muscovite put it, "When you got sick, the first thing you did was get on the phone and call your friends in high places."

By late 1992, clout was diminishing as a necessity, and access to medicine and a healthy way of life became one of those luxuries that could be bought and sold like everything else. When one Russian woman's father needed lung surgery in early 1993, her family pooled all their savings, pulled all their strings, and got him in the best hospital in Moscow. The cost, not counting little fees for the nurses to give him a blanket and for the orderlies to mop the floors, was one hundred thousand rubles (about $200)—a steep price for someone who earned ten thousand a month, who had no medical insurance (which was scheduled to arrive only the following January), and who still had to find money for postsurgery care and drugs sold only in the Western markets.

Suddenly, like elsewhere in the world, medical care—both the best and the worst—came at a price. There were clinics emerging that provided painless treatment for a broken tooth or an abortion or a broken arm. Powerful Western antibiotics, once so scarce they were reserved for the elite or sold on the black market, were available in the cities for a powerful Western price. Only in the state hospitals were old, Soviet-style antibiotics still administered by injection three to six times a day. The problem was that the alternatives to state treatment—the drug kiosks on the streets and private doctors' salons—were unmonitored by any government agency. There were charlatans and faith healers practicing in one "center," while legitimate doctors breaking away from the Soviet mediocrity were running another.

A state-run hospital or city clinic would operate a private section to help pay for the rest of the hospital. And the doctors, whose status was low compared to Western countries and whose salaries virtually disappeared in the years of hyperinflation, would take private patients or extra jobs to boost their income. I knew one who moonlighted as an interpreter. Another worked part time as a veterinarian for a small private clinic where, in 1995, his vet's salary more than outweighed his doctor's pay.

* * *

With the end of the Soviet state, two basic forces were at work in health care. The state system, already in decay in many areas, was deteriorating rapidly, and the newer private system, virtually uncontrolled, was becoming a medical bazaar.

Of the many physicians I saw in Russia, two were particularly distressed about what they saw happening to the nation's hospitals and polyclinics. One was Dr. Andrei Vorobiev, one of Yeltsin's first health ministers. An elegant man with the demeanor of a diplomat, Vorobiev was alarmed by the breakdown in government control of health care.

"There is a real lawlessness out there now, " he said, speaking slowly as though he felt the heaviness of each word. "I don't think we will realize change in this place while lawlessness reigns."[4]

The other was Dr. Mikhail M. Kuzmenko, who was president of the Health Workers' Union of Russia when I went to see him in late 1992 about the status of Russian doctors. As he talked about the doctors' lowly status, their meager salaries, their lack of equipment, his voice rose angrily.

"Our health care system is on the brink of ruin. If the government doesn't find the means to finance or to run it, it will stop by itself," Dr. Kuzmenko fumed. A large man with a dark mustache and dark hair, he sat behind the standard-issue laminated wooden desk in his dimly lit office on the south side of Moscow.

"We have no money for medicine. No food for patients. Our doctors? They make less than bus drivers. [For some reason, the comparison was always to bus drivers]. Last year we lost ten thousand doctors [who emigrated]. And who were they? They were the best because the worst— what could they do abroad? The good specialists—they are gone or going."

Dr. Kuzmenko grew so agitated that he stood up, walked a few feet, and then returned to his chair to finish his message. The amount of the Russian GNP spent on medicine was about 3.7 percent. "Do you know what 3.7 percent is?" He shook his head, in disgust. "Even in Africa, they sometimes spend 5 percent. Or more."

Like many Russians, Dr. Kuzmenko was angry and embarrassed that the powerful Soviet Union was viewed suddenly by the rest of the globe as just another third-world nation, struggling to provide people with their most basic needs. For decades Soviet doctors had managed without the necessary supplies, equipment, and medicines, but they could hide such deficiencies behind a largely secret and greatly feared superpower. They had taken hope in the idea that their social experiment was a few years away from the goal of everyone moving forward together, as a community. Now, the system was a very public failure, and even the old tricks for nudging it along no longer worked.

"Yesterday, I called a friend of mine who was ill, and she said she called the ambulance and it had not come. So I called the ambulance," he said, pointing a strong, short index finger into his chest. Normally such a call would mean that the ambulance went to his friend's apartment immediately. Instead, he learned what everybody knew in that period—a free ambulance wasn't worth its price.

"And what did they say, the ambulance drivers? They said, 'How can we come if we only have analgesics as medicine? How can we come if we only get five to seven liters of petrol allocated each day?' And how safe are they? Maybe eighty percent of all ambulances should not be allowed even to go on the roads."

By 1995, the *skoraya pomoshch,* which literally means fast help, had become a sad joke. Ambulances could take hours. They might never arrive at all. The day a bomb exploded at the newspaper offices of *Moskovsky Komsomolets* on October 17, 1994, killing one of Russia's top investigative reporters, Dmitry Kholodov, his fellow journalists measured the time from their call for help to the arrival of the ambulance. It was over thirty minutes.[5]

One evening in late 1993, I stood on a major street in Moscow trying desperately to hail a taxi. Actual taxis were rare in this period, and virtually any private car would double as a taxi—with all but the new rich offering to carry someone across town, even out of the way, for an extra few rubles. That evening, however, a sleek new Volvo ambulance responded to my hand. The driver assured me that he was off duty, and there was no equipment in the back of the vehicle. But I could not help wondering if the waiting time for an ambulance now included the detours taken for taxi service as well.

"There are many examples of the destruction of our medical system,"

Dr. Kuzmenko had concluded on that day in late 1992. "For the first time in recent history, this January, the mortality rate is bigger than the birthrate in this country. This is the general state of health—deterioration."[6]

The huge all-union centers that had served all fifteen Soviet republics and were expected to provide the very best medical care in the U.S.S.R. had become in many ways the most forlorn in the early 1990s, when fancy respirators and aging emergency care machines died for lack of parts, taking their patients with them. Expert brain surgeons, like those at the prestigious Burdenko Institute in Moscow, dreamed about the old days under Brezhnev when they could make out elaborate shopping lists for Western equipment—an era that one Burdenko specialist wistfully called "the golden age of stagnation."[7]

Some of the less famous hospitals, the ones that treated ordinary people for free, had never been fully equipped but now found themselves without basic necessities such as plasma, surgical thread, and bandages.

"We lost two patients last week because there was no plasma," Dr. Zakhar Simchovich said matter-of-factly one day as we sat in his office in the summer of 1991, a few months before he emigrated to Canada.

"I had to sit in an emergency room next to a man who was in a car wreck," said a woman patient during the same period. "He seemed okay. The next day he was dead, they said, because they did not have plasma."

The lack of supplies was a chronic problem that grew even worse in the late 1980s and early 1990s. Even the best Russian doctors were forced to spin treatments out of stern advice, strong tea, massages, and a few doses of whatever medicines they had. Daily they were faced with the task of deciding who got supplies and how to make doses for ten reach fifty instead. Sometimes they diluted whatever was in the storeroom. Sometimes they sent people home to get better on their own or die.

The lack of supplies and the erratic distribution—some through legal channels, some through networks of thieves who specialized in medical equipment—meant that nurses and doctors often broke the rules. Ekaterina Burova, a dermatologist who lived with her son in an elegant old apartment behind Moscow's Arbat Street, was about to take over a major job in early 1993 running an analysis laboratory in Moscow. She had taken a tour of the facility where she planned to work and was horrified by what she found in the section where people were tested for AIDS. Practitioners had used one kit to test blood for four to eight people. "How would they know if anybody had AIDS or not?" In earlier years, the U.S.S.R. Ministry of Health had allowed ten to fifteen blood samples to be taken per test.[8]

For all her indignation, the question remained: how do you test or treat patients when supplies are not available? In early 1993, a report was released from the Russian health ministry that stated what had been suspected but not officially acknowledged by the government for years: 42 percent of the hospitals had no hot water, and 12 percent had no running water at all.[9] Faced with a shortage of scalpels, surgeons told of using razor blades on the operating table. When the laundries broke down, they reused linens—instead of one sheet per patient, one sheet per day on examining room tables. One doctor became somewhat famous for using the cotton "snow" from the hospital's New Year's display when surgical dressing had run out.[10] Patients were given cancer drugs, and if they worked, they were told to go out and find more of the chemical they needed in the street markets.[11]

An American doctor who helped set up new procedures for clinics in early 1992 said that Russia's medical system provided about the same level of care as America had sixty years earlier, when the nation's hospitals and clinics and doctors' offices were hobbled by the Great Depression. Several Russians suggested that the best description of Russian medical care in the 1990s—especially polyclinics, which provided the most rudimentary care in cities and rural areas—was written by Anton Chekhov almost one hundred years earlier in his story "Ward Number Six" about Dr. Andrei Yefimovich Ragin, the doctor in a rural clinic.

"To give serious help to forty out-patients between breakfast and lunch is a physical impossibility, and the upshot can only be total fraudulence. . . . Moreover, if one left theory out of it and stuck blindly to the rules like other doctors, then the crying need was for hygiene and ventilation instead of dirt; for healthy food instead of stinking sour cabbage stew; and for decent subordinates instead of crooks," wrote Chekhov, himself a doctor, although he practiced medicine only occasionally.[12] The description was altogether too valid a century later.

At Hospital No. 4 in southeast Moscow, the care provided in the waning Soviet years was better than in Chekhov's Ward Number Six, but not vastly better, considering what was happening to the medical profession else-where in the world. The images of Dr. Ragin haunted the staff, especially the chief administrator, Dr. Aleksandr Stepanov, who saw his role during the early 1990s as trying to keep his sprawling medical complex from turning into the prerevolutionary prisons for the sick and dying.

No. 4 had begun as a warehouse for the poor, established in 1763 to fulfill a promise made by Catherine II when her son Pavel was gravely ill. If the boy recovered, she would build a medical facility for the poor, the tsarina swore. Pavel survived, and she had a series of wooden huts built on the once-rural site outside Moscow.

In late 1991, when I went for the first time to Catherine's hospital, a black metal gate kept all but authorized cars away from the complex. It still spread over a large area, almost three blocks in each direction, but the hospital was now in the center of the city, within view of a cluster of industrial smokestacks in southeast Moscow. Inside the fence, people in starched white coats and towering, cheflike hats pushed aged trolleys or carried piles of documents from building to building. Through the worn doors of the administrative wing, past the messages on health from Lenin, sat Dr. Stepanov. The room was neat and spacious by Russian standards, and Dr. Stepanov, a tall, gentle-looking man who spoke so softly that sometimes it was hard to hear him, had agreed to help me understand the shape of Russian medicine in this period.

He did not mince words about the problems, but later, when I had written about how sad and miserable it seemed, he gently scolded me for not including the successes. In particular, Russian doctors had learned—out of necessity—to find substitutes for drugs. Western doctors, especially Americans, seemed to turn too quickly to powerful and disruptive drug therapies, he said. Even if these medicines were available, Russians would want to try massage, acupuncture, and relaxation therapy to help with pain and recuperation. A famous hand surgeon in his hospital had found a way to treat hand injuries without heavy doses of antibiotics and the results were as good as, if not better than, results with those who had all the wealth of the Western apothecary, he had said.[13]

Russian ingenuity would serve the world health community well, Dr. Stepanov had argued gently. Whether it could cure the vast numbers of patients in Russia was a different question.

On my first tour of the complex, I noted that most of the buildings, which were painted a faint yellow color and looked reasonably fresh from outside, were actually in desperate need of repair. The peeling paint was part of a general deterioration of equipment and facilities at the hospital that ranged from drafty windows to broken pieces of the heart-monitoring equipment. The dominant building in the complex, built in 1807 to replace the huts constructed by Catherine, was a beautiful structure that still managed to look elegant when I last saw it in 1995. But it was far too old and drafty for a hospital ward and operating rooms, a reality that Dr. Stepanov acknowledged when he took me through it on my first visit.

It was one of those cold autumn days that would have been winter anywhere else, but as we walked outside from an administrative building to the old wards, Dr. Stepanov wore only his white coat over a shirt and his white doctor's cap. I was shivering in a long thick sweater but he seemed oblivious to the cold and to a non-Russian's delicate constitution. "We have lost control over the personnel," he was saying as we walked into a dark hallway of the main building. "Among them there is no will to work. The increases in salary will not help. It does not change a doctor's qualifications, and for a nurse, it's a very difficult life. This is a real proletariat that has nothing to lose but their chains. They can quarrel with patients. They can drink on the job. They can insult the patients, and what can we do? There are no elephants anymore to do the hard work."

Dr. Stepanov, in a few short phrases, had managed to describe the sad state of the medical worker at the end of the Soviet era. The laborer, the elephant who once took on tasks with the zeal of a believer, was angry at his fate, surly about his clients, a disgruntled slave ready for the revolution that would come a few months later. In most cases, doctors had been trained in schools where medicine seemed a by-product of social politics, and many were barely qualified to do their jobs. The nurses, especially the older ones, were often the linchpin for a big hospital like Stepanov's. The dedicated nurse knew what the doctors were supposed to know, even though she usually made far less money, and in spite of the fact that the hospital had maintenance workers to do the heavy cleaning, the nurse often added scrubbing and sweeping to her duties.

As Dr. Stepanov led the way up the stairs, I could not help noticing the cigarette butts and the dirt, mopped into little triangles in the corner. He saw me looking and sighed.

"The government tried to pay more for work, and these workers accept more money, but they do not do the work," he said tiredly. "We imagine medicine to be a special sphere, but here it is a stepdaughter of the government. At one time only the most talented were accepted to medical institutions. Now, they take almost anybody. People who cannot learn these complicated matters, we take them anyway."

The pay, the lack of status, the lure of the West had begun to take its toll on the pool of doctors. As we turned a corner, Stepanov nodded to a nurse who was gray with exhaustion but who managed a respectful greeting. She was one of the good ones, he explained. "We survive with a small percentage that are dedicated, fanatically so."

In the once-grand building, the hallways were large enough for a few extra beds, and the patient rooms were cavernous. There were enough beds but not enough painkillers, only analgesics. In one room, a seventeen-year-old boy named Sasha was sitting on the side of his cot after having his bandage changed. His hand had been mangled by a wood-processing machine, and he had been through two operations, complete with promises that his hand would work well when he was released. I asked about pain. Nothing during the operation, said Sasha, who did not know how lucky he was. But afterward yes. It was very painful. Dr. Stepanov leaned away from the boy's bed and whispered, "Sometimes the patients have to stand pain. Our analgesics don't work as well as they should."

Then he turned to the boy, and for the first and last time during our several meetings, I saw the stern physician that Russians talk about, part healer, part drill sergeant. Women told me stories about having a doctor chastising them during their labor, slapping them and saying, "Stop your howling. This is what you get for having sex." Or when things got unbearable and a woman began to cry, "Don't be a little girl. We have enough babies in here."

Dr. Stepanov turned to the boy and corrected him: "You don't cry out in pain, right?" It was a challenge for the boy to be a man, an order from the top doctor.

"Right," agreed Sasha firmly.

Later, we walked into a women's ward, where five patients were in one room with eight beds. The room, like many other hospital rooms I would see around the country, had the look of a small communal dormitory, and it was clear when we arrived that these patients had become part of a minihospital commune. In Russian hospitals, patients stayed three times longer than they would in the West, and in this cardiac care ward, patients were kept sometimes for months, with the understanding that only here would they get well. At home, they would pick up the shovel or go out to stand in the lines.

Marina, a pensioner whose head seemed oddly bandaged in a thin cotton towel, was the only one lying in bed. The others were sitting up, writing or drinking tea made in pots brought from home. They cooked their own food, and the strongest often cleaned their room. As Marina turned her head to look at us, a small cluster of white coats that included doctors, nurses, and a journalist, she made a pitch for better conditions.

"It is so cold in here," she moaned. "The sheets have not been changed in a month." She touched her head and its towel to help make the point, but it wasn't necessary. It was indeed cold, even by Russian standards. Patients were issued one blanket, and in most hospitals, a small tip or bribe could have brought others, I was told later. When it became clear that her complaints were being ignored and had even brought frowns to the faces of the director and the head nurse, Marina suddenly changed her tack, hoping perhaps that praise would bring rewards, now that complaining had proved unsuccessful. "We get good care here, the best. Our doctors are the very best," she could be heard saying as we were leaving.

Dr. Stepanov wanted me to see the whole ward including the outdated equipment, which could not be replaced when parts broke either from wear or ill-treatment. At one point, he opened the door to a cupboard where two old women were lying on their sour hospital beds. The room smelled heavily of urine, and an open jar that had been used as a bedpan was sitting on a chair near the door. The jar must have been there for some time. Even in the cold, flies circled it noisily.

One of the women raised her head at the sound of the door opening and began to screech: "What's happening? What's happening?" The terror in her voice was contagious. Another doctor with us assured her there was nothing going on, nothing to worry about. As her head dropped back to the pillow, I saw that the woman was blind. She was sixty-nine years old, the doctor said. I would have guessed at least eighty, maybe ninety. The other one, asleep, looked a little younger—eighty, I estimated. She was sixty-four, Dr. Stepanov informed me a few minutes later.

As he shut the door, Dr. Stepanov asked me not to write about the old women for my newspaper, because technically it was against one of the government's many rules for them to stay in the hospital. But nobody wanted to send them to the places where they belonged. "It is like a charity that we have them here," he explained. "There are houses for the elderly but they don't want to go there. They lose their apartments, and all their worldly goods are sold to pay for their care. And the state homes are terrible," he said. "They are places without joy."

"Worse than this?" I asked. He nodded.

Later, back in his quiet office, we talked about how his hospital would survive since it had been funded by the government, which had less money to give, and by a few particular industries, most of which were struggling even to pay their healthy workers, much less subsidize their sick ones. This was not the top of the line for hospitals, but because it had the status of a teaching hospital in Moscow, it was not the bottom. But he vowed that it would not become a clinic, and as I left, Dr. Stepanov said the hospital had no plans to become part private, as many facilities were doing in order to raise money for their public operations.

"Now, the situation is so hard that the only idea for us is to survive and at least conserve what we have," he said.

Three times I went back to see Dr. Stepanov's hospital. On one occasion, in 1992, a load of Western aid arrived, and I went to see the boxes being crammed into tiny offices and the barely used operating tables stacked in an enormous warehouse. The head nurse opened one box, her eyes shining like a child's. Inside were hundreds of pairs of disposable gloves, needles, and intravenous kits. "These are to throw away afterward?" one nurse asked incredulously. The American who accompanied the equipment said, "Yes, they aren't for sterilizing." But he knew as all of us knew that, somehow, they would be washed, the way people wash plastic bags and still darn old socks in a society that cannot afford to throw away anything that is or may be of use. After a while, the head nurse, who had looked warily at the packets with their instructions and labels in English, managed a some-what begrudging thanks. "We need it all. We need everything," she told the American who had arranged the massive delivery. Almost two years later, during one of my visits with Dr. Stepanov, he said the help lasted for what seemed like only a few weeks. Then he was back, juggling his budget to try to wheedle drugs and money out of the Russian and Moscow governments.

In late 1992, when I visited Dr. Stepanov again, he sat in the same office behind the same spare desk. But he looked thinner, and during most of our talk, he sighed and kept his head slightly bent like a man who could feel his powers to control his institution slipping beyond reach. When I asked if anything had changed, he took a long breath and stared, first at me and then down at his hands. I thought that he was marshaling the reasons not to talk this time, that my questions had become an irritation, another burden in an already overburdened existence. Finally he began to speak, the anger building even though his voice stayed low: "The situation has not improved; maybe it has not grown drastically worse, but there have been no changes for the better."

He ticked off the old problems, but this time he added an especially cruel new twist. Drugs, once scarce, were now available, mountainous stacks of them slowly losing their potency at central warehouses. The problem was that they were exorbitantly expensive, even the generic ones that public hospitals like his had to buy with their dwindling share of the state budget. The patient load seemed to be shrinking, he said, as those with money went to private hospitals or those without any faith in Soviet medicine simply stayed home and treated themselves. Health statistics in this period explained why the bigger hospitals like this one were dying, like too many of their patients. The Soviet Union had boasted 132.8 hospital beds per 10,000 people compared to about 50 beds per 10,000 in the United States,[14] but the figures had always puzzled Western medical experts who saw extra hospital beds as unnecessary and costly.

"I don't think the state will really let us die," Stepanov said that day. "You can close a factory, but you cannot close a hospital, and so we are not really afraid about our future." It is simply that the future will be less like the prestigious teaching hospital of the past and more like the big-city public hospitals that are famous in America for taking all who make it to the emergency room doors.

"Probably this is our destiny," he said. "We will have to cure only the poorest people."

It would mean that the future for Moscow's Hospital No. 4 would be its past. What began as a pauper's hospital would, he feared, return to its original mission 230 years later.

Today's Russian medicine may not be as good as in the West because of communism, but it is far better than what the Bolsheviks found when they were creating the Soviet state. As Lenin put it in 1919 when he outlined the need for health services to stem epidemics after the revolution, "Either the lice will defeat socialism or socialism will defeat the lice." Between 1916 and 1924, estimates of deaths attributed to epidemics ranged from 3 million to 10 million. Typhoid, smallpox, dysentery,—these were the diseases threatening to wipe out Lenin's peasant revolution, and there were few qualified physicians to control them.[15] With civil war raging, many doctors died from battle wounds or disease. In one province on the Volga, a single physician was left behind in 1921 to deal with fifteen thousand victims of typhus, a lice-borne disease.[16]

The first wave of modern Russian medicine, like many of the nation's major historical changes, began with Peter the Great, who imported Western doctors and expanded medical care for the military, the aristocracy, and the industrial centers.[17] In 1706, a medical school with fifty students opened in Moscow, another in St. Petersburg a few years later.[18] By 1883, a few clinics had been set up to serve the poor in St. Petersburg, originally to treat outbreaks of diphtheria and scarlet fever, but the death rate and infant mortality rate in Russia from these diseases and other causes were still far higher than in Europe.[19] According to physicians' estimates of the day, life expectancy in the late 1880s was around twenty-nine years—a figure skewed by the high infant mortality in this era.[20]

By the late nineteenth century, the local, or zemstvo, governments had begun to establish a ragged health system for the peasants, and the zemstvo physicians moved into the countryside, some of them like intellectual missionaries who came to save the "dark and deaf" masses. The peasants sometimes viewed these urban doctors as suspicious aliens, and a number were murdered over the years as they tried to peddle medical science over superstition. Still, the numbers of zemstvo physicians grew steadily into the beginning of the twentieth century, and by the time the Bolsheviks took over, they served as a base for the new Soviet health system.

Historians in the past have often argued that these community doctors established a force of socially conscious physicians who believed that the only way to improve Russia's abysmal health system was to change the form of government. In the 1990s, however, that view began undergoing some revision. Other historians now contend that these local doctors were often as conservative as the city physicians who catered to the upper classes. There were some doctors who wanted to expand health care beyond the elite. The Pirogov Society was a collection of physicians who argued that it was time to discard the tsars' system of "medical police" and make the doctor independent of the government. The Pirogovists wanted the doctor to control how the patient was treated, but even with their relatively advanced views toward populist medicine, they were among the first to be disappointed when the Soviets took control (even though a number of the Pirogovists quietly joined the Soviet medical establishment and began to work for Lenin's medical reforms).[21]

After he took power, Lenin set up the Soviet of Medical Collegia in 1918 to centralize medical care and discredit the powerful and independent-minded doctors. He lumped the Pirogovists with the rest of the physicians, their reforms deemed insufficient for his revolution. Lenin then described his new medical system as "the highest medical organization of the workers' and peasants' government"[22] In this new order, Lenin had given more power to the feldshers, literally the field barbers, who had served through the years as paramedics or doctors' assistants, and they were told that part of their task was to "cut the doctors down to size."[23]

In some ways, robbing doctors of their status was considered a great pleasure by peasants, who saw the medical profession in two hostile ways: either they were viewed as courtesans—physicians for the rich—or as medical police whose real job was to kill off anybody who diluted the nation's reputation by not being appropriately robust and healthy.

During the cholera epidemics of the late 1800s, people rioted over the treatment their government provided for those unlucky enough to contract the deadly disease. One doctor recounted tales of the government's *sanitaires,* unsavory people who roamed the streets picking up the sick or dead, carrying them to the hospitals or the morgue. Russians whispered that these health workers were really officially sanctioned ghouls skulking through the dark city streets and seizing not only the dead and dying but anyone sleeping off the night's vodka. These unfortunates were picked up like fish, with a large hook, dumped in a cart, and carried to the cholera hospitals, where those presumed dead were showered with lime, thrown in a pitch coffin, and buried in an unmarked grave.[24] To do Lenin's bidding—to cut the medical profession down to size—suited many of the ordinary Russians, who feared the old doctors and yearned for new ones who would be competent and sympathetic to their sufferings.

The communists quickly opened medical training to virtually anyone who wasn't from the "exploiting classes," which vastly expanded the numbers of medical workers.[25] Women were encouraged to go into medicine, especially after World War II, and although administrators, surgeons, top researchers, and medical scientists were often men, the workaday doctor for most Russians in the Soviet years was a woman. By 1950, 77 percent of the Soviet Union's doctors were women (a percentage that began to drop slightly in the 1980s, when women were encouraged to stay home more and tend to their families).[26]

The medical profession, like medical care, was given a lower priority by the Soviet state. Medical personnel were officially labeled as "nonproductive",[27] unlike the industrial engineers or defense workers, whose pay and status were much higher. The result of all this leveling down of the medical profession in the Soviet Union meant that by the early 1990s, doctors were threatening to strike because their wages were lower than those of most bus drivers. In later years, analysts of the Soviet medical system would suggest that the loss of status for doctors in Russia occurred as medicine increasingly became women's work in a traditionally sexist society.[28]

Whatever the connection between the increase in women doctors and the decrease in status of the profession, what worried many physicians, even those loyal to the state, was that the drive to push more doctors through medical school would lower the level of medical care. A move toward quantity meant an automatic move away from quality, they told one another privately. Few spoke out about their concern; to do so meant writing your own death certificate. Aleksandr Krasin, a professor at the prestigious First Leningrad Medical Institute, complained officially to his colleagues in the fall of 1934 that the government was "more interested in increasing the number of doctors than in how they were trained," as his daughter told the story years later. Two weeks after he protested the change in policy, he was arrested and never seen again by his family—one of an estimated five thousand doctors who were executed during the 1930s for not following Stalin's political or medical line.[29]

At about the same time, Stalin's health ministers experimented with teaching doctors in brigades, so that one class of several hundred students passed through six years of medical school as a group. When it became clear that some individuals knew almost nothing as they stared down at their first official patient, the system was phased out in favor of individual exams.[30]

There was always a way to bypass the official system, of course, and the ardent young Communist Party member could get his diploma by waving his party badge at the examination board. Mark Field, whose 1957 book *Doctor and Patient in Soviet Russia* was one of the first glimpses many Westerners had of medicine in the U.S.S.R., tells the story of a doctor asked to substitute on the medical examining board, where he found one candidate "particularly weak" in the skills of medicine. He decided to give the young student a three (top score was a five) and made his decision known to the rest of the board members. The other professors were horrified, the doctor recalled later, and they whispered that the student was a Komsomol (Young Communist) activist whose grade average would be damaged by this mark. The substitute professor suggested they try the exam again later, and he heard that on the second round, the boy had passed with a 5.[31]

Politics became crucial, and even though many students resented the Marxism-Leninism courses, they studied them as rigorously as, or sometimes even more than, the medical subjects. "You could flunk surgery, that was all right, but not political courses," one physician said, explaining why so many doctors got their degrees long before they knew how to treat patients.[32] Shortly after World War II, Soviet medical schools were requiring students to have 250 hours of political studies a year, compared to 216 for biology and 213 for general surgery.[33]

Although the political training at medical schools lessened during glasnost and virtually disappeared by the late 1980s, most doctors practicing in the former Soviet Union in the early 1990s had spent long hours at medical school learning the communist line on their field of expertise. In the early 1980's, one doctor whose children wanted to be doctors decided the only way to deal with the Soviet education system was to teach them medicine himself. By day, his offspring attended a Soviet institute; at night, they learned doctoring at home.

Almost every Russian in the early 1990s had a story about malpractice, that, once committed by a Soviet doctor, could not be challenged successfully by a mere patient. *Trud,* the official trade union newspaper, wrote about a fifteen-year-old girl who died from appendicitis in Kazan on the Volga River because four different doctors with Soviet degrees had misdiagnosed her case.[34] A 1991 report on Soviet doctors estimated that two of every five new medical school graduates in the 1980s could not read an EKG.[35]

Dr. Yevgeni Chazov, minister of health under Mikhail Gorbachev, was appointed to try to improve the deteriorating health care system in 1987. At the time, he sent a letter to the Politburo; this may have been the "first time they recognized just how bad the situation . . . actually was," he told a Moscow newspaper reporter.[36] Among the revelations in that letter was Chazov's assessment of how many untrained physicians were practicing in the U.S.S.R. He had determined that 40 percent of students graduating with medical degrees were "completely devoid of medical skills."[37]

As Russia began trying to revamp its medical system after the end of the Cold War, many of the most talented physicians and surgeons had emigrated or quit medicine, at least officially . One doctor, making a sad joke, told his colleagues that Russia did at least have one thing to brag about in the medical sphere—the biggest tumors in the world. It was because they were so often misdiagnosed, especially in the provinces.[38]

As this communist era ended, medical schools were trying to limit their numbers for two reasons: first, they had less money to educate doctors, and, second, there were too many doctors. In 1991, Aleksandr V. Telyukov, an economist at the Soviet National Planning Committee (GOSPLAN) issued an important report on the Soviet medical system. In it he said:

The number of doctors per 10,000 population in the Soviet Union is 44.3 and remains unmatched by the world community (U.S. has 28.8 per 10,000). Leadership of this kind is obviously meaningless, because providers are severely under assisted by people of other medical occupations and the so-called physicians have to spend 40 percent of their working time acting as nurse practitioners, medical registrars, and the like. . . . The professional skills of physicians are quite poor, as a result of the depressed economic and societal status of the health sector, low salaries, and bad labor conditions in medical practice."[39]

Because of the problem of trying to maintain a deteriorating medical system, the exceptions were all the more astonishing. Good doctors could be found in surprising places—rural outposts, children's hospitals, centers without support or glamour. I saw a children's cancer hospital in eastern Russia where Dr. Valentina V. Mityaeva and her colleagues treated their patients not as cases but as human beings.

Dr. Mityaeva,[40] whose center was in downtown Khabarovsk, had created a warm, clean, and loving place for children with cancer. She battled the tangle of bureaucracies and tried to convince Western aid officials that she desperately needed chemotherapy drugs to keep many of her patients alive. By taking children who had been rejected at some of the large cancer hospitals because they were deemed incurable (a problem not only for the child and family but for the hospital's statistics), she faced the possibility that her own hospital's death rates would be higher. But Dr. Mityaeva felt her job was to comfort the sick, even if she couldn't heal them.

As we walked through the clean corridors and into a wing for the most serious cases one day in late 1992, Dr. Mityaeva opened the door to a room where Anna, a frail young girl without hair or color in her skin, stared at television set, its silent screen bouncing with the happy faces of Russian cartoon characters. Anna's mother sat beside her, a luxury in children's hospitals, where the family and those who were ill were often separated by the hospitals' rigid rules of treatment. (One mother I knew who was a doctor slipped into a Moscow children's hospital in her white robes to be with her son during his tonsillectomy. When she was found out, the nurses were furious, she said, and ultimately she was asked to help out by washing the walls and floors of her son's ward. Others simply convinced the weary hospital staff to allow them to serve as unofficial cleaning women to be near their sick children.)

In a similar way, Dr. Valentina Lukyanova, head of the clinic in Chapayevsk, had tried to treat people whose ailments were directly related to the fertilizers and other chemicals being produced nearby. Dr. Lukyanova's facilities were dilapidated, and her possibilities for real treatment were slim. Still, Dr. Lukyanova was energetically doing what she could to provide advice and medicine for her stream of patients. As we sat in her office one day looking through Soviet medical files still marked "top secret," part of the ceiling fell on my lap. She looked at me, apologized, and smiled in embarrassment. Now I knew what it was like, she said.[41]

There were thousands of doctors like these two women and Dr. Stepanov at Moscow's Hospital No. 4 who struggled every day to heal the human suffering around them. There were also the extraordinary doctors who grew to be Soviet legends, the state's brilliant surgeons or scientists who pursued their work with the approval and support of the state. As examples of Soviet ingenuity and expertise, they were rewarded with money, equipment, the best of anything they wanted, from anywhere in the world. Svyatoslav Fyodorov was perhaps the most dramatic example of this bureaucratic extravaganza. In the 1970s he convinced the state medical establishment to allow him to start an assembly-line eye surgery to do his operations, primarily for shortsightedness. By the 1990s, he had converted his hospital into an elaborate private business complex that included optical instruments, car rental services, an agricultural training system, and a luxury hotel.[42] The hotel was built around a courtyard with a massive copper-and-brass eye staring down from the courtyard ceiling.

The son of a cavalry general who disappeared during one of Stalin's purges, Fyodorov grew up in Ukraine, a young man trying to become a doctor despite the crucial black mark against him, that his father had been branded an enemy of the state. In 1955, after he learned that his father had been in a prison camp in Siberia, son and father were finally reunited and, as Fyodorov told one interviewer, "His face was sad. When a man has not laughed for a long time, he can only imitate a smile."[43]

Dr. Fyodorov has said the memory of his father's face turned his life into a crusade. "I want to destroy the Stalinist bureaucratic system," he said in 1989. "I hate it because it has ruined everything—culture, nature, generosity."[44]

In the old days, Dr. Fyodorov once called his hospital "a medical factory for the production of people with good eyesight" or sometimes "medical factory"[45]—a description that turned out to be true, not mere Soviet hyperbole. The Moscow Research Institute of Eye Microsurgery was a strange place where the production methods of Henry Ford were adapted to the practice of medicine. Patients even in the 1990s were given an eye anesthetic and then placed on a table. The table began to move along an assembly line to the first of five surgeons. The first surgeon stopped the bed and performed the first part of the surgery. Then the bed moved to the second surgeon for the next procedure. The entire operation usually took about ten to fifteen minutes.[46]

More than 220,000 patients a year passed through his institute by the time I arrived in Moscow. They were paying for relief from glaucoma, cataracts, or myopia. Dr. Fyodorov, who pioneered the surgery for near-sightedness, called radial keratotomy, in the 1970s, still faced many skeptics as his techniques were viewed firsthand in the late 1980s and 1990s. Doctors from abroad worried that the surgery, which involves cutting the cornea radially like a pizza to change the shape of the eye, is unnecessary— a grave risk to take with your eyes just so that you will not need glasses or contact lenses.

Within the country, there were those who began to wonder whether his goals were great medicine or the pursuit of a rich lifestyle. Besides his apartments, dachas, car phones, and airplanes, the Soviet Union's most famous eye surgeon had more than fifty horses. The institute owned two yachts, and one visitor to his office put it this way: "His spacious, paneled office on the third floor of a hospital eleven miles from the Kremlin would not embarrass a Rockefeller or a Ford."[47]

Fyodorov was an example of how the medical profession—like the Soviet society—had two layers, the privileged and everyone else. In the case of medicine, as I have mentioned, this division was also sexual. The elite, powerful doctors, the heads of institutes and hospitals, were mostly men. Underneath them was an army of doctors who did the rest of the work, mostly women.

Women often undertook the tough, unrewarding tasks—performing the 7 million legal abortions reported each year in the Soviet states, managing

Dickensian children's hospitals that broke all but the hardened doctors' hearts, supervising the state *rodilnye doma,* or birthing houses, that were so inhumane and dangerous that they forced many women to choose abortion or abstinence. Most provincial clinics and many urban polyclinics, where treatments were crude and drugs scarce, were run by women. After praising women doctors for having the warmth and selflessness necessary for medicine, Soviet émigré Dr. Vladimir Golyakhovsky noted in 1984: "While men account for less than 30 percent of all Soviet physicians, they have appropriated for themselves practically all well-paying jobs, leaving drudgery to women." He added that because these women had also to do housework and shopping, cooking, and taking care of the family, "Most Russian women doctors are strikingly passive; they have no time for enterprise or initiative. However, they fit nicely into the system of socialized medicine."[48]

There were exceptions, women whose energy and dedication were beyond my comprehension, and I tried for months to find a certain female doctor whose patients mentioned her name in a tone of almost religious reverence. Finally, on a cold sunny day in October 1992, she agreed to meet me in a Russian friend's kitchen, where we sat for most of the afternoon drinking tea and talking about her life of trying to make people well.

Although I met many women doctors in my tours of Russian clinics and hospitals, Nina Ivanovna was the only one who would not let me use her family name. "This is the new Russia," I argued. She shook her head and said simply, "You never know when they could come back. I still have family here."

As we were laying the ground rules for her discourse, I could not help staring at this woman who had earned such awe and respect among Russians I knew to be cynical about anybody who was successful and privileged under the old system. Her hair was white and her hands knotted—that was to be expected of anyone born eighty-six years earlier. But her eyes were what startled people who met her for the first time. They were black and penetrating, and she still possessed the clear direct gaze of a thirty-year-old. At one point, she read a letter presented to her without squinting or using glasses. Half her age, I could barely make out the letters without my magnifiers. Had she been a patient in Fyodorov's operating theater? I wondered. She shook her head, no.

When I asked her my first real question—about her background and how she got into medicine—she stared at me for a few moments as if my face or my eyes or perhaps the way I held myself would give her some sign, some indication, of how much she could say. Finally, as if I had passed this silent exam, she began talking for what would turn out to be the entire afternoon, telling stories of the war and her family, of the time the KGB had come to get her and she had worn two dresses in case she was moved directly to prison (she was not), of how the war years were so terrible that people burned whatever they could find for heat, including her Ph.D. dissertation on Rh factor.

As she talked, the people who had loaned us their kitchen and who had known her for years and who had been treated by her since some of them took their first howling breath, sat listening in virtual silence. Only the wife left occasionally to quiet a child, to make more tea, to spread out a lunch of meat and pickles and fresh steaming potatoes.

Nina Ivanovna was born to a Polish aristocratic mother and a military father. She met her husband at a ball, she said, adding that it was not something they talked about afterward, in the days after communism arrived. Still, she went to the best schools in Moscow, and after graduation as a pediatrician, she was sent to the faraway town of Kheta to help with the resettling of Siberia. "Because I had no children, I was sent there. All of us were sent in trucks, and we drove for two weeks. Many people were being sent away [to Siberia], and every night people were hammering on the trucks, crying to be let in. Trying to get help. If one person fell ill in the family, the whole family was put off the trucks."

"And they were left to freeze? To die?" I asked.

"Who knows?" She shrugged, in the Russian manner of saying, I don't know and I cannot afford the pain or worry of thinking about it. She was called back to Moscow for the war, and there her husband died mysteriously. "I tried to find out, but"—she shrugged again—"I got nothing." The army just told her that he died. Somewhere. It was not her business to know and especially not her business to try to find out.

So she dedicated herself to her work and became known as the children's doctor that anyone with clout tried to see in Moscow. "I have now treated sometimes three generations of families," she said. "Some are perfect. But others . . ." She waved her hand over my notepad and declared that what she was about to say was off-limits. Then she talked, without naming names, about the drinking and the child abuse, about men leaving their wives when the women became fat or inconvenient. It was not just Russia, I assured her. We are all learning the horrors of broken homes and child abuse and vicious, mindless crime, the man-made epidemics of our century.

"But we have more than that," she said, as if to make certain I knew we were not the same. "We have the most frightening problem of all—our children." The children were growing weaker, she said; Russia's latest generation was thin and spindly, plagued by illnesses that were rare or believed eradicated thirty, maybe forty years ago.

"I have seen our children for over sixty years, and what I have witnessed now is something terrible that is happening to them," she said, her voice strong and angry, filling the tiny kitchen where four adults sat transfixed by stories that seemed to define a century in Russia. "The health of our children now is very poor, due to ecological problems, our air, our water, our food. Most of our children have some kind of allergy, respiratory problems, asthma. It is becoming worse and worse. Thirty years ago, we saw single cases. Now, it's a pandemic problem.

"The quality of food is so bad now, and women are weaker. They have more difficulties giving birth, and a larger percentage of children are premature. There is an absence of highly qualified medical help, and clinics can provide only so much. Achhh, the unsanitary conditions." She stopped and shook her head.

Others were beginning to make the same point publicly. In late 1991, two youth experts, Georgi Serdyukovsky, then director of Soviet Health Ministry's branch on young people, and Col. Grigori Filchenkov, deputy chief of the Soviet department on juvenile delinquency prevention, laid out the depressing realities about the younger generation. Fewer than one in 10 schoolchildren "showed normal physical development" and only 12 percent to 15 percent of the Soviet army conscripts were "considered healthy." "The picture is truly catastrophic," said Serdyukovsky.[49] The headline of an article in *Argumenty i Fakty* weekly newspaper expressed the question many people had begun to ask themselves. It said: "Do We Have a Future?"

In the long hours with Dr. Nina, she talked about what the stress of such a life was doing to her people. Russia's minister of health, Dr. Andrei Vorobiev, had also talked with me earlier about the wages of stress, but he had been talking in the abstract. He had warned that people trying to cope with the unknown, the chaos of daily living after communism, were being worn down, becoming easy targets for disease and susceptible to strange psychological behavior. Nina Ivanovna confirmed his theory in the particular.

Recently, she said, a man called and asked her to come see his eight-and-a-half-month-old son. Even though she had no time and little extra energy, she went to the man's apartment, where she found that the child was not only sick but totally disabled, blind, and perhaps deaf. She quickly wrapped the child in a blanket and got the man to take them to a hospital. He offered to drive her home, and as they were riding, the man grew more and more upset at her for taking the boy to the authorities. "He cried and yelled at me that I had ill served him. He said he would not come to the hospital and see the child. He was so angry I thought he was going to eat me. Then, when he calmed down a little, he explained that he had brought the child from the south to Moscow so that it would die. He said, 'I am rich. I could pay thousands of rubles for a lethal injection.' I said, not to agree but because I was curious, 'Why didn't you do it at your home?' and he said, 'It would be easier here. So many thousands die every day.' "

At the next stoplight, Nina Ivanovna jumped from the car and walked to the nearest subway. " 'I will not help you with such a sorry business,' I told him before I got out of the car. But I knew I could not just leave it behind or someone else would." So, she called the wife, who said that her husband had returned to their place like a rabid animal. He raged. He pounded the walls. He broke dishes and glasses, all the time telling her he wanted a divorce. The wife was hysterical. At first Nina Ivanovna thought it was simply because of the child, but it was more than that. "She asked me, 'Do I need to kill my child now because he will be a person of disability? Otherwise my husband will divorce me.' " The wife was torn between wanting to keep her sad child and wanting to stay married to her rich husband.

"It was the first time I had ever heard of such a thing in my sixty-two years of practice," Dr. Nina concluded.

A good doctor from the old days, Dr. Nina Ivanovna was horrified by the new ones. In the past, she had run a private network for the families she felt needed her—some privileged, some merely lucky. Even now, officially retired, she was treating grandchildren of former patients and providing these services, in most cases, for virtually nothing.

Most people were not fortunate enough to have such care. They were shunted into the Soviet medical machine, dumped into institutions built in the Soviet years for the glory of institutionalism, not concern for individuals. Even before the end of the Soviet era, people had begun making their own decisions about whom to see and what drugs to take. Perhaps the best example of this skepticism was that few people we knew had their children vaccinated against the normal list of childhood diseases. Russian friends explained to us that even their doctors had warned against it. Unsterilized needles caused infection and perhaps AIDS, they were told. The sera made by Soviet factories were sloppily produced, they said. Some of their information came from articles like those by Vladimir Umnov, who wrote in *Komsomolskaya Pravda* in 1988 that the most basic vaccine, the DPT that vaccinates against diphtheria, pertussis (whooping cough), and tetanus, had been made with an antiseptic that caused allergic reactions so severe that an unspecified number of children had died after taking the shots.[50] The antiseptic had been banned for human use in the West.

In this period when long-hidden truths were being aired everywhere in public as part of Gorbachev's glasnost, *Trud* newspaper told about how over a hundred children in the southern city of Elista had been infected with AIDS. Medical workers had not sterilized needles, but simply moved them from one young patient to another. In the hospital, logbooks that were supposed to show how hypodermics were sterilized were destroyed by a mysterious flood.[51]

By 1994, some Russians looking at the health data were talking about "Russian genocide," and even the language sometimes used to describe what was happening to the population of their country had frightening undercurrents. An Itar-Tass report of research released in April 1994 by the Russian Academy of Sciences provided one example. The Academy survey warned that the population of Russia could decrease by half in fifty years. Under this headline, Itar-Tass reported that one million fewer Russians were born in 1993 than in 1992 and that by the year 2001, the present population of 148.4 million would decrease to 146.5 million. This loss of population was especially "severe" among ethnic Russians the report said—noting that the share of Russians in Russia would soon be down to 70 percent.

"Social, economic, and political factors are beginning to have a direct effect on the depopulation of Russia," the news report concluded. "The scale and nature of that trend needs not only to be made public but demands direct government intervention to prevent Russian society from dying out and *to forestall the degradation of the nation's gene pool* (emphasis added)."[52]

Such language in the state news agency had the ominous sound of a nationalism that pitted "true" Russians against other ethnic groups around the country. The deterioration of Russia's health was taking its toll, not only physically but politically.

In late 1993, I returned to see Dr. Stepanov at Moscow's Hospital No. 4. By then the first small changes after the end of the Soviet state had blossomed into startling and showy differences between Soviet and non-Soviet Russia. Ordinary shops sold kiwi fruits and Bénédictine. Mercedes, BMWs, and Volvos roared through the streets, sending the tiny Soviet models coughing into the slow lanes. And while the rich celebrated their ability to show off their new finery, including an array of bodyguards, there were more old women begging for change at the entrance to Moscow's once-elegant Metro stations.

On that afternoon, when I drove into the compound, Hospital No. 4 seemed like a descent into the past. It was the same ragged place. The noise of the cobbled street outside was far away. Up the stairs to Dr. Stepanov's office, Lenin was still reigning along the wall on one floor. The administrator's office was still pin neat, a few pieces of paper carefully stacked on his desk.

"How are you?" I asked the American question, noting that now, at forty-seven, Stepanov's hair had grown much grayer in the year since I had seen him.

Stepanov laughed gently. "Society still needs us so far," he answered, glancing through the sheer curtains at his small empire outside.

The problem for him, as for hospitals all over Russia, was money, in his case to cover the cost of his nine-hundred-bed facility. (There were 884 patients in residence that day, he said.) The system had changed, but the need for the director to scramble was the same. "We are consumers now," Stepanov explained that afternoon, suggesting that only the term was different. Before, they were simply beggars, their hands out to the state, the city, and the remaining factories. No longer did he wheedle and coax supplies from central warehouses, using clout and whatever worked. Now he scrambled for money. For a few hours that day, he talked about his hospital's plight; the way university students paid a few rubles for lectures so that his doctors, who made about $70 a month, could make a little more money. For patients, his hospital still was free, he said.

For everyone?

Stepanov smiled. Yes, but there were often ways for patients to pay. If they were from outside Moscow, the hospital could charge them or their companies or their families for the care. Or if the hospitalization was for something not vital.

Like the managers of all institutions in this period, Stepanov had figured out the hospital's assets—a group of talented doctors—and tried to figure out how to market them. Several of the hospital's surgeons were specialists in cosmetic surgery—more for burns and industrial accidents than wrinkles and noses—but now was the time to adapt old skills to the new needs. Moscow's rich wanted face-lifts. Stepanov was planning to offer them a place to be surgically rejuvenated—for lots of money.

"There is a big demand," he said, explaining that he had only recently received approval from the hospital's board to go ahead with a cosmetic surgery ward. "I don't know yet whether it will work."

When I saw him in 1995, Dr. Stepanov seemed like a far different person from the stern doctor I had first met four years earlier or even the dispirited man I had visited in late 1993. As he opened the door to his office, unchanged except for the new stack of medical journals and newspapers covering his desk, he smiled and explained that he had a recent acquisition, as he called it—a limp, the result of an Achilles tendon torn during a volleyball match. The injury had left him recuperating in bed for most of the month. "Everyone is laughing at me now, of course, because I have been a lifetime fanatic about sports," he began as he took my coat and walked me to the chair near his desk, where I had spent so many hours in earlier years.

How had things changed since I last saw him? Well, he was thicker around the middle now at age forty-nine, he laughed as he patted a barely rounded stomach that would be the envy of most Americans his age. He was wearing a gray striped jacket and striped shirt with a bright tie in red, orange, and yellow. "I try to do sports," he continued chattily, "but, now, it is only for the rich." As he talked generously for the first time about his life as a sportsman—his various attractions to body building, then Ping Pong, then volleyball—Stepanov began to relax and reveal a few details about his family. It was the first time I had heard about his wife, for example, who was in charge of the hospital's cardiac care unit. She was a workaholic, he said, a lively woman who loves her job. ("There are arguments on TV now about whether women should work. I can't imagine taking away her work. She loves her job. She's interested in everything. She is there from eight to eight, and I phone the office less often than she does.")

His daughter was in her third year of medical school, he said proudly, and his son was becoming a physicist. "He is the one I worry about, the one who may never find work," he said, only half joking. It was a reference to the thousands of engineers and physicists produced by the Soviet state who were spending most of their time now adapting to low-level jobs in business. The family, including his parents who fled from Baku when the Russians were made unwelcome there, now lived together in one noisy apartment.

As I listened to this funny, self-deprecating man boasting about a family that clearly deserved his pride, I wondered why someone you have known as somber and quiet suddenly becomes not simply happy but almost effervescent. Perhaps this was his real personality, hidden for all these visits under the Soviet doctor's white cloak. I had seen the strict head doctor lecturing a young boy about the need to overcome pain. I had seen the kindly physician who made room for two miserable old people rather than send them to a nursing home. Now, it seemed, this was an almost giddy Stepanov, a man who had something to celebrate. Only later, after visiting the wards, would I realize what it was.

Hospital No. 4, which looked cleaner and better maintained than I had ever seen it, simply had money for the first time since the full-stagnation days twenty years earlier. Patients no longer risked their lives with a system of injections that depended on whether the nurse had properly sterilized the needles. Disposables were used and then, unlike in the past, they were not reused. The walls, the floors, the rooms would not yet pass a Western test for cleanliness, but the care was better than two years earlier, when patients often diagnosed their own illnesses and bought their own medicine. The system of funding the hospital had changed, and now the money came not merely from the state and from leftover Soviet industries that still donated funds for their workers' care, but also from a massive new state insurance fund that had begun operating about a year earlier.

For patients, the hospital may have seemed cleaner and the medicine more abundant, but the real miracle was that it was still basically free. The exception, besides the gifts and extras that were still part of the tradition, was that those from outside the hospital's designated service area had to pay for their care. But even those outsiders were often reimbursed from their own area's insurance funds, Dr. Stepanov said.

The fourth quarter in 1994, Stepanov's budget was 4 billion rubles ($800,000), he said, but his budget would increase by about 40 percent to 50 percent in 1995 because of inflation. The hospital was being financed well enough to do its job, and some of the inequities of a few years ago had begun to disappear.

Like the problem with pacemakers a few years earlier, he continued. The patients on the heart wards in the early 1990s were told that if they needed a pacemaker, they could go out onto the open market and buy one. Siemens was recommended, $4,000 each. That meant that in the communal wards in Russian hospitals, some heart patients who needed pacemakers had them and some did not. Some thrived, and some died—the differences being not merely their vital signs or their doctors' skill but their family resources.

A few patients, World War II veterans mostly, bought the pacemakers as suggested and then wrote the health ministry to complain. Eventually, these complaints changed the way hospitals did business. Now, Dr. Stepanov said, the doctors could decide who gets a pacemaker, and in most cases the insurance fund would pay for it.

Still, it did not always work as smoothly as he made it sound, he admitted. One man came into the hospital with a heart problem and his son, a young rich entrepreneur (with no medical experience), wanted him to have a pacemaker. The doctors refused, saying that a pacemaker would not improve the old man's heart or his life. But the son insisted, and he purchased the pacemaker, then demanded that the doctors install it.

"So"— Dr. Stepanov shrugged his shoulders—"we put in a pacemaker for him. Of course, it did not help much."[53]

The hospital, for all its improvements, still had its problems, he said. The government was trying to take back full control of the medical system, a move that would deny hospitals like Stepanov's their independence and mean that clinics like one nearby would continue to remain open even though he believed their care was minimal or even hazardous to the local clientele. Dr. Stepanov's plans to build a private ward for cosmetic surgery were also moving more slowly than he had hoped. A year and a half after he had received his first approval of the idea, nothing had changed: he was still drawing up plans and begging various government agencies for their official approval.

But overall, he was much improved, he concluded—his hospital, his life, even his leg.

It was a short visit, and I had wanted to see the hospital again after several years, but Dr. Stepanov asked a nurse to serve as a guide, mainly to the hand surgery ward. There, under conditions that would alarm any Western doctor, one of Russia's best-known specialists in hand surgery, Vyacheslav Fedorovich Korshunov, performed about four hundred operations a year, on people who had damaged their hands on everything from axes to computers. The patient load was down that day to forty-six in a ward that would hold sixty people, and there were no beds in the corridors as the last time I had come. (The entire hospital had 700 patients in all. Usually it was about 900, on some days as many as 950.) This week had been a holiday and the elective surgeries had elected to go to the parades celebrating the victory over the Nazis in World War II.

As always in Russian institutions, a visitor is required to see the top available official first. Dr. Sergei Nikolaevich Yesekhin, chief doctor of the hand surgery ward, greeted me in a small office and escorted me to a place where we could talk. As we moved through the hall, patients were coming down the corridors. Each of them had one hand bandaged—wrist, fingers, some up to the elbow—while the good hand held a flat bowl of food: meat, potatoes, and cabbage piled in one unappetizing mound. Dr. Yesekhin, who gave a quick history of the hospital, proudly concentrating on its beginnings, said that No. 4 had experimented with a cooperative three years earlier, giving private quality service to some who paid private quality prices, but that it had not worked. Doctors had to labor a full day then participate in the private practice after hours. The cooperative, called META, meant that most doctors worked from 8 A.M. until late at night.

A few minutes later Professor Korshunov, the hand specialist, emerged from his operating room . He was a small man with a coarse smoker's voice and the weathered face of a farmer. He had seen about one thousand patients a year in recent years—four hundred operations done personally, he said. At the posh government hospital, he also performed ten to twenty operations a year as requested. When I asked about whether he would be part of a cooperative, possibly to perform face-lifts and other elective plastic surgery, he pointed up and said, "That's not us. It's the Svetlana cooperative upstairs."

When our interview was over and he rushed back to his patients, I asked the nurse to take me to the cooperative upstairs. At that point, I was totally confused about what it was. Dr. Stepanov had said he was working to build a private plastic surgery clinic and that it would be several years away. Now, it appeared that there was one. Was it attached to the hospital? Did it rent the facilities?

The nurse agreed to take me upstairs, but she said she knew little about the clinic, except that it rented space from the hospital. This would be the first time she had ventured past the thick double doors—upstairs was off-limits to her. But she smiled and noted that nothing was off-limits to a foreigner anymore. She opened the doors and came along, as much pro-pelled by curiosity about Svetlana as I was.

As we moved up one floor to the private ward, we did not so much see a change in the standards of the facilities as we saw an improvement in the decorations. The walls had been recently painted a soft green, and the new wooden doors on the cooperative announced the name. It was Natasha, not Svetlana, and I thought later that by getting the name wrong, Dr. Korshunov had given some indication of how he thought about the medicine being performed beyond his reach.

As we walked through the door, a young man stood in the hallway with a briefcase. He looked like a businessman, but he may have been a doctor, a drug salesman, or a *mafiya* thug for all we knew. When we asked about the cooperative, he shook his head, ducked into a room, and brought out a woman he said was the head nurse. As the woman stood in front of us, a hand firmly on each large hip, we stared at her uniform. It had been white, yesterday or maybe the day before. Now it had a large smear of blood across the front.

She began by giving out information warily, short answers to specific questions. Yes, there were two patients now, she barked, nose jobs. Both of them.

The nurse gave me a telephone number to call for more information and said that the plastic surgery clinic had been renting the space from Hospital No. 4 for over a year. As she talked she began to warm to her subject, losing the tone of an employee being interrogated by an outsider and increasingly sounding like a saleswoman for her new firm.

Natasha did everything, she boasted. "What do you want?" She stared at my face, body. "We make things bigger. We make them smaller."

"What exactly?" I asked.

"Anything. What do you want?" Noses. Breasts. Thighs. Buttocks. She patted her behind gently.

To look at her, with her dirty smock and her starched white hat, I was reminded of the women who worked in the markets selling meat—by the kilo, by the handful, whatever you wanted could be carved to the right size. With an ax.

As we left, I peered quickly into one of several empty rooms saved for Natasha's high-priced patients. Before it had been a ward for emergencies—general casualty, as the Russians called it. Now, instead of eight or ten beds, there was one. Perhaps the Russian love of company had taken me over, but the one bed looked forlorn in the dark room with its towering ceilings.

As we scurried down the stairs and the nurse breathed a sigh of relief to be back in her own ward, I wondered why anyone would pay this group 2 million rubles ($400) for a silicone breast implant. It was cheaper than in the West, but even there, they could be dangerous, stupidly so. Why would anyone let this woman care for their nose job, especially the rich in Russia, who were now extravagantly rich? They could go to Paris, to Texas, to Hollywood to get the best face-lifts in the world.

Later, when I thought about Dr. Stepanov's mood contrasted to the empty feeling of Natasha, the private clinic, I began to realize why he was so cheerful. The new insurance system seemed to be doing what it was supposed to do. It had boosted the chances for hospitals like No. 4 to continue treating most people for free, to continue some form of universal health care, Russian style. Any new system like an insurance fund was an opportunity for abuse in this chaotic Russia, but in almost sixteen months since the beginning of the new system, the ordinary medical care for patients at Hospital No. 4 had clearly improved.[54] It was only one hospital in only one city in an enormous country, but it was a reason for hope in a place that could certainly use it.

5

Alternative Medicine: From Herbs to Hocus-Pocus

During times of great disturbances in Russia, a large number of sorcerers has always appeared.
> —Valentin Pavlovich Pokrovksy, president,
> Russian Academy of Medical Sciences,
> October, 1991[1]

When freedom came to Russia, especially after the failed coup by aging communists in August 1991, it seemed to open all doors at once, like a national amnesty that freed the innocent and the guilty, the hero and villain, the gentle suffocated artist and the violent underworld don, all in the same intoxicating moment. Not only were people free to leave or to publish, free to gather and grouse and pray, but they were also free to become street hucksters or pornographers, school dropouts, part-time prostitutes, political fringe groups, and haters of all sorts.

For an outsider watching this explosion of possibilities, not all of them for the better, one area seemed particularly dangerous. It was the surfacing and public acceptance of quacks and visionaries, extrasensory perceivers and health wizards, "medical engineers" and stargazers. After decades of being considered outlaws, they were free to advertise themselves as instant healers who could outperform the official health care system with a vast new repertoire of expensive miracles and elaborate spells. And they were encouraged by increasing numbers of patients, who came bearing a very Russian suspicion that the old cures, no matter how tenuous their attachments to science, may have been better than anything created in the last seventy years.

Outside the medical establishment, there were really two brands of alternative medicine that began expanding as rapidly as the official health care system deteriorated. One was what I called kitchen cures, recipes for homegrown potions that were distinctly Russian versions of the traditional grandmother's apothecary of balms and poultices found almost everywhere in the world. The other was a world of ethers and electronic fields, crystals and wordless chants, all concoctions of an old breed of charlatan who was sent scurrying underground during the communist years but who surfaced in the new free market to peddle worthless remedies for exorbitant prices.

For centuries, Russians living far from the towns or cities have known how to use the leaves, seeds, barks, and roots from their gardens and forests to cure common ailments. During the hardest times, even in recent decades when Soviet medicine was supposed to provide twentieth-century relief, teas were brewed to ease heart pain or give relief from chronic stomach problems. Some doctors encouraged these cures because they were natural, believing that anything concocted in a chemical factory would tend to harm the body; others suggested the medicinal plants because there was little else.

As people found themselves caught between private medicine that was too expensive and public medicine that was too unpredictable, they were forced to look for help wherever they could. Many people grew herbs in their summer gardens, not to make food taste better but to heal aches and wounds the natural way. A group of young women we knew had among them one herbologist who knew each weed and flower that could be used safely and cheaply to cure a cold, menstrual cramps, stomach complaints, and rashes of all sorts.

Cranberries, honey, and hot water helped a cold (one version adds a dram of vodka to "increase the medicine's natural potency"). For "general suffering," some Russians cut a hole in a black radish and filled it with honey. The radish then went in the refrigerator (or on the balcony), and after two days, when it had rotted sufficiently onto the plate, it was fed to the patient. For flu or even pneumonia, mustard plasters were still in use. *Gorchichniki* were the mustard plasters for the back or chest—twenty minutes per treatment—and *gorchitsa* is common dry mustard that sometimes went in woolen socks at night to keep a patient warm, feet first. Sunflower oil was deemed the appropriate balm for bee stings or burns. Elk's milk was good for ulcers. Socks made of dog's hair were said to cure arthritis, and for the hair of the dog—a standard hangover remedy is to drink the brine from pickle juice.

Many were beyond a Westerner's abilities to imagine, and when I grimaced at the idea of onion-juice nose drops for a sinus condition, one Russian recalled the old saying "What will cure a Russian will kill a foreigner."

An American colleague had her own story about the Russian way to cure a chill. When she came down with bronchitis during one of her winters in Moscow, she decided to go out into the streets and ask people for advice. Teas with honey, mustard in her shoes, feet in hot water and head under a towel, hot fat applied to the neck, and cupping—heating jars and placing them on the back and chest—were among the suggestions from a variety of street counselors. What came as a surprise, she said later, was that not one person had suggested she try a doctor. (After testing the Russian methods, including cupping and the heated fat collar, she went to a Western doctor for Western antibiotics. Such quick fixes aren't easily available to most Russians, who would be wary of them even if they were. When I resorted to antibiotics for my daughter's earache, Russians frowned in disapproval. They viewed such treatment as destructive of a child's immune system.)

Lyudmila Kim was one of the better-known philosophers of the home remedy culture. Her recipes were among the most popular in late 1992 when her book *250 Folk Medicine Prescriptions* hit the Russian streets with the latest in kitchen healing. "Medicine is one hand, with five fingers. Folk medicine is one of those fingers, and hospital medicine is another," Kim said of her role in the Russian health picture. A trained chemist of Korean descent, Kim's cures included one for baldness that certainly must have required the patient to stay in his room during the treatment. She said to take one hundred grams of cow brain, an egg, fifteen drops of ammonia, and two tablespoons of castor oil. The paste was to be mixed and spread on the head for three days. For a backache, patients smeared a combination of crushed chestnuts, camphor oil, and fat onto a piece of black bread. The thick goo was then applied to the ailing part of the back.[2]

When I met the head of the Russian Academy of Medical Sciences, Valentin Pokrovsky, and the Russian minister of health, Andrei Vorobiev, in 1992 to ask about the increasing number of medical quacks in the new Russia, both men made certain that I understood that there were two kinds of nondoctors practicing medicine—the fakes and the babushkas. They wanted the quacks in jail, they said, but the collectors of folk remedies deserved respect and thanks; they had preserved a tradition and probably saved more lives than they had lost in these last difficult years.

"There are extremely talented persons who use age-old experiences with popular medicine," Pokrovsky told one interviewer. "Their experience and knowledge must be carefully studied and used to the benefit of the people. In the final analyses, contemporary medicine evolved from popular medicine. Many folk medicines and herbs are widely used nowadays. So we have to respect the knowledge of our predecessors. . . . Nobody will reject these days such methods as acupuncture, [controlled] breathing, and other exercises, because all of them are based on serious knowledge."[3]

The harmless home remedies and the genuine research in herbal medicine were not what the medical establishment began to worry about as the government's control over health care weakened steadily in the early 1990s and people lost faith in the Soviet form of science.[4] More and more Russians began turning to what American Southerners used to call hocus-pocus medicine—healing earrings that helped sinus trouble or electrodes that sucked evil spirits out of the spinal cord or a newspaper photo that would ease pain or a special vacuum-cleaner-like gizmo that could rid food magically of nitrites.

The tendency to believe some of these people was not altogether new. Even Brezhnev had his own personal spiritualist, a strange woman called Djuna Davitashvili, known simply as Djuna. Her work in the 1970s was part of the privilege of the powerful, but when the old society ended, Djuna opened her own faith-healing center to the monied public. By the mid-1990s, she could be seen at events around Moscow—a large, brooding creature wearing a Soviet general's uniform and dark glasses. Around her were the new signs of power, a covey of bruisers whose job was clearly to protect Djuna from more than the spirit world.

(At a press conference in March 1995, Djuna announced that she had invented a device to record, decipher, and then reproduce the healing currents that came from her hands. The new machine was described thus: "Influence of ecological factor on human health and how to correct it with the help of DJUNA-1 apparatus for biocorrection. Technical revolution in the field of nontouch bioenergetical massage." Djuna by now had begun referring to herself as an academician, specifically the vice-chancellor of the Open International University of Complementary Medicine of the World Diplomatic Academy under UNESCO and UN.)[5]

Djuna and her kind were technically practicing medicine illegally. The law was supposed to protect people against these charlatans, as former health minister Andrei I. Vorobiev called them, but the law was vague, the officials either corrupt or too busy with the new surge of murder, rape, robbery, and corruption to go after self-made doctors in their instant unauthorized clinics.[6] (The same Russians who were told a decade ago to think as a communal nation and to believe their medicine was the world's best were now told to shop for their own doctors, to think for themselves, and not to trust every authoritative-looking figure in a white coat. There was little to help them find the good doctors except word of mouth, but the warnings about unqualified doctors were everywhere.)

A Russian doctor I knew who worried about this explosion of healers peddling their expensive potions was particularly concerned about a new place in Moscow called the Traditional People's Medical Center. As she described it, the people's center was a one-stop clinic for everything from yoga and herbal remedies to astrological readings and psychosurgery.

For a place that sounded so large and busy, it took a surprisingly long time to find. The medical profession was stubbornly unhelpful, of course. Even though I talked with a number of people who had heard about it or knew someone who had gone there, they seemed almost intentionally vague about the location, as if they were embarrassed for a Westerner to know such things were now a part of their society. Finally one day a piece of paper with the address in a handwriting I did not recognize appeared on the keys of my computer at work. When I called the telephone number, a woman answered and gave the hours, the prices, and the location. On a sunny June morning, I set out with Slava Zelenin, who joked about being slightly nervous for this descent into the world of warlocks and sorcerers. From the Sokolniki subway stop in the northeast section of the city, we tried to ask directions from people as they passed hurriedly, shaking their heads before we could even blurt out our request. A young woman finally stopped for a few breathless moments and gave us directions. It was across the street from the graveyard, she said, pointing toward an area overgrown with weeds and surrounded by a small white fence. As we walked past decrepit tombs, some with bouquets of plastic flowers and aged photos fading in the sun, I wondered if the cemetery served to remind those looking for help at the center that no medicine man can work his magic forever.

Beyond the high wall and into the rambling red brick building, we asked for the director, and a young woman whisked us into the office of Yakov Grigorievich Galperin, who looked and acted a little like the wizard in Judy Garland's land of Oz. Galperin was wearing a three-piece suit, but not for us, since we had come unannounced. He was slightly round, with gray hair and a cherubic face, and he ushered us in like royalty. A good bedside manner, I would say, no matter what degree of skill went with it.

Out of many such healers I met during 1992 and early 1993, Galperin was one of the more ambitious. He had a clinic, a school, a newspaper, and a network to more than a dozen similar operations around Russia and the other former Soviet states. His office was a large room with grand bay windows that made him rich in sunlight, one of Russia's most precious commodities. The morning light spread over his workplace, the conference table covered with papers and old books; it played on crystals and healing pyramids around the room. It was like a summer place for Merlin, and only such things as a high-tech phone and a large Japanese television set brought the office back to the twentieth century.

"We are trying to contribute to the revival of the oldest traditions of health and culture," Galperin began as he settled into a chair at the head of the table. "I must tell you that the people who preserved the tradition through these years are those who do not have any medical education. That is why official medicine has treated us in a negative way."

Exactly how and why he was mistreated was difficult to find out. Questions about his past or even his credentials were treated with a studied haziness. When I asked his age, he answered with a nice grandfatherly smile. "I was born an Aquarian in 1927," he said, offering a range of about twenty-nine possible birthdays and an age of sixty-five. I began to realize that, barring a full KGB investigation, which might have been possible for a price in this era when everything seemed to be for sale, Galperin's hidden past would stay that way. He did reveal that in 1953 he helped with a Soviet army lab investigating parapsychology and telepathy. Trained, he said, as a psychiatrist, his job was to determine the mental state of those working for this particular lab. "Luckily I saved a lot of talented people—biotherapists or people who had seen UFOs—from being sent to the nuthouse. I became a kind of savior for these people," he explained.

After that, his career would remain somewhat undocumented, but in 1987, he opened the center in the old hospital clinic. To have this huge institution meant that someone in the top layers of power believed in Galperin and his mission. It was not impossible, given the news about Brezhnev's stargazer and stories that Russian president Boris Yeltsin had a team of astrologers provided by his security forces through the early 1990s.[7] When I visited Galperin in June 1992, his hospital was expanding month by month. He already boasted five academicians, sixteen professors, six Ph.D.'s, and twenty-five candidates for Ph.D.'s. Self-financed, as Galperin explained it, the center saw about twelve hundred clients a day, who paid fifty rubles (about fifty cents) for ten sessions. Before 1987, Galperin explained, such places were illegal, but with other freedoms under Gorbachev came the one that allowed nongovernment healing centers.

"Previously when healers declared that they could fly to other planets or put their hands on people to cure them, they were considered either charlatans or people who were mentally ill," he said. I nodded, trying to look understanding. Galperin clearly concentrated on more than herbal therapy and folk remedies. His center also experimented in netherworldy matters such as something he called psychotronics. This involved trying to control a microlipton, which he said was thirteen times smaller than a lipton. When I looked bewildered, he explained. "We consider ourselves conductors of a higher intellect, which allows us to heal people. This may mean God to religious people, and you will see that many of our healers are very religious. To scientific people, they may understand this as part of the cosmogonic brain."

After this explanation, Galperin took us on a tour. We wound downstairs and through narrow corridors with high ceilings. Everywhere there were people waiting, sitting on chairs in the hallways and the landings. First came the seance room, which Galperin said was one of their most popular attractions. He escorted us into an old hospital auditorium, about the size of a small movie theater. The midsummer sunlight filtered through thick greenish curtains, giving the room an eerie, underwater look. Around the walls were icons, crosses, and bouquets of mint, cumin, coriander, and a mysterious weed that gave the hall a heavy smell like freshly turned earth. Roaming through the aisles was a youngish man with a full beard, Aleksandr Yeremin.

Yeremin's clients, mostly women suffering from ailments that ranged from minor complaints to serious illnesses, sat shielding their eyes with thin pieces of metal that looked like aluminum masks, as they listened to the tinkle of Eastern music and the gruff chanting of their conjurer. The session lasted about an hour, and at the end, each patient would close her eyes, remove the shield, and concentrate deeply on having the irregular heartbeat or the chronic sadness or the aching gout disappear. Then, at the appointed end to the hour, Yeremin would perform his grand finale: he spat a mouthful of "energized water" into each wincing face.

This prerevolutionary, perhaps even ancient, healing scene was one of many strange new services that were available at the Traditional People's Medical Center. If it seemed a bit too ethereal, there was urine therapy. I had heard about this ancient Eastern cure from women in the Russian baths, but Slava was stunned into silence when an elderly man, who looked like an ordinary clerk or librarian, named it as his field of expertise. Slava, schooled in the best of Moscow's excellent educational institutions, was having trouble understanding whether this could possibly be what he suspected it was.

"What is it?" he finally whispered to me in English, shaking his head slightly as if to ward off the answer.

"They drink their urine," I explained, as he grimaced. "Ask him," I advised. Slava turned to the old man and asked about the treatment, as suggested. People were asked to filter their urine and then drink it, the man explained as matter-of-factly as if he were a pharmacist describing how to take a cold tablet. This was supposed to restore vigor, especially to people with diabetes.

Later I learned that the relative of an artist I knew was going to the center to follow the urine treatment for her diabetes. I asked if I could talk to her, but the artist kept refusing. At first she said her relative had gone to the center because she had trouble getting a decent and steady supply of insulin. I knew from other people that this was true. State stores tended to have limited supplies, and often what insulin was available was the wrong dose. The woman, who had decided to shed this troubled existence and go to Galperin's people for treatment, was too embarrassed to talk about it, she said. Older Russians did not like to talk about their ailments, especially something intimate enough to involve one's bathroom habits. A few months later when I asked again, she was too sick. Shortly after that, she was dead.[8]

We continued on our tour of Galperin's center and wandered past rows of morose people in hallways and along corridors. They were waiting for their turns to go into one of the various tiny rooms where healers ministered their individual concoctions. In one small room, there were three clients lying very still on their backs while three small candles burned around their heads and music from a Russian rock group screeched from a cheap tape deck. Healer Igor Verbitsky, a tall young man with an unruly beard, introduced his patients, pointing to "lymph cancer," then to "cerebral palsy," and finally to "brain hemorrhage," who lay deathly still.

In another cubicle, a young woman in her underpants and panty hose, breasts exposed, was receiving manual therapy which seemed to be a form of massage, performed by a man with large, muscular-looking hands. Her own hands were clenched in front of her, either in pain or to shield her nakedness from her manipulator and from us. Her neck and shoulders were a bright and rough-looking red. "Does this hurt?" I asked Galperin. He nodded as he whisked us elsewhere.

The center's main healer, a young man who made a brief appearance in a blue satin robe, was not available for an interview during the tour. But we saw his therapy room, littered with bouquets of flowers from his patients, mostly women. Finally we met a nice-looking woman who had the manner of a chirpy young housewife. Her specialty, she explained, was an operation that transferred pain into herself, which she then eradicated by putting herself into a mysterious, trancelike state. She could perform this operation, she said, even long-distance.

At the center, as at other such places I visited, I found that some clients saw their sessions as auxiliary or complementary to their treatment from the official medical establishment, while others saw them as something to try when everything else had failed. Aleksei Stepanov, a sixty-three-year-old retired engineer from Moscow, was standing in the main waiting room of the people's center, under a fresco of the zodiac signs in glaring primary colors. As he steadied himself on a cane, I stopped him and asked why he was here. "So many problems. Very many," he began, smiling at a foreigner in the open way some Russians have, always surprising given the years of counsel they have had against it. He studied my face and clothes, the way many Russians did, probably trying to remember details for telling friends later about the strange American he met that day. Finally, remembering the question, he answered with a sweep of the hand.

"Everything, everything," he said. "Heart, kidneys, lungs, and others," not ready to be more specific.

"I went to the clinics and the hospitals, but they didn't help me," he said.

"And have they helped you here?"

"No, not really, but I feel comparatively better. Psychologically, I try to influence myself, and that feels much better. It's worth the fifty rubles because money isn't worth anything anymore, and when someone is ill, they are ready to pay anything."

He smiled and leaned on a makeshift cane. "I come here, and if I get a good rest for an hour, of course, I feel better. But really, I know. I know it is more business here than medicine."

If people like Galperin had a hard time surviving the communist years, it was in part because the Soviet government was trying to spread science-based medicine and eliminate the conjurors who roamed the countryside during the prerevolutionary era. The most famous of these was Grigory Rasputin, a peasant who declared himself a religious healer and a man of

God. He wore a priest's robes yet reigned at orgies and private seductions, often at the higher levels of prerevolutionary Russian society. Rasputin, who became infamous for his powers over the tsarina after he persuaded her that he could control her hemophiliac son's bleeding by using a kind of hypnosis, was murdered in 1916 by a small battery of men who poisoned him with cyanide, shot him three times, beat him with a truncheon, and finally threw the famous visionary's lifeless body into a canal. What surprised me about Rasputin's legacy in Russia was that some people saw him less a demon than as a variation of the well-known Russian healer.[9]

When the Soviet system began officially barring these visionaries from openly proselytizing, those who practiced the ancient trades of *znakharstvo,* spiritual healing, went underground. The *znakhari,* (whose name literally means the knowing ones) had practiced laying on hands and chanting their paganlike prayers since before the days of Christianity in Russia, and their silence and persecution did not mean they had disappeared.[10] Some worked secretly or kept their old notions to themselves, passing their knowledge on quietly to some trusted member of the next generation. Aleksandra Sychkova was one of those who surfaced in the mid-1990s as a classic *znakharka.* On her deathbed, Sychkova's mother had whispered the chants and methods for the old cures, and when controls began to weaken with the new freedoms, Sychkova began working openly in Moscow. By 1995, this woman with almost no formal education was known as one of the leaders in the oldest form of Russian faith healing, and her powers were widely believed by many people in the area, especially if they were practicing Christians, since, as she explained, her powers would not work unless the patient had been baptized.

Without the heavy hand of communism, the healers, religious and otherwise, had begun to surface, and even though Rasputin himself had not managed resurrection (in spite of a few suggestions that this was still a possibility), the methods of some of the healers we met seemed to offer at least the possibility of Rasputin-like cures, involving a seduction of both spirit and body, especially for women's ailments.

Once, when I was feeling especially lethargic from the cold and depression that can descend in the darkest days of November, a Russian woman asked if I wanted to use her method of treating such common Muscovite complaints. Fine, I said, thinking we were going to try a dab of camphor under the nose. Instead, a few days later, she arrived, pulling behind her one of the largest men I had ever seen, her own masseur and healer, who was introduced only as Andrei. Andrei's black hair seemed to brush against the ceiling in our small apartment, and his dark eyes were staring at me with an intensity that people in the West associate with either a hypnotist or a serial killer. I feared my obvious anxiety was reinforcing his strong notion that I needed help. Andrei walked over to me as I sat frozen in a chair, and when I focused on what was happening, I realized he was holding out three limp carnations, the traditional gift a Russian brings when he comes to a stranger's house.

"Andrei has come to give you a massage," the Russian woman offered brightly.

I glanced at Andrei's hands, which seemed big enough to snap one of my arms like a dry twig.

"Thank you, but I feel fine," I said, trying to sound equally bright and healthy.

"You need my help," Andrei replied, sweeping his hand over the space about four feet in front of me and finding something terribly wrong. He shook his head in dismay. "Your spine is troubled. Everything else is dislodged. Just give me a few minutes."

A friend of mine who was baby-sitting for our daughter suddenly jumped in and agreed to Andrei's advances, more to spare me the embarrassment than because she wanted a massage, she confessed later. They went into a tiny bedroom and came out about fifteen minutes later. Her face was red. She said it was a rough massage and that she had been required to take off her shirt and bra for the treatment. As Andrei left, he gave my aura one last stroke and shook his head.

Did she feel better? I asked the baby-sitter after he left. She shrugged and laughed. "No, but maybe Andrei feels better."

Russia is not the only country with freelance healers like Andrei, of course. Some of it is relatively innocent—the sale of crystals and the reading of palms is an international addiction, a costlier version of reading the astrology guides or knocking on wood after courting disaster with such phrases as "I am really happy." Russians indulge in these superstitions, although instead of knocking on wood three times, they pretend to spit three times over the left shoulder if someone has proclaimed their good fortune.

What was different in Russia was that people from all education levels appeared to believe more deeply in things mysterious and supernatural. Practically every Russian I knew talked about the power of forces and fields that affect people's health. Sometimes magnetic fields would be blamed for a surge of fatigue or minor illnesses. Radios should not be held too close to the ear, not because they affect hearing but because they emit other electrical waves besides sound that were considered far more dangerous. The lore was only beginning to take shape over how to operate cellular phones or computers or microwave ovens.

One of the most bizarre beliefs for me was the concept of the evil eye, which has an especially odd meaning in Russia. I learned about it from a well-educated Russian woman who was trying to explain why I was getting such stiff or strange responses when I smiled or cooed over a young child in the metro or on the sidewalks of the city. When a child gets sick for no apparent reason the way children do, the mother will sometimes try to think back about who has cast an illness on the child. If a stranger has smiled at the child or, God forbid, touched him, the outsider has given the child the evil eye. I had heard about this sort of reaction in peasant societies of the last century, when strangers from other villages had been beaten or murdered if something bad happened while they were around. But I thought such ideas or their modern-day adaptations had been wiped out of this new order. "Isn't this evil eye just superstition?" I asked this woman. "No," she answered, surprised that I would question the idea. "It's the truth."

On another occasion a Russian woman, an educator with a great deal more learning than most teachers on her level in America, saw a stack of books and newspaper articles about Russian healers on my desk in Moscow. She picked up a newspaper ad for a man who transformed ordinary tap water into energized water by praying or chanting or staring deeply at it, and her face became red in alarm. "Do you believe in this?" she asked urgently. "Of course not," I told her. "I am merely writing an article about it." "It is a terrible thing," she said, turning the picture over as if trying to prevent its ethers from contaminating our apartment.

A devout Russian Orthodox believer, she said that such healers were ruining many young Russians. I thought she meant by this that people who were sick failed to go to genuine doctors, but it was worse than that, as she tried to explain. These people, she said, these healers actually bring the forces of evil into people, the devil, if you will, and it takes priests and nuns a great deal of time and effort to remove it. "Like exorcism?" I asked. No, that was something else. These were evil energies that harm the person's health both physically and spiritually. This was a very intelligent woman, and I thought we had similar views and philosophies, even though we came from different cultures. That day, I knew what every foreigner learns over and over again in Russia: an outsider is always an outsider. I could observe, listen, ask, and take notes, but I would never truly understand.

The healer who had provoked my friend's outburst was Alan Chumak, a prominent medicine man with his own television program broadcast from 10 to 11 P.M. on Tuesday evenings in Moscow. The first time I caught his show, I thought there was something wrong with the television set. There on the screen sat a pudgy, well-dressed man in steel-rimmed eyeglasses. He was mouthing words I could not hear, and he seemed like any other television analyst except that something was wrong with the volume on my set. He did not look crazy—no long hair, no rotating eyeballs—so I turned up the sound. At full blast, I heard only an occasional mantralike hum and the soft crinkling of his clothes as he waved his hands, mostly in circles, to cast his spell.

When it was over, Chumak's real voice suddenly blared from the television, sending me racing back to the volume button. He was telling viewers to drink a glass of water that he had asked them to put in front of the set before his performance. The water was now charged, but Chumak warned that after they drank it they might be overexcited. This overexcitement would pass as the healing took place, he advised as he closed the show, giving mysterious messages to a select few of his many believers. Later I found that Chumak was a regular feature in a popular Moscow newspaper, *Vechernyaya Moskva,* which advertised that his picture, which had been charged like the water in front of the television set, could cure readers of a variety of ailments if the photo were placed on the source of pain or illness for ten to fifteen minutes.[11]

This is not to say that only Russia has its Alan Chumaks. In New York, sorcerers take to the public airwaves intoning their spells and promising relief. The American South offers a variety of voodoo queens, and California visionaries seem at the epicenter of otherworldly vibrations.[12] What made Russia's plague of conjurers so distressing was how little skepticism there was among the educated and elite. Even for a people known for their mysticism, the reliance on palmistry, astrology, and other mysterious forces was strangely medieval.

With the idea of medicine suddenly expanding to include virtually anything, the healer-merchant had made his very public appearance. In a manner that harkened back to the wild West or my home in the South, medicine was hawked like shoes. As a result, the organizers of the marketplace—the various *mafiyas*—were always circling the clinics that made money.

I was never certain whether a health *mafiya* had taken hold in Moscow, but across the park from my office was a place that made me wonder. It was a yellow stone building with an expensive brass plaque that announced the offices of Anatoly Gritsenko. Gritsenko ran the elaborately titled Medical Engineering Center for the Restoration of Segmentary Innervation of Organs and Tissues, and although he had several trained physicians working for him, Gritsenko had the air of an old-fashioned snake-oil salesman.

I would never have visited Gritsenko or even known he was there except that one morning in the fall of 1992, someone stepped out of a car driving through the park, lifted a handheld grenade launcher like those used in Afghanistan, and launched a small incendiary device at Gritsenko's office. Gritsenko, as it turned out, was elsewhere, but the explosion shattered his windows and damaged the wall of his office.

With my friend Dr. John Collee, a physician who writes a column on medicine for *The Observer* in London, I went to see Gritsenko after the bombing. When we rang the office bell, a large man whose job was clearly not healing opened the door. He appeared to be ready to throw us out when Gritsenko himself suddenly arrived in his flashy Western car. As he swept inside, surrounded by several large bodyguards, he carried us along with him.

Gritsenko was a small man in an expensive-looking Western suit, and he wore a carefully clipped mustache that gave him the look of a European businessman. His office, except for the boarded windows, was fancier than those of most Western doctors I had known, with its thick carpets, giant Japanese television, and broad wooden desk. His secretary, who came in twice to talk to him while we were there, wore a cocktail dress with a spray of sequined netting on one shoulder, and a large percentage of her ample bosom showed each time she leaned down to whisper into his ear.

Could the grenade launcher have been one of his 110,000 patients, upset after paying twenty thousand rubles for the promise of being fully cured? "Certainly not," he said in English. In Russian, he added, "It is definitely not personal, but an ideological motif here."

Ideological?

He eyes darted around the room constantly like those of a man who expected trouble. The problem, he said, was that he had this elaborate plan to cure victims of radioactive poisoning from Chernobyl, and if his system worked, many doctors would be deprived of millions of rubles in research funds from the West. Even in this strange lawless time in Russia, Gritsenko's version of the bombing sounded far-fetched. It was hard to imagine a Russian scientist taking out his frustrations with a grenade launcher.

What about some kind of medical *mafiya*? What about the medical establishment? The answer seemed to be a thousand layers away. We were strangers asking questions that many of the insiders probably did not know how to answer. I suspected that, like many people in this time, Gritsenko was pulling every lever, grabbing every sweet opportunity to make and enjoy his money while the government still allowed it. For many people who started getting rich in this era, there was never any confidence that this was the beginning of a new order. It may have been simply a window, a moment to wallow in excess before the joy police came back to power.

Besides his private patients, Gritsenko had managed to gain some support from the medical establishment, or at least the Russian government. His clinic was set up in part with funds from the Russian Ministry of Social Welfare as a place where employees could be treated for less than the normal fee. And he had several trained and well-educated doctors on his staff to treat cancer, glaucoma, heart disease, diabetes, and childhood disorders, all with a combination of drugs and manual therapy that was, as he put it, his own secret system.

After listening to Gritsenko talk about engineering feats and electrical mumbo jumbo, Dr. Collee decided that the man was a medical fraud, and he became interested primarily in how the operation worked. But my dislike of Gritsenko was more visceral. At some point, Gritsenko seemed to sense my feelings about him because as he was talking about how 70 percent of operations were not necessary if you used his secret method, he suddenly pointed to my left breast and declared aggressively, "You have a tumor in your breast and I know that you don't know about it." Our translator sat silent, refusing to pass on the bad news, so I translated it myself for Dr. Collee and told him that I'd just had a mammogram. Still, it was unsettling, and I was left with a small gnawing doubt, which it took me several days to shake. The scene also made me realize how much more vulnerable Russian women would be to a man who says, so freely, that they are in danger, especially since former Soviet doctors were masters in the art of avoiding a diagnosis.[13]

Few medical officials spoke out against these new clinics, perhaps because they were too busy with the problems of shifting from communism to a market economy or perhaps because they were desperately trying to shore up the old system, its hospital and clinics, with drugs and equipment from the West. Or perhaps, like many people in this period, they saw any control as part of the past; the country had thrown out the old order, even the parts of it that might have been worthwhile.

One of the few trying to warn people about the failings of these practioners was Dr. Georgi Komarov, editor of the doctors' newspaper *Meditsinskaya Gazeta*. Alarmed after he picked up a pamphlet advertising how breathing could cure most of the ills of mankind, Komarov began his own investigation of Konstantin Buteiko, the well-known practitioner in Russia of willful breath control. Komarov, who is a medical doctor and researcher as well as a journalist, recalled a young woman in his home republic of Kirghiz in central Asia whose physician suggested that she stop taking asthma medicine and start controlling her breath, according to the Buteiko method.

After two years of trying to control her breathing, she began to feel dramatically worse and finally rushed back to the regular doctors for help. A medical exam showed that not only did she need more powerful drugs for asthma but she also had a large inoperable tumor in her breast. She later told the doctors in Bishkek, the capital of Kirghizia, that her own doctor at the local town clinic had known about the tumor but had advised her that the Buteiko method would heal it as well. "She went into a cancer hospital and, unfortunately, never recovered," Komarov said the day I went to his office to interview him. He gave me a copy of an editorial he had written on the subject.

"How can you recommend breathing gymnastics to treat genetic, immunological, and morphological violations?" the editorial concluded. "Isn't it criminal to declare that holding your breath gives hopeful results during the treatment of AIDS cases? There is no greater sin than for a doctor to intentionally misinform a patient and lead him away from science-based, though not altogether perfect yet, treatments."

A few weeks after I talked with Komarov about the breath doctor, Buteiko decided that his cure for AIDS needed to be shared with sufferers in the West. He wrote to Magic Johnson, the basketball star who is HIV-positive, promising to rid him of the virus without harsh medicines and their detrimental side effects. "Only my method can save you," Buteiko's letter said. "I am offering you my help."[14]

My reaction would have been to laugh at such nonsense, to poke fun. But when I actually went to the places where people were sampling the new assortments of medical alternatives, I realized how desperate they were for relief, how they yearned for someone to care and to treat them gently. I became convinced that in some cases, after seeing state doctors for less than five minutes and hearing what was always bad news, even if it was just that there was no film for the x-ray machine, what mattered was the attention. Call them frauds, but these people looked the patient in the eye and listened intently to the complaint.

One of the new centers for alternative medicine, which included trained doctors and nurses who had left the official system, was set up at VDNKha, Moscow's huge park for "the Exhibition of the Accomplishments of the People's Economy." (The park was briefly up for grabs in 1992 before merchants took it over with kiosks and converted it into halls for selling rich Italian leathers and oriental clothes. By 1994, it had been so overrun by these shops that the Russians had nicknamed it "the Exhibition of the Accomplishments of the Peoples of Germany, Japan, and Korea".) But on this day, the park was still a territory for babushkas and young children, who came more out of a tribal Soviet memory than for any real view of the achievements being boasted there.

Beyond the imposing steel statue of the worker and peasant woman that was on every tourist's prescribed route of the Soviet Union was a small makeshift clinic. It was clean and inviting by the standards of most city polyclinics, but the cost was two hundred rubles a visit (which when I went was about fifty cents, but still a lot of money for many Russians). It was there that I met a homeopathic doctor who was treating a woman for ovarian cysts. Tatyana Bulanova had short hair, what would have been called a sedate bubble in the 1960s, and a large smile. As she buttoned her shirt, she talked about why she came here. It cost her a lot of money, not only the visit fees but the price of medicinal gold that she said had made her feel better.

"At the hospital, they told me they were planning to do a hysterectomy if the cyst did not shrink. What could I do? Nothing. The doctor only told me that we could wait and that it was growing. So I come here now regularly, and I also keep going to the regular doctors. They tell me now that the cyst is shrinking."

She smiled triumphantly, and as she left, a woman slipped into the tiny room and changed the top sheet of the examining room bed. This was the way it was supposed to work everywhere, but it seldom did. This woman was probably getting the best care available to her by balancing the paid practitioner against the unpaid government doctor.

But she was probably an exception. Down the hall from this room was a bioenergy pathologist, as he referred to himself, named A. M. Makeyev. Makeyev was a cheerful man who used his hands, a piece of wood, a salve that smelled like turpentine, and a strange, electric-looking machine to sweep away illnesses, especially of the spine. As he worked on a Chechen woman who had accompanied me to the clinic and who volunteered for a massage, Makeyev talked about how his grandmother had been sent to the camps for practicing people's medicine and how now, even though there was no Stalin, there were still scoundrels to make the ordinary person's life miserable. The members of this ad hoc clinic had wanted originally to start a school for people's medicine, but the head of the project had absconded with the funds and was now in jail. The managers of the big VDNKha park had then moved the group to the present building temporarily, and it was embarrassing. The sign over the door said: "Veterinary Exhibition." It put some patients off.

As I sat there thinking that Russians were learning that freedom was far from easy, Makeyev suddenly grabbed my hand and jerked me into the center of his examining area. My problem, he said, was my sinuses. I had not mentioned that I suffered constantly from sinus allergies, but it probably did not take a medical genius to hear my sniffling and to see that my eyes were red and slightly swollen, a chronic ailment when I traveled through the polluted streets of Moscow. Before I realized it, Makeyev was massaging my head, flattening my nose against my face, and moving my eyebrows in excruciating circles. After it was over and I could barely see for the pain, I managed to thank him, mumbling that I should pay for my treatment. "No charge," I could hear him saying as I began to focus and my eyes rested on the hands that had just been kneading my face. They were filthy, the nails blackened with what looked like axle grease. He saw me looking and apologized. He had been fixing his car before we arrived, he explained. "We doctors have to do a lot of other things besides medicine," he said, giving a large toothy grin and showing a fine set of Slavic cheekbones.

For several days after that, my hair follicles ached from having the scalp moved around the head as part of Makeyev's treatment, but in all honesty the sinuses were quieter than usual. I will never know whether the face massage helped or the weather changed that week. Whatever it was, I knew a little about why a person who couldn't get antihistamines and needed to live in a polluted city would pay half a week's salary for a facial massage from a man with axle grease under his fingernails.

In many ways, medicine had become like other aspects of Russian life. It too was a marketplace, a wide street with scientists and doctors on one side, spiritual healers and shamans on the other. Most Russians, even the well-educated ones, seemed to roam along freely, sampling advice and potions from both.

6

Sex:
Slaking the Oldest Thirst

It is often said here that in sexual matters we are lagging behind America twenty years, but that is not true. We are forty years behind.

—Dr. Nikolai Oleinikov, one of Moscow's
first private sex therapists, 1992[1]

People seem to have nothing better to do than describe every imaginable way of having intercourse, homosexual or hetero-sexual.

—Elena Bonner, Andrei Sakharov's
widow[2]

A good Soviet citizen was officially a prude, a stalwart worker who courted by touching hands, married for love, built a tiny nest, and produced new comrades for the state. Sex was virtually unmentionable, and for those charged with the task of creating the next generation, even the worker-peasant position (street slang for the male on top, the female on bottom—i.e., our missionary method) was to be understood somehow through poetry or intuition or, at the very least, natural instinct. It was a tidy portrait, sternly enforced through the years by teachers, doctors, and many parents, and like most Soviet versions of reality, it was narrow and unreal. Privately, Russia was seething with unorthodox passions, secret lusts kept under a Soviet cover that was slowly becoming thin and transparent in the last years of Soviet communism.

By the time I had arrived in Moscow in early 1991, Russians were in the process of shedding old layers of Soviet control, not only over their government and their economy but over the most intimate details of their lives. Timidly at first, and then with a roar that seemed all too natural after such forces had been contained for so long, Russia in the early 1990s went on its first public sex binge in more than six decades.

Sex, or the promise of sex, seemed to be everywhere in the new Russia. At the tiny book tables in the Moscow subway, *The Story of O* began nudging out Agatha Christie as the commuter's best-seller, and a display of steamy novels, nestled perilously close to a stack of children's comics, bared more young, glistening flesh than most Russians had ever seen outside their communal bathhouse. Russian *Cosmo* slipped into the news kiosks in early 1994, at a hefty $3.50 per copy, with its advice about fashion, business success, and orgasms, three areas of life that were either unnecessary or unmentionable a decade earlier. Russian *Playboy* arrived just in time for the new young Russian playboy entrepreneur.

In the hotels, casinos, and restaurants for the rich, the prostitute, who had been secretly servicing apparatchiki and visiting foreigners for years, began to make her public reappearance for the first time since the early years of the Soviet revolution. Once a state secret—since the street whore was considered a symptom of capitalist decadence—the sex trade flourished along with other new markets in Russia's cities. Full time and part time, male and female, adult and underage, the hookers patrolled well-known pickup areas in the cities. Some loitered in parks, where big cars with dark windows circled slowly; others, the lucky ones, draped themselves late at night over the bars like the one in Moscow's elegant Metropol Hotel or the Europa in St. Petersburg. The unluckiest whores could find business only in places like Moscow's Belorussky train station, where the rings of sad, dirty hookers were being proffered by a group of local policemen.[3]

Movie producers, who had been limited to a short stretch of violin music in the past to hint at the Soviet idea of romance, quickly understood the cinematic power of X-rated sex. Female breasts made their first appearance in the late 1980s and were soon followed by rough and even violent sex scenes, which seemed a requirement for every successful new Russian film. If these scenes proved tempting, the Russian consumer could find more sex, minus the interruptions of plot or context, at the new video salons that opened throughout the cities. At a decaying Soviet sports complex in southeast Moscow, I once opened the thick glass door of a small X-rated shop to see what was inside. The narrow room featured rows of video cassettes, their covers promising every untempered fantasy. On a television screen on the counter, two bodies writhed in constant orgasm, and a small man scowled darkly at me from over the counter until I felt uncomfortable enough to leave.

Outside on the streets, Western condoms were being hawked by boys too young to do more than peddle these exotic devices. The first striptease joints began trying to lure male customers in Moscow and St. Petersburg. The first sex shop opened in Moscow in 1992, charging twenty rubles (about a dime) just to ogle skimpy lace underwear or Taiwanese dildos. Gay men and lesbians paraded in the streets; they openly handed out pamphlets on AIDS, revived pre-Bolshevik homosexual literature, and partied all night at lavish gay discos.

The evidence was everywhere that Russia had shed its Soviet corset and begun to loosen up, to let it all hang out, to finally make itself easy for the first time since the decadent prerevolutionary days. This sudden invitation to feel good was ecstasy to the young. To the middle-aged, it was a curiosity; to the old, a disgrace.

The story about sex in Russia in the late 1980s and 1990s was of a society virtually unprepared for choice. For many, there was comfort in the old public prudery, and the day I first began to get some idea of how the educated Soviet viewed sex or even sexiness was when my husband put up a few posters in his office. The white walls, decorated only with maps and bookcases, needed something to remind him that there was life beyond Moscow journalism, and for just such an occasion we had brought several posters given to me by an American friend. The posters were bright, lively things: a steamer in pastels, an oriental-looking scene of women in silky yellow and gold robes elegantly drinking tea, a Picasso-like beach scene with bathers in full frolic, the sun warming their plump, rosy bodies in a way that took away some of the cold seeping in from outside. After taping the posters to the doors and walls, my husband stood back and admired his work. As he turned around, however, he saw two Russians who were so embarrassed they could only look down or out the window.

"Did you see this?" one asked as I walked into the office a few minutes later. She was shaking her head; her face was a bright crimson. In a kind of half-joking, half-chiding way, she pointed at the bathers. For the first time, I noticed that their wet bathing suits clung to their bodies and the women's breasts were painted in luscious, if somewhat unreal, detail. To me, it was merely a playful illustration suggesting the joys of sitting in the sun, but to these middle-aged Russians, it was nothing less than pornography.

My husband thought they were joking. I soon learned that they were not. This was a society that had even censored art on occasion—not merely modern art that could be deemed anti-Soviet but also the classics. Although some nudity was allowed—a copy of Michelangelo's *David* loomed in one hallway of the Pushkin collection in Moscow and Greek statuaries existed in the government museums—there were also well-known cases of how censors saw sex in mere suggestiveness. One now famous story is of a Leningrad publishing house that refused to publish a photograph of the *Venus de Milo* in a brochure about aesthetics in the 1950s, calling the famous torso pornographic.[4]

Discussion of sex had been such a taboo that the entire subject often had the aura of a state secret. When I decided to find out how people were coping with what I called Russia's sixties, meaning their version of the sexual experimentation era that had hit the West thirty years earlier, I found it one of the most difficult subjects for the Russians to discuss with an outsider, especially when the Soviets still had some power over their lives. It was not that people had controlled their sexual urges (clearly they had not, since they managed to continue the species); they simply did not like to talk about it to aliens like me from the West. Men who blushed and shuffled at the mention of sex were also the same ones who pinched any suitable behind in the streets, whose vodka-fueled passions often drove them to persecute women of any age with their propositions, whose bawdy talk had become a powerful folk art form, whose leers across a restaurant or a parliament hallway or a subway carriage could leave no question about what they were suggesting. The Soviet society had not actually tamed its more adventurous sexual urges, of course; it simply did not acknowledge them. What the Soviets did was what all truly puritanical societies do; they lived two lives—one real, the other for show.

By the 1990s, people in the cities were beginning to see a different spectacle, as unreal in some ways as the purity that had been officially sanctioned before. They now saw visions of free, unencumbered sex, the pure passionate act of lovemaking—minus the love, the precautions, the cares about pregnancy, or the concern about disease. It seemed that with the tons of new information about sex, the Russians still could not find out the plainer truths about it. If the adults were still shy about talking and the videos instructed only in how to achieve orgasm, how did people learn about pregnancy and birth control? Did anyone talk to them honestly about AIDS? Or foreplay?

I decided to ask some of these questions to a Russian woman I knew well. When the time came, I prepared tea. It was a mistake; I should have served vodka. It began in my living room one morning, after I thought I had made certain my friend was comfortable, finished the preliminary questions about her family's health, and given the latest news of mine. Then I tried to slide my question into the conversation gently, using the Western word *seks,* since I couldn't find a suitable term in Russian that wasn't either too biological or too obscene. "Did your parents tell you about sex?" I asked, thinking we knew each other well enough to speak so directly. "Your doctor? Your friends? Do people learn about this when they teach it in school?" After I finished, the room grew silent, and my friend's face had turned bright red, either in anger or embarrassment, I could not be certain. Before either of us could speak, however, the phone rang and I left to answer it. When I returned, she had composed herself completely and said that she was extremely lucky in matters of sex because her parents had explained everything to her when she was a teenager and that now she knew "all that had been necessary to be healthy and happy or happy enough." It had the sound of a carefully crafted response, balanced between an effort to respond to a Westerner's questions and a desire to say nothing at all on this uncomfortable subject. Considering the amount of effort it had taken for her to say this, I could not torture her with other questions.

Another Muscovite from the Caucasus was more helpful, if a little off base. At first she began telling me dirty jokes. (What do they call the middle lane in the highway that had been reserved for the big ZiL limousines full of party apparatchiks? It's the "members' lane," she had whispered, giggling over the pun that is the same in Russian as it is in English.) After we'd enjoyed her repertoire, however, I explained that what I was really interested in was how young people learned about sex. She shrugged, as if to say they manage well enough, and then promised she would introduce me to Tatyana Zubkova. "She is the best," my friend had said mysteriously.

When I first heard about Tatyana Zubkova, I had expected something else—a madam, maybe, or a doctor. Tanya, as it turned out, was a high school teacher. She taught biology and geography at a fairly progressive state school in southeast Moscow, and the course I came to see her about in late 1992 was called simply Anatomy and Physiology. When I walked through the echoing halls of her school one afternoon and found her science laboratory, with its faintly nostalgic smells of formaldehyde and freshly ground pencils, it felt as though I had traveled back in time to my own feeble sex education classes forty years ago in rural Florida.

"Welcome to my sex laboratory," Tanya smiled as she escorted me into her classroom. She swept her hand over the standard Soviet double desks and small-looking chairs, all worn but spotlessly clean. There were mock skeletons of reptiles and small mammals, safely contained in glass cases. On the walls were ancient-looking maps, one displaying the chart of evolution and another of a country that no longer existed, the Soviet Union.

I sat curled in a student's chair while Tanya perched easily on a short stool. She had thin blond hair pulled into a ponytail, and her face was narrow, surprisingly delicate for a woman who had been strong enough to talk about sex not only to giggling kids but to their embarrassed parents. On the day I saw her, Tanya was wearing a blue cowboy shirt, jeans, and rubber boots, horseback-riding gear that she wore after school to teach at a stable nearby.

"Boys and girls are separate," she began. "The girls are much more experienced, but they can be so different at this age—one can play with dolls, another read Faulkner, and two in my class are afraid they are pregnant. As far as the boys go, well, some look like young roosters who have more crow than actual experience in the barnyard.

"We start them by age fourteen or fifteen," Tanya said. "But, by then, of course, it's already too late for many of them."

In spite of stern warnings from their parents and the conspiracy of silence in the Soviet society, the Russian youth had found ways to mate freely in empty apartments, cars, even snowbanks. Teenagers hot with passion had been known to take a walk in the forest, carve out a cave in the snow, and copulate like ad hoc Eskimos. Many first learned about sex in the easy summer months, they said, taking a break from their enforced summer camping to engage in an unmonitored sport in the lush woodlands nearby.

Some of them quickly began to experiment with their new pleasure, practicing one particular sexual aberration, anonymous sex, that in a strange way seemed to mirror the worst of Soviet society. In the most secretive years, doctors and others leaving the U.S.S.R. explained how these couplings could occur anywhere: in a darkened corner of a building, never a hard place to find in Soviet Russia; a basement warmed by heating pipes; the bathroom on a train; the bushes at Gorky Park.[5] There were no names, no reports, no documents, just a moment of much-needed pleasure.

For the young, there was also another way of taking the idea of communal society to another extreme: group sex. Some former Soviets have told researchers that the most notorious of these games was the daisy, an act that was sometimes done willingly, at other times as an initiation forced on those who wanted to join a local gang. The daisy girls took off their clothes, lay on the floor, and put their heads together, their legs spread in a large replica of their floral namesake. Boys would move like bumblebees from opening to opening, as long as they could last.[6]

What was missing from the years of underground experimentation and the new avalanche of pornography was the kind of education about sex that Tanya tried to give them—the biology, the technique, how to prevent pregnancy and disease, and the ways sexual partners should treat each other.

"They've seen a video; they may have even tried it; and they think they know it all." Tanya shook her head at the stupidity—innocence, really—about a subject that seems so simple at first blush. "I don't make fun of them. I let them ask questions. It is then that I know that most of them know nothing.

"At first, all they want to know are the techniques; they want to know how to do the things they see on videos. There are a lot of porno videos now, and they have all seen them. But it comes as a big surprise to some of them when I tell them how sex makes babies, that the baby comes out of the same place that gives the pleasure," she said. As she talked, she laughed occasionally in a low guttural way that must have been the stuff of a young boy's daydreams, and I suspected that the students adored her, not only because she told them the truth, but because she had a worldly manner and an infectious confidence at the time when teenagers are the most green and anxious.

We talked for a long time about what she taught in these classes, and in some ways it was far better than in the United States, where fear of disease is often the primary reason for bringing the subject to a young person's attention. She explained about homosexuality and lesbianism; she told them that it was okay for the woman to be on top, a subject of intense discussion after the 1988 movie *Little Vera* showed Vera and her boyfriend having sex in this manner.

Such subjects might never come up at home, Tanya explained. Parents were still incapable, many of them, of explaining sex to their children, and on occasion, the adults would come rushing into Tanya's room after the first few classes, horrified that their child had heard a teacher talk about such unspeakable things as condoms. "Usually by the end of our conversation they are relieved that I am telling the kids what they should be telling them but can't."

Tanya told the girls that sex gives pleasure, but she also added quickly that every form of birth control except abstinence has its hazard. The rhythm method "does not work"; IUDs "are difficult because it is hard to find a doctor who will insert them"; spermicides "lead to disease"; and condoms "are expensive." "Birth control pills?" I asked. "They are dangerous," she decreed.

"Dangerous?"

She nodded. It was the official line of the medical community, I would learn later and it was a view that remained in spite of the flood of Western contraceptives into the Russian marketplace. Birth control pills caused breast cancer, some medical officials had informed the public. When I asked one Russian woman I knew whether she had used oral contraceptives, she had snapped, "What, you want me to grow a beard?" Then she added that the real reason she had not used them was that she was never confident that they would be available and that most of the pills were so strong they made women feel all the worst symptoms of pregnancy. Later, when I asked Russian health officials about their views on birth control, some would say that the Soviet and new Russian pharmaceutical industry could not make decent pills. (The figures on use of contraceptives vary from group to agency, even years after the end of the Soviet system, which massaged figures until they looked good enough for the state. According to the Russian Association of Family Planning and the International Planned Parenthood Federation,[7] some Russian women were beginning to try modern forms of birth control, especially in the cities. Some estimates suggested that about 13 percent used birth control of any kind; others said about 5 percent or less—compared to the estimates that at least half of the women in Western countries use contraceptives.)

For many women who did not want to be pregnant, the only recourse was abortion, still the method of choice. The Russian abortion rate has been widely estimated at 98.1 per one thousand women of childbearing age, compared to 20 per one thousand in the U.S. and 10 per one thousand in Canada.[8] Tanya did not lecture against the state's abortion mills, which performed most of the operations without anesthetics. "Yes, I mention that it can be painful, that it can ruin a girl's ability to have children," she said, shrugging one shoulder at the realities that virtually every grown woman in Russia learned, often with the first trip to the abortion factory. Still, there was only so much change she could bring to her youngsters. If she told them the truth about disease, they would know more than most.

As we walked through the empty hallways past old women mopping the floors, I asked how many others there were teaching kids about sex. She shook her head. In spite of help from Western women's groups and some effort from the Russian ministry, most teachers preferred talking about the glories of true love and the responsibility of producing for the community.

"There are only a few, but it's better than it was before," she said as she walked me to my car.

How Tanya had become such a rarity in this huge, lusty country was part of the story of the Soviet state. Along with many other areas of Russian life, sex was an uncontrolled part of human nature that the communist leaders needed to fit somehow into their Soviet machine. This effort to tap sexual energies for the state was an unnatural act of government, and it left a deep scar on the Russian people that became truly visible only as the U.S.S.R. disappeared.

In some ways, the nation's stunted libido was trying to take up where it had left off. At the two ends of the twentieth century, before communism and after, the Russians savored all the bizarre variations of free sex, allowing the bawdier side of their character to reappear. For many, the line between freedom and decadence became very thin.

At the beginning of the twentieth century, Russian students and bohemians were consumed with sex in a way that some historians have said was unparalleled in the country's history,[9] even its very early days, when pilgrims from Europe were shocked at Russia's raucous sexual folklore.[10] When censorship was repealed after the Revolution of 1905, bringing an eruption of erotic poetry, homosexual writing, and even cheap sex novels, Russians began to read the works of such people as Mikhail Artsybashev,[11] who spawned the term for a lifestyle that focused only on sex and death— or *artsybashevshchina*. A more serious writer of the era, Vasily Rozanov, argued for sexual transcendentalism. The only way to discover either reality or God was through sexual experience, wrote Rozanov who mocked Jesus as a man who never fulfilled himself by laughing or taking a wife.[12] "We are born to love. And as long as we do not fulfill our love we shall languish in this world. And as long as we have not fulfilled our love, we shall be punished in this world," Rozanov concluded.[13]

As the Russian revolution progressed—one writer describing it as a "voluptuous shudder"[14]—the Bolsheviks wisely avoided condemning the free-sex advocates until after they took control of the country. One of the most famous of these sexually liberated Bolsheviks in the early years was Aleksandra Kollontai, who became the commissar of public welfare in Lenin's new regime and who argued that the old morality was a key link in the chain that needed to be cast off by the proletariat. Campaigning for a "winged Eros," which she described as a spiritual union on behalf of the new society, she favored "the love of worker bees," with life being like a beehive, the woman as queen, her children raised by the hive. One of her famous characters (fictional) said that sex itself was a bodily need, of no greater significance than relieving thirst by drinking a glass of water.[15]

The tasting of sexual pleasures by the young eventually provoked Lenin to complain that such activities were a waste of a good communist's energies, and he suggested that Kollontai's winged Eros was like "an Indian saint . . . absorbed in the contemplation of his navel."[16] But Lenin did not clip Eros's wings. It was Stalin who took Lenin's concerns and cast them into an ironclad puritanism,[17] whose government banned the mention of Freud, who forbade questionnaires about sexual habits, whose controls led to a society so uninformed and frightened about sex that during one of the first U.S.-Russian television shows of glasnost, a Russian woman became furious and famous when the discussion of the two societies strayed into matters of sexuality. *"Seks? U nas nyet"* ("Sex? We don't have any"), the good Soviet matron huffed at the cameras. The phrase quickly became a joke, especially in the kitchens of Russia. But like all good Soviet jokes, it was perilously close to the public reality.

Even in the Soviet years, anyone seriously interested in sex issues in Russia went to visit Igor Kon, who was renowned as the U.S.S.R.'s premier expert on the subject and whose very name could make older Russians blush. Late one day in October 1992, I went to his tiny office in the academic center of Moscow, a relatively luxurious section that was still called Lenin Hills. I listened as "Mr. Sex," as one Russian called him, talked generously for hours about sexual mores, sex education, and homosexuality. He was a small man with a slight beard, which made him look not only like a professor and intellectual but also like a psychiatrist. In a country where Freud was virtually unknown and regarded as perverse and corrupt by most who had heard the name, Kon was probably among the few in Russia who would not have been insulted if I had said that he looked a little like the pictures of the world's most famous psychotherapist. In his tiny cave of bookcases crammed with a personal library that deserved at least two other rooms, the sixty-four-year-old sociologist worked over a large, outdated personal computer, churning out books, articles, lectures, and course outlines.

"It was wrong to say that in the 1920s the Bolsheviks were liberal. It was simply that they were not yet in control," Kon began, referring to the era when Lenin allowed the free-sex advocates as part of his political experiment.

"Stalin remedied that lack of control, and over the years, Russia was rendered 'sexually ignorant and mute,'" Kon said softly. "Now, we are paying the price for that."

Ignorance, violence, disease, and unwanted pregnancies were all part of the sexual picture that had begun to surface when the Soviet media was finally allowed to explore subjects that had once been banned from public discourse. For all the problems facing his country, Kon was full of hope about future attitudes towards his specialty. He had begun getting calls, not just from journalists or academics or publishing agents, but from schoolteachers, who felt that it was time to start following his advice in the public institutions of Russia.

While conservatives from the church or the old order protested that the new licentiousness simply needed to be curbed, some thoughtful people were beginning to see that the young needed to be educated about sex. In late 1992, almost a year after the Soviet system had collapsed, the director of the Dnepropetrovsk town center for preventing AIDS, Boris Estrin, tried to stop the local paper *Sobor* from printing its rapidly expanding section of personal ads. Peddling sex was dangerous in this period when people had no idea about how to combat AIDS and were being told by a sleepy health ministry that it was still a disease confined to Paris and San Francisco, Estrin argued. "Better that they should advertise condoms," Estrin said of his local newspaper. "In [our] region, twenty-three percent of the people never saw one, and seventy-three percent cannot explain how to use it."[18]

The Soviets had tried sex education before, and to most adults who had been educated in these classes, it was like trying to get information "from a stone wall," as one former student had explained it. The school subject called Ethics and the Psychology of Family Life made its brief appearance in the 1980s, with teachers talking about Marx, Lenin, nineteenth-century love poetry, family life, housekeeping, almost anything but sex.

Even in the dullest days of stagnation, there were some efforts to fill the gaps. One educator, Sergei Amirdzhanov, ran a program for twelve- to eighteen-year-olds in Moscow in 1964, but unfortunately, the lessons were not as direct as they could have been, considering teenagers knew almost nothing about the subject they were about to be taught. After one session on human reproduction, a bewildered group of fourteen-year-olds began comparing notes and decided the teachers had been talking about the hazards of cigarette smoking.[19]

On the day I saw Kon in his apartment, he had wanted to show me how society's opinions were changing in his favor, and he invited me to join him a few weeks later at a Moscow-area technical school where he would counsel teachers on how to advise their students about sex. When I met him at the school early on the appointed day, he was upbeat about the lecture, which he had been yearning to give teachers like these for years. As we drank thick coffee and ate delicate shell-shaped pastries in the principal's office before his speech, Kon explained that he was ready to talk about anything—from romance to contraception to oral sex. He was prepared to explain not only how to teach about exotic sexual matters but even to explain what they were.

The school auditorium where Kon would speak did not seem the kind of place where Russians could talk about anything so difficult and socially embarrassing as sex, but the teachers at this technical school had worked hard to make it comfortable. They had laid out a lavish spread at each of about twenty tables that filled only the front half of the meeting hall. Pepsis, homemade cakes, pads, and pencils were arranged neatly for those who needed them. The walls were a peachy pink color, and in spite of peeling paint and curtains that were a little worn, the place was scrubbed to a high sheen. Still, if people were supposed to be chatting easily about an intimate subject, an auditorium, even a peach-colored one, was not the setting. As the teachers arrived—all but two of them women—I began to feel a wave of tension spreading across the room. A few of the newcomers stood in a cluster, whispering to one another as though they were part of some naughty, adults-only outing.

Kon began with a short description of his mission. He explained how important it was to advise kids who already knew what body part went where but little else. He talked about how he went to a children's camp on the Black Sea, where there were three young boys in their early teens "with sex experience vaster than my own, but without any basic knowledge about it. I found it almost impossible talking to them, because they did not understand the words I used and I didn't know their slang." (I later learned more detail about one of these camps that Kon had visited. The youngsters had created an elaborate sex club, with ritual rapes of initiates, both male and female. What these young teenagers knew, they learned from one another, from slightly older children, and from drunken parents, Kon would explain a few years later.)[20]

After he spoke, talking first about the need to tell kids about safe sex and birth control, then about morality and the need for foreplay, a middle-aged woman stood up and addressed the group of about fifty teachers. "What we need is, not this, but a comprehensive program that explains the poetry of love, the joy, the magic. This is so cold and bloodless. It is not about love," she said, her voice rising with each phrase. Passionately waving her hands, and coming near tears in her emotion about the horrors of demystifying the sex act by explaining it, this woman with her clenched fists rallied behind the saccharine poetry of romance and stern warnings about aberrations as the only way to teach the young about sex.

Kon suddenly looked tired as he listened to her, and when his time came to answer, he spoke quietly, his voice showing his displeasure and disappointment: "They've already heard enough from us about poetry. Now they need to know the facts."[21]

As we walked out of the room, a cluster of younger teachers followed Kon to a small reception area, where he would continue to talk for hours.

"Poetry?" I asked him along the way.

He shook his head. "It may take longer than we think."

In the next few months, as I talked to young people in the streets, in their homes, or even in their clinics, I could see that Kon was right. Many bright young Russians, even those who thought they were part of the new Westernized society, lacked the information they needed to have healthy sex lives. Many still viewed birth control as the woman's job and abortion as the solution to pregnancy. Diseases like syphilis still came as a surprise to those who caught them. And for too many of these young adults, good sex meant rough sex, the kind now being glorified in the movies. "Long denied and exorcised, 'Soviet Sex' has broken its chains and appeared as uncivilized, ugly and violent as almost every other aspect of the Soviet Social life, producing in a society a state of shock and moral panic," Kon wrote in late 1992.[22] The young still needed help to break away from these old patterns that so easily caused pain, disease, and sterility. Their parents, however, were not so sure, and even the most modest steps by government officials drew intense criticism. It was as if by stopping any official information about sex, they could halt the sexual revolution already going on around them.

One September evening in 1992, the Russian health ministry decided to take a first step in educating the nation's teenagers about sex by airing a film focusing on abortion. With little or no warning, the ministry's documentary, called *You Can Go Mad*, appeared on a regularly scheduled youth hour, a time when teenagers came to the television set expecting to see a rock video or a program about how to get a driver's license. Instead, they saw a grisly message from Russian doctors instructing young people that there were other ways to prevent pregnancy besides abortion.

I went to the health ministry to see this video, and when Inna L. Alesina, a counselor on medical issues for the Russian Association of Family Planning, took me to a laboratory for the showing, she warned that it was a very graphic film. This was not the usual animated cartoon or the series of forlorn, downtrodden kids confessing their sins while adults scolded about the cruel wages of sex in the former Soviet Union, she explained. The classic matron's advice about sex, "Die, but never give a kiss without love," was not a part of this film, even as a joke.

The film began gently with pictures of a couple meeting and falling in love. Music, flowers, poetry, fuzzy soft backgrounds—it all looked like an advertisement for some new soap or cigarette, like those now becoming common on Moscow television. With a cinemagraphic jolt, however, the scene suddenly shifted to an abortion clinic—the dimly lit waiting room, nurses in their starched uniforms, doctors with the blood on their white coats. Perhaps the most horrifying part of these real-life pictures was that it was so routine, patient after patient rolling through the procedures like trucks going through an assembly line. The clinking sound of utensils echoed against the tile-lined rooms. In hushed tones, the terrified patients begged for painkillers that worked, and they pleaded for support from doctors and nurses too exhausted to give it.

"I am always tired and in a bad mood here," one nurse groaned as she prepared for her next client. "I want to give up, but the same questions are always there, asked in a trembling voice as I'm preparing the next miserable patient."

International statistics showed that Russia had more than a tenth of the world's 30 million estimated abortions. In 1991, 249,000 girls aged fifteen to nineteen underwent these legal abortions.[23] The number for illegal ones was unknown.

Abortion had been the contraception of choice in the Soviet Union, except for the period between 1936 until after Stalin's death, a period when the Kremlin wanted women to have more children. After Stalin's death in 1953, it became clear that birthrates had not risen as dramatically as deaths from kitchen abortions, and the procedure was once again legalized in 1955. Russia's abortion rates then grew steadily to become among the highest in the world, and the rates dropped only slightly in 1992, when Russian women in the cities apparently had more regular access to contraceptives.[24] Still, most Russian women used abortion as contraception, a leftover from the Soviet years. Some gynecologists said the abortion factories suited the gynecological establishment of the Soviet Union, which required work for many lower-level doctors, who could perform this relatively simple medical procedure. Others suggested that it was the only method for a society that did not want to expend vital resources—i.e., cash and capital outlay—on mere contraceptive devices (and thus decreed that they were unhealthy).

A third reason sometimes given by those analyzing the abortion rate was far more sinister. By providing advice about how to avoid pregnancy, officials would be admitting to a kind of immorality that was not part of the Soviet propaganda landscape. An abortion, which meant the girl was whisked away from school or work a day or two at most, meant that few people need even know about the problem of unwanted pregnancy. And if they did find out, it would be viewed as an isolated incident, not part of a sweeping national trend of premarital sex. Abortion during the Soviet years became what one Western analyst called "the silent solution."[25]

The video showing how this solution was performed seemed to go on forever that day in the Russian ministry. It showed the girl being rolled on a medical bed through the long, darkened corridors; the painkiller in her arm leaving a trail of bright red blood; the stirrups for her feet; and finally the stream of fetus and placenta dropping into a steel pan. Then suddenly a smiling baby waved into the camera, a shot that was followed with another picture of the bloody mess of an aborted fetus in the metal container. Baby and abortion. Back and forth. This was not kid vid, and when I watched it with a Russian woman in her late twenties, she hid her eyes and shuddered.

For most people outside Russia, this film had the feel of anti-abortion propaganda, similar to the ones like *The Silent Scream* that would arrive in Russian cities in 1993 and 1994, courtesy of the American evangelists and antiabortion advocates in the United States.[26] But *You Can Go Mad* was against abortion primarily on medical grounds. This program also tried to explain to the young and sexually active that there were better methods of avoiding childbirth or preventing pregnancy. Condoms were shown, pills and IUDs were mentioned as possibilities, even abstinence was suggested. The message was not that abortion was wrong, but that it was unnecessarily traumatic and unhealthy. Abortions may stop the immediate pregnancy, the youth were told, but there was a price. After several such abortions, many women became sterile. To many young women who watched the program that night, this was important and troubling news.

After the show had aired, however, the television station and Russian health offices were besieged with angry calls from parents, suggesting that the program promoted sex among young people. Nobody was outraged by the graphic nature of the film in the abortion clinics, the authorities said.[27] The idea that sex can cause pain was acceptable. What was unacceptable was the frank explanation of ways that sex could be enjoyed without becoming pregnant, without enduring the abortion clinic. This was like an invitation to purgatory, as far as the protesting adults were concerned.

"The youths were interested in the program," said Inna, referring to the news that other options were available to limit disease and pregnancy. "But the grown-ups were"—she looked for a way to describe the outcry—"not happy," she said finally.

"For old people especially, they thought it was propaganda for immorality."

One cold October day a few weeks after seeing *You Can Go Mad*, I went to a downtown market in Moscow to talk to young people about the things they seldom heard from their parents. I began talking with a twenty-year-old who called himself Maxim, who was perfectly happy to whisper about the *mafiya* and the problems of his life until the subject turned to sex. Then he began to fidget and look over his shoulder to make certain his friends weren't listening. I asked whether he used condoms. He scoffed at such an idea.

Did he worry about disease? Of course not.

Pregnancy?

He laughed, shaking his head and frowning. Condoms would slow down the rush to these new freedoms he and his friends had seen being demonstrated on videos and their well-fingered magazines. "We let the state worry about that. It's up to the government."

By that he meant that he did not worry about it: babies or abortions were women's work.

If the Russian young were still unschooled in the concept of birth control, they knew even less about venereal diseases. Some had heard about SPID, the Russian acronym for AIDS, but the ones I talked to like Maxim did not worry. SPID was a foreign disease that had not really made it to Russia, they said. It affected only people who used dirty needles in New York, they argued. It was a disease for homosexuals and Africans, they explained. Oddly, even though they professed not to believe the government about other things, they found it convenient to follow the state line that AIDS was not a Russian problem. Condoms were either Western and extremely expensive, or they were the Soviet rubbers, so thick that more than one wearer likened the experience to "wearing a shoe."[28]

As for other venereal diseases, I had seen small articles about how the rates of syphilis and gonorrhea were suddenly soaring among the young. It was difficult to get authorities to talk about it, and almost impossible to get ordinary Russians to discuss it. Finally, a Russian woman I knew helped me find one of the few VD clinics in Moscow, where the director, Dr. Olga Loseva, was known for her progressive ideas. One of her avant-garde proposals sounded familiar: she wanted the schools to tell students details about venereal disease, an idea that was literally unspeakable in the 1970s when she first started quietly pushing for it within the medical and education systems.

I went to find Dr. Loseva in one of the city's working neighborhoods, an area that still had cobbled streets and worn, prerevolutionary buildings that gave it more character than the industrial-looking apartment blocks elsewhere in the city. Her health center, set safely behind a battered wrought-iron fence, had been part of a church hospital before the revolution. From the tree-lined street, bypassers could be expected to notice only the elegant old clinic, an intricate redbrick design still managing to look decent in spite of years of decay. Behind this building was an ancient church that during the communist years had been used as a medical records library. Now it was empty, its doors nailed shut, a sign that said *remont* (reconstruction) dangling from unused scaffolding.

As I walked past the old church, a woman was slowly sweeping the walk, and I asked her where to find Dr. Loseva. She stared at me for an instant, trying perhaps to judge what foul disease I had, and then pointed to a concrete gray slab of a building with severe iron bars over every window. If you wanted to build a clinic for the society's pariahs, this one would do nicely.

Down the long hallways, past young people who waited on overstuffed couches and kept their eyes cast downward, I found Dr. Loseva. In a narrow office, she sat hunched over her case histories, feverishly trying to finish a stack of reports before I interrupted her. She was a frail-looking woman, too delicate it seemed to spend her long working hours explaining to fifteen-year-olds why they had strange sores and rashes, swollen glands and ugly discharges. Most of them had never heard of syphilis or gonorrhea before they arrived in her hospital, she explained. Even a popular newspaper that had begun warning about AIDS did not go into detail about these less deadly illnesses.

The treatment here was basic, she began, the best an impoverished state government could afford. A patient with syphilis or gonorrhea spent a minimum of twenty-eight days in the hospital. Without money for powerful Western antibiotics (available only for a steep price at the new private clinics), her patients received only the old Soviet medicines, which were far less potent. The antibiotic was administered by injection every three hours. That meant 224 shots before a sufferer was cured. When Dr. Loseva's patients were released, most could barely sit down during the bus ride home.

As she described the treatment, a red-haired girl stuck her head through the door. Cheery and confident, with strikingly translucent skin, Lyuba (a name she had chosen for the interview and which, oddly, means love) promised to tell her story as long as it meant that she wouldn't miss lunch. This agreed, she bounced into the room like any ordinary teenager and sat down slowly, like an old woman.

Aged fifteen—I would have guessed twenty-five—she wanted to be a cosmetologist, and she was dating a boy steadily (having sex since age fourteen). One day they had a fight. To make him jealous, she went out with someone else she did not know.

"And what happened?" I asked

"He gave me bad blood," she said, a shy giggle covering her embarrassment. Bad blood. It was the phrase for VD I had heard growing up in the American South.

At Dr. Loseva's gentle coaxing, the girl began explaining her symptoms. It had started with a rash that would not go away, Lyuba said. She went first to a dermatologist, who gave her a salve, she said, rubbing the back of her neck as she talked about the first trips to a doctor. When the rash got worse, she went a second time. The doctor then suggested a blood test. After the results came back, she was sent to Dr. Loseva.

In the old Soviet days, this had been a very common route to the kinds of hospitals where venereal disease was being treated, and over the years, physicians who left the U.S.S.R. reported that statistics on VD had been hidden behind the label "skin disorders" and treated in separate clinics. Syphilis and gonorrhea were supposed to be decadent Western problems, cleansed from the perfect society. By the 1990s, the teenagers came to Dr. Loseva from many different clinics and doctors, their disease no longer a political secret.

When I asked Lyuba whether she had learned about sex from her parents, she laughed and rolled her eyes.

"A girlfriend told me about sex," she said. Then, with a sad little girl's smile, she added, "She didn't tell me the whole story."

After Lyuba came Natasha, also not her real name. She was an angry young woman, who learned that she would spend a month in this hospital when the boy she had been dating called to tell her that he had syphilis. It was the last she had heard from him.

Natasha sat sullenly in a flowered robe. Her hair was thin, desperately in need of vitamins, and in an attempt to brighten it, she had dyed it a wan yellowish blond. Natasha was slightly overweight at age nineteen, and she had the look of someone who would grow thick and leaden with the years. What did she want to do? She did not know. How would she live? She shrugged. Already there was a bitterness with each monosyllabic answer, which I suspected she would not shed easily once she was outside these walls.

"Would this experience change the way you have sex in the future?" I asked her.

She looked at me out of the corners of her eyes, and I tried not to shudder. I would not want to meet this one on her own, I was thinking, wondering if she had been a moll or a hooker. Suddenly, just as I thought she would growl some obscenity at me, she sighed and looked frail, as if she wanted to cry, which, I suddenly realized, she probably did.

"Sure, I will be more careful," she said, her watery blue eyes looking at me directly for the first time. "But what do you do when you meet somebody? Do you interview him? Do you take out a card with a list of questions on it and say: 'Do you have this? Do you have that?' "

She shook her head, as if to say it was hard enough just getting the boys to be with her. Any interference, any demands would just make things worse. Any more questions also seemed like torture. I wished her luck, which I knew she would need, and watched her shuffle tiredly out the door.

Dr. Loseva had held her face in a neutral expression while Lyuba and Natasha were talking in the office. She did not show disapproval or reprimand them, as I had expected; she was matter-of-fact and direct, the way the best doctors often are in such situations. But when they were gone, she slumped over her desk and shook her head.

"Parents," she whispered. "They should do this, not us. It is not the job of the government to tell them about this."

Many parents of her patients had, in effect, turned their children over to the state when they were in kindergarten. The state had taught them to read, to write, to be prepared to do some task, however menial, in society. But when it came to complexities of love and the hazards of sex, the state had failed.

"Most parents of these children are separated," Dr. Loseva said. "Many are less than ideal parents, and most are working. They don't know how to relate to their children. In our collective society, too many parents just put their kids in the kindergarten and backed away from them."

Now, society was paying the price for lack of attention to the young, she explained, as she told of the lack of morality, the deadened young souls who learned early to grab at pleasures no matter whom they hurt, even themselves.

"For these reasons, we are seeing more and more sex among younger and younger children," Dr. Loseva said, citing the increases in fifteen-year-olds with sores and lesions. I asked her for any numbers she had showing this increase, and Dr. Loseva shook her head. "I don't know about recent data," she said, her voice so soft it was hard to hear her. "I can only tell you that there are many, many more than in the past few years."

While the girls had been telling their stories, an assistant brought Dr. Loseva stacks of documents that looked as though they were carbon copies of typed manuscripts. To try to answer my questions about data, she opened one of the folders and began to explain about her other work as a specialist—her surveys on teenage sex.

In 1976, less than 1 percent of girls had tried sex before the age of seventeen; her latest survey, in early 1991, revealed that more than 28 percent had sampled sex before age seventeen. Since 1991, she explained, she had been too busy treating teenagers for syphilis and gonorrhea to do another poll on their sex habits.

If little was being said about disease in the newly liberated society, even less seemed available on the subject of lovemaking. The city metros and news kiosks were full of lurid suggestions about technique, of course, but as the society raced to modernize itself, the more thoughtful books on the joys and responsibilities of sex were often hidden under the piles of glossy magazines. While the young and the sex starved began to feast on these new possibilities, a sight often compared to sailors on shore leave or ripe young students on their first unchaperoned outing, there was little time to concentrate on repairing the damage of the past. One had the feeling that Russia had to settle down a bit, to become sated and spent enough to deal with the deeper sexual problems inherited from the Soviet years.

* * *

If there are no jokes, as Freud is often quoted as saying, the nonjokes I heard from women in Russia were particularly telling. One vibrant and interesting Muscovite offered this one in the last months of the Soviet era. Question: "What's a Russian man's idea of foreplay?" Answer: "Olya, what's wrong with the TV?" In these quips and stories, the outside world began to understand how many ordinary Russians viewed the side of life that came closest to the Western concept of private. The lack of information in the Soviet years may have been useful somehow to the government or respected by people who had an almost religious view of sexual morality, but the official prudery made it extremely difficult to repair any sexual difficulties or even simple misunderstandings. A doctor who had moved West several years earlier remembered a farmworker who was stunned to learn that his wife was not becoming sexually aroused when he played with her navel.

Without access to the Western manuals or even porn videos that circulated only among the top circles of the government and the bottom levels of the black market, most people learned about basics from their peers. Any problems encountered in this process were often viewed as bad luck, an unmentionable and irreparable human weakness.

If the male couldn't perform (afflicted with what some women called the "6:30" problem, referring to the hands of the clock), most of their Soviet doctors could barely tolerate hearing about it—if the afflicted had the nerve to ask. A woman's frigidity might have been worth a laugh or even a divorce, but any possibility of cure in the old U.S.S.R. would have been little short of a medical miracle.

What was worse for many women was that their men often seemed to prefer a kind of sex that we would call abuse or perhaps even rape if it happened in Europe or America. In an interview after she left the Soviet Union in the mid-seventies, a former ballet dancer and sometime hustler named Regina Savitskaya talked to a writer about sex in Russia. Her stories were about mad, drunken sex, when the man who is angry about the rest of his existence takes it out on the woman.

"Four hundred years of the Tartar yoke, the Golden Horde, Ghenghis Khan—it's all had an effect on Russian behavior. The Russian has a barbarian in him. He sees women as slaves," she said.[29]

Far worse than the Golden Horde may have been the Soviet system, which tried to civilize this ancient tendency too often by turning men into obedient and docile beings. Many, as sexologist Igor Kon explained after the end of the Soviet state, were meek only at work. With their women, they felt free to show their anger. "Either [the Russian male] must be a brute, be cruel, proving himself to be a tyrant, or he is nothing."[30]

I found these statements difficult to believe since most of the men I knew seemed gentle and even sweet. Their wives were often the ones with the noticeable passions—often for politics or religion or the theater and, of course, their children. The male was the quieter sex, who drove the car and laughed at the jokes and seemed always to be there when the wife had overextended the family resources or broken the fragile Soviet-made (or, later, Chinese-made) vacuum cleaner.

Some Western women I knew who became involved with Russian men listened to me and scoffed. One suggested that the ordinary male seemed to believe that a good lover was something between Rhett Butler and John Wayne. Another told about a very gentle, sensitive-looking Russian man who seemed the perfect mate until they went to bed, where he suddenly was transformed into a sexual bully, more ape than Tarzan, as she put it. Jean MacKenzie, an American who has written a number of sour columns in *The Moscow Times* about her encounters with Russian men in Moscow, once lamented the fact that Russians did not celebrate Valentine's Day. "It's not really Fedya's fault that he doesn't get it," she wrote a few days before the holiday in 1995. "What do you do in a country where romance went out the window with the October Revolution?"[31]

Some Russian women were even more direct. Anya Vakhrusheva, a young writer who had spent some time in the West as a student, decided after she returned to Moscow and got a job that she would avoid Russian males, not as a general rule, she said, but as an absolute one. As she declared simply, "On the one hand, Russian men are very juvenile, and on the other hand, they are very aggressive to women."[32]

Others saw strength and manliness in their Russian mates. Sure, the brutes existed, they explained, but many Russian men were romantic, arriving at your door with their arms full of flowers, helping you with your coat, being protective and gentle at the same time. "After the American male with all his hang-ups and uncertainties—what's right, what's not allowed, what's proper—I enjoyed the self-confidence of the Russian men," one American woman said after several encounters. "They were not afraid to try to sweep you off your feet, to make you feel beautiful."

Romance is always a delicious pursuit, and when it works, it is worth all the poetry and flowers and wit and drama that this powerful nation retains in its vast romantic arsenal. When it did not work? When it turned aggressive and ugly? Reports of sexual harassment and violence were still relatively rare, but the growing number of specialists who began dealing openly with such problems suggested that there were signs these abuses were increasing, even if the official numbers had not substantially changed. Although men had been known to suffer badly at the hands of women judges and prosecutors in the old Soviet court system, by 1992, the women did not fare well when complaining to the authorities about a sex-starved boss or a violent mate.

Rape, for example, was often viewed as the woman's fault, and once the assault occurred, there was seldom help for the victim. If the woman went to the police, she could expect to find a policeman whose first instinct could well be to think she had lured the attacker into his crime. If she went to a hospital or clinic for treatment, she was told to go to the police. As a result, most women's groups said they believed that many rapes were not reported and that the thirteen thousand rapes registered with police each year were a small percentage of the true numbers. Natalya Gaidarenko, who runs Moscow's Sexual Assault Recovery Center, and a few other women had begun by 1993 to try spreading the word that rape is a crime, not a sex act, but the old views and values were still solidly entrenched. In early 1995, one woman went to see a psychotherapist after she was raped, only to have the doctor tell her that the best way to get over her fear of sex was to go to bed with him, Gaidarenko told a press conference in April 1995.[33] Another woman who was raped went to a lawyer who told her that there was not enough evidence to support her case against her attacker. He suggested that she return to the man to see if he would try it again. This time, she should bring a witness.

Most of those dissatisfied with their sexual lives had far less drastic problems.[34] A few women I talked with about sex complained that Russian men understood little about how to make their wives or girlfriends happy, or that orgasm was a male phenomenon and women were supposed to lie back and, if not enjoy it, then survive. Men saw some women as too strong, too bossy; others were too weak from the strains of daily life to try some of the *Cosmo* recipes for a better sex life.

I suspected from the few hints dropped by older Russian women that many of them enjoyed the idea of sex more than the reality, but it was hard to imagine the young Russian woman—a strong, smart, and demanding creature, as a rule—living only for her dreams. Surely she would ask for her share of life's pleasures, I had thought. But at a press conference on contraception in late October 1992, a young woman who worked for a Russian newspaper asked Inga Grebesheva, head of the Russian Association of Family Planning, how women could enjoy sex. It was as much a plea as a technical question, but Grebesheva's answer was surprising and distressing. "In our society you have to work too hard, and if you work so much, day and night, you will not even be able to think about sex," she said.[35] "During sex, women are not thinking about sex. They are not thinking about relationships. They are thinking how not to get pregnant."

As for the men, Russian medical officials by early 1993 had begun to register a surprising increase in impotency, which they attributed to the stress caused by the changing society.[36] Others suggested that there was not an increase in actual numbers of impotent males but a surge in the numbers of those willing to come forward to be counted and treated.[37] The upheaval in society was taking its toll, and until people began to live more luxuriously and talk about sex more openly, the idea of sexual pleasure was considered a luxury even in the mid-1990s—a brief joy for the young or a coveted ritual for the rich and powerful.

Treating sexual problems was still rare as the Soviet Union died, but in Moscow, there was already one private and professional sex clinic. Opened in 1989, it was an experiment by a group of doctors who had decided to leave their state practice and begin a private clinic for those suffering from sterility, frigidity, and impotency, among other problems both physical and psychological. The costs were steep by Russian standards but not unbearable, and although other private clinics had opened to help the increasing numbers of women who had problems having children after several Soviet abortions, for example,[38] MIR was the best known and the most widely respected for treating a wider range of sexual problems.

MIR, which stood for *Meditsina i Reproduktsiya* (Medicine and Reproduction), was housed in a large prerevolutionary building in one of the nicer northern sections of Moscow. The first time I went, in the autumn of 1992, the structure had a fresh coat of turquoise paint, and like many such operations evolving into private enterprises at the time, it was a strange collection of shops, clinic, and offices, in this case, generally having to do with sex. It was, for example, the site of Moscow's first public sex shop— *Intim*, or Intimate.

The day I arrived, a row of large black limousines with reflecting windows rumbled outside in the MIR parking area, their drivers keeping the motors alive so that their rich or powerful passengers could speed away at any moment. It was not the clinic these customers had come for, I realized once inside the door, but for *Intim*, the small two-room operation that, in October 1992, cost twenty rubles (less than a nickel) to enter, which apparently was all that most people did in those earlier days. For those with the money, like the men (and they were all men) from the limousines, the store sold mostly products from Poland, Taiwan, and Korea—condoms, blowup dolls, dildos, manuals, skimpy underwear, and, oddly, "Save the Panda" stationery.

MIR was farther inside the building, and their offices and medical facilities covered more than two floors. In 1992, there were already plans to expand as soon as the landlord or the profits allowed. The corridors were dark, in the Soviet fashion, but the smell was clean and the tile floors were newly patched, the walls freshly painted. The sign on the entrance gave the list of services, from birth control to helping people have babies, with the prices in huge letters beside it. After passing my calling card through the small slot in the office window, I was directed to a room where, with little of the usual formalities, Dr. Nikolai Oleinikov quickly began to assess the fallout from years of Soviet sexual repression.

"It is often said here that we are lagging behind America twenty years," he began, using a phrase that he would repeat several times in his discussion of sexual medicine. "But that is not true. We are forty years behind."

It was not that his kind of work was forbidden during the years before perestroika, he explained. It was simply that any research on sex was being done at an academic or theoretical level. A male patient who was impotent in those years would go to a urologist. If he was lucky, the doctor might give him more than a lecture about accepting his fate. Those doctors who did try to cure their patients' sexual problems now had begun adapting to different demands from their patients, even advertising the specialty that they had performed in secret for many years.

"For many patients now, only the sign on the door has changed," Dr. Oleinikov said. "Earlier, if you went to a urologist, you might, if you were very, very lucky, find a good sexopathologist. Now if the plaque says sexopathologist, you might find a urologist in the room," he said.

During my long talk with Dr. Oleinikov, on subjects ranging from sterility to sexual hysteria, I became increasingly aware of the gap between the West and Russia on these issues. In this case, when he had been talking about urology, he began to review other problems that were more complicated than the usual prostate infection or female cystitis. "Often problems are not simply biological," he said. "Sometimes they are more psychological." In terms of cystitis, a painful ailment that many women suffer not only for biological reasons but sometimes because of stress or stressful sex, the idea that the mind could make the body worse seemed so obvious that it need not be said. It was at times like that that I realized he was doing what he did every day—trying to educate patients and even other doctors in a world that had missed much of the West's obsession with the id and the psyche.

The subjects he taught these newly freed Soviets were basic. Many men had to be convinced that masturbation was not a vice that would destroy their brain and their manhood. Early Soviet doctors, often using outdated views from the West, seemed to find proof that masturbating weakened the body. Among them were followers of one sexual theologian who said that such activity was unethical, that it decreased a person's mental ability, and that after four thousand times, a man became impotent. (Some Western preachers had promoted this view since the eighteenth century, after an anonymous tract called *Onania, or the Heinous Sin of Self-Pollution and All Its Frightful Consequences* was published in London. European doctors in the nineteenth century cited masturbation as the cause of tuberculosis, fits, indigestion, blindness, acne, warts, and even insanity.[39] By the 1950s and

1960s, most urban Russians knew that such theories were ridiculous, Oleinikov said, but the subconscious continued to play tricks years later.)

Still, in some areas he had seen progress. The day before, a "friendly doctor" (one who thought MIR was providing a useful service) had sent a woman to him who was so hysterical that she had been tested for epilepsy. Many Western doctors had suspected a connection between female hysteria and sex, but the idea was still new to Russia's Soviet-educated medical profession.

"I felt that the problem was not epilepsy but sex," he said, "and when I started to look for sexual reasons, she said that the last time she had had sex was four months earlier, although she had strong sexual desires. I asked about her husband. He did not come up to her standards, she said, and he did not match previous partners. He was too shy and wouldn't do many of the things she wanted him to do. She couldn't adapt to this relationship, so after years of suffering, she took over as the master of the family. She did everything, sacrificed everything. She became a martyr, and her husband was a nuisance, and she was just tolerating him, until slowly the problem of hysteria built up in her. He may have been more intelligent, she had said, but he was isolated by this intelligence. Withholding sex was her revenge, but it had hurt her as much as it did her husband."

The avalanche of information about sex, after years of silence, had helped in some ways by bringing problems like hers out into the open, he said. For others, like the women whose husbands had seen pornography and even erotic literature and taken it home to the wife as a suggestion, the freedoms had created a whole new category of anxieties. Was this kind of thing okay? they wondered. Was it healthy? Moral?

As I left Dr. Oleinikov, he sounded like the other experts in his field. What was needed was candid information, he said, sex education that could keep people from turning a source of love and pleasure into a personal tragedy or neurosis.

Real information about sex, books for young people that explain everything directly, the good and bad, were still hard to find in the early 1990s. The day I visited Igor Kon, I asked whether any such books were available. He reached across the pile of papers and fished out a volume that I had never seen on sale anywhere, even a year into the new Russia. It was a copy of his own work, *Forbidden Fruit*, which included much of the art, poetry, and advice that Kon said had been missing for five decades. The first printing of fifty thousand copies in early 1991 was gone shortly after it went on sale in the bookstores. Two thousand copies were stolen immediately, Kon said proudly. The others went into the black market. (A friend of mine, on hearing I wanted my own copy, finally spotted one at a bookseller's table outside Moscow. It cost more than twenty times the original price, and she and I would not be its first readers.)

The book I scanned quickly that day had an introduction to such basics as the *Kama Sutra*, the erotic statues of Pompeii, and the revolutionary idea (in Russia) that homosexuality could be a preference instead of a perversity. There were photos from *Playboy* and a primer on erogenous zones: it was a digest of human sexuality, too much in too little space. But it was a start.

Kon, watching me become so engrossed that I was beginning to waste his time, gently took the book from me and flipped to a page that he said was his triumph, a section he tried to publish for years. I expected something unspeakably lewd, but when I looked at the page he picked out, I was more shocked than I had been at anything for sale on the streets. The illustrations showed a woman examining her breast for cancer.

"They don't pass these out at the polyclinics [where women went to their doctors]?"

He shook his head. "No, they don't. Not even this."

7

A Stranger in the Family

Let's Turn Red Square into a Pink Triangle
—Planned slogan for fledgling gay group
in U.S.S.R., 1990[1]

We are still considered scum here. I think we always will be.[2]
—Aleksandr Korotkov, St. Petersburg
homosexual, 1995

The nervous crowd of three thousand gay men and lesbians, the "blues" as they called themselves in the slang of day, flooded the city of St. Petersburg on a warm June weekend in 1993 to celebrate their new freedom. Two months earlier, the Russian government had abolished Stalin's dreaded Article 121, which made the crime of "man lying with man" punishable by at least five torturous years in prison. As an instant member of the "degraded" caste, a prisoner convicted on 121 became a "rooster," a thing to be raped and abused within the cruel prison society.

Now, although they were free to gather for the Christopher Street Days, named after the center of gay life in New York City, the Russians met nervously, glancing over their shoulders as they moved from gay discos into the eternal twilight of St. Petersburg's high summer. After years of living with fake wives and underground lovers, after fearing that each encounter would uncover a turncoat who would demand money or gifts or enslavement to the KGB in exchange for silence, they now faced a chaotic new world, where having the law on their side meant little on the city streets. Guards hired to protect those attending gay discos had been known to sample the local vodka and allow their old animosities to emerge. Apartments leased under agreements that were seldom totally legal suddenly disappeared if the landlady suspected two roommates of the same sex were gay. Jobs became harder to find and easier to lose. A young woman who had been elected president of Triangle, the first nationwide organization of gay men and lesbians, appeared at a press conference in Moscow in August 1993 wearing a paper bag over her head. On the bag was this notice: "I cannot show my face because of society's attitudes toward homosexuals."[3]

Even though the law changed, the system was taking its time about letting known homosexuals wander freely on the streets, fearing that these men and women would add another decadent choice to the tantalizing buffet of sins now being offered openly to the nation's young people. Yuri Yereyev, president of the Tchaikovsky Foundation for Cultural Initiative and the Defense of Sexual Minorities, told the audience at one point that June weekend that any effort to release homosexuals from the dungeonlike prisons of St. Petersburg had so far brought "smirks and indifference" from prison authorities. New laws did not make new people, Yereyev had said. Still, outside the prisons he believed that attitudes were beginning to change. As he had walked along St. Petersburg's gracious boulevards that morning, Yereyev had asked a few dozen people how they felt homosexuals should be treated now that they were no longer operating illegally in Russia. "Only one said he would want to kill us," he reported.[4]

Yereyev's poll may not have been scientific, but it was certainly more comforting than the major survey four years earlier. Pollsters from the All-Union Public Opinion Center asked about twenty-six hundred people in 1989 how they should deal with homosexuals. Here were their responses:

Six percent wanted to help them.
Ten percent were for leaving them to themselves.
Thirty percent wanted to "isolate them from society."
Thirty-three percent wanted to "eliminate" them.[5]

* * *

When I arrived in Moscow in early 1991, a Russian homosexual still had a fairly simple choice between the closet and prison. Although the young celebrated a new openness about sex, at least in movies and metro stops, where they could buy cheap pornography for exorbitant prices, most people lived with the emotional heritage left by the Soviet education system. That system had decreed that homosexuals were deviants and criminals, and even people who knew better intellectually still felt that being gay was an unmentionable flaw, shameful at best. Once a Russian woman and I began talking about a new exhibit in Moscow of the works and life of Marina Tsvetayeva. She had not seen it, and neither had I, but we were considering the possibility, weighing the problems of scheduling kids and finding tickets. "You know she had a very difficult, very unusual life. She had added hardships," my friend said. "Yes," I answered, "she was a lesbian, wasn't she?" My friend winced slightly. Yes, she nodded, and without correcting me (Tsvetayeva was actually bisexual), she swiftly moved the conversation to a new subject. An erudite woman with a great deal of knowledge about the West, she had difficulty with the word "lesbian," even from a Westerner. In Russia, it was still a rude word.

For ordinary Russians, it would take a long time before homosexuals were considered normal people. The man in charge of the anti-AIDS program for the U.S.S.R., Valentin Pokrovsky, told an interviewer in February 1991 that homosexuality should never be made legal because it is "not so much a disease as a depravity that has to be combated, precisely by legal means."[6] The view was so deeply imbedded that the Russian Interior Ministry in June 1993 published an official guidebook to warn newcomers about the perils of visiting Russian cities. To avoid crime one must avoid "criminal types," which include "prostitutes, homosexuals, dealers in stolen goods, and currency vendors." The guidebook was still being distributed long after homosexuality was no longer a crime.[7]

For all his official new freedoms, the Russian homosexual (who had begun to adopt the English word "gay") stepped timidly into a world that believed he was a criminal, a carrier of AIDS, or a psychotic who needed to be cured. I suspected that Russia's attitudes toward gay people in the 1990s were not much different from America's in the 1950s. Outside the most cosmopolitan of cities—New York, San Francisco, and New Orleans—the idea of homosexuality somehow challenged a young man's virility to the point that he and his friends would routinely beat up any available "queer" as some kind of rite of passage into heterosexual manhood.

Russian gay people knew this type only too well. They were called *gayee bash-'ers* (gay bashers), Vladislav Artanov told me one October afternoon in 1992 as we sat in the darkened hallway of Moscow's first clinic for homosexuals, a place where gay people could also meet to talk about the psychological and sometimes physical problems of their underground world. Artanov, a biochemist, was one of the first gay activists in Moscow after the beginnings of glasnost and perestroika. He had started *RISK* magazine in 1990, and its circulation had grown to about five thousand, mostly homosexuals looking for a community in a hostile communal society. The magazine provided relief for these lonely people, but it was full of warnings about the real world for a Russian gay person.

The Russian gay bashers ran in gangs, and they had their own term for stealing, beating, and in some cases killing gay victims. They called it *remont*ing, an especially chilling use of the favored term for renovation. With the old Soviet structure suddenly being revamped, apartments being sold, stores being redone, restaurants and cafés being opened, the sign "Closed for *Remont*" was everywhere, often a signal that some new venture was on its way. *Remont*ing gays meant that these gangs viewed homosexuals as things, structures that needed to be molded forcibly from their old ways into something new. In too many cases, that meant restructuring a living person into a dead one.

"There are a lot of horrible cases now of murders of gay people in their own homes. There are nine, no, ten cases I know about personally," Artanov began. When I asked for details, he responded as he would often that day, with a gentle shake of the head. "The primary reason for these murders is money. The gang members pretend they are gay; we invite them home and then we are robbed, beaten, or killed."

It was not a new system. In a famous article in 1984, a respected defense attorney named Yakov Aizenshtadt had described one of his clients, a sixteen-year-old named Dima Sorokin, who had been arrested for *remont*ing gays. Sorokin told his lawyer how his group worked: they chose a target, and one of their group acted as bait. The "homo," as they called him, would be lured into an empty building, and then the rest of the gang would rush in, beat him over the head with a metal rod, and rob him, tie him up, and leave him, presumably for dead. Even if he lived, the "homo" would never report the crime, and Aizenshtadt wrote that he believed the boys were actually working as a renegade arm of the local police force. Sorokin faced trial, not for what his gang did to homosexuals, but because they attacked a heterosexual woman who complained noisily to police.[8]

Artanov saw the same police-sanctioned hooliganism years later, and when I asked about specific examples that afternoon, he stared at me for a long time, perhaps thinking of some friend who had been *remont*ed, perhaps trying to judge why I would ask about such matters.

In the moments he took to think, I found myself staring at him, thinking how easily he would blend into the crowd walking the streets of Moscow. Artanov had clear brown eyes, a thin face, and disheveled brown hair—a very Russian face, more gentle perhaps than some of those seen scowling in the streets after work or ogling girls from their the makeshift construction scaffolding that now seemed to cover most of the older buildings in the city. He was wearing cheap gray trousers, a big V-neck sweater, and lumpen Soviet-made shoes with a heavy layer of Moscow mud around the soles. He did not fit my image of the Western homosexual— usually handsome or stylish in some personal way—but looked like all the people on the metro who traipsed from home to job to home, a drab army in misshapen clothes that I once heard described as having been carefully crafted by Soviet manufacturing committees so that "one size fits nobody." Ex-Soviets had learned the art of blending into the crowd because standing out meant trouble. Even though others in the new Russia had begun to enjoy looking different, wearing bright colors that seemed jarring to the old Soviet eye or appearing in public wearing rich Western labels, Artanov and his homosexual friends had retained the old self-protective skill of looking like everybody else.

"It is not necessary to kill them," he said finally. "They know they aren't going to the police. In many cases they are more afraid of the police than of the robber."

With the change in the law, there came some hope that this harass-the-victim mentality by the police would also change. But old habits did not die with a set of new guidelines from the chief of police. Russians I knew, heterosexual and gay, did not see the police as guardians of the peace so much as arbitrary enforcers of flexible laws or agents of corrupt courts and deadly prisons, all of which sullied everyone who approached them, even if they needed help. Talking to the police was, at best, a lottery. A call for help could bring a decent officer to the door, a policeman who would try to investigate, to pursue the criminal, and to follow the law. The same call, however, might mean the arrival of a criminal in uniform, a cop who would offer to help for money or maybe the TV. He would operate by his own law, his own personal prejudices. For anyone who was different, this could mean trouble. Dark-skinned people from the Caucasus, Asians, black Africans—they were nervous about bringing their cases to officials who might have a basic distrust of anyone who was not Russian. For homosexuals, there was the same fear of being an outsider, an alien.

When I asked Artanov that day if the police could ever help, he sighed and shook his head. "When a crime is committed, they investigate the victim first. They take personal letters; they investigate the names in our notebooks. As a rule police investigate the private life of the person robbed more than they do the crime. They find letters, papers, literature that proves his sexual preference. Then, they are the ones in trouble.[9]

"It is not worth it to report a crime, and there are many cases when gays are robbed precisely because the burglars know they will not report it," he said. "But then, sometimes they resist, and that is when they are killed. About one murder every month or two months that I know of in Moscow alone."

I asked Artanov about himself as our interview ended, and he talked with some relief about a life that had been, as he put it, difficult but satisfying. He was thirty-nine when we met, and he had spent the last twenty years in Moscow. His father had constructed power plants, and the family had moved around the Soviet Union from city to city. He had two brothers, and he was the only homosexual, he said, adding, "as far as I know," with a rare smile.

"I was twenty-one when I learned I was gay. I had a happy meeting that opened my eyes," he said without elaborating. He was married at the time, but there were no children. "I think she knew, but we never discussed it."

Artanov never told anyone he was homosexual until he entered the gay underworld. Now, although he was one of Moscow's first gay activists, there were some places where his sexual preference remained secret—such as with a boss or landlord.

"I have had a partner for five years. We rented flats together, but we had to move pretty often because of the neighbors or the landlord, and, as you know, it is not easy to move here. I have moved five times in five years," he said. "Now, my partner and I, we share an apartment with my former wife."

Centuries before Stalin and the Soviets, Russia had a reputation as a huge uncontrollable territory full of peasants whose lifestyle was earthy and free. Russians were more tolerant of gay people than the Europeans, and in some rural areas, peasants tended to view the entire idea as a source of humor rather than a sin against nature.[10] The church did not approve, of course, in part because of the problems homosexuality caused for them in monasteries, but man-to-man sex was the subject of so many jokes and raunchy stories that some Europeans who visited Russia in the sixteenth and seventeenth centuries returned home to report that the Russians were a crude and lusty people.[11] Peter the Great, who wanted to make Russia a part of Europe, adopted the first state laws against sodomy in 1706 and 1716,[12] changing a Swedish version that required burning at the stake to some form of corporal punishment. Death for a homosexual came only if he raped a soldier, according to Peter's code.

The laws barring sodomy, or anal contact, as it was called, grew more severe in 1832, depriving those convicted of all rights and sending them into exile for four to five years. For seduction of a minor, the penalty was hard labor for ten to twenty years.[13] By 1903, the law was scaled back, resulting in jail for no less than three months in some cases and giving harsher punishments of up to eight years only in aggravated circumstances such as rape or abuse of a minor. But sodomy laws were enforced rarely in the prerevolutionary era because aristocrats, artists, writers, composer Tchaikovsky, and ballet master Sergei Diaghilev had made such behavior more acceptable, at least unofficially. Homoerotic art and poetry began to appear, and intellectuals openly discussed the idea of same-sex love.[14] When the revolutionaries spread throughout the country, many hoped that they would bring with them a new tolerance for love and romance in all its various forms.[15]

The Bolsheviks, in those early years, did not seem to have a clearly defined policy on homosexuality, and Lenin apparently preferred not to provide any guidance about such matters. For almost seventeen years, homosexuality was legal, even though it was treated officially as a sickness—a sign of what was ahead for those who practiced homosexuality. One writer, Mark Sereisky, suggested in the late 1920s that Soviet doctors must help homosexuals find a "trouble-free" life in the new collective by using "cures," such as transplanting heterosexual testicles into the scrotum of a homosexual.[16]

During the early 1930s, Stalin's propagandists began a campaign to link homosexuality to the bourgeoisie,[17] and by 1934 sodomy was an unmentionable crime punishable by a prison term of up to eight years if the act involved violence, threat of violence, or a minor.[18] Although there are no public documents showing how many were sentenced under these laws, Soviet sex expert Igor Kon and others estimated that about one thousand a year were selected for prosecution. As long as they did not flaunt their sexuality, drawing public attention to the way they were breaking the law, certain artists, dancers, and other celebrities enjoyed relative immunity. "Once they overstepped the mark, however, the law descended upon them with a vengeance," Kon has said repeatedly in his lectures, books, and interviews.

Prison was a desperate and forbidding place for any Russian, but for the gay male it was often worse, especially for those who were not tough and aggressive but assumed the role as "female" partner in their relationships. Prison made this homosexual "the bottom of the prison heap," as Pavel Masalsky told reporters after the law changed. Masalsky, who had been in prison in the early 1980s because a partner decided to testify against him for revenge, said, "Nobody respects them, but everybody tries to satisfy their sexual demands with them. If the person tries to resist, the best that awaits them is a beating, the worst is a terrible death."[19]

These "roosters," or "degraded ones," may number as many as 10 to 12 percent in colonies for general criminals, and as many as 20 percent in juvenile colonies, for people under the age of eighteen, where they are hazed constantly, forced to eat mice, to put lightbulbs up their anuses, and to endure other forms of abuse. The prison system, like most such establishments, had its layers of severity. The stricter regimen could be the nightmares so well documented by Solzhenitsyn and many others. But for gay people, these more controlled environments were preferred to the easier prison regimens because guards watched prisoners more carefully. At prisons with the milder regimens, the inmates had more power, and their control usually meant that the degraded ones were treated like slaves or animals. Gay rights specialists in Moscow estimated there were approximately one thousand roosters in 1993, whose status would not change because of changes in the law.[20] One group of Russian Orthodox church members visited the degraded ones housed at Squad 6 at St. Petersburg's Yablonevka prison and reported that the prisoners refused anti-itch cream to relieve sores and scaling. The prisoners said the skin problems tended to ward off sexual predators, who feared lice and disease.[21]

Masha Gessen, a Russian lesbian who moved to America when she was fourteen and has since become an international advocate for gay rights in her home country, visited St. Petersburg's dreaded Yablonevka prison, where she asked to see gay men in the "depraved" ward. Even though Gessen had trouble letting her eyes adjust to the darkness and the lack of air, the prisoners said they were treated better than at other prisons because they were separated from the others.[22]

Such contact with an advocate for their cause came later, when society had opened enough for priests and outsiders like Gessen to try to help and when the news had begun to spread beyond homosexual cells that their treatment was as bad as or worse than that of some of the more famous political detainees whose tortures were widely documented in the West. In the stagnant Soviet years, the conspiracy of silence about homosexuality was so widespread that Igor Kon said even in academic journals he could not refer to phallic cults and pederasty in ancient societies. In 1974, he said, he submitted an article called "The Concept of Friendship in Ancient Greece" to a scholars' history magazine, only to be told that when referring to Greek homosexuality, he could say only "those specific relationships."[23]

In the meantime, homosexuality was viewed as a pathology and a crime, a vestige of the bourgeois West, and it was not until about 1987 that glasnost helped air more tolerant views in a variety of popular newspapers and magazines. At first this new surge of publicity helped the gay movement; then it almost destroyed it. One young homosexual named Roman Kalinin decided that glasnost had finally given him the freedom to air his views on sex. If he had stood naked in Red Square, he could not have shocked more Russians.

Kalinin made his mark on the Soviet citizen in 1990 when he gave "the interview," as it became known, to a small Moscow-area paper. The interview, which was quickly picked up by all the major Soviet news organizations, gave a name and voice to a parent's worst fears. His words, in fact, were so detrimental to serious homosexuals trying to promote tolerance that they left many in the fledgling gay movement wondering what Kalinin was really trying to do—open the doors for homosexuals or bring out the storm troopers. Kalinin, who at first denied that he ever gave the interview, later told friends that he talked to the reporter late at night, when everyone was stupefyingly drunk, and that it was all a joke.

The ordinary Russian did not take it as a joke. Here is a part of the interview:

> "I'm not involved with children myself, but the Alliance's [Kalinin's group] position is clear: we want the article on corruption of minors taken out of the criminal code. We are opposed to violence, but if it does take place by mutual consent, this is normal at any age, in any combination of the sexes. Where do they get the children from? They have their own channels: a child costs between 3,000 and 5,000 [rubles]. The pedophile gets the enjoyment he seeks, after all a young child has a beautiful body and soul, it doesn't do anyone any harm. . . ."
>
> "What about dead bodies for necrophiles?"
>
> "No problem either; you get necrophiles working in morgues, in the ambulance service, at cemeteries. Others come to an arrangement with them."[24]

Within days TASS, the party press, and the St. Petersburg television program called *600 Seconds* had picked up details of the interview, which also included a resounding endorsement of sex with animals. Protest movements were organized at factories and offices. Parents were up in arms.

The public outrage, far from slowing down Kalinin's operation, seemed to fire his loftiest ambitions. Within a few months, he had announced his candidacy for president of Russia and began giving out free condoms at metro stops in Moscow. One TASS report, translated into English for Western readers, noted Kalinin was running for president on the Libertine

Party ticket. Later it became clear that he was running as a Libertarian, but either TASS was making a joke, which would be difficult to imagine, or the differences were lost on a Soviet translator.

I tried to interview Kalinin during the brief period of his candidacy, which was clearly little more than a publicity stunt, since at twenty-four he was too young to be included on the ballot. The interview was repeatedly put off, and later I was told that Kalinin had been in the hospital after one of his campaign stops handing out condoms. The details were not available, but an associate explained that Kalinin had been beaten to "near death." What was true at that stage I did not know, but it was not hard to imagine a gang of young Russian workers energized into an instant assault squad by watching Kalinin pass out the silver packets to anyone who reached out a hand. (I was later told that Kalinin had tired of his performance as a candidate for the presidency and had ordered people answering his phone to tell reporters he was in the hospital and unavailable.)

Professor Kon and others have suggested that Kalinin's enemies were legion, and that not all of them came from the conservative antigay side of the political structure. As Kon himself put it in a 1993 essay on sexual minorities: "If Kalinin's purpose was to court popularity at any price, he certainly achieved that. Yet, one is bound to ask whether such notoriety actually improves the status and reputation of gay men and lesbians, and helps them to gain political allies in the fight for civil rights." Many moderates working to decriminalize homosexuality found their path much more difficult when they followed in Kalinin's wake.[25]

Masha Gessen, in a conversation with me in 1994, described Kalinin as "a child," adding that "he did a lot of good things very early on, and I think he has burned out. It was really too much attention for a twenty-four-year-old to handle."

By the time I visited the headquarters for Raduga (Rainbow), which had been formally registered in August 1992 as an organization to combat discrimination and to provide support for homosexuals, Kalinin had been shunted into the background, at least for the time being. Although many psychiatrists outside the cities continued to believe that homosexuality was a form of psychosis, reasoned voices were available finally to combat the real problems for homosexuals—the spreading of AIDS and the acceptance by families that their gay sons or lesbian daughters were not psychotic criminals. Raduga, I was told, was the real center for gay people in Moscow—not the park near the Bolshoi Theatre or a secret disco or an underground passage at a prearranged metro stop, although homosexuals could be found in all those places. It was a safe house where they could meet, not to pair off, although that happened sometimes, but to get help and to discuss their problems.

Raduga headquarters, the first of several in the cities across Russia, was in the MIR building, a long corridor away from the sex clinic or the sex shops. It was narrow room lined with standard metal chairs, the bare walls a bilious green. In this drab place, Dr. Nikolai Oleinikov and others had started Raduga. Dr. Oleinikov, as one of Moscow's few sex therapists, seemed just the sort of person who could help. He was authoritative but comforting, not embarrassed to talk about subjects that were still taboo outside on the streets.

"We felt that our work with gays required higher qualifications for doctors; only sexopathologists can really work with gays at this stage. Gays have their specific sexual problems. Some are similar to those of other people, such as impotency and inability to relate. Now we are treating four lesbians and trying to make them sexually compatible. Two of the four have finished treatment, and I am told they are happy. One couple has had a relationship for eight years, one couple for five years.

"One lesbian couple adopted a child. One decided to give birth to a child," he said.

"Artificial insemination?" I asked. Dr. Oleinikov shook his head, as if the question came from another world. "No, the normal way, with a man," he said, not hearing the irony of his comment.

Lesbianism, although never specifically illegal, was far more widespread than imagined in the old Soviet Union, especially in prisons. In her heartbreaking story of years behind bars for being a Christian, *Gray Is the Color of Hope,* Irina Ratushinskaya describes putting her ear to the utility pipes—the prison's communication system—to hear the keening of women who believed their female lovers in the prisons were being untrue or losing interest.

Prison folklore and some underground or *samizdat* music was full of references to the lesbian culture in the Soviet camps, but the subject was virtually off limits in public discourse before the 1980s. Even in 1991, the first time I ever heard anyone mention lesbianism in Russia was in connection with the city of Ivanovo, a famous textile center which was one of the first in the post-Soviet days to fall on very hard times. Westerners who visited the city were stunned that it was populated mostly by women, and although they still did not talk about their love lives to foreigners, virtually every Russian knew that Ivanovo was a place where the joys of Lesbos went hand in hand with the miseries of factory life. Dr. Mikhail Stern, who published a book called *Sex in the Soviet Union* in 1979, told interviewers that he had been in prison with a man who met his wife in Ivanovo and, after the wedding, found that she had almost no interest in sex. Finally, he asked her why not, and she explained that she liked sex with women. He didn't understand and asked her to explain. She went into the details of how women make love, and the husband, finally catching on, became so enraged that he picked up a flatiron and killed her.[26]

The practice of lesbianism was considered so abnormal that its treatment was often barbaric. In the Soviet medical encyclopedia used by most physicians in the 1960s and 1970s there is no mention of female-to-female sex. In a famous book by A. M. Svyadoshch called *Zhenskaya Seksopatologiya* (Female Sexual Pathology), published in 1974, the endocrinologist recommended that women be treated with a combination of hypnotism and drugs to cure lesbianism. First the patient was given injections of hydrochloric apomorphine and then shown a picture of her lover or lesbians kissing or touching one another. Hydrochloric apomorphine induces vomiting or, in sturdier people, the violent urge to vomit. The association of vomiting and woman-to-woman sex would eventually work, he said.[27] In other cases, women diagnosed as lesbians underwent a regimen of pills, shock therapy, and isolation.[28]

In my years living in Russia, I never met a woman that I knew to be a lesbian. Several found their relations with men constantly souring in ways that both sexes seemed to be at a loss to understand. Others took on what appeared to be old-fashioned roles as schoolmistress and spinster— preordained, it seemed, to slip quickly into old age with its black, shapeless costumes and its rituals of shopping, praying, keeping the young, and carping at the middle-aged. But would they have become open lesbians in another society, or were they simply women who had been discarded into old age? I would never know.

The best-known lesbian in Moscow was Yevgeniya Debryanskaya, and I tried repeatedly to find her in early 1992, shortly after the end of the Soviet system. I would later hear many reasons why she seemed to go underground in those years, at least for a reporter from a big Western newspaper. Still, I would occasionally get word that she had been seen, organizing a movable pub for lesbians or making money dealing cards in the new casinos. The lore about Yevgeniya, or Zhenya, made her all the more intriguing, but it was not until November 1993 that I managed to find her.

Zhenya agreed to talk to me during a break in a literary event at the Central House of Literary Writers in Moscow (once the meeting place for some of the Soviet Union's most talented apologists). The gathering of perhaps five to six hundred people was being held to celebrate a Soviet underground poet and a new homosexual play, now being performed openly and without official persecution. As I climbed the stairs to the concert hall, I passed a wall of photos of the most-honored Soviet writers. Some were in military uniform, their chests laden with medals. Their faces were stern and disapproving, in the Soviet fashion, as the crowd of people they would have considered deviant or criminal paraded freely underneath. Still, the audience of gay people and intellectuals climbed the stairs quietly, none openly mocking the old order that had persecuted them. They also seemed to have none of the flamboyance that could be seen in similar groups in the West. As with Artanov, they were still testing their limits in the new society.

After a poetry reading that barely hinted at homosexuality and a dramatic scene between two males that seemed only vaguely suggestive by New York standards, I searched for Zhenya at the break. I found her sitting on a low overstuffed couch, where she had promised she would be. She was a slim, attractive woman, with a thin, bony face that was relieved only slightly by eye makeup and tiny, diamond-like earrings. A black leather baseball cap was shoved down on her head, the brim almost covering her eyes. Her hair was cut so boyishly close that her ears stood out in a way that seemed unnecessarily jarring, but I thought that she was pretty, a compliment that I feared she would take as an insult. After years of fighting not only the establishment but society, she looked hard, lean, and ready to pounce on any possible slur. Undoubtedly there had been plenty of battles in her past, and I suspected there would be many more.

As we talked, two very husky blond women stood near her, watching me, watching the door, making eye contact with Zhenya every few minutes. At first I thought they were friends or girlfriends, but I soon realized that the two women, both in black outfits, were bodyguards.

Zhenya talked for a while about how long she and others had been working for acceptance. Her male homosexual friends had a change in the law on their side, a frail but important form of progress. For lesbians, the freedoms—to speak out, to publish, to meet—were still enjoyed hesitantly. There were "several hundred" lesbian groups working in the cities across Russia, she said proudly, but they were still nervous about outsiders. It was an anxiety or even fear that was understandable, and I felt it most tangibly when I asked Zhenya about herself, hoping to find out what was lore and what was real about this well-known Moscow activist.

"What about you?" I asked. "When did you know you were lesbian?"

Zhenya grew restless and looked down at her hands as she began to talk, in the vaguest way, about her own life. She had known since she was fifteen that she was gay. Now, at forty, she was working full time at a commercial operation, which she did not identify. Her family "knew for a long time" that she was a lesbian, and her mother "at least knew relations between women are possible, in principle, even though it was probably not all that pleasant for her" to find out that such a possibility existed in her own family.

As I asked these questions, the two women in black drew closer. One offered Zhenya a cigarette. Another gave her a cup of coffee. Neither of them looked at me, but they had a protective way about them that made it clear I was tresspassing onto private territory. After a few more questions that drew little more than shrugs in response, I changed the subject.

Even as she was answering the political questions, Zhenya seemed more frightened than tough. She looked at strangers fleetingly, her eyes only briefly making contact in the manner of one who has been singed many times in human relations. Like many of the people who milled around with her during the break in the program that evening, she seemed more a victim than a powerful force for her cause.

It would take a long time before homosexuals could feel strong enough to be a real political force in their society, like gay people in America. Zhenya's battles were still on a very basic level. The old law that had been repealed had not mentioned lesbians, and the women in psychiatric hospitals were lost in a world where medicine, not law, had control of their fate.

"It is hard to get the homosexuals out of jail now, yes, but it is even harder to get out the lesbians from the hospitals," she had said at one point. "When we contact government or the psychiatric hospitals, they say that they do not possess information, because such information is private, to protect the patients. It's the doctors' secret."

Zhenya and her male colleagues in the gay movement had shifted the focus of their concerns by the mid-1990s. As it became clear that homosexuality would no longer be illegal, gay people moved from trying to change the law, which turned out to be less difficult than they had assumed, to the more difficult task of changing the way people thought about homosexuals. Such conversions could take years, maybe decades, but if Zhenya was concerned about the attitudes of the medical profession, so were some of its own members. "It's the attitude that will be the hardest," Dr. Oleinikov had predicted on the day I saw him at the Raduga center. "After the Soviet [years], more work is needed on such a very basic level." He shook his head, undoubtedly imagining how hard Russia would be to change. "We need to do the kind of work that will allow these people to face society. Recently, we published an interview with the mother of a homosexual, and we got a lot of letters from a lot of mothers. Many of these letters were even compassionate."

The ones that weren't?

He shrugged. The usual. In the period since they had been treating homosexuals for the psychological and even physical distress caused by their status in society, he said, most of their problems had not been with friends, but with their families.

"The families are usually more strict. There may be silent acknowledgment, but many prefer that it stay that way, and in only about fifty percent of cases have we managed to get parents to adapt to the realization that their child is gay. No one wants to acknowledge that there is a stranger in the family."

Dr. Oleinikov had said "stranger," knowing it was a loaded word in

Russian society. An outsider can be treated hospitably, but he is always apart, and there have been eras when strangers, not only from another country but even from the next village, were viewed as forces for evil, responsible for the community's misfortunes or unexplained disasters. In the Soviet years, outsiders, and Westerners in particular, were seen officially as the purveyors of what was wrong with the twentieth century. After a brief period in the latter stages of the Soviet Union when everything non-Soviet seemed preferable to something made or thought or done under the communist rule, Russians by the mid-1990s were already beginning to settle back into their natural state of being wary of outsiders. Being different could be exotic and worthy of fascination in Russia, but it was also alien.

"And of course, it is also evident that the whole Russian culture is heterosexual," Dr. Oleinikov continued that afternoon, "and the control over the individual is still very strict here. Outsiders don't realize how hard it is here to be an individual. Those who do not fit into the mass are still being pushed into it. Relations with children are not easy, even when they are heterosexual. It's easy to realize how difficult it would be if a child is homosexual."

Dr. Nikolai Neparade, a young associate who helped with Raduga clients, broke into the conversation to talk about one of his specialities, the difficulties homosexuals were having with their families. "Sometimes people take changes of behavior in their children as a personal insult. Many can be compassionate with friends, but when they see their own children, they blame themselves and they grow angry."

Dr. Oleinikov, who said he lectured around the country trying to change people's attitudes towards homosexuality, found some success in the attitudes of the young. "Recently we asked two hundred students about their attitude towards homosexuals. Less than five percent wanted them to be eliminated," he said, noting the improvement since the 1989 survey, which had quoted 33 percent of all ages wanting death for gay people.

"But still only thirty percent [of the young] said it was a personal matter," he said.

One aspect that was not entirely personal was the spread of AIDS. Officially it was not considered a major problem in the early 1990s. In my own interviews with the minister of health, Andrei Vorobiev, and Valentin Pokrovsky, the deputy health minister for epidemiology, the two men virtually in charge of controlling AIDS said that the disease was not widespread in Russia and was primarily a scare perpetrated by the media. Vorobiev said in 1992 that there had been thirteen new AIDS cases in Russia, down from eighteen in 1991. By late 1994, the health ministry still only listed 752 HIV-positive cases throughout Russia. At about the same time, the World Health Organization and other agencies were estimating ten thousand to twenty thousand in Russia with the virus.

One of the reasons that the official numbers were low may have been simply that people who feared they had AIDS or HIV stayed away from state-run clinics. The government was known to be testing secretly for AIDS, especially when a young person came in for a blood test for syphilis or gonorrhea. Once the test for HIV was positive, the patient was required to fill out a form from a government agency with a very Soviet-sounding name—the State Committee for Sanitary-Epidemiological Surveillance. The form required anyone who was HIV positive to inform partners and medical personnel about their condition. If they had sex without inform-ing their partner, they could be liable to up to five years in prison. If they infected anyone, the prison sentence could go up to eight years. After a Russian went to *poliklinika* for blood tests, many became suspicious when the nurse called and said the tests needed to be redone. The "broken test tube" too often became a way of getting a patient back into the clinic, not only for more tests but to sign the dreaded government forms.[29] The stories about the transmission of AIDS were the most depressing for people like Kon or Dr. Oleinikov, who had tried even in the earlier years to get the medical establishment to look at the scientific and medical data coming out of the West and to use that data to advise Russians how to remain uninfected.

Some of the warnings about AIDS in Russia had already backfired, giving health officials a wariness about dealing with the issue. In the summer of 1990, 122 children in the southern Russian town of Elista were identified as contracting the AIDS virus from unsterilized needles used in routine hospital inoculations. Medical officials from Russia said that the AIDS virus originated from a Russian soldier who was infected in the Congo. He gave the virus to his wife, who then gave birth to an infected child.

When word got out about the infections, however, the Russian health ministry and medical establishment viewed the problem as a matter of hospital procedure—the unsterilized equipment—not the first warning signs of a sexual plague. Almost nothing was said in larger newspapers and magazines about the ways to combat AIDS—public discussions of safe sex were still virtually taboo. (The story fueled a rising panic among Russian parents about the possible hazards of having their children inoculated against childhood diseases, adding to fears about the poor quality of Soviet vaccines that had been part of several investigative news stories. Health officials later blamed the rise in diseases such as diphtheria on the media, even though increases were undoubtedly also due to deteriorating health and sanitation.)

"We had a chance to do something here," lamented Artanov when I talked to him about AIDS in 1992. "A few years ago, it was very favorable for gays here in that respect. The only positive thing about the Iron Curtain was that it kept out gays from the West. Unfortunately, it also kept out information about safe sex. Two years ago, gays never used condoms. We do our best now to convince people that it is absolutely necessary. Now, I think in a personal relationship, it is only with a condom, it's more normal. Two years ago, it was considered a negative."

If a homosexual tapped into the growing network of magazines, hot lines, and discos that began appearing in the cities, he might know about the need for a condom to fight the sexual plague of the twentieth century. But most people I knew thought condoms were either too expensive—i.e., they came from Europe or Taiwan—or a joke. (On the streets, the word *gondom* was a powerful insult that meant, generally, a useless person, an idiot or jerk.) The average Soviet condom was so thick and unreliable that some men said they wore two, which may not have provided any more protection but certainly ruled out any unnecessary pleasure. At one point, health officials boasted that clinics were giving out condoms free—three a year to males aged fifteen to fifty-five.[30]

In early 1993, the mass media were only beginning to talk about the need for sex education and protection against AIDS and pregnancy, and they were still of little help to homosexuals. Because of state control of media distribution networks in Russia's cities, gay people often could not convince ordinary news kiosks to sell their publications. In Moscow, an alternative distribution network was set up briefly on small card tables in designated metro stops. The system worked until police raided the tables as pornography. Dom Knigi, the elegant bookstore in downtown St. Petersburg, agreed in 1993 to carry one expensive journal about gay life. But the bookshop owners put the journal in the medical section.

Fears about distributing and publishing gay news grew worse after an incident on October 13, 1992, when storm troopers from Pamyat, a rabidly pro-Russian group that is anti-Western and antisemitic, raided the newspaper offices of *Moskovsky Komsomolets*. *MK*, once the newspaper for the young communists, or Komsomol, had become one of Moscow's most lively and adventurous publications. It covered topics like Western music, drugs, AIDS, sex, and homosexuality. The morning after the raid, when *MK* staffers arrived at work, their desks had been ransacked, machines were broken, and leaflets were tossed around the newsroom that said: "All Pederasts and Komsomol Members will soon perish." Pamyat's leaders, who were eventually jailed for the incident, accused the newspaper of "engaging in propaganda of homosexuality and lesbianism." From the gay point of view, this accusation came at a strange time. They saw *MK*'s coverage as sarcastic or heavily ironic when they wrote about homosexual events—a tone that had upset or angered many of Moscow's gay readers.[31]

"The directors at the television network are afraid of violence against the TV station, against correspondents," Dr. Oleinikov said to explain why there had been so little coverage of Raduga. "As a rule, a homosexual here is considered violent and aggressive. There is a fear here that homosexuality also provides a means to express one's own aggressiveness as well."

"Or what Freud calls transference," interjected Dr. Neparade. "When people begin to be afraid, they also transfer aggression to the object they fear," he added. "Also, the stereotype of a homosexual here is one who seduces young boys. In part, gay people themselves contribute to this perception because for the last ten to twenty years the homosexual explained himself to society by saying he was raped or seduced at an early age. If he is an adult and still practicing, a normal reaction here is, 'How long will you continue to seduce our children?' "

"When people begin to understand [about homosexuals], the public aggression will diminish," said Dr. Oleinikov. "It is in part fear of the unknown."

A few years later, television in the cities would have interviews with gay people, whose sexuality was legal as long as force or a minor was not involved. One later program on Russian homosexuality, which identified two gay men at a Moscow "blue" beach, resulted in both of them being identified by coworkers and family. Both were forced to quit their jobs.[32] The open discussions about gay men and lesbians may have vented some of the old passions that had been kept hidden for decades, but they also ignited Russians who saw homosexuality as a form of depravity, a disease. Because this freedom came with democratic movement, with the new market economy, with the end of the Soviet state, for some Russians they were all part of a Western conspiracy. One Moscow psychiatrist, a man known for opposing the repressive nature of Soviet psychiatry, decided in early 1994 that gay liberation had gone too far. In an article now famous in gay circles, Mikhail Buyanov wrote that homosexuality was alien to Russia and that it had spread in recent years with American and British ideology.[33]

During most of my interview that afternoon with Dr. Oleinikov, a phone rang plaintively in the corner. The bell had been turned down as far as possible, so that it was a gentle tinkling sound that did not interrupt so much as it gave the feeling that I was holding up the center's business. When I asked, Dr. Oleinikov apologized for the interruption.

"We have a hot line," he said, nodding to the phone in the corner. "But we need someone to answer it. We started to look into this possibility because too many young people came to us in a crisis of homosexuality. It's especially hard here for someone, when they have had their first love, usually a man with his first woman, and they have been rejected and insulted as too small or too inadequate. It becomes a very serious problem, so we decided to create this center."

As it came time for me to go, I wanted to know whether Dr. Oleinikov had a personal understanding of the pain suffered by homosexuals in Soviet society. I asked in English whether he started Raduga because he is a homosexual, but the male translator accompanying me that day changed the question in a surprising way. In Russian, he asked, "Why did you start Raduga?" There was a momentary silence, and Dr. Oleinikov must have wondered why such a question would come, long after he had already answered it. So I interrupted, and asked him again myself, this time in Russian. "Are you a homosexual, and is this why you are working here?"

"No, I am not a homosexual," answered Dr. Oleinikov, smiling as he realized how a Russian man and an American woman would view my question from such separate cultures. "But it was still possible to understand the depth of these problems," he added as he escorted us to the door.

Later I asked the translator why he had balked at asking Dr. Oleinikov if he were a homosexual. "It wasn't necessary," he said, his tone indicating that the very idea of such a question would be rude or impertinent to the esteemed doctor. "It was clear he wasn't a homosexual."

The remark should not have surprised me as much as it did, given the fact that to call a man a homosexual or even a "hunchback" homosexual would still invite a fight in the streets of Moscow. But even after almost two hours listening to reasons why homosexuality was not a blight on the human character, this cosmopolitan Russian male's views had remained the same. Homosexual was still an insult, a dirty word.

8

Lessons for the Young

In this country, it's better not to plan.
> —Maxim, a twenty-three-year old street
> merchant in Moscow[1]

The sign outside Detsky Sad (Kindergarten) No. 1179 in downtown Moscow was freshly painted in the fall of 1992, not by an exuberant child but by some hurried adult. Waiting to meet a parent of one of the children in this kindergarten, I studied the paint oozing onto the walls and wondered if there were some larger philosophical excuse for not staying within the lines of the appointed task. Perhaps it was that any precision—a straight edge, a mitered corner—was a symbol of pettiness, of a soul overly restricted by little rules and tiny details, much like the rigid Soviet catechism that had been taught for decades at the school beyond the new steel door. The time was 10:20 A.M., my appointment set for 10 A.M. to meet the person who would introduce me to the kindergarten's director. The November sun was breaking over the tops of surrounding apartments, making its appearance briefly in the snow-covered courtyard. As I surveyed the rusted children's playground, the door sprang open suddenly behind me and in two perfect rows, out marched a small army of four-year-olds, each in a thick coat, hat, scarf, mittens, and grubby winter boots. I had heard mothers complaining that it took so long to dress three dozen kindergarten kids that by the time the last ones were in full outfit, the first were sweating profusely, which made them easy targets for the colds or grippe that had already begun working their way into the city for the winter. Ten-forty-five. The parent had forgotten. Feeling a little like a voyeur whose presence would bring out some stern woman with her besom to shoo me away, I decided to go into the building and at least get an idea of what a kindergarten looked like in the post-Soviet era.

Inside, the kindergarten was warm; the comforting smell of cabbage soup and frying cutlets gave promise of something hearty for lunch. My footsteps echoing on the tile floor alerted someone above, and a door swung open noisily. Out stormed a woman with a hawklike face who padded in her *tapochki* to the stair railing and glared menacingly at the intruders. For an instant, my companion in this adventure, Slava Zelenin, was rendered childlike under her gaze. He apologized, lowering his eyes as he explained who we were and what we would like to do. She knew nothing about this visit, she said sharply. Her mouth pursed, her eyebrows raised, she looked at one of us then the other, as if to make us confess who had started a fistfight in the playground. We persisted; I brought out a business card. Finally, she swept us into her office, sat us down, and offered us the prime token for adult visitors in this era—instant coffee.

Valentina Stepanovna Popova had been running Detsky Sad No. 1179 for twenty-two years. When I met her that morning, she was an aged fifty-three-year-old with gray tousled hair and sharp, craggy features that softened only slightly when she smiled over us in the narrow storeroom that doubled as her office. Before she poured coffee, she opened a locked compartment on the wall and drew out one of several sacks of sugar in plastic bags, treasure made safe against the pilfering of one of Russia's perpetually understocked commodities. After she had settled us in our chairs and given us the luxuriously sweet coffee, she excused herself a moment, and we could hear her padding down the short hall. The clicking of heels announced her return, and she was wearing a full array of lipstick, powder, rouge, and bright blue eye liner. Properly dressed, Valentina Stepanovna then took us on a tour.

Most of the children were still outside when we climbed the narrow stairs to the top floor. In a large room, newly painted a warm beige and filled with light, sat ten students. They had new desks, new toys, and a nice new rug. This was the Lycee, Valentina Stepanovna explained. The Lycee was the paid kindergarten. A private group had leased the top, and best, floor of her school that summer, had redecorated it, hired a teacher from downstairs, and had begun charging a whopping $4 a month, a steep fee for most parents and one that would rise precipitously in the years ahead.

Downstairs, in the section funded the old way, by the government and a local factory, was shabbier. The paint was peeling from lockers, and the toys were well worn. A sleeping area, tiny hand-painted beds crammed into a room that brought to mind the tiny sleeping loft for Disney's seven dwarfs, was clean and well kept (a nap from one to three was a standard part of *detsky sad* regimen). But the group here was twice the size of the one upstairs.

The detsky sad had been a constant source of complaint for many mothers in the Soviet years: "Every mother cried when she left her child there," my friend Masha Ryzhak said, shuddering as she remembered working at one kindergarten to ward off the beatings and abuse that landed on any boisterous child. "They are horrible places, just horrible." But in the new Russia, any day care seemed destined to become a luxury. The state continued to pay grants to public kindergartens and to provide them basic foods, but such support could not keep up with the needs of each institution, and it was up to the principal or head of the school to find a way to pay for continuing in business. Some did it better than others. Valentina Stepanovna was at least surviving.

"There is no money for new toys this year," Valentina explained that day about the regular kindergarten. The Lycee would not begin paying rent until a few months later, and then, perhaps, the money would go for extras downstairs.

As she took us through the rest of the school, Valentina boasted about the cook, who had been there for ten years and who served the same food upstairs and down. And she was so proud of her kindergarten that her only grandson, Maxim, was going here this year, she said.

"Which kindergarten?" I asked as we left.

She cocked her head at such a question.

"The Lycee," she answered, looking faintly embarrassed.

* * *

As I talked to young people and wandered through their schools as the Soviet state changed into the new Russia—privileged English schools, technical schools, and even a cooking school, where the teachers were forced to use plastic food for demonstrations because real food was too expensive—this kindergarten became a basic symbol for me of what was happening to the youth of Russia and the system set up to guide them into adulthood. The schools, the teachers, the parents, and the young people were, in a word, schizophrenic, with one foot in the old way and one in the new. The institutions and the individuals struggled to adapt while their society of equals was being rapidly divided into rich and poor, paid and unpaid. Values like "the group" or "the community" were being replaced with an individualism that sounded blatantly selfish and opportunistic to the old ear. Money, never a way of determining status, began to matter. It was like a chorus: *Naoborot. Naoborot. Naoborot.* Turn it over, they meant. On the contrary, Grandfather. It is the opposite of what you said, Professor. The child was the father of the man.

As the educational system tried desperately to adapt itself to the up-heaval in society, schools like Valentina's kindergarten survived by allowing private and public to exist side by side. It was not an unusual method for keeping an institution going in the early 1990s, and there was something communal and familiar about letting the rich help pay for the poor. High schools and special schools (as well as many other institutions like hospitals) had begun offering services for pay to help fund the services that once were free. The paid services were almost always better, more luxurious, better equipped, less painful. Some principals insisted that the education was the same, paid or unpaid, and that the students with money bought only extracurricular activities, but it was impossible to believe at that point, even for those who were trying to sell it.

The larger issue, of course, was not what education cost but how it succeeded in preparing young people for their lives. Some students simply deserted the stern disciplinarians in the schools, opting instead for the hard lessons of the streets. Some stayed, continuing to believe that a good education would give them a better chance in any version of their world. But the relationship of Russia's young to previous generations had reversed overnight, and the young became not only the teachers, but in some cases the providers. Most of the young people I would talk to in these years lived with aging and increasingly impoverished parents who, for all their poverty, still had an apartment and knew the backdoor routes to cheap food and supplies. If the young were in school or had gone into the army, the whole family lived on what seemed like nothing. If they were working in the new shops or enterprises, these children often made more than the adults who cared for them. The best young ones helped provide for the household; others simply disappeared into the chaos.

Data about the young—little of it good news—poured out of the bureaucracies and into the media. Suicide rates had risen among youths, jumping 18 percent in 1992 overall, and increasing dramatically among those between the ages of fifteen and nineteen. *Izvestia* reported that the increase was due to drug and alcohol use.[2]

Rabochaya Tribuna, the workers' paper, featured a poll in 1993 that said one in seven young people was ready to break the law to get money. Specifically they would try, or had already tried, prostitution, money laundering, or simple theft. The writers noted that 70 percent of those polled "approved of the desire to make easy money" and it was only in "the bucolic countryside that [the youth] still defies this ugly outlook, with less than 50 percent sharing these lusty ambitions."[3]

The Soviet schools had been among the best in the world for teaching children to read, write, and understand basic math. The system, well documented elsewhere by many fine scholars, was so rigorously controlled that across the eleven time zones of the Soviet Union, children would be studying the same chapters during the same week in school. There are many examples of how this automated education system worked; many of how it failed. One artist who was employed by the Soviet schools outside Moscow was chastised because he tried to teach children how to paint *matrioshkas*—the classic Russian nesting dolls—during a week when the curriculum guide made it clear they were supposed to be learning to draw animals.

Parents often said that above all, the schools taught their children how to exist in a society that demanded obedience, creating a group mentality that required children to help one another and report on one another. One Russian woman told me that she counseled her children every evening about what they could say and not say in school. "Never, never talk about what has happened at home," she had said, fearing that a slip about some book being read or friend visiting could have caused problems. Girls learned to be little disciplinarians. Little boys, whose mothers may have allowed them every license at home, had to become tiny mute soldiers at school. The imprint had been made early on Russia's children, and I was often reminded of the story that Russian journalist Pavel Felgenhauer told about a visit to a city that had been closed previously to all but a few Soviet military experts and their families. Reform, still in its infancy in Moscow schools in the early 1990s, had not reached this city, and when the visitors toured a local school, one of their stops was a fourth-grade classroom. As the strangers moved to the back of the room, the children stared straight ahead. There was no giggling or gawking.

The teacher began, "You may now turn around and look at the visitors."

The class turned in unison.

"That's enough," the teacher said in about a minute.

Like a tiny drill team, the ten-year-olds turned their heads again, eyes front.

By the time I began to look at the youths and their schools, teachers were losing authority as they tried desperately to learn enough to stay at the head of the class. One thoughtful educator explained the problem for those trying to guide Russia's 19 million undergraduate students. Teachers, some of them masters in the intensely difficult catechism of Marx and Lenin, were now buried under an avalanche of reading matter that had been outlawed under the old system.

"Because of this lopsided and ugly system we had, people are only now reading books they should have read long ago—Freud, religious books, some Western literature," said Evgeny Yamburg, principal of an experimental school on the southern edge of Moscow. "They are confused now. They don't have time to digest it all, yet in a short period we have to master what most people do in a lifetime," he said.

If a teacher is twenty-five, it is possible, he explained. "If you're two years short of retirement, it's a tragedy," said Yamburg, shaking his head.

* * *

The division between the rigid and the adaptable, the rich and the poor, the successful and the failures, showed itself most dramatically in the way the young were educated in these early years of the new, capitalist Russia. Public schools grew more crowded, with most schools forced to have large classes of students coming in two shifts per day. Textbooks, many rendered out of date by the events that these children had witnesses firsthand, were in short supply. Some teachers simply kept teaching what they had always taught. In early 1994, students were still being asked in one quiz, "What do you do if the enemy attacks using biological weapons?" The correct answer was "Defume and quarantine." The question was asked by a teacher who viewed the changes as destructive to Russia's society and used the word "democrat" in his classes as an insult.[4]

At the same time, private schools were flourishing in the cities, with an estimated 640,000 private academies established in the country by early 1994. These new lycees included church schools, business institutes, and general education institutions of the kind that operated for the wealthy elsewhere in the world. Moscow alone had over 160 private institutions, including some that cost about $12,000 a year and provided not only handsome facilities, decent education, and a swimming pool but also security guards to protect the children of the Russian rich from being harassed or kidnapped. St. Petersburg's array of private schools included a school of manners, where modern Russian youngsters learned nineteenth-century etiquette, including table manners and ballroom dancing. The students, who paid about $360 to attend the 1993–94 school year, often wore period costumes to city concerts. Teenage girls floated through the academy halls like princesses, and their head matron addressed them quietly and politely as "fair maidens."[5]

The experiments in new schools, however, were not all successful. One Moscow establishment decided that since academia was in a slump—with full professors near poverty—these experts could be used at private academies. The young would hear the best physicists, the best experts on literature, the best musical historians. It sounded far better than it was, and experienced teachers and troubled parents virtually abandoned the idea a few years later.

I watched one early effort by a Russian and an American, an "advanced English" institute which was called the Soviet-Anglo-American School. The school directors rented space from a local high school in one of Moscow's better academic areas, but in most cases, the SAAS classes were held late in the day, often when students were tired from a full range of classes and activities at their regular school. Still, the Soviet-Anglo-American School lured some of the city's better Russian students briefly during 1991–92. By 1993, parents had begun to take their children out of the school when it became apparent that the Americans imported for the school were simply students or recent graduates who had answered ads in college newspapers. Most had little or no experience in teaching, and one parent told of a young American who spent most of the crucial classroom time reading newspaper articles out loud in English, more for his own edification than for the children.

Some parents sent their young to schools that, for all their promise of luxury and academic achievement, had no license or accreditiation. Only about 11 percent of Moscow's private schools were accredited in late 1994. Other children began at a private school, only to have rates raised so precipitously that the parents were forced to send their children back to state institutions. The Russian newspapers were also full of stories about renegade private schools that took money and handed out diplomas "made of nothing but paper," as one Russian woman put it. I tried to find one such school, which had advertised learning as a visual matter best done with movies and videos, but even with the help of several astute Russian friends, I could never locate it.

To Russians who had become very demanding of their education system, it did not take long for the glamour of the private school to wear off. If the worry was that the private schools would destroy the public school system, it was not happening immediately, and President Yeltsin had at least made pronouncements that the state would keep giving money to the public schools. These schools still had to find extra funds—rallying parents' groups for fund-raisers as most PTAs do in America. But the public system was also helped by increasing dissatisfaction with the full-time private schools.

One incident served for me as a classic example. A Russian woman, a member of the old intelligentsia class, told me that she had put her son in one of Moscow's top private schools as the public school system seemed incapable of adjusting to the rules of Russia's new society. The experiment had lasted about a year, and when she took him out of the school (which by 1995 cost $500 a month), he was trailing behind the other children in the public school classes. Age five, he could read well enough, but he could barely write, she said, embarrassed by what she saw as a doubly costly mistake. Also, there was another reason, she added, one that may have had even more weight than the money or the academics. "He was being taught by homosexuals," she said, shaking her head in horror. "I could not have that."

My own experience with one of Moscow's first private academies was better than that, in part because *Dom Stankevicha,* as it was called, was designed not to replace the state schools so much as to complement them. *Dom Stankevicha* was housed in an elegant prerevolutionary mansion in the middle of Moscow, and in the early 1990s, it provided some of the city's brightest students with extra training in Western literature, culture, and languages. One of the school's American teachers offered an inside look at this transitional school as well as an outsider's view of what the Soviet education system had done to its students.

Sarah Wieben was age thirty when I first heard her talking about Soviet education in late 1991. She was an energetic woman, a heavyset Midwesterner with a deep romantic attachment to Russia that ebbed and flowed like any tempestuous love affair. On the day I met her, she and her Moscow academy were near divorce. First, Sarah could not tolerate how the administrators yelled at the students, belittling and demeaning them to their faces in ways that most Americans would reserve for an offending umpire a hundred yards away. Second, the students cheated.

"The first time I realized it was when I asked them to write about something they had read. Three students turned in the same theme—I mean exactly the same, word for word, mistake for mistake. I was stunned and said, 'What is this?' They couldn't understand what was wrong with it," she said.

"We're not talking about bad kids here. These are the top of the line. I explained it again and again, and they all say, in effect, 'So what? I cheated. No one else is going to hold it against me except this crazy American teacher.'

"Asked to explain why, they say obtuse things, starting with, 'What is the problem here? This helps everybody. The whole class gets ahead.' And they told me that in many cases, the teacher sees cheating and just looks the other way. Perhaps it is accepted that a lot of what they had to learn was garbage or that if the kids fail, it's the school's fault. But what happened was that they lose the ability to differentiate between what is important to learn and what they can cheat around.

"We are taught that change is natural, a good thing." Sarah fumed. "They are taught that any variation is dangerous or bad." Far from the Socratic method, Sarah found that her students did not want to discuss their ideas or argue themes of the literature or culture she was teaching. "They want you to tell them what to say about it," she said.

Russian acquaintances chuckled when I relayed Sarah's experience. Cheating the teachers was a necessary lesson if one were to grow up understanding how to manipulate the Soviet system. Teachers always knew who was bright and who wasn't, even if the whole class moved along together, and a battery of exams determined who was accepted to college (the exam was an especially terrifying rite of passage for young boys, whose failure meant a barbaric tour in the Russian military).

One particularly savvy Russian I knew, Masha Lipman, explained the code, the basis of which was that it was considered a grave offense not to help a friend.

"First of all, the word is a little different," Masha said. "The Russian is *spisyvat*—which means not to cheat, but more precisely to copy. It is a much more innocent word in Russian than in English."

A math whiz, Masha remembered sitting in the front row in class, and when friends would go to the blackboard, she would slowly edge her chair forward to get within whispering distance of them. To make it less obvious, the other students on the row would move with her. After a while, the teacher would say, "All right, you in the first row, all stand up and move your desks back."

The teacher would make a pretense of punishing Masha. With a grade system ranging from zero to five, she would give Masha a one but would write the one in such a way that afterward, it could be changed easily to a four. Many other teachers simply accepted this moral code of students helping students (and undoubtedly gave Masha the fives she deserved).

By contrast, one young woman I knew in Moscow, Katya Reznichenko, recalled studying in the early 1990s in Connecticut, where one of her strongest impressions was how badly the American students cheated. "I came out of an exam one day, and there was one of the students from my class asking me for the questions," she said. "She seemed startled that I would not give them to her, but it was our final exam.

"In our community, if you promise on your own personal honor that you will not cheat, then you won't. Otherwise, you will," Katya told me as I sat in her parents' apartment, where she lived in 1993. "But this matter is different here than there. Our society is based on the principle of community. It was, at least. Now, it is changing."

Other Russian colleagues told about taking exams or writing papers for the lesser intellects in their class, understanding that the value of friendship was far greater than any respect for the system. "If someone asked you to help and you said, 'No, I abide by the law,' you would be regarded as an outcast," one graduate of the Soviet system explained.

Could a school teach morality? Some did, adding pronouncements from the Russian Orthodox church or from other religions to combat what one young woman called "a new flatness" of the soul. But the larger question was how educators would prepare the young for a world that they, as adults, could not understand. What subjects would a child need to succeed in a time of chaos?

By late 1992, as the schools were losing their control and educators were talking earnestly about how young people were missing their chances to be educated, learning instead only the dark lessons of the streets and the trading that some called *biznes* and others called crime.

On the day I visited Sarah Wieben's school, her students sat in a semicircle and began to discuss their new society. Some looked to Sarah for guidance. Others, like Natalia Kholina, had their own strong views. Natalia announced in precise and excellent English that she did not look kindly on the new market economy that had invaded her country.

"I wouldn't like to be a businesswoman," she began. "I went two months to a school of business, and I didn't like it. I became very nervous when I couldn't sell something. Once I remember we had a business game, but most of it was very dull."

Natalia was the daughter of Moscow intellectuals, and she seemed to carry herself with a self-assuredness that was unusual for someone her age in the West. At one point she appeared to conclude what others seemed to be feeling privately—that they had been trained for a higher order than mere trading. "Most of my friends are humanitarians," Natalia said proudly. "They don't want to be businessmen."

For an educational institution that had once been an advanced school to train professional Communist party functionaries, the academy on Gottwald Street in downtown Moscow had a particularly shabby look by 1995. Gottwald had once drawn party leaders from around the world to study Marxist-Leninist philosophy, literature, and economics. The Higher Party School had been ousted after the August 1991 coup and restructured as a university for humanities, literature, and business. Now, there were holes in the stone facade where the old party sign had been pried from the wall, and the doors looked warped and untended, the glass covered with dust and hand prints that once would have been buffed away every few hours.

The school's official title was the Russian State Humanities University, but it was known among the young I met there not so much for its literature and humanities departments as for its less strenuous computer and business schools. There were better business schools in Moscow but this one provided a modicum of marketing along with a way to stay out of the army.

On the day I visited, the students were taking exams, and I watched them from across the street for a few moments before the traffic allowed me to cross. They did not act like students who were anxious about the tests going on inside. No one was studying. No one was cramming in the last fact, jotting the last idea for an essay. They milled. They smoked. They whispered in cool little clusters. A group of girls compared fingernails, and one circle of boys stood pawing the ground like anxious young bulls.

My first effort to talk with the boys was not particularly successful. I approached a young man in a double-breasted sports coat who looked from a distance like someone headed for a corporate vice presidency at the very least. But as I grew close, the business executive suddenly turned into a frightened young man. He kept his eyes down as I tried to ask him questions, and when I turned to ask a question to another boy standing beside him, two youths rushed up to the sports coat and drew him away with a force that did not look altogether friendly. The three of them then sat huddled on a cement fence, and when I looked their way occasionally, the two seemed to be giving the boy a stern lecture. I imagined that they were warning him about the danger of talking to anyone, especially such an obvious stranger.

Such warnings apparently did not bother another young man, who surveyed the small disturbance I had started and then ambled up to introduce himself. "Andrei," he said, hand out in American fashion. Andrei wore a maroon double-breasted sports coat, businessman's slacks, and brogans. Even with one more year of university, he already had the weary look of a metropolitan adult.

Andrei was practicing a form of business on the streets—probably using methods that his teachers warned were illegal and dangerous. He had two cars, he said, and the business—well, it was "straight business." A friend of his would later amend that to be "part legal, part illegal like everybody else." When Andrei was asked what he sold, he said, "mostly food." Asked again whether he worked in a kiosk, he grimaced at such a thought. "We *deliver* to kiosks," he said, obviously making a grand distinction.

With two cars, a suit of clothes for an ordinary school day that would cost a judge's three-month salary, Andrei was already doing well financially. So why was he in this school? School was to "know more, to get further up the line" in a company, he said. The street trade was for the young who would never go anywhere else, and at some point, he acknowledged, he would be thirty. Maybe even middle-aged. By then, he hoped to be rich, like the people who could glide through Moscow in long white limousines, with a car or two of bodyguards riding nearby for protection.

It seemed an understandable reason for staying in school, until later, when Andrei began talking about his parents. They were Russians who had been living in Grozny until Chechnya became a war zone. His father was a retired army man, and the family had returned to Moscow and relative safety.

Andrei shook his head at the idea of military duty. "Not for me," he said quietly. Young men who were drafted faced the possibilities of disease, starvation, a deadly form of hazing, and, now, the perils of a dirty war in the Caucasus. "I'll do whatever is necessary to stay out of the army," he said. "Ah," I said, finally making the connection, "like stay in school?" Andrei smiled. It was one way to avoid the draft that was legal and beneficial at the same time.

A friend of Andrei's, who would not give even his first name and who said he went to another school, stood by with a car radio under his arm. He listened to Andrei and nodded, often making grand philosophical statements about why to avoid the draft, why crime had invaded his country, why the young knew more than the old. "You have a car?" I interrupted at one point. I had seen several young men carrying their radios and wondered if this was some teenage fad or whether they actually had cars to go with them. "Of course," he said, surprised at the question.

The car was necessary, not so much for racing through the streets or pursuing girls as for business. It was part of a life that sounded as hectic and bloodless as the schedule for a commodities exchange broker in the United States. These young men were deadly serious about their work, and they were focused on a life's goal that seemed immediately within reach. Fun was in the budget, on the calendar. Andrei's idea of a good time, for example, was to go to a club or disco. Once every two weeks. "It's on the schedule," his friend said, not smiling.

The friend also said that they drank, of course, but they were not drunks. And drugs were too time consuming—"You'd have to be a complete fool now to do it," Andrei's friend said. Their hunger for money, felt with little residual Soviet guilt, had become their drug of choice. If they were not killed before they graduated, I thought, they could be very very rich.

As we stood talking, a cracking noise suddenly echoed against a building and a dark Volvo sped past, its shaded windows open only enough to see the top of a blond head. We looked to see if anyone had been eliminated, and then decided that the noise was not another gangland slaying but a firecracker. Andrei smiled. Perhaps among the junior *mafiya* it was a favorite joke.

"We are not the real students, the best students," Andrei's nameless friend said. "You should go inside and talk to the botanists." The "botanists" were the misfits I had seen walking past these groups of young entrepreneurs. They were still wearing lumpy Soviet clothes or cheap new Western outfits that mimicked the styles of the rich. The botanists were good students who attended on full scholarship. They came to this school primarily to study, not merely to avoid the draft or make contacts. Rodion, a rosy-faced youth well into his second year at the computer and information section, clearly fit the image. When I grabbed him to talk, he smiled brightly like a young person with little to hide. Rodion wore a matching blue jeans outfit that had a leisure-suit quality about it, and over his arm he carried a new backpack, one of Moscow's many imitations of the American trailblazer look. He received sixty thousand rubles a month (about $12) as his student's stipend, and with his parents' support, it was enough, he said. Still, his goal was to be a successful banker, although he seemed far too innocent for such a dangerous profession in the new Russia. As he left, Rodion managed not to see the looks of disdain from his classmates, and I suspected that over the years he had adopted this foggy exterior to filter out such teenage abuse.

The botanists, even ones like Rodion who dreamed of being bankers, were not the students who made the old party school into a new phenomenon. What gave the humanities university its sense of promise was the group of young businessmen like Andrei preening outside the door that afternoon as if someone had already stamped the words "future millionaire" on their foreheads. While their sisters, parents, and grandparents were losing ground, these new business boys were among the society's winners. The chaos and the upheaval that had forced everyone to learn how to operate from scratch gave an advantage to the young. Andrei and his friends clearly planned to use it.

As the possibilities for education expanded for some young people, many others believed that their schools were not teaching them the necessary skills to exist in the new Russia. Thousands of young people left or skipped their classes in favor of the hard but lucrative life on the streets. As they moved from being restless students to apprentice street merchants, many of Russia's young found a brutal world where money reigned, criminals muscled out the weakest competitors, and the future was nothing to think seriously about.

In late 1992, I went to the Arbat in Moscow, constructed as a Soviet showplace, a model street designed to demonstrate how the Soviets could have cafés and little shops, quaint lampposts, and well-tended sidewalks, just like those in London and Paris. A year after the end of the Soviet state, the Arbat had become one of the city's most active bazaars, where tourists and Russians could buy dollars, rubles, drugs, and, of course, souvenirs. It was here that a fast-talking, fast-moving crowd tried to be at the crest of a money wave that had the power to make them rich or wash them down the gutters of the free-market economy. The Arbat had by this time become a maze of rickety tables jammed so close together that it was increasingly difficult for potential customers to walk from one side of the market to another. The buyer had to weave cautiously through the aisles, careful not to dislodge the mounds of fur hats, military gear, Russian shawls, overly bright paintings of St. Basil's, birch bark ornaments, wooden toys, black laminated boxes, and *matrioshka*s of snow maidens or Soviet leaders or the world's latest political superstars. The city government would eventually rout the table trade as too uncontrolled and too visible. But on the cold October day I visited, it was still an open market like many in Russia, a tiny fiefdom ruled by its own cruel laws.

An early sleet had suddenly begun layering the displays of goods, rendering sable hats instantly sodden, their fluff turning to peaks of watered fur. Slush decorated military medals on another table, and the young salesman was trying in vain to clean up enough to appeal to the rare browser. What was most strange to an outsider, of course, was that these young merchants stayed when there were almost no customers. Russian weather was not going to scare off a Russian, they boasted to me later. Napoleon, Hitler—the alien had never recognized the Russian's power to overcome cold. Also, they added quietly, their bosses would not let them leave.

Pavel, who like all of these boys refused to give his last name, had the perfect face for his job. At nineteen, he looked clean and innocent, his teeth slightly crooked in a way that gave him a mischievous and alluring look when he smiled.

"I attended the Moscow Law Institute, but I quit after a year. I didn't find it interesting," he said, shrugging his shoulders in the all-purpose gesture of dismissal. Other jobs also were deemed inadequate. Either people were too rude or the pay was too low.

"So now I sell *matrioshka*s from 11 A.M. to 5 P.M., then I go home. I live in the apartment with my mother," he said.

It did not work to stretch the mind and become a lawyer, he explained. The money was better on the street. The previous day, "not a good day," he had made the equivalent of a doctor's monthly salary. On a good day, he earned double. Most of his money was spent, he said, on his hobby—going to bars with girls. He chatted amiably about them, in a nice, overly cheerful tone that disappeared instantly as soon as it was clear I wasn't going to buy anything.

"Ach," he groaned, shaking his icy fingers. "This is an awful life. I want to move to Great Britain next year. I have some friends there. One of my girlfriends is working in a supermarket in the middle of America. Where, I don't know. It doesn't matter. Detroit, maybe. Do you know if it is possible for me to get a job in a supermarket there, in Detroit?

"It is everybody's dream to go now," he explained. "If I go to Great Britain, I will never come back. This fucking shit. It's crazy."

While we talked, a thick middle-aged man wearing sunglasses stared at us from an automobile about twenty yards away. Pavel pretended to show me a *matrioshka* and explained that this was the "tax collector," the man you paid in order to work. Then he nodded at a policeman loitering under a building nearby. The police watched a sale—this was supposed to be an "exhibition of Russian wares," not a market, they said—and when it was over, the officer took from five hundred to one thousand rubles per day. We stood quietly, listening to the ice sliding along the rooftops and slapping against the sheets of plastic covering the tables nearby.

Elsewhere around the cities, the system worked much the same way, and estimates of those selling on the streets were impossible to find or difficult to believe. Pavel and most of his friends were officially at school. Others had not registered as unemployed, and some were simply runaways, lost, undocumented kids. One particularly miserable-looking group was the young teenagers who began selling gasoline on the streets of Moscow so that drivers would be able to avoid the gas lines that appeared each time there were rumors of a price increase. For every one hundred rubles they earned, they paid twenty rubles to the collectors. In one case the collector was a seventeen-year-old, who then paid most of his earnings to the true dons—gang members whose leaders were in their forties and fifties. The dangers of not paying quickly were obvious to those trying out the gas trade. Dr. Shamil Buranov of Moscow's Hospital No. 29 said in the spring of 1992 that each night his emergency staff ministered to about fifteen badly beaten youths age seventeen to twenty-one, sometimes even younger. When the physicians asked what happened, the kids said they fell down the stairs or shot themselves with guns accidentally.[6]

The street hardens children quickly, and like Pavel, the young Russians began to believe in little more than survival. "I was religious for a while," Pavel had offered that cold day as a covey of religious believers in saffron robes and woolen hats scuffled past his tiny shop. "But after my grandfather died, I thought, 'If there is a God, he is an unjust God.' " He shook his head when I asked how his grandfather died, saying only, "I believe now in myself and in love. In this world, there is not much else.

"I think about what I want here. I dream about it. I really want to be a rebel. I want to wear a black jacket and drive a Harley-Davidson and join a motorcycle gang," he said as he pranced from foot to foot in the cold. Shuffling feet did not work for me. I was shuddering in the icy rain, and Pavel took his hand out of his pocket to shake mine in a proper Western good-bye. The icy hand in my glove was stiff from the cold, like an old man's.

"Where are your gloves?" I asked, suddenly sounding like one of the babushkas whose prime job, it often seemed, was critiquing the way the nation's young dress for winter. "In my pocket," he said sheepishly. "It's hard to sell in gloves."

The girls on the Arbat that day would not talk to me. Natasha, age seventeen, was the only one who would answer questions, but they were the responses of someone terrified to speak outside her salesgirl's routine. Her head down, a gesture meant to dissuade me from continuing, she mumbled her age and a name, almost certainly not her own. "I do nothing," she said sullenly. "I just work here, almost every day." She went to the eighth form, had a boyfriend, and lived with her mother, with no father around since she was seven.

As I talked to Natasha, or rather to the top of Natasha's head, a cluster of boys moved around me. They had given up selling, it appeared, and had come closer to ask questions and answer them, to boast and to toy with this stranger, and, of course, to make certain Natasha was okay. I talked with them while my friend Lyuba Aratieva listened to their asides, knowing that they would be saying one thing and quietly talking to one another in a street slang I would not understand. After we left, Lyuba reported that most of them had simply feared that their bosses or police "guardians" were listening, or that would I tell the authorities. They finally decided I was relatively safe after one of them pocketed a business card from me. He stored it carefully in a way that I suddenly thought would make it possible for Eleanor Randolph of *The Washington Post* to appear later in some different human form, probably asking for press seats at one of Moscow's new all-night bistros.

We had been standing outside the Lyubava Café when I invited them inside for coffee. They waved some sign at their keepers and hurried through the door. Once we were inside, the harried-looking waiter grumbled at us: no coffee allowed without food. But he let us stay in the warmth for a while.

After a few minutes of relief from the sleet, the young merchants began to chatter like the teenagers they were. They lived with their parents, often a single mother. They chased girls, never worrying about the consequences if they caught them. The talk lasted more than an hour as we stretched out a time that was warm for them and enlightening for me. Rather than dissect it, I will try to give some of the flavor of the exchange, which was full of banter and laughter and undoubtedly more truthful than any of us had expected when we met a few hours earlier.

Anton was nineteen, handsome, and dark, his light Western jacket keeping him fashionable but certainly far from warm. He was the kind of boy whose smile was slow and sensual. It was undoubtedly good for seductions of all varieties, including street sales. "I live with my momma. If I like it I will stay. I have my life; she has her life. We are in two rooms, and it is crowded, but I prefer to live with her because . . ." He paused.

"Because of your stomach," interjected a friend from the sidelines.

"Yes," said Anton sheepishly. "She cooks well, and I like it because, well, I had a girlfriend until the day before yesterday. She was fun, but I had problems with her mother."

The friends laughed.

"Her mother wanted me to marry her. Now." He smiled, making it clear that the girl was pregnant. "But kids, those small pretty little things. No, I do not want them until I am a man."

As we talked, another youth circled. On the second lap, I stopped him. He was nineteen years old and said he was called Alex. "The racketeer," one friend called him, and he had the manner, not of a racketeer in the Western sense, but of a smart-ass newcomer to an executive trainee program. He had short brown hair and soft brown eyes. A lady-killer.

"I know about marriage," he said confidently. His compatriots nodded for reinforcement. "I know about divorce."

A year ago Alex got married, he said; twelve months later, he was divorced. "She wasn't happy with the way I make money. She wanted me to have a full-time job."

Now he was a hard-currency-exchange boy. Like the others, he had gone back to the free sex, the street drugs, and illicit riches on the street.

"Let me explain," offered Maxim, who stood in front of the others and suddenly exhaled his views in a way that seemed like a confession. "Everything here, *everything*, is at a low, wild level. When sex happens, it happens in a wild way here. AIDS is not a worry as in the West. There is some advertising for it, but nobody pays attention to it. We won't worry until it affects someone we know."

I asked if they knew anyone with AIDS. They all said they did not. In the West, I offered, young people have to think about this all the time.

"You people should take better care of yourselves," said Aleksei, laughing.

In the other marketplaces, young merchants had explained the need for something extra to pass the hours. The favorite in 1992 was *travka,* or marijuana, but the more adventurous were trying cocaine, heroin, and something called *vint,* a mixture of iodine, a kind of cold medicine, and phosphate water.[7] Outside I had smelled marijuana, and I knew the word for it in Russian, so I asked, not about drugs in general, but about *travka,* the weed.

Maxim, the oldest, spoke first. "No. That's terrible. Terrible stuff," he said, shaking his head scornfully.

The others looked at him, then at me, and began to laugh.

"It depends on what kind," offered Aleksei. "I take drugs. No injections, of course, but I have a lot of friends who do. I take cheap grass."

I had never heard of cheap grass, so I asked him what it was.

"It comes from beautiful red flowers that grow here in the summer and all year in the south. We smoke it." I looked at this boy who was talking so bravely and found myself stifling a maternal lecture about what opium does to people.

The opium boy, Aleksei, came from a good home, he said. He lived in a large apartment with his parents and grandmother. He also rented a one-room apartment with a friend. His father was a military man, his mother a doctor, and he said that in the future he wanted to be "a software programmer. I want knowledge of marketing. I think this is a good beginning."

Grand plans for the future versus the day's tempting platter of drugs, girls, and money. These were the two basic instincts at war in this round-faced youth. Smart, well connected, and dangerously arrogant on this afternoon, Aleksei clearly believed he could have it all, and I yearned to see him again in two years, ten years, but he would not give me his last name.

The nineteen-year-old Alex, the divorcé, was smiling at all this talk of sex, drugs, and undocumented cash. Then he leaned over toward me—he was very tall—and whispered in English: "It's very difficult without drugs on the Arbat."

Alex had argued that in contrast to other places where youngsters found work, the Arbat was safe. "I worked at the Intourist Hotel a few years ago. Currency. Bought and sold. My girlfriend, then wife, she said it was much more dangerous for me there. She said, 'They will kill you. I will be a widow at nineteen.'

"I want to move to the West," said Alex. The States, Belgium, Holland. "I don't live well here. I want to go there."

"But there you would have to work," said Max dismissively.

"I'm not afraid," said Alex, smiling. "I would not be afraid to do work, even work that was legal."

Nine months after I visited these youths, I tried to call them. One after another, the numbers were wrong, the voices at the end of the line either irritable Russians or the abrupt operator's recording that chastises you for dialing ineptly. I went back to their market, but the Arbat was empty. It had

been cleared by police a few months earlier because it had become impossible for clients to walk through the maze of tables and because the drug
trade had become an important sideline, drawing with it the underworld
characters whose deadly traffic was heroin, cocaine, and other illegal
seductions for a new, untapped market. It was now a walkway for Russia's
tourists. I asked a young woman where the schoolboy merchants had gone,
and she spat a curse on them. "In prison or in the grave," she said. Probably
in one or maybe even two cases, it was true. Others, I suspected, were at
other street bazaars or they were among the young people who could be
seen in Moscow in the mid-1990s driving BMWs and Land Rovers and
wearing watches that cost a cabinet minister's annual salary.

Russia's young had little guidance about how to act or how to survive in the
new society after communism. On the streets and in the new businesses,
their parents' experience counted for little: their education was too often
out of date. A top degree that meant stability and privilege in the past often
earned little respect from the wild new entrepreneur. He was looking
instead for a new kind of worker untainted by the old Soviet enterprises,
which encouraged sloth and tolerated a certain amount of pilfering by the
employees.

As a result, the better jobs went mostly to the young—those who were
strong, able, willing, malleable, and cheap. Some of these young people
quickly drowned in the new freedoms their instant money could buy—
drugs, sex, clothes, Western cars, the vast array of things that had been
impossible to own or even to imagine only a few years earlier. The best of
them brought home money to take care of their stunned parents or
grandparents who were suddenly out of work and unable to adapt. In
short, the burdens of adulthood rested early on their shoulders, and the
young became Russia's new providers.

9

Suffering for Culture: A Ballerina

When I see Swan Lake, *I forget that we don't have enough to eat.*

—Teacher at MAKHU (the Bolshoi's ballet
school), 1992

"If I see Swan Lake, *I think the communists are back in power.*
—Response from Moscow teacher
Lyudmila Melekhova[1]

Aﾠs we arrived in Russia for the winter of 1991, Soviet culture was deteriorating into its inevitable finale. The structures were still alive, with their once-lofty names and their elegant buildings—the big, pink Bolshoi crumbling on Moscow's central square; the Central House of Writers, with its books and wood paneling; the Mosfilm industry, which seemed to spread its Soviet-style Hollywood over a park-sized area of Moscow; the Conservatory, with its ghosts of musical genius; the art supply houses, where paints sold for kopecks; the publishers, who still put out collections of poems and art books that cost the consumer little more than a loaf of bread.

The state that had supported and strangled the arts was steadily decreasing its rations to the hungry old culture giants. Like most Westerners, we hoped that freedom from the Kremlin would bring an explosion of creativity around the country, allowing new voices to be heard, new ideas aired. Instead, the chaos unleashed artists who seemed more confused than energized by the possibilities around them. They had adapted to the controls—either by creatively resisting the state or by peacefully producing for an all-powerful patron. Now they appeared stunned, like subterranean beings suddenly thrust into the sunlight.

What added to, or reinforced, this shock of liberty was that culture suddenly began to collide with commerce. In one of the many ironies of the era, the people's artists learned that the only way to make up budget losses was to appeal to the lowly masses, who often had a vastly different idea of culture. Publishing houses that had once printed thousands of thick books by writers who were paid by the word were suddenly stalled into silence, while those who pirated an old Jacqueline Susann or a new Jeffrey Archer grew instantly rich. Talented artists often painted tourist souvenirs to sell on the streets and sold their valuable works abroad (even though technically it was illegal to export a work of art). Musicians faced the world-market price of a violin or a piano—instruments that had been virtually free in earlier days. And finally, Russian ballet, an expensive art form that had survived in both tsarist and communist Russia, began to suffer from lack of funds—the totalitarianism of the U.S.S.R. being traded for the "despotism of the dollar," as some Russians called it.

In the first draught of freedom, culture had stalled in midair, and it was during this strange interim that I began to know a Russian ballerina, Masha Ivanova, and her family. Masha was not a star at the Bolshoi, to her despair; and, to her relief, she was not a member of some distant Siberian dancing troupe. M. Ivanova was a principal dancer at the Stanislavsky and Nemirovich Danchenko Musical Theatre in Moscow, and for me she offered a glimpse into the cruel and once-secret world of Soviet ballet, as well as a lesson in the unseemly scramble that followed it.

When the padded steel door to Irina Mikhailovna Ivanova's two-room apartment had been firmly bolted against the dirt and ugliness of the Soviet streets, new visitors like me often stood silently for a moment, reverently entering a tiny museum for Russian antiques and the once-illicit memories that went with them. Irina had invited me one winter evening in 1991 to talk about her daughter, Masha. Irina and her mother, called Babushka by her adoring family, led me into their miniature salon near Moscow's Oktyabrskaya metro, savoring the effect it had on someone who had long tired of seeing the dreary, plasticine Soviet furniture, the homes laden with thick ceramic lamps, the cheap wall mirrors, and rangy plants yearning for a few hours of direct sunlight.

In this flat, large pieces of furniture meant for grand drawing rooms with high ceilings were crammed into every corner, set against every wall. A harpsichord stretched over most of the tiny entranceway, and in the cramped sitting room, oversized paintings in their elegant prerevolutionary frames were tilted away from the walls so that we could sit comfortably under a roof of pastoral artwork. In an ancient cupboard of a warm rosewood color that comes only with love and age, tsarist teacups preserved and probably hidden for decades were now stacked openly for visitors to admire. The grandmother brought them out and asked me which one I would like for my tea. I chose a blue-and-white one with a faint line of gold along the lip of the cup and the rim of the saucer. Even filled with tea, it felt like an eggshell in my hand.

Masha, who was at the theater that evening preparing for a production of *Giselle,* reigned in silence, from the pile of black scrapbooks on a nearby table to the satiny pink pointe shoes in the corner of a bookcase. Her haughty ballerina's gaze bore down on us in an unsettling way from photographs on the piano. She seemed to be overseeing her family's discussions about the privileged life of a Soviet ballerina, at first about the pride and the honor, and later, about how she had been "ravaged" by the Bolshoi ballet school and had struggled for a decade to overcome "the best ballet training in the world."

My friend Svetlana Makurenkova, who introduced me to the Ivanovas after I had asked about the changes in the ballet world in the last years of communism, was not certain that they would talk about the school. To return to Masha's graduation ten years earlier from the Bolshoi school would open old wounds, and so, we began slowly, analyzing the sad state of culture in the world, the troubles in the marketplace, and the family pride in the grandmother's beauty as a young girl. From her place at the table, Babushka coquettishly handed over an aged black-and-white photograph.

Now, in her seventies, she curled over the lace tablecloth in the posture of old age. In her twenties, she had been a proud beauty, her hair pulled back carelessly to highlight the large green eyes and high cheekbones that had left a trail of swooning young soldiers.

Finally Masha's mother sighed, glanced at Babushka, and then softly touched my hand. "I want to talk about this," she said. "I want you to know what happened. It was Masha's tragedy, her personal tragedy. Eight years she worked so hard at the school, and she endured such abuse. One terrible teacher called her 'horse face.' How I hated them, but I kept quiet because she was the best. She was always the best; she was the one chosen to dance *Coppelia* in the school performances. She was the star of her class.

"Once, when she was getting ready to go onstage for a school performance, she was playing *Coppelia,* she just happened to turn her pointe shoe upside down and a shard of glass came out of it." Irina paused a moment to catch her breath. Then she began again, almost in a whisper. "Someone had put it there to cripple her for life. They were all jealous of her. They were desperate to get rid of her."

"They managed it somehow," Grandmother said quietly.

The details of how Masha had been the top student at the Bolshoi's ballet school but had, on graduation, been rejected by the Bolshoi Theatre came out slowly that evening, over tea, fish salads, and sweet, doughy cake. In 1981, it was still the era of Leonid Brezhnev's stagnation, and the Bolshoi meant something close to luxury for its chosen artists, not only apartments, privileges, and decent medical care, but the right to go abroad to show the world the power of Soviet culture. When the day arrived for the competition to become one of the elite three hundred dancers in the Bolshoi Theatre dance troupe, all sixty-seven graduates were competing against one another. Normally one or two were chosen from the school after the year-end competitions, but that year, the Bolshoi Theatre chose thirteen students, including Georgian Nina Ananiashvili, who went on to become a Bolshoi superstar. If they had selected only one, as they did in some years, it would be understandable, or at least tolerable, but how, with thirteen, they asked themselves, could they have overlooked Masha?

"We tried to find out why. The women at the school, they loved her, she was so nice to them, they cried for her," Masha's mother said, her own eyes brimming with tears. "Much later we learned that Grigorovich [Yuri

Grigorovich, the director of the Bolshoi from 1964 until he 'resigned' in 1995] had said that Masha would ruin the line of the corps de ballet. But at that time, we had no explanations.

"They said her *form* had changed." "Form" was a word that referred not to technique but to a dancer's body. As they grow into adulthood, these young talents change. Sometimes there are "accidents of nature," as the teachers say. The neck is too short. The feet are too long. Irina Mikhailovna did not elaborate, but it was the world of ballet that made such things important—not only in Russia but everywhere the art was practiced.

"Oh, she suffered so," the grandmother said, remembering the despair of her eighteen-year-old granddaughter a decade earlier.

"She was so bright, so cheerful before," Masha's mother added, "and then, after, she could not even walk past the Bolshoi for a long, long time."

At the end of the evening, as my friend Svetlana and I were putting on our coats in the darkened hallway, I saw a small futonlike cot under the harpsichord. When Irina Mikhailovna noticed me peering at the makeshift bedding, she nodded. "I sleep under there sometimes," she smiled. When I looked concerned, she shook her head and reminded me that for someone like her, who teaches music and lives music, it is better to sleep with music. "No, no, for me it's a nice place to be."

I had told them that I hoped to meet Masha and to watch her dance, that I wanted to follow a dancer or group of dancers through the tumultuous changes of the 1990s. But in some ways after this evening, I did not wish to go to the theater where she would be appearing soon in *Giselle* as Mirtha, the queen of the spirit world. I suspected that there was a problem with Masha's body or looks or style that a mother and grandmother could never see or at least never accept.

Several months later, when I finally saw the production of *Giselle* at the Stanislavsky, it was clear what was wrong. Masha would indeed spoil the corps de ballet. She was a little taller than the regulars on the Bolshoi chorus line, where the preference was for small, fragile-looking dancers, and her form was less sylph than Circe. There were curves where the Bolshoi preferred a taut, almost boyish body in its ballerinas. When she danced she looked like a woman, not a will-o'-the-wisp. Still, Masha commanded attention each time she leapt, walked, or even stood on the stage. She had the aura, the excitement, of a self-made principal, not one of the troupe. I yearned to meet her the same way the young want to meet a movie hero or television personality. A Russian ballerina, even one who did not work at the Bolshoi, was still a very glamorous person.

One of the most important aspects of this disorderly era was that people like Masha would talk openly about their jobs and their lives, grousing and complaining about their superiors in a way that would have been suicidal a decade earlier. The horrors of the Bolshoi ballet school, the political chicanery that gave some dancers better roles than others regardless of their real talent, the bribes, the fear of brutality—none of it would have been mentioned to a foreigner in the old days, except by those over the border.

Now Masha and her friends were free to debate the values of the two systems they knew—the staid old Soviets versus the tawdry new *Kapitalisty*. The old tyrannical order preserved classical Russian ballet, and some said the preservation was more like petrifaction into lifeless but technically perfect performances (one critic compared the Bolshoi to a still-sleeping beauty).[2] Still, it was vastly superior to the avalanche of mindless sub-cultural entertainment that came streaming into Russia from the West after end of the Soviet state. What was better—a staid *Swan Lake* at the Bolshoi or a snappy *Field of Miracles,* as the Russians called their version of *Wheel of Fortune?* What was preferable—a politically rigged ballet system or a commercial company of dancers who took any trip West, no matter how trivial, to make money?

For some of Masha's friends, the great and famous sopranos, sculptors, artists, architects, prima ballerinas, composers, and poets, the way out of Russia's difficulties was easy: they simply left the country. They packed their bags, sold their furniture and their apartments and their tiny automobiles, and departed for the West, waving their international reputations at the border guards and receiving acclaim elsewhere in the world. But for those like Masha who were not stars but who were well regarded among Moscow's stern society of ballet critics, leaving Russia would bring too little money to make up for a loss of country, home, family, and stature. Because she stayed, Masha and her colleagues gave me a glimpse of what happened in "purgatory," as they called the chaotic interim that came after the old protective order disappeared and before a new one had replaced it.

I had arrived in Russia with the deep respect for ballet that comes from years of painful classes, each an embarrassing struggle to pirouette gracefully or keep the feet aimed outward or simply drape a hand in the air like a true ballerina. In those years, even to see ballet in distant Russia seemed an impossibility. As a result, very shortly after we arrived in Moscow, I took my daughter to see her first ballet ever, *Swan Lake,* at the Bolshoi Theatre. We had students' seats, as it turned out, and from our spot close to the Bolshoi's ceiling with its lofty Muses caressing their harps and lyres, we could look down at the arrow-straight parts in the dancers' hair as they whirled and leaped almost, it seemed, underneath us. Still, the magic reached even the cheap kopeck seats. My five-year-old daughter, Victoria, stared at the prince and the peasant girl gliding across the stage while I whispered to her what was happening. Finally she turned to me and gasped in alarm. "Mommy?" she asked, putting her tiny hand to my cheek. "Are you crying?" It was the first time I would explain to her that sometimes people cry not when they are hurt or angry, but when something is agonizingly beautiful.

My own reactions paled, however, in comparison to those of the Russians I would see in other ballet audiences over the next few years. They cried, they shouted, they swooned, they glared angrily at some flaw or excess that only a true balletomane could understand. Over time, I began to realize that the Russians have a depth of feeling about classical dance that is both proprietary and visceral. On a good night, a performance had been known to unite a Russian crowd, workers and intelligentsia, new democratic right, old Soviet left, into one rapturous animal. Its rhythmic cries of approval would thunder through the hall as dancers took bow after bow, their elegant arms gathering roses and carnations brought to the stage or thrown from admirers in the aisles.

To see this audience made it hard to believe that the Russians did not, in fact, invent ballet. Instead, they imported it from Europe in the 1700s, and then they took command of it, nurturing it, giving it life and passion, and, in the last analysis, allowing "this hothouse flower," as the Bolsheviks had called it, to survive in their cold and brutal country. As the late Arnold

Haskell, director of the Royal Ballet School in London, once explained, "In one sense, all ballet is Russian, for without Russia, something called ballet or more appropriately, 'toe dancing' might have lingered on in reviews or musicals, something as inane and vulgar as the plump plastic doll won in the fairground hoopla."[3]

Once performed by serf theaters for the Russian nobility, ballet became an obedient servant to the Communist Party for most of this century. The Soviet leadership became involved in the grand designs of the theater as well as the smallest details of the ballet world: The Central Committee, whose mission was control of the state and obedience of its citizens, once issued a notice to prima ballerina Marina Semyonova to lose weight. She was growing too chubby for her waifish parts, the powers in the Kremlin decreed.[4] Other changes in the nation's cultural world were more serious. Andrei Zhdanov, Stalin's brutal censor who launched campaigns of vilification against some artists and sent others to prison, enforced the idea of socialist realism that required positive heroes and politically acceptable villains who danced to simple music created by obedient composers. Strange rhythms and dissonance were not allowed, just as there could be no hint of sex, no introspection, no real agony of the soul.

Giselle, thought to be too mystical, was made more acceptable when the cross on her grave was replaced with a humble comrade's tombstone. *Swan Lake,* too beloved to be scrapped, was given a new, upbeat ending in the later Soviet years, so that the swan and her prince survived, able to walk gracefully back into what Stalin had once labeled "the better world" of communism.[5]

Soviet ballet, like the Soviet expertise in the Olympics, was part of the pride of the state, and ballet stars, especially at the Bolshoi, often lived in a comfortable but controlled existence. A staff of twenty-five hundred people provided for the Bolshoi's every need, from ballet slippers to medical care to apartments in the best section of Moscow. Most important of all, the better ballet dancers, the students as well as the adults, were fed the best food available: proteins and vegetables, instead of the bread, fatty meat, and potatoes that served for much of the population.

In many ways Russia's classical dancers had not progressed very far from their imprisonment on the landowners' estates. The great Bolshoi dancer Maya Plisetskaya, who moved to Europe shortly after Gorbachev opened the borders, once talked about the "serf theaters," not of the tsarist days, but of the communist ballet system.[6] "Everything was based on slavery and fear. Rebellious slaves ran away (Baryshnikov, Nureyev, to name a few). Everything was forbidden. It was forbidden to dance new ballets, to invite new choreographers. I managed to direct a few ballets but with great pain and fighting."

By the 1990s, the pain and fighting were not caused by the bullying state authorities. The ballet world's efforts were now focused on ways to find the money to perform. Some Russian dancers, nostalgic for the Brezhnev days, began to remember one of the old Soviet ballet themes—the idea that artists in the Soviet Union were secure; in the West, they were starving. Before the 1990s these stories seemed as unlikely as a girl turning into a swan. The famous *Lost Illusions* was one ballet that depicted an artist in France being destroyed by the capitalists. Other Soviet ballets told the stories of young ballerinas being forced to strip in dance halls to survive. In most cases, these artists were restored their dignity when they returned to the Soviet state or were saved by Russian soldiers.[7] By the mid-1990s, some struggling dancers and artists could hear the echoes of Lenin's famous question to artists and writers: "Are you free from your bourgeois public, which demands pornography from you?"

For someone like Masha Ivanova, who was not a big name in the West and not able to command a huge fee for a few star performances, the new order meant hours spent with booking agents, spare time used not to practice or to dream but to peddle her talents in the world market. It had been simpler before—what the Stanislavsky theater did, she did. But now each individual or each couple (she toured in this period with her then husband, Stanislavsky dancer Andrei Glazshneyder) had to be a small business. Like most mom-and-pop operations anywhere in the world, these two dancers were so busy that their lives made an American's look calm and sedate. I saw Masha for fleeting moments over an eight-month period. Once, after a performance, she shook hands and said "hello" in proud English. Another time, at a social occasion, she signed a pair of ballet shoes for my daughter. Before she autographed the satin shoes, ragged by Western standards but still beautiful to any clumsy fan like me, she put one of them on her worn-looking foot and stood for an instant in a grand arabesque. "What joy," she whispered rapturously before she came down to earth and presented me with the slippers.

For a serious talk, however, it took months. She was out of the country. She was out of the city. She was locked in rehearsals, then back on the road to Europe, to Japan, to the United States. I had the image of someone always leaping, jetéing, at breakneck speed through the cultural centers of the world. When she finally agreed on a time to meet in late 1992, she offered a gentle warning. I had to be at the back door of the Stanislavsky Theater at exactly 9:50 A.M. if I wanted to watch her in class before the interview. Classes started at 10 A.M., she said, and she could not wait for me.

I waited in the cold, 9:50, 9:55, 10 A.M., when suddenly, from across a back alley, I saw her, not walking but not quite running, with that elegant grace that signals a ballerina, this one in a fox fur coat and black knitted hood. She grabbed my arm and we hurried through the back corridors of the Stanislavsky, a beautiful old structure, its massive outer hallway curved along the edge of the theater. On that morning, it was dark and silent, as if full of sad ghosts from the grand era when dancers performed while the Germans were preparing to invade the city in 1941. The smell was old and stale, musty from upholstery that had been worn decades beyond its time. We rushed up the stairs, past columns and elegant gilded curlicues faded in the gloom. Finally we reached a bright corner room, where faces and lithe young bodies that I recognized from the Stanislavsky stage were warming up in the cold. The classroom had a high ceiling, and the walls were a light apricot color. Yellow-green curtains, once lavish if not beautiful, were gray with dust. Tattered ballet bags sat under an ebony piano, where a handsome dark-haired man with blue eyes sat playing and, oddly, chewing gum. American gum had appeared suddenly in the street kiosks, and veteran smokers like this one had learned the placebo effect of Wrigley's.

A tall handsome student with dark eyes sprinkled the unwaxed wooden floors with water to keep the dancers from slipping. He wore a black sweater and jogging pants. Everything from the waist down was filthy, and his shoes were almost transparent, as though they had melted into his feet. There were nine students at first, all wearing very Western, very worn-looking warm-up gear. One student was practicing in a long warm-up cloak with little patches in bright Russian colors. Was this cloak an old

good-luck piece carefully patched by his grandmother or a carefully calculated look of disarray? He checked himself every few seconds in the mirror,
the feet, the posture, the cloak. Later a tiny, older ballerina arrived, outfitted in a creamy white wool sweater that stretched from chin to ankle.
Unlike her young colleagues, her dress was cleaned to perfection—an
example, I was told later, of how some traditional Soviet ballerinas had
preferred to appear, even at a rehearsal.

As the class chattered, their teacher arrived. It was 10:25 A.M., and as he
said good morning, he was greeted with a chorus of gentle whistles and
raspberries. He laughed. He was late, he explained, because his underground subway train took forty-five minutes instead of the usual twenty.
The class bayed in mock sympathy, but we all knew the problems with the
Moscow subway. The rate had risen that day from one ruble per ride to
three, the second increase in six months. At my stop, they would not take a
three-ruble note, only a new plastic *zheton*, or token. The line for *zhetons*
was almost out the door, and I could hear two trains stopping and then
whizzing past as I waited. The system, faced with another adjustment to the
market economy, had trembled and shuddered, leaving most of Moscow
with a good excuse for being late to work.

Masha had begun to disrobe. Her leotard was an iridescent turquoise,
with a black plastic warm-up suit that stretched from under the arms to the
ankles, presumably to help lose weight. She was obviously the teacher's
favorite. She did everything well, with great energy and enthusiasm. Her
long neck, held always so proudly, made her seem suspended in the air, and
her arms moved in soft waves to the music.

After the lesson, which closed with kisses for the teacher and a nuzzle
for her husband, we sat outside in the dark corridor to talk. There was no
heat that early in the day, and the corridor was damp and cold. Masha
dismissed the idea of a chill with a Russian's pride, but I knew she had just
come from an hour workout. I put my down parka around her, and she
took the offer graciously, making the old army green coat somehow
instantly fashionable. As we talked about her trips abroad, she pulled the
coat around her, conscious of the cold. As everywhere in Russia during the
first year after Soviet rule, the topic of conversation was how to make
money, how to survive.

Life here for a star of the Stanislavsky theater was better than most, but still not enough to support two people and their parents, she said. "There was a short period in early 1991, about one and a half months, when the prices were still low and the salaries went up to four hundred rubles [$80] a month each. My mother at the time was making three hundred rubles [$60] a month. It was the first time we could live on our salary for the whole month."

Now, in December 1992, she and Andrei each made ten thousand rubles (less than $20) a month. "We can't live on it. We must go abroad to work." She shook her head. "It is a misfortune. Not terrible, like someone close to you dying, but unpleasant."

An earlier package tour to America had brought Masha and Andrei about $1,600 for two weeks when they danced in Wilmington, North Carolina; Boise, Idaho; California, Pennsylvania; and El Paso, Texas. Chicago, the big stop on the tour, had been canceled for reasons that were never adequately explained to her and Andrei.

"It was a nice trip, but the main problem was that the entrepreneur is an operator," she said, using a word that, from her, was an insult. Artists were not supposed to care *only* about money, and this self-styled producer of ballets in the West had been taking a huge cut of the profits earned by the dancers. "For an impresario he is too greedy and too money crazed," she said, shrugging her shoulders as if that was what the new Russia meant. She had received less than $400 per appearance for dancing at night and sleeping by day on buses, rehearsing on warped and even dangerous floors, and scrambling in the afternoons to see at least something of the places where they landed.

"The first time I went to America was last year, and no matter how often I'm invited, I will go," she said. "It is still a mysterious country to me. Although, I would not want to live there. I cannot understand what it is, but there is such a drastic difference between our two countries. I can't understand it, even though I try. What is it?" She smiled and laughed at a question far too large for the time we had that morning. Then she looked down at her hands and continued.

"Our debts, we expected them to be paid with a trip planned for London in March with a good company. For artists, it is very important whom you dance with. In many cases, the people are very unpleasant. People I had to work with on other tours were very unpleasant. In London we would have danced with other professionals, worked with professionals.

"But, yesterday, they called and told me the contract will not take place," she said, explaining why she seemed distracted and down. It would be the first hint that the Soviet-trained dancer was no longer an exotic creature in the West. The dwindling interest was a problem not only for people like Masha, whose trips to Europe and Japan became less regular with every season, but also for the vaunted Bolshoi as well. The Bolshoi's grand tour to London was canceled in 1994 after ticket sales dwindled to levels that were widely described as "humiliating."[8]

"My husband is an optimist," Masha continued. " 'Soon we will find other work,' he says, 'don't worry. As long as we are together, we will pay off our debts. There will be other trips.' " She shrugged. "I don't know."

I had just seen Andrei with his fellow ballet students, and besides his reputation as an excellent and spirited dancer, he seemed to be someone who made people smile when he came into the room. At the end of the session, when Andrei and Masha had whispered to each other in the back of the hall like two young lovers, I thought about all the women whose husbands had faded into angry hopeless people, human shells who had left their spirit somewhere, in school, at work, in the streets, these men who drank and beat their wives and spent their money on schoolgirls. She was lucky, I thought. Masha seemed to read my mind.

"We spend a lot of time at home now. It is nice," Masha said, "with Andrei. I am very lucky. My husband never says, 'that's your job, and that's mine.' I am *very* lucky." She laughed in her deep husky voice, which made others around her smile, even though they could not hear what she was saying.

"We have to have an apartment," Masha said. "We have to sleep; we have to eat. Also, I have to earn my money to help pay for our new apartment—$15,000 we bought it for, but this is not so terrible. If we are not able to pay it off, we will sell it and it will be profitable. Oh, maybe for $40,000."

Masha shook her head, barely dislodging a strand of brown hair that had been slicked back into a severe bun at the nape of her neck. They were dancers, not entrepreneurs, she said. They were not trained to think too deeply about money, only art.

When I had mentioned the idea that most Russian dancers wanted to leave Russia now, Masha did not agree. In the West, there is more money but not so much love of ballet, she explained. "I am not like diplomatic wives—yearning for black bread or crying for the birch trees—but I just want always to come back," she said.

In many ways the Russian dancer—like the poet, the writer, the very Russian artist—saw the vast territory beyond the border as a place with more wealth than culture. It was only in Russia where they felt there were the real critics with eyes that missed nothing.

I was curious about how Masha survived in the new Russia but I was also interested in her past at MAKHU, the Bolshoi ballet school that her mother and grandmother had remembered with such bitterness. It was a period in her life that she now could talk about openly without fear of serious repercussions within the Russian dance world. The school still had its reputation as a breeding ground for skilled ballet dancers, even though by the mid-1990s critics had begun to say openly that the dancers were too mechanical—their virtuosity bordering not on ballet so much as sport. "They could teach a table leg to dance," Masha's mother had told me a few years earlier, and she had later explained that such a skill was not so much the school's strength as its weakness.

Masha began her interest in ballet as a child, she said, and her family, with its ties to the Russian intelligentsia, had taken her to the theater, the ballet, the cultural events that dominated Soviet Moscow. At age ten, young Masha managed to win a spot at the Bolshoi school, gaining a position that was coveted by hundreds of young girls and their families across the U.S.S.R.

When we began talking about the school, technically called the Moscow Academic and Choreographic School, Masha seemed to transform herself before my eyes from a confident star into a nervous young woman. Her straight back curved into something close to a slouch, and she took a cigarette from a passing friend for support.

"Earlier, it was a place where talented small children would go to school. I cannot say when, but at a certain time, it changed. In 1973, when I entered, it was already a top school for elite children." Masha used the word "elite" in a way that meant privileged, the ones whose connection to power made life infinitely easier. "From time to time, there were a few let in like Andrei and me who were not famous and not well connected, ordinary people with some talent."

She paused, thinking how to say it concisely. "The school was not a very nice place. I don't go there anymore because I have a lot of unpleasant memories."

She sat and waited for specific questions, willing to be polite but not anxious to dig around in a painful time. Someone brought her a glass of warm tea and she offered to share it. I told Masha that I was trying to meet the director of the school, Sofya Nikolayevna Golovkina, who was said to control MAKHU like a Soviet despot. Masha smiled and rolled her eyes.

"The worst thing that she did, because of her strong will and strong character and because she always wanted to be at the center, was that she made many of the best teachers leave the school. It did not happen in one day, one hour, but over a while.

"A really good school is supposed to have a good atmosphere. But the feeling is"—she struggled for a word—"that the school has become rotten, a garbage dump [pomoika]. Of course, it was not only this school; everything in the U.S.S.R. was that way. Sofya Nikolayevna is cunning and smart. She would surround herself with top people—she was the good friend of Brezhnev's wife and the culture minister. The granddaughter of culture minister Ekaterina Furtseva (who also served as the Kremlin's cultural censor) was there at the school, but as soon as Furtseva was no longer minister, she dismissed the girl."

Like others, Masha listed the granddaughters of Gromyko, Gorbachev, and Andropov as those whose talent was as great as their connections and who had studied at the school as a result. "I come from intelligent, honorable people. None of my family would kill or rob, but we had to be operators, like everyone. But I was like a white crow [an outsider, a black sheep] in school because I would pretend not to understand what was happening around me.

"At one concert, when I was Coppelia, I started to put on my stocking to dance, and there was a razor blade inside it." Her mother had said shards of glass were in her shoe, I told her. She shook her head. No, she corrected, it was a razor blade. "Those things happen in any theater, but how were children taught to do that? I have no doubt that Sofya Nikolayevna has ruined so many children, her arms are up to here in blood." Masha reached down in an imaginary vat and then pulled her strong arms upward, as if to allow the blood to run down over her body. She shuddered and pulled the coat around her.

"My husband didn't see too much of that. It was somewhat easier for boys; there were fewer of them, and so they were more valued by the ballet establishment. Usually there were two times the number of girls than boys, and many of the girls were dismissed—for many reasons, it could happen so easily." She shook her head at memories of friends who disappeared one day and returned to dreary lives in the industrial cities of the south or Siberia. "The real problem for the school was that the children were ruined morally. There were cases when they were forced to take special pills to lose weight, and then after that they were not very healthy.

"The doctor's checkup," Masha continued. "We dreaded them; they came every four or five months. It was not only to make certain they are healthy but to be sure that their bodies are turning into ballerinas. If you are too fat, too tall, too ungainly, it is over, good-bye, pack your things. Unless you had political clout. Of course."

Masha's face had grown taut with anger. Her eyes darted toward people passing by, and she talked very quickly, as if to expel her impressions, to get rid of them so that she could return as rapidly as possible to the jokes and the stories about the ballet.

"She is very despotic, a political prostitute. In a different system, she would not be a director. But will she be replaced? Only if there is drastic political change. Or her death."

Masha's story was not unusual, as I was told later by those who watched Olympic gold medalists or heroes of the Soviet space program suffer many of the same difficulties. Once the goal was established, in this case to be the best dancers in the world, no human problem could stand in the way. These children were being sacrificed—their health, their mental welfare—to the Soviet ballet world. The ten-year-olds who entered the school complex came out, for better or worse, as dancers eight years later. Not to dance—or even not to dance at the Bolshoi—stamped the Bolshoi school student as a failure (Even though some, like Irek Mukhamedov, graduated and went elsewhere before returning to star at the Bolshoi Theatre). The Bolshoi school, with its long list of ballet star graduates and its tsarina-director, Golovkina, had many admirers, but it was not until the era of glasnost and especially the end of the Soviet Union that outsiders were allowed to look closely at what was happening to these student dancers as human beings.

To understand Masha's disappointment and bitterness, to determine whether it was much different from the heartbreak suffered by hundreds of young dancers every year who fail to make the big ballet companies in the West, I felt that I needed to go back to the school. I wanted to see a little of this ballet terrarium where Masha had learned her formidable skills and to meet the director who could make dancers like Masha shiver in disgust and anger a full decade after their graduation.

The ultimate reason for the existence of the Bolshoi school was to feed the most famous ballet theater in the world. The Bolshoi Theatre was first constructed in 1780 as the Petrovsky Theatre. It burned in 1805, was rebuilt by 1824, and burned again in 1853, when the structure that could be seen in 1995 was erected, using parts of the older building that had survived the last fire.[9] After World War II, the Soviets made the Bolshoi the official ballet showplace of their society, thus downgrading the Kirov in St. Petersburg (by then called Leningrad), which had previously been the Bolshoi's main competitor and often its superior in the battle for top position in the world of Russian ballet.[10] Every year in the late 1980s and early 1990s, the Soviet and Russian state leaders had talked about repairing the theater, and by 1995 the pink wedding cake decorated with its bronze sculpture on Teatralnaya Square was shedding patches from its outside walls as if under siege.

The Bolshoi school traces its origins to the opening of "classes of theatrical dancing" at a Moscow orphanage in 1773. In 1888, the school had evolved into the Imperial Ballet School, and after the Bolshevik Revolution, it became a state ballet academy, commonly referred to as the Bolshoi ballet school.[11]

On a gray November afternoon in 1992, when I drove to the address given for the school, I thought I had made a mistake. The building looked like a walled corporate office, an institute, or a Western prison. It commanded most of a city block in one of Moscow's nicer residential sections, and it was not until I saw a cluster of young boys whose gait had a grace that tends to be uncommon at their age that I realized this was the correct place. The teachers would call it a small city, "a ballet town," where six hundred students aged ten to nineteen lived, studied, slept, ate, and competed friend against friend for a place in the Bolshoi Theatre.

I had been wanting to visit the school and meet Golovkina for months after Masha's grandmother had suggested that it warped children the way the hardened toes of satin ballet shoes can distort a dancer's feet. It had taken months to make an appointment. The first call in the summer of 1992 brought a terse response from the director's assistant: "Call back later." When later? "Next year." Slava Zelenin, who would act as my interpreter for the interview, tried again the next month. "There is an epidemic of chicken pox," the voice on the telephone explained. We called again, a few weeks later. "No, not this week. The children have exams; call next week." The next week, the director herself got on the phone and said that there was a diphtheria epidemic in Moscow. Slava informed her that we had been inoculated against diphtheria and that I had received a booster inoculation in August. Finally she relented. I would be allowed a *brief* interview on November 24, almost five months after the first call.

Sofya Nikolayevna Golovkina was seventy-seven years old the day she finally ushered us into her long, narrow office. The room, with its glass windows overlooking a barren cement courtyard, looked a little like a seaside gift shop of the kind that sells crystal animals, waltzing china ballerinas, and a variety of frivolous things that seem to appeal mostly to very young girls and older women. A piano dominated one end of the room, while chairs were arranged in a perfect line against the other wall. Her hand rolled like a ballerina's to point to a chair, a thronelike seat that had golden birds for armrests. As I settled in, I felt like an extra who had been elevated to a temporary peerage in order to sit before a queen of Soviet culture, still one of the most powerful people in the international world of ballet.

Shortly before this visit, I had reread earlier reviews of Golovkina as a dancer, which described her as popular and energetic, like a brand-new rubber ball.[12] The Russian critic Vadim Gayevsky had been even more scathing. A few months before I saw Golovkina, I sat in his tiny apartment, his wife silently serving tea while he talked about how, in the past, Russian ballet had always had some magical ability to find a great talent during times of trouble. "But in this case, it happened upside down," he said. "Golovkina became the school director; it was anti-art, antiballet. I've seen her on the stage, as a dancer. She is the most vulgar ballet dancer of all times and peoples. She is also crazy on self-determination." Not like a state or a people. A dictator, he meant.

I had these reviews in the back of my mind to help me from being intimidated by this queenly woman. Sofya Nikolayevna sat down slowly and gracefully, and while looking through the papers of her desk, she began the interview by saying, *"Ya slushayu."* "I am listening," it translates, but in this case it also clearly meant, I am busy. State your business.

When I explained that I was writing a book for an American publisher and that I worked for *The Washington Post,* facts that she already knew but for some reason had chosen to forget, she suddenly changed from haughty and dismissive to exceedingly pleasant, the voice mellifluous as honey and the attitude helpful. She was so happy to have me, please; ask me anything, she said.

I asked her how the school had changed since the dissolution of the Soviet state. I knew from those inside the school that the days of having anything she wanted had ended. The support from the Russian government was still there, but it was not as lavish as it had been. The first winter after the end of the Soviet state, Golovkina had stored sacks of potatoes and root vegetables in the school basement to insure against a famine that did not come. Golovkina now had to work hard for the school's money, and she had begun taking foreigners for a fee—a step that some teachers saw as pure desperation—and she had taken the best students abroad to perform and to teach for hard Western currency.

Foreign students paying $1,500 a month, wasn't that a dilution of the rigorous standards of the school? I asked provocatively. Golovkina smiled, dismissed the idea with a royal sweep of the hand, and answered in English. "So they are living under communism," she smiled, making a joke a year after communism had ended. "They are living under the communism that everybody was always dreaming of." By this she meant free food, free housing, an excellent education, and free medical care—all for $1,500 a month.

The goal for the foreigners is to go back and improve their own ballet theaters, she explained. Oh, yes, foreign students take part in the school performances, but will they be accepted as dancers in the Bolshoi Theatre? Golovkina shrugged off the thought. "No." She frowned. "Not the Bolshoi Theatre. You have to be really great to dance there."

It was a sharp reminder that many Russians believed that ballet could not be performed expertly by anyone but themselves. In the chaotic days when Soviet pride had been destroyed and nothing had yet replaced it, some people consoled themselves by believing they were still a superpower when it came to culture. The poets had begun to warn that Russia could lose this peculiar superiority as the frivolous and pornographic began to replace poetry and art. They railed against the new, unbridled passion for money that seemed to dampen the desire for things spiritual. But for some, such a loss seemed an impossibility. Russians could change their governments, but a true Russian would always cry over a treasured poem or swoon over a great moment on the stage. No mere government or social system would ever change this durable part of the Russian soul.

"Nothing has changed," Golovkina stated, even though she had seen six leaders and two opposing forms of government since she took over in 1960. "No changes. Politics doesn't affect us at all. We are given full freedom; we teach children now as we feel is necessary. Politics has never influenced us."

With this response, stated as though there could be no other possibility, the director had contradicted every other person I talked with about the school. Students, teachers, ex-teachers, and critics repeatedly said that Golovkina was so attuned to the politics of the moment that in any other society she would have been a minister, a chief of state. With the Russian worship of culture and love of the ballet, she traded in an important commodity—the children or grandchildren of the powerful. Masha the dancer and Vadim Gayevsky the critic had both talked about the grandchildren of Mikhail Gorbachev, Andropov, the culture minister, and the other powerful figures whose offspring did well at the school.

"Golovkina assured the grandmothers that their grandchildren are very gifted, but I see nothing wrong with this system, if it helps money and feeds the people in the school better. The only suffering ones are the grandchildren," Gayevsky said the day I visited him. "Had Andropov remained in power, I believe *Swan Lake* would be danced now at the Bolshoi by Mademoiselle Andropova," he added.

When I asked Golovkina about the relatives of famous Soviet leaders, the question made her eyes blink and her mouth tighten. "Politicals?" She repeated the word as if I had just thrown a tomato onto the stage. "No, no. They are no different. Like Gorbachev's granddaughter; she attended school not as a Gorbachev but as an ordinary girl. Nobody knew who she was. She is a normal girl. She dances like all the rest."

As for political influence, "It is not possible," she said indignantly, dismissing the idea with the perfectly poised hand. "Nobody can influence me. I am Golovkina. I am a pedagogue. I have my name."

As she talked, my eyes strayed above her to a portrait of a young blond woman with a dancer's tiara in her hair. It was in the place where normally a portrait of Lenin would have been in the Soviet days or, now, in the new Russia, at the very least an early Bessmertnova or some revered talent in Russian ballet. In the new era, Russian president Boris Yeltsin had not been elevated to this altarlike position in most offices, and people were free to choose their own honorees. Golovkina had chosen herself.

"That is I," Golovkina said in very stiff English as she saw me looking at the picture. The very position of the portrait meant that there should have been no doubt that she had been one of the great talents in Russian ballet history, but it served only to prove that she was a master at the kind of self-promotion that she felt was necessary to keep the ballet school going the way she wanted it to go.

In her crowded office, Golovkina did indeed look like a person who would have control of everything around her until her last breath. She was firm in speech and clearly free of doubt about her ideas, her history, her purpose. Even for me as a grown woman, she was frightening. For a young girl, it must be like trying to perform for an angry and all-powerful Medusa.

"This is a ballet town," she said, reeling off details in a way she must have done thousands of times before. "Twenty rooms for lessons. There are three hundred boys, three hundred girls."

"Not more girls than boys?" I asked, remembering Masha's version. She continued as if I had not spoken.

"Each year there are one thousand applications, and in the spring I invite only sixty. There are three tests. The first is body condition. Second, the doctor checks for health. And finally, artistic talent. Can she or he do this or that? I am the one who chooses, and I invite only the ones I want. We invite only children who have talent. If there is not a good body, good movements, they don't come."

"Even the foreign ones?"

She nodded. "Money doesn't matter."

Golovkina, clearly not planning her own retirement, talked about her plans for the future, and there was a feeling that she believed somehow that she would continue on for decades to see it through. "I dream about an artists' ballet school in the twenty-first century. We are in the process of humanizing education and our children perfectly. We want to create an artistic personality, one who knows everything about the arts. I have changed my school curriculum. Earlier we used to teach according to the [state] plan for all institutions. Now, we give more history of ballet and not communism. History of religion comes now, and it is very difficult for many because it is new. We have added aesthetics. It is hard for the teachers to change. History was the hardest."

What percentage of those who come to the school graduate?

"Sometimes there are surprises of nature," she said. "At nine to ten they are invited, and we test them, but maybe a girl is too big for pas de deux, a boy's feet are too long. They didn't count on this."

This is the only reason that Golovkina will give for people leaving the school. Of the fifty who graduated the previous spring, she said twenty-six were invited to dance at the Bolshoi. Twelve went to the Stanislavsky, six to Kazakhstan, eight to other republics. It added up to fifty-two, but undoubtedly like many people who had sat in that office before me, I kept my thoughts to myself.

"There is no problem for them to get work. Every graduate has three invitations. The Bolshoi choices depend on how many have retired that year. I had to give my place to Plisetskaya and Maximova. They wouldn't let anybody take their place, though. Some of them are sixty-five and still want to dance."

Plisetskaya, one of the great stars of Russian ballet, had left the Bolshoi after a battle with Grigorovich and had spoken harshly about the Soviet ballet establishment. Still, she had appeared in Red Square a few months earlier as part of an artistic extravaganza, and at the impossible age of sixty-seven, she had danced the "Death of a Swan." The audience that evening had applauded her for almost fifteen minutes.

"Does she come back to her old school?" I asked of Plisetskaya, knowing that it was unlikely, if not impossible. Golovkina stared at me to see if I knew what I was asking.

"No, no," she said finally. "She is now making contracts outside [i.e., outside Russia and outside the Bolshoi]. She cannot dance and she lives in Madrid," Golovkina snapped. Then, relenting: "Oh, sometimes maybe she can do ["Death of a Swan" from] *Swan Lake.* But ballet is for the young. Normally they dance for twenty years, but it depends on the condition of the artist."

Plisetskaya was in the West. Irek Mukhamedov was in London and spent his time on European stages. Many had fled over the borders in search of more money and an easier life. Golovkina did not argue with the fact that many had left, only with the wisdom of it. Why would a true Russian artist leave Russia?

"It makes no sense because now they can live here and also go touring there. Also it's not that easy there now."

She mentioned one dancer who went to Belgium but could not get a contract. Another dancer was in the movies, one was teaching at an "inferior" ballet school. Golovkina sniffed at how the greats had fallen into petty lives surrounded by things but lacking in soul and culture.

"There is no Balanchine now. No Nureyev. No Baryshnikov. No Diaghilev. Nobody to teach the Russian tradition abroad anymore. Only Russia has managed to preserve the tradition of classical ballet," she said proudly and with a finality that forestalled any argument and, for all practical purposes, ended my visit.

I came away from the meeting with Golovkina knowing I had encountered a rare Soviet icon who had managed to hold on to her power long after her natural era had ended. A steely-eyed babushka, she had kept a major world ballet institution alive for three decades, albeit at a cost that will be many more years in the counting.

As I left, she handed me a brochure, signed as a souvenir. In it were the lists of all the great dancers and the ballet teachers associated with the school. Graduates include such dancers as Bessmertnova, Vasiliev, Lepeshinskaya, Maximova, Plisetskaya. Great teachers featured in the brochure were P. A. Pestov, N. V. Zolotova, and Aleksandr A. Prokofiev.

Pestov was still at the school; I could not reach Zolotova, but Prokofiev agreed to see me. A respected teacher who was part of a group that had left the school in the late 1980s and early 1990s, Prokofiev provided another strong piece of evidence that the Bolshoi and its school no longer had a monopoly on people of talent. They were moving to other Russian companies being formed by those with more youth and energy than money, or they were leaving the country.

Prokofiev agreed to see me two days before our Western Christmas in 1992. The Young Pioneer Palace in Moscow where we met was a strange cavernous building, like most Soviet showplaces, and it was designed to have everything a child could want—rooms stocked with games, trucks, dolls, trampolines, all watched by guards whose job, it seemed, was to protect the toys more than the children.

We sat in the lobby, the banks of blinding white snow behind us as Prokofiev talked about how the school had treated its teachers. A thin fifty-year-old, with gray-blond hair, blue eyes, and the smoke of a string of Marlboros creating a haze around him, he seemed to find difficulty keeping still, as though pacing a stage floor was the only way to keep him settled in one place and on one subject.

His parents, who were evacuated from Moscow during the war, were not involved in the arts. "Prokofiev, the composer?" I asked. No, he smiled, no relation. His father had played the guitar and young Sasha (Aleksandr) had danced. "Then one day they brought me to a house of Young Pioneers, and I jumped and ran around and danced, and I was selected to go to the Bolshoi ballet school. It was 1952, I was ten. I was invited after graduation [1962] to go to the Novosibirsk Ballet Theatre. I worked there five years. Then one day, I had a very serious knee trauma at a rehearsal. . . . After my trauma, I spoke to my teacher, who said you will not be able to dance as before. But I decided to give it another try. Then in rehearsal, another trauma, and my teacher advised me to become a teacher. He was at the State Institute of Theatrical Arts at the time I entered in 1966 and until I graduated in 1971.

"In 1969, while I was still at the institute, I was already invited as a teacher to the Bolshoi, where I worked for twenty years," he mused, listing some of the names that had grown up under his tutelage. "Some of the best dancers of Europe came through me."

"I left in 1989," he said, ending that era of his biography. The papers had been full of news the week I spoke with him that he had started his own company, called the Aleksandr Prokofiev Ballet Company. The new company was working with Isabelle Fokine, granddaughter of one of the greatest choreographers in ballet history, Mikhail Fokine. Prokofiev had famous Russian émigré dancers returning to work with him, and like many Russians, he was most interested in talking about these future productions. He wanted to focus on the soaring possibilities now that he was free from the Bolshoi ballet school and its rigid interpretations of Russian classics. I wanted him to talk about his twenty years at the school and why he left it.

"Why did I leave? Golovkina," he said, virtually spitting out the name of the school director. "Frankly speaking, I couldn't be in that atmosphere which she had created. I would lock myself in my room and teach the way I liked. With the years, Golovkina got to be worse and worse. The same year I left, thirteen teachers quit because we could not live under her dictatorship. We couldn't live being humiliated by her, not just in private but in front of the students. Of course, no teacher with any dignity would tolerate this."

I told him that Golovkina had said the school had lost so many teachers because a few wanted Western money and others did not work well with children. Prokofiev scowled and pursed his lips as he listened. Whatever his first reaction might have been, he checked it. Instead, he said quietly and patiently, as if explaining to one of his young students, "You can tell that a teacher does not like children when they come and go in two or three months. But twenty years? Of the thirteen who left, some two or three were young, but she doesn't have a right to smear the whole group." He took a deep draught from his cigarette, exhaled, and then gave his verdict on her accusation.

"That's a lie," he said finally.

Whatever reservations he may have had about talking to an American about this great Russian establishment quickly began to disappear. Words and phrases began to tumble out rapidly, broken only by an occasional moment to smoke or light another cigarette.

"She created an image of elitism, inaccessibility, but the reason it is hard to get in is that a lot of things would not be liked if people found out about them. The school is open to all of her friends, of course."

The politicals?

"Aaah, yes," he sighed. "Many never had any talent at all. But there was no question why they wanted their children to go to this school. It provided the very best education (math, writing, reading, literature, English); it *is* an elite school. Children during the days are always busy studying. They do get an education. And all the privileged people want to bring their children because even if they wouldn't become dancers, they would have a great cultural education."

Like an experienced teacher, Prokofiev would begin to lecture occasionally to make certain his listener understood the complex background of Russian ballet, of the Bolshoi, of the Bolshoi school, of the culture of the dance world. One of these explanations was about the status of ballet in Russian society and how seductive the ballet culture can be for young people, even some of those with almost no talent for the dance. This was why 70 percent of those who entered MAKHU managed to graduate and why almost all of those graduates went to ballet theaters around the country.

"It is like an illness; you cannot get rid of it," Prokofiev said of the life of a dancer. "Nobody can go anywhere else. There are even boys that never had any skills as ballet dancers, maybe they are good in math, maybe they would have been good engineers or scientists, but you know they will choose dancing even though they know they will carry that spear for years and years. Ballet in Russia is a different world. They have their own humor, slang, interests. If they are in normal company, after a very short time they are bored because, really, they want to speak only about ballet."

He stopped talking about the school for a moment and smiled. "Recently some of us got together and we decided we would not talk about ballet," he said. "And then we took a glass of champagne and"—he snapped his fingers to show how quickly such a notion evaporated—"we started talking about ballet and talked for hours and hours, all night long."

When I spoke with Prokofiev and later with Masha, I kept wondering how Golovkina, so feared and despised by many, could remain in power. It was a new era, I said to Prokofiev; this was no longer the Soviet Union. How did this woman who was almost eighty years old survive when the rules of life, work, and politics everywhere else seemed to be changing virtually every day?

"It is not a matter of art. It's a political question. If it were a question of art, she would have been sacked long ago," Prokofiev had said sharply. "She is worse than average. In order to be a good director, she needs to give the school a good atmosphere."

Already, it took everything a good teacher had to keep the children separated from the politics around them. "Usually, what I did was, I concentrated on the work and tried not to pay attention to all the dark things around us in the school because there was nothing we could do about it all. But many children see the humiliation and insults. And when they come into the theater, it shows. They lose their air of youth, and they get to know life at its worst far too early.

"We say your life shows on your face when you are on the stage," Prokofiev said. "Over the years, we have seen less and less soul there." On the stage of the Bolshoi, dancers had increasingly been criticized for losing their spirit. Ever since the first signs of glasnost, after stars like Plisetskaya began speaking out, some Russian critics had also begun to talk of the technical expertise that lacked creative energy.

I asked Prokofiev what he meant by "dark things." It was worse for the girls, he began. The pressure to stay in the Bolshoi was a constant terror to these children, who feared, more than anything, the transition into womanhood. Budding breasts and rounded hips could spell a quick exit to the dreary schools back home. When the angular child's body began to soften, these girls took diet pills or routinely vomited after their enforced meals at the Bolshoi's walled city.

"A lot of very talented girls are expelled from school as they start to form into women. And some have gone to other schools and become great dancers, but at fourteen or fifteen—that is when the girl's body starts to get formed, and that is a dangerous time for them, that is when they can be expelled," Prokofiev said.

"So if you know you will be thrown out, you start taking pills and you are ready to do anything. There were cases when girls fainted during performances or they were shaking, convulsing in class. They would never eat; they were under huge pressure; they were so nervous. It almost never happened to the boys."[13]

Masha Ivanova's grandmother, a woman of spare but precise words, had described the way these young women stunted their personalities and bodies to become dancers. She said, "They are like buds that are not given a chance to blossom."

Even in the mid-1990s, the selection process for the Bolshoi Theatre appeared to be one of the most arcane and secret of those still left in the old Soviet capital. Russian ballet critic Irina Dezikova had once said of the screening process at the Bolshoi: "Soloists are selected by height. People with relatives in high places have the best chance of making it."[14] The same could still be true of students chosen to enter the Bolshoi world. Each year during graduation exercises, a commission was set up to examine the year's crop of dancers. Grigorovich and Golovkina were not the only members of this commission, but they were the ones who decided, Prokofiev said. "The teachers are never asked, and this doesn't make sense. These teachers are the ones who know everything about these dancers, how they do every day, not just then, at that moment," he said.

"About a third of the Bolshoi dance troupe doesn't have the right to work there because their professional level is not up to the Bolshoi's standards," Prokofiev said, stating what others had said quietly, not for quotation or certainly not with their names attached. "The Bolshoi troupe is very big, three-hundred strong, at least. Some can hold a sword in *Giselle*. Some can be toreadors in *Carmen*. In principal, a theater must have these kinds of people, who will stand holding the spear twenty years and cannot be placed anywhere else."

In Russia's ballet theaters after the Soviet years, their places would increasingly be in jeopardy, their pay minimal. The Bolshoi, moving to a contract system in 1995, had begun to demand more than loyalty on the stage. Masha's Stanislavsky theater, now busily adding sponsors who seemed to pay for the stage and the costumes, paid dancers at salaries little better than a state pension. And when the Stanislavsky took a break to restore the old theater, Masha and her colleagues were paid even less, a holding salary that could barely pay for ballet shoes.

Even with the luster fading rapidly, the schoolchildren at MAKHU were told that their highest calling would be the Bolshoi. "The idea of the Bolshoi Theatre, going to the Bolshoi, is always cultivated in these students.

No matter what, no matter how, you must get to the Bolshoi," said Prokofiev. But some of the dancers had begun to understand in the late 1970s and 1980s that the Bolshoi was not always the best place to start a career as a dancer. To go to the Bolshoi at that stage meant being part of the corps de ballet, and some of the students had grown to believe they were too good even to start out at that level.

"Some of them were very talented, and they wanted to have leading parts," he said. Instead of joining the Bolshoi, where he would be a member of the corps instead of a principal, Irek Mukhamedov went to Perm, a city in the Urals best known to many outsiders as the site of many notorious Soviet labor camps. "It turned out to be a wise decision because then Bolshoi director Grigorovich had a very public quarrel with his lead dancer, Vladimir Vasiliev. When Vasiliev left the Bolshoi [to return only in 1995 as Grigorovich's successor], there was no male lead for *Golden Age* and Mukhamedov was asked to come to the Bolshoi as its new male star.

"Who knows what would have happened to Mukhamedov if he went directly to the Bolshoi?" Prokofiev said. Like many who felt this way about the Bolshoi, Prokofiev quoted Gayevsky, who once said: "The Bolshoi is the cemetery of talent."

Listening to Prokofiev that afternoon had tended to make me more and more angry about Golovkina and her imprint on thousands of Masha Ivanovas. Then I asked about her replacement. His answer startled me and made me wonder whether she was a dragon naturally or by necessity.

"I don't know who should replace her," he said, "but I know it should be a man. Women are too emotional and erratic. Women are more into intrigue, and women ballerinas are always worried about their physique and physical appearance.

"A woman is a woman. If she feels sorry, we all must feel sorry. Most cannot spend nine hours every day in school. A woman must have a family and stay at home so much to care for them. Also, one needs real physical strength for this job.

"Vasiliev, Lavrovsky maybe," he said, citing the names of two of the school's most famous graduates. "But they would not take the job. It's very difficult to find an adequate successor. You can't restore the school from what it is. It is my opinion that you should sack all the teachers and students and start again with a new director. All of them are spoiled by

Golovkina. You cannot restore a rotten school. The staff will smile and pretend to change, but if a new director is not eaten in a month, he will be eaten in a year. These people will appear to change their ways and smile, but they will eat you anyway—because Golovkina looked after these people and educated them."

I left Prokofiev wondering how he could wipe out a whole school because of his disagreements with its tyrannical director. There was something disturbingly familiar in Russia about the idea that the old order must be obliterated before something better could be created.

Many ballet lovers saw the Bolshoi and its school as one of the few places where Russian classical ballet could be preserved. Whatever the problems with the school, they said, it was capable of turning out dancers who knew the intricate culture of the ballet. On this point, Prokofiev, Masha, Golovkina, and the critic Gayevksy agreed. All but Golovkina and her supporters, however, questioned the methods, not of teaching dance but of intimidating the students.

The discipline at the school was another way in which they controlled and destroyed the children, Gayevsky told me the day I went to see him. "It is barracks discipline," he said. "It is done with sticks. They are beaten with sticks, and the intimidation there, it is even worse. They are threatened all the time, one way or another. They are threatened to be thrown away, to be dismissed. It all starts with threats of not being taken into Bolshoi, of not being taken on tours abroad. Even if you are a member of the Bolshoi, the threat is that you won't get any good roles."

Gayevsky's charges were not merely the musings of an outsider. *Literaturnaya Gazeta* newspaper in May 1992[15] had published a letter from Natalia Kasatkina and Vladimir Vasiliev, who were then directors at a competing theater in Moscow called the Classical Ballet Theatre. The two wrote to ask for help from the government and the police to protect Bolshoi school students, who felt they were being threatened because they were considering offers to work outside the Bolshoi system.

The two directors charged that Golovkina's son had threatened a talented young dancer who considered refusing a contract with the Bolshoi. " 'Do you know what part of the fist smashes the head?' " the son said. " 'You will find out if you go to work at the Classical Ballet Theatre.' " The threats were not taken lightly, the writers said, because one dancer, Vladimir Molokhov, was beaten up three times and refused to return to Russia, "being afraid for his life."

The letter went on to say that one girl was threatened by an officer at the Bolshoi school in this manner: "We have long arms; we'll get you anywhere if you go to the Classical Ballet Theatre." Others were told, "You are property of the school, and are obliged to tour with Sofya Nikolayevna Golovkina."

The letter concluded: "It has been well known for a long time about the situation in [the Bolshoi school] . . . and not only students suffer from it, but teachers too. Some of them could not tolerate it and just left; however we encountered it on a mass scale only this year. Concerned parents ask: 'When could the kids admit that they are going to you [the other theater]? What if they give them bad grades? What if they mutilate or cripple them?' "

Shortly afterwards, *Literaturnaya Gazeta* printed a second letter, this one from teachers at the Bolshoi school and signed by eighty-five school supporters. Their long letter portrayed the young ballet students as innocent dupes who were persuaded to sign contracts with the Classical Ballet Theatre without knowing the consequences and without proper consent from their parents. The contracts signed before graduation were illegal, the Bolshoi staff said, and went against every ballet dancer's secret wish, to dance at the Bolshoi.

"The parents today have addressed the leadership of the school, the teachers and the parents' committee, asking for help in escaping from this trap, and from this dirty story."

One of the newspaper's writers interviewed some of the students, who basically denied the Bolshoi school version and told about being called up before the students and teachers and "grilled" about their contracts. "It wasn't nice, all of it," one student said.

Gayevsky had talked about this unseemly side of the Bolshoi. Like the swan, whose feet are peddling furiously to make things look so elegant on the surface, the system had an underside that indeed "wasn't pretty." "We all know who these people are. The whole institution is very *mafiya*," Gayevsky said, meaning in this case that it was run by a powerful group that made its own rules. "I was threatened on the phone. They threatened to hurt my wife after one of my stories half a year ago. This world is very horrible. Don't you think it is nice," he said, wagging a finger at me but not breaking his stride.

Gayevsky then began talking about banks and currency, dangerous deals and international finance—all of which for him meant that the ballet had become a part of the seedy commercial world in the new Russia. "They are not writing poems, they are trying to make money," he said, now speaking softly.

Gayevsky's wife watched him as he talked his way into a sadness and anger that she had undoubtedly witnessed many times before. "I was going to explain everything on a high artistic level to you," he said finally, "but you took me aside to look at other things."

The Bolshoi ballet school was like much of the old system. It had been corrupted at the top, but it had preserved a school for Russian ballet that gave hundreds of students a chance to dazzle audiences of people when a part was danced exquisitely, as it so often was. The communists may have ossified classical Russian ballet, but they also preserved it for most of another century. The Bolshoi ballet academy may have scarred Masha Ivanova, but she had spent her life dancing—in Moscow, in Europe, in the Far East.

On a rainy evening in the spring of 1995, I returned to the apartment of Masha's mother and grandmother. It was still among the most beautiful I had seen in Moscow—small and overloaded with grand antiques. The harpsichord was gone, sold to help pay the price of living in the new Russia. And there were four cats chattering constantly at one another—three white ones and an old, ill-tempered tom.

Masha's mother, Irina Mikhailovna, was now so busy with twenty-two full-time students that she seemed oddly Western. The table was not set when I arrived, an impossibility in the old Soviet days, but as she scattered music over the room to make a place for the food, she explained how her new school was working and overworking everyone who participated. I helped with the table setting, an event that Babushka Antonina protested was not done. In America, I said, guests almost always help, and she smiled at the assurance that the new ways were not giving offense.

As we sat around the table, Masha arrived, a flurry of activity and apologies, as she carefully removed her black hood to show the tight ballerina's chignon underneath. It was the first time I had seen Masha in this room, and I felt a certain anxiety from her mother and grandmother as their prize offspring settled into the chair and cuddled one of the cats with a rough love that made it howl in protest. Masha, at thirty-three, was still beautiful, but when she thought no one was looking, her face settled into an angry frown. She had new lines around her mouth, and her deep voice, so sultry before, now seemed to be moving toward a harshness that did not suit her.

Nine months earlier, for reasons she would not make clear to her mother and grandmother, she had filed for divorce. A friend of Masha's had suggested that Andrei had moved into commerce and had begun to take up a "different life" while Masha had begun to want security and children. Masha's mother could only explain that her daughter was "traditional," but whatever the reasons, she now wore her sadness heavily, and every few minutes as we talked, she would look at her watch and sigh. She needed to get ready for a tour of Bratislava, she kept saying, but clearly she also wanted to get away. As a group, her mother, her grandmother, and the inquisitive American wanted to know too much.

A safe subject seemed the nature of ballet, and we argued more than talked about the new order at the Bolshoi. What did it mean that Grigorovich, the man Irina Mikhailovna and Masha had both called a tyrant a few years earlier, had now been ousted in favor of his enemy and former protégé, Vasiliev? Masha shook her head vigorously and defended Grigorovich. For all the rejection she had suffered from the old director, the change was not for the better. Grigorovich was a true ballet master, Masha decreed, her voice booming over the table, her head shaking firmly. He merely did things his own way. Vasiliev was mediocre. Ballet had become less of a force in Russian society, and the Russian ballerina was now a worker, she said, not a superstar.

The Stanislavsky was about to close for three months for *remont,* or renovation, and Masha, like the other members of the troupe, knew that there was no such thing in Russia as a three-month renovation. It would take six months at least, maybe a year. In that time, they were paid holding salaries of a few dollars a month. "We are all scrambling now for work," she said.

When I asked Masha what she wanted to do after she could no longer dance, she said she wanted to teach. It was the same answer as three years earlier, with one change. This time she would confine her teaching to adults.

"No children," she said, firmly. "That would make me crazy. I would like to teach at a theater." Like the Stanislavsky.

As I listened to her, with a voice so deep and hard that it sounded almost manly, I realized that she would be an excellent teacher, with a new toughness that all successful teachers needed. And before she left, rushing off to pack for her trip, she decreed that in the time I had known her, life in Russia had changed for the worse.

"Personally," her momma corrected.

"Personally and professionally," Masha said as she kissed us all dutifully and hurried out the door.

After a long silence, Irina Mikhailovna sat shaking her head. "I fear she is doomed to be like me," she concluded. When Masha was young, her mother had also endured a divorce, and the little ballerina had become the focus of her life. Somehow, Irina worried, she had passed on the love of culture, the cruel infatuation with ballet, without giving the ability to make the rest of life work properly.

As I looked at the Ivanova women, soon laughing and talking about a recent concert or the scandals at the Moscow ballet houses, I thought Irina was wrong. Masha had been lucky to live in this house, even with her disappointments. Before she had hurried away that evening, Masha had said that even now, dancing made all her problems disappear. Irina's love of great music could do that; the timeless poetry on the Ivanovas' shelves could take away troubles for a few minutes at a time. Many others around them had suffered divorce, poverty, confusion: the society was stricken with panic about how to survive. Russians like the Ivanovas would find relief in art, and for that, they were among the fortunate.

10

The Spiritual Bazaar

*Spiritual competition, which like the economic kind has sud-
denly become the order of the day, is not a Russian tradition.*
—Pavel Gurevich, expert on mysticism
and religion[1]

The proselytizers came to Russia in
the early 1990s like a conquering army, crusaders marching onward past
the rusted Iron Curtain, their faces beaming with sanctimony, their arms
full of free Bibles and Korans and Torahs and the complete works of
scientologist L. Ron Hubbard. They stormed into a massive new territory
that many believed was as religiously backward and deprived as the world's
jungles and uncivilized deserts of a century earlier. They moved with
incredible speed and determination in a race to stake out a claim in this
luscious heathen land. Their appearance mystified, amused, and intrigued
most Russians, who, in the early stages, at least, were curious about all of
the outside ways that had been prohibited for so long.

It was on a cold day in the early spring of 1991 that I first heard the
chant of the Hare Krishnas echoing through the alleys near Moscow's
shopping way, then still named after Mikhail Kalinin, a top official in
Stalin's era. The area looked oddly Western, with its wide boulevard and

rows of boxy glass buildings; a Russian architect had once told me that it was Khrushchev's imitation of a modern glass and cement city that had so blighted this particular area of Moscow. In the crowds of people, who roamed and stared more than shopped in this earlier era when the stores had little to buy, the Krishnas always seemed just beyond the next cluster of Russians. I wandered past the woman selling kittens out of her coat pockets and the men smoking and nodding in small groups. I passed the lonely news kiosk that only a year later would be crowded out by a long line of miniature shops and stalls and tables selling everything from sugar to birth control pills to Italian leather gloves.

I shoved my way through the lethargic crowd until I found them, a covey of exotic creatures, their bright orange robes in blinding contrast to the dead Soviet grays and blues around them. On this icy morning, when most sensible Russians had on felt boots and fur hats, the Hare Krishnas were not as transported beyond the elements as one could expect. They wore combat boots, thick pants, and jackets under their saffron robes. On their mostly shaved heads were woolen caps. A hole had been cut in each of these caps, and out of it sprouted the famous redemptive pigtail, kept always in view in case they were ready to be yanked into Krishna heaven.

A frail-looking old woman was yelling at them in animated Russian, for disrupting people, for not working, for not being soldiers, for doing this weird street hooligan thing here, *here,* less than a mile from Red Square and Grandfather Lenin's tomb. A young Krishna, undoubtedly failing to realize that this woman was enjoying herself immensely, kept trying to calm and convert her, a daunting task that had his Russian audience chuckling in sympathy and understanding. The young man's colleagues watched idly and continued chanting, their hand cymbals chinking rhythmically for the curious and amused city crowd.

In early 1991, the Krishnas were an oddity. By the end of 1992, they were claiming seven hundred thousand in Moscow alone and had brought in pop singer Boy George to lure the young into a concert hall where the Krishnas could try to convert them. In the same wave, the Baptists arrived from all over America. The Mormons came. The evangelicals and the Baha'is. They were on the streets, in the parks, everywhere, it seemed— christening, baptizing, holding hands and declaring communion, singing, chanting, and speaking in tongues. The blossoming of religions and sects mirrored the sudden explosion of choices that Russians faced in every other sector of their lives. Not only did the Russian have to decide what to do and how to live and what to buy, he was also asked to choose a religion that would fill the void left after the years of communism.

Many of the young shopped for creeds as they did for Western clothes, and others began to see their ancient traditions surface after years of terror and hiding. Jews were allowed to practice their religion freely, to give their children bar and bat mitzvahs without fear of the state. The Old Believers, a group that had split centuries ago with the Russian Orthodox on such questions as whether to use two or three fingers for crossing themselves, began to explore their differences openly, as did those practicing other variations of Russian spiritualism and belief. And finally, the mother church, the Russian Orthodoxy with its roots deep in the Russian culture and psyche, began to rebuild the power and grandeur that Lenin and his successors had destroyed so methodically in the name of the state religion of atheism. Not only had Lenin's state confiscated the church property and killed or imprisoned many of its priests but the Soviets had eventually co-opted the church, allowing it to exist as long as these servants of God also kneeled obediently to the Red Star.

As the church began to pull to its feet, keeping as always a link to the state, whether it be tsar or party leader or president, the Russian Orthodox establishment found itself in the center of this massive competition for Russian souls. In the late 1980s and early 1990s, Orthodoxy seemed to be winning easily as a wave of teenagers and young people arrived at the nation's churches. They asked for baptism; they had their civil marriage vows reconstituted by a priest. They wore lacy headdresses and elaborate Orthodox crosses, heavy metal decorations conspicuously dangling on their young breasts. They bowed and chanted in the cavelike churches with their walls of saints and glittering icons; they lit the long golden tapers for grandmothers who had long ago whispered promises that someday the church would open its doors and bring back the ancient beliefs and the smell of lovely incense. And then, once having converted and stood through a number of long mysterious services, where only those who are lame or near death are allowed to sit, the young seemed to wander back to the less sacred business of struggling for food and scrabbling for money in their new way of life. Of the many young Russians I talked with over the last few years about the difficulty of their religion, the most concise was a young man selling souvenirs in Moscow. When asked whether he considered ever going to church, he answered, with a slight roll of the eyes, "Yes, of course. I went." He meant once or twice, not much more.

Even as these freedoms opened the spiritual world to people who had been told to believe only in the power of the human masses, it also unleashed the furies that ride with such passions, the ugly side of belief that excludes or hates the nonbelievers. The Soviet Union taught atheism. The new era offered belief as an antidote to the new greed, the cheap American TV culture, the spiritual emptiness that had become a favorite complaint of the day. But few seemed ready to preach tolerance. In some ways, the religious turmoil was a reflection of the basic political problem in Russia in this era. Just as Russians had no real experience with either the joys or the problems of democracy, I felt when talking to religious people that there was no basic emotional understanding that freedom of religion meant freedom not only for your own beliefs but for everybody's.

The Russian Orthodox church seemed the most offended by the influx of alien religions. Orthodoxy was a cumbersome giant, pulling itself off its knees, and it had little time or patience for the distractions of Baha'ullah or Presbyterianism or even the more liberal forms of Russian Orthodoxy.

A winter visitor to Soviet Russia, the eye desperate for relief from the gray skies that reflect the deadened landscape below, was drawn to the beauty of Russia's Orthodox churches. In the middle of a bleak little town, full of broken-down apartments with greasy windows, the snow melting over mounds of scrap metal that littered what should have been parks or gardens, there would suddenly appear the tiny remains of a church. In early 1991, when we could roam the countryside only with the permission of the foreign ministry, we could occasionally see them. A tiny jewel with blazing blue onion domes sat tauntingly off-limits on a distant hillside. An old white church, its busy geometric designs like some strange magician's plaything, would wait untended along a pitted dirt road.

Most of these places, we were told, were not churches. They belonged to the state, and the authorities had taken a malicious joy in using houses of worship for more earthly matters. Part of this revenge against the church came from Father Lenin, whose internal diatribes about the corrosive nature of religion and how more priests needed to be executed became known to most people in their searing detail only after the latter stages of glasnost.

In the late 1980s and early 1990s it was altogether too easy to forget why Lenin's antireligion views held sway over so many of these spiritual people. The church, now trying to regain its strength, had been exceedingly powerful before the Bolshevik Revolution, and its rich establishment had been a strong force supporting the tsar and his court. In 1897, there were 87.3 million Orthodox believers, almost 70 percent of the population. The church had more than forty-eight thousand houses of worship and a vast empire of schools, monasteries, and publishing houses, as well as wineries, farms, tanneries, and small factories. In European Russia, the church establishment owned more than 8.1 million acres of land,[2] and the average priest was ten times richer than his parishioners. The church, however, was not so widely beloved that belief in God and respect for the local priest went together. One famous nineteenth-century painting, called *Tea Drinking in Mytishchi*, by Vasily Perov, shows a grossly fat priest eating while a servant tries to get rid of two beggar children clearly interrupting him.

Before the revolution, the church was also a powerful force for the status quo. Soviet historians have written that "the cornerstone of the Church's entire social doctrine was the view that the division of society into the rich and the poor was eternal."[3] The rich were, in principle, condemned if they refused to give to the poor. The poor were condemned even more stridently if they tried to protest their lot.

Thus, when Lenin arrived in the name of the people, these men of God were among his favorite targets. Many priests were arrested, imprisoned, and killed. In one notorious act, Lenin rounded up one hundred priests from a parish that resisted him and had them hanged, their bodies left to putrefy as an example to others.[4] Church properties were confiscated and adapted, often in ways designed to make a point graphically, to remind any remaining believers of what the new authorities thought of their faith. Although some churches were turned into offices, warehouses, or small factories, many in the countryside were used to store manure for the fields. A Soviet doctor, Vladimir Golyakhovsky, recalled that when he came to Moscow's Botkin Hospital in the 1960s, physicians had moved the morgue into a nearby church. Bodies were dissected on a marble table that had once been the altar.[5]

The list of humiliations for believers was long. When the Orthodox church finally negotiated the return of its six-hundred-year-old Simonov Monastery in Moscow, only a corner of the original remained. In the 1930s, much of the old structure was destroyed for the Torpedo Soccer Stadium and the Palace of Culture (a stage, meeting place, and recreation area) used by workers at Moscow's ZiL automobile factory. Another section of the monastery was converted into small factories producing fishing rods and Lenin busts, which were much in demand in the latter decades.[6] Lenin's atheist state made its point with other religions, as well. One Moscow synagogue, for example, was turned into a reptile museum.

By 1992, the religious were beginning to stake their claims on old sites. In Moscow, the patriarch took over St. Basil's, the bouquet of cupolas on Red Square that is the backdrop for virtually every outsider's book or television show or movie about Russia. The legendary site of Moscow's Cathedral of Christ the Savior was finally returned to the church. The cathedral, built to commemorate Russia's victory over Napoleon, had been destroyed in 1931 by Stalin, who had wanted to put a palace in its place. It was an act that was done not only to please Stalin but to anger and dishearten any who still believed in the old "cult" of Christianity. The lore whispered afterward was that a distraught believer had put a curse on Stalin and the architects, and when they tried to excavate for the foundations, the earth grew spongy and soft, as though an underground river had suddenly been routed through the site. Defeated, party leaders finally built a heated swimming pool, a year-round recreation spot that, on winter evenings, gave off vapors of steam that writhed like anguished spirits over the once holy place. In late 1994, city workers started clearing the site and putting a fence around it for the reconstruction of the church, and by 1995, the 1.1 trillion ruble project being funded by city, local corporations, and individuals was remaining true to turbulent history. While the religious saw the rebuilding of the church as a way to wash away some of the sins of the communist era, others wondered whether the money for this cathedral could best be spent on some more earthly need such as housing. One construction worker on the site spoke for many who saw the costly new structure as simply another monument to those in power. "You could compare it to the Egyptian Pyramids," he concluded.[7]

In the countryside, the restoration of the village church was far less grand and undoubtedly closer to the ideal of the Christian faith. In many ways, this rebuilding was a way of restoring life after the Soviet era, and one of the most powerful images in the late Soviet period was from a movie called *Repentance,* which used the destruction of a village church to describe the villainy of their totalitarian state. At the end of the movie, an old woman is looking for directions, asking for the road to the church. Told the church had been torn down, she says: "What is the use of a road if it doesn't lead to a church?"[8]

In the town of Kuznetsk, about two hundred miles southeast of Moscow, the elders had begun trying to restore a church that had once been the center of village life. The Soviet secret police had stormed the town one day in 1945 and demanded the keys to the church. When five of the elders refused to hand them over, they were shot. The priest was sent to prison and never returned. In 1992, Kuznetsk was restoring its "heart"—its church—a few bricks at a time. With little money, pensioners foraged for building materials. At one point, a group of pensioners came to the church bearing an offering of rusted nails. They explained to the priest that they had carefully pulled them out of the walls of their already decrepit homes in the village.[9]

The Orthodox church was also rebuilding in the cities, restoring not only its properties but also staking its spiritual claim over the nation's new leadership. Patriarch Aleksy II could be seen at state functions now, routinely putting the church's blessing on each step toward Russia's new society. The top church leaders also attempted to negotiate an end to the violence in October 1993, when Russian president Boris Yelstin dissolved the parliament, bombed the White House, and abruptly put an end to the giddy hopes for a smooth path to democracy in the former U.S.S.R.

But for all the busy revival of its old prerevolutionary powers and its new attachments to a new state, the Russian Orthodox church was an institution that found freedom as troubling as some of the other structures from Russia's more recent past. Not only did the outsiders threaten competition, but even within the church, priests began to peddle their own disruptive message. The Orthodox leaders at once began to crack down on those it deemed threatening. The church punished the priests who challenged its authority, including some of those who had asked for a "purification" of Orthodoxy after documents showed that some of the church leaders had doubled as KGB agents during the communist days—a connection to the Soviet leadership that was deemed necessary to keep some vestige of their religion alive. The church leadership also chastised those who wanted to change the rituals, in particular by conducting them in modern Russian instead of Old Church Slavonic.

Two stories made the point most dramatically that the church had resurfaced as a powerful force for a conservative, even nationalistic Russia. When the patriarch defrocked Father Gleb Yakunin in the fall of 1993 for taking part in Russian politics, it was a particularly bitter disappointment to those supporting the democratic movement in Russia. Father Gleb was a famous dissident in the old days. He had spoken out against the Soviet bans on religion, a dissent that had earned him time in a rank Soviet prison. The fact that his sacrifices had not also earned him tolerance within the church sent a powerful signal that the church was not planning to adopt the freedoms allowed elsewhere.

Yakunin, who persisted in referring to the church leadership as the "church nomenklatura," talked about how Patriarch Aleksy II had summoned him for the dismissal. At one point the patriarch told Father Gleb that he had been a deputy himself during the Soviet years and that it had been a spiritual burden. Yakunin, whose real sin may have been his efforts to publicize the names of KGB agents within his church, told reporters that he replied, "Why did His Holiness not condemn the all-encompassing powers of the KGB and the Communist Party when he was a deputy? Maybe that is why his soul is troubled."[10]

If the defrocking of Yakunin sent a signal to the international Christian community that the church hierarchy was turning inward, it was the demotion of Father Georgi Kochetkov that angered many ordinary believers who hoped that after its years under the Soviet yoke, the church would shed some of its old authoritarianism. Father Georgi was decreed a revolutionary within his church in the early 1990s because he dared to hold services in modern Russian. The accepted language of the church was Old Church Slavonic, a language that was considered mysterious and beautiful by many believers but was virtually incomprehensible to all but a few.

Father Georgi had been holding his services in the Sretensky Monastery Cathedral in Moscow, a beautiful old church built in 1679 to commemorate the arrival of an icon to help save Moscow from Tamerlane's Tatar hordes and used during the Soviet years as a workshop for art restoration experts. When Father Georgi took it over, a refrigerator stood where the altar should have been, and the sanctuary was partitioned into workshops. In three years, the priest and his parishioners had helped lovingly restore the church, its frescoes painted in 1707, and other religious relics returned by old parishioners. Then, early in 1995, Father Georgi was called to the diocesan council and told that he was being demoted for changing church procedures without approval of the proper authorities. He would be transferred to a small parish church, very plain and, by Russian Orthodox standards, unattractive—no frescoes, no icons. (During the Soviet years, it had been a naval museum.)

His transfer did not take place with the simple packing up and moving from one church to another. Cossacks came into the cathedral one day and drove out his followers. Witnesses said the men rushed into the church like the barbarians of earlier days. They shouted and pushed; they even used whips on worshipers who were slow to leave. "They threw icons and books," Father Georgi recalled in horror a few days later. "It was a real pogrom."[11] Still, the priests who most offended many Westerners, like Metropolitan Ioann in St. Petersburg, were not publicly disciplined for their nationalist, even anti-Semitic, rhetoric. Ioann (John) was quoted in 1992 as saying that "the *Protocols of the Elders of Zion* [the document faked by the tsar's police] have not only failed to become outdated but have actually become more precise and their views are promoted in our day."[12]

My first Easter in Russia, I wanted to see the patriarch's church, not on Easter Day, an event that by 1991 was already a mob of politicians, priests, media, and curious worshipers, but a few days earlier, a normal day, a normal service. Yelokhovsky Cathedral, the patriarch's home parish, is a nesting of domes and facets surrounded by a wall of grim buildings, leftovers of Soviet architectural committees. The day I went, the sun played on its strange color—a dusty aquamarine accented with gold-and-white filigree, curling upward to the bell tower. Inside were the bones of St. Seraphim of Sarov, which had drawn long lines of worshipers, each leaning to kiss the casing for their holy relic. Old women, their heads wrapped in scarves and their eyes glowing with religious passion, were chanting and pulling themselves down onto brittle knees to pray and kiss the marble floor. The icons shimmered in the light of hundreds of long candles, each an effort to pass on earthly pain to a higher being, and the smell, after the pungent odors of the city, was intoxicating, like freshly ground spices from some Eastern market.

For all its splendor, however, the cathedral's spell was shattered as soon as I left the church. On the doorsteps, literally, were two wiry young men trying to peddle a thin, badly printed newspaper. As worshipers left the darkened cathedral and came squinting into the sunlight, the youths, who wore old tsarist army uniforms, would show them the paper and ask for money.

When I approached one of the men, he would not sell the paper to me. "What is it?" I asked. "It is for Russians," he mumbled, "not for you." I had my pockets full of small change, one- and three-ruble notes that I undoubtedly would have given to the women who stood outside the church bowing and pleading for charity. I pulled out the wad and handed most of it to the young man. He grabbed it, handed me the newspaper and left, pulling along his friend with him. The paper, called *Zemshchina*, was full of stories about Jewish curses, hints that Russia was suffering from practitioners of the infamous *Protocols of the Elders of Zion*. Within a few months such newspapers had gone beyond hints, and groups like the Union of Orthodox Brotherhoods had begun to spread their ugly message. In one of their bulletins, they announced, "Hasidism is a secret cruel teaching, the followers of which practice bloody human sacrifices. . . . As a fanatical human-hating religion, Hasidism must be banned on Russian territory."[13]

At the top of the church, however, there were occasional efforts to combat the anti-Semitism that loitered on the edges of the Orthodoxy's new surge in popularity. The patriarch Aleksy II on a trip to America in 1994 had met with Jewish leaders to assure them of his stand against such intolerance. The best-known anti-Semitic group, Pamyat, leveled its angry abuse not only at Jews but at Christians as well, a revelation that made it far easier for some Orthodox leaders to turn away from them. Pamyat, which means memory, drew squads of angry young men who wore black uniforms and preached hatred of all but the pure Russian—a purity they defined in their own arch and bitter terms. In one book published in 1979 in Paris, a screed that some Russians believe was the starting point for Pamyat, the writer lamented the beginning of the Russian Orthodox church and called for restoration of the gods Svarog, Dazhbog (the god of sun and celestial fire), and Perun, "destroyed by Prince Vladimir in 988, after which free Russian people became slaves of the circumcised Christ."[14]

Such antichurch propaganda was easier for the Orthodox leadership to combat than leaflets like the one that began to appear near Russian churches in 1993, which said: "Pray for the salvation of Holy Orthodox Mother Russia from the evil Jewish yoke. Only the Orthodox Tsar will defend us and our children from ritual Jewish slaughters and keep our Church from the evil schemes of Judaic Satan."[15]

The church seemed tainted by these "true Russians" and by the years when the leadership worked for the KGB, whose intrigues were beginning to surface in the early 1990s.[16] When I suggested to a Russian friend that it would be hard to respect or bow to someone who might have been whispering once a week to the secret police, she shook her head in alarm. I did not understand, and I would not understand until I met a priest named Otets Nikolai, Father Nikolai. His reputation was as a good man, a holy priest who could explain the reasons to be a believer now, in this chaotic time.

By the time I actually met Otets Nikolai, more than a year later, I knew his family well—a situation I believe was in some ways part of a spell being cast on our family by a group of believers who tempered their association with ungodly Westerners like us by trying, in every way possible, to convert us either to their religion or, at the very least, to one of our own. Not one to take my daughter to Sunday school with any regularity, I was in danger of raising a heathen, they feared, and they were perpetually coming to the rescue. When I needed a baby-sitter, Tanya, the daughter of Father Nikolai, arrived. Shy, gentle, and vastly overtrained for this job, she nevertheless took it on like a mission. She played with my daughter and prayed over her. As the new ugliness invaded the streets, rudeness and anger exploding at every corner and kiosk, criminals in fine suits grabbing their take, Tanya would stand every day as a strong reminder of the powerful goodness that could remain underneath this ugly surface.

In time, Tanya introduced me to her family. Her niece, Irina, was eight when I met her; she was playing the piano at the culture center at a physics institute nearby. The hall had been filled with people, all listening to this child, in her blue velvet dress and long hair pulled back with a Victorian bow, playing Mozart, Bach, Schubert, Beethoven, and Mendelssohn. Irina (whose name the family had anglicized as Iron) would come to our apartment, where she was on orders to play with the dolls and the vast assortment of American games. After four hours at the piano a day, every day, she needed to be not a child prodigy but merely a child.

Irina's mother was a musician and music teacher. Her father was a violinist in the Conservatory who spoke passably good English, all of it learned from a book. Tanya's other sister, quiet and religious, was the kind of person who needed to be protected from the new Russia. Olga had been trained as a doctor, and when she went to the hospitals to work in the early 1980s, she could not bear to watch the pain of children suffering without their parents, who were routinely considered an inconvenience to be kept out of the way. Tanya told me how Olga's job had made her ache and cry at night, and once when I saw Olga, who was looking for some other kind of work, I asked her about her years as doctor. She shook her head, held back the tears, and simply said, "Please. No."

At one point during the period I knew her, Olga had tried to get a job in a Westerner's home so that she could make enough money to pay for treatment for her son, an extremely intelligent child who appeared to have some kind of attention deficit disorder. After a week of scrubbing and cooking and baby-sitting, the woman fired Olga and refused to pay her for the week's work. Olga was bewildered and angry, as were the rest of us, although we were not allowed to help. She later found work at the church newspaper, a job that finally satisfied her financially and consoled her spiritually.

So when Tanya's mother and father appeared one day for a long-arranged interview, I thought I knew about them, or at least about him. As with many such meetings, it was more than I had expected, and afterward, even though I resisted a part of his world view, the part that I found surprisingly intolerant, I could see he was a good man. In a chaotic new world that seemed overrun with corruption and self-indulgence, a priest like Otets Nikolai could indeed inspire belief and loyalty.

* * *

Asked to come for an interview and dinner at 6 P.M. on a warm June evening in 1992, Otets Nikolai Anatolievich Vedernikov and his wife, Nina, rang the doorbell at our apartment as the clocks tolled the hour. Bursting into our narrow entranceway, their arms laden with hats, raincoats, and flowers, Otets Nikolai and Nina greeted us for the first time with hugs, kisses, and blessings. Nina, a small woman with a warm, smiling face, touched my daughter's head gently and whispered that she was "beautiful, a gift from God." Otets, a man with a carefully cut beard, who wore a standard Soviet suit instead of his usual long robes, reached out for both of my hands and kissed me three times in the Russian tradition. An Orthodox friend I had invited to help me fill in the silences (which never came) approached him reverently and, after saying hello, stood before him, her head bowed. He blessed her, his hand on her shoulder while he said a short prayer. I expected him to actually make the sign of the cross over our heathen doorway, but if he did, I did not see it.

The Vedernikovs, having been greeted in what I hoped was a polite Russian manner, walked into the apartment like tourists, staring at the roominess and the excess of things, showing less disapproval over these luxuries than I had feared. But as I placed them on the American-sized couch that dominated our Soviet-sized living room, Otets Nikolai sat upright like a man who believed the softness of the cushions would envelop and corrupt him. With his wife beside him and his hands clasped firmly in his lap, he faced me in the manner of a soldier ready to be interrogated, even though I knew from his daughter that he had been willing, even anxious, to talk to a Westerner about his church.

I began by asking him about his background, and in a firm voice, enunciating each word as he must have done in his sermons, he listed the events of his life—his interests, his school, his religious training. It was not until halfway into the recitation that I realized that he had not mentioned his wife, who punctuated each point with a vigorous nod and an occasional pat on his hand for reinforcement. It was a strange omission, I would realize as they began to talk about their lives together.

Nikolai and Nina met when they were teenagers, she told me later. They were married when she was nineteen, he twenty, and now, at sixty-four and sixty-five, they had grown together like the trees that I had once seen braided in the forest at Tolstoy's estate Yasnaya Polyana after young lovers decades earlier had wrapped them together in testimony to their passion. As she sat beside him that evening, they seemed inseparable, answering each other's questions, finishing each other's sentences. She was warm and loving and tough, not simple but not leadenly complicated in her religious belief. She was supportive as he spoke, nodding and adding detail, but she also quietly hissed her disapproval when he strayed into territory she found alarming. I quickly became accustomed to hearing them support and edit each other, and I was certain that when they died they would go within weeks of each other.

The biography he gave that day was spare. He was born in 1928; his parents were "teachers," as he put it, even though his father was actually a well-known expert in adult education. Nikolai went to "normal" grammar school, but "at age seven I began playing the violin, and I studied three years, and then, after that, I went to Moscow's Central Musical School," he said.

Without elaborating, Otets Nikolai had just told me that he was a very talented musician. To be accepted at this school at age ten meant that he was one of hundreds, perhaps thousands, trying to enter. Later, when he played our tiny spinet piano, making it sound like a grand instrument full of fun and laughter as he elaborated on themes we made up for him, such as "cowboys in the wild West" or "Russian snowstorms," we had some idea of what he might have become in the secular world.

With the arrival of the Second World War—the Great Patriotic War, as it was known in Soviet Russia—young Nikolai went to stay with his grandfather, a professor of eye diseases, who lived in Ufa. When he could, he returned to Moscow, graduating from Moscow State Conservatory, first from the regular course and later from the composers' school in 1955, at age twenty-seven.

In his early teens, Nikolai began going to the cathedral, where I had seen the disturbing young men wearing their old tsarist uniforms. But back then, he had to slip into the church to help the archbishop as a kind of altar boy. It was a dangerous gamble for a young man, since good Soviet teenagers were supposed to be part of the Pioneer Corps, the Soviet version of scouts, and later the Komsomol, the Young Communists League. "I did not get into trouble because the head of the school was a believer and he was quite understanding," Otets explained.

When a patriarch was elected during this period, Nikolai began to help the new church leader during services. As he talked about this era, he made it sound like just another youthful job, and what was not said was how he could only have been a member of the Russian elite to do these lowly church tasks for such high church officials.

"I was very fond of the Russian Orthodox service, and at that time, I felt I wanted to join. Probably it was my father's idea; he was a strong believer, and he always dreamed that I would participate in church life. At that time, during the war years, Moscow had many bishops and more acceptance of the church. When I came to the church of St. Elija, one of the priests asked me to participate in the service because there weren't enough acolytes. He put the clothes on me and asked me to hold some of the church's holy objects for him. I began coming to church regularly after that."

Nikolai seemed to be describing a young man who was infatuated more with the trappings of the church than its beliefs. It is not hard to understand how a sensitive youth in the Soviet war years would look for a quiet, beautiful place to grow into manhood even though it meant turning away from the atheist society around him. "At first, I didn't have a desire to become a priest. I felt that working with people, being responsible for their souls, caring for them, would be very hard, and in the Russian church there is a deacon, or junior priest, who does not really deal so much with the congregation. I just dreamed of being that deacon so that I could participate but not be responsible for people's souls."

Like many powerful men who are modest in talking about themselves, Otets Nikolai had to be led from subject to subject. I asked about how his music and religious life worked together or tugged him apart. He listed his accomplishments quietly, and a friend of his would tell me later that what I viewed as a career sacrificed and confined to the church, he viewed as an honor and a gift to his chosen religion.

"As a composer, I wrote music for the church, and it was performed in church. My first experiment was when I was fifteen years old. I wrote the processional music for Patriarch Aleksy and also a composition to celebrate God's mother. In the seventies I created more church music. They were performed at the Monastery. I have done more than ten pieces, maybe

twelve to thirteen. They were all performed, yes, but not together, sep-
arately." His music had been folded into the grand repertoire of the church.

When he became a priest in 1958, Otets went to the patriarch to ask for
his assignment. The patriarch first wanted Nikolai to work for him, and the
young obedient priest complied, but he did not want to talk about that
early period. His brush with the politically savvy church fathers may have
made him see that his religion must too often survive its leaders. What
Otets Nikolai did want to talk about was his first parish, the Church of
Christ of Nativity in a suburb of Moscow called Izmailovo. There, in a place
that by the 1990s had become a major tourist market where one could buy
trinkets, rugs, puppies, and stolen icons, Nikolai had served as a deacon
until 1961. Then, one day, he was called in and told that he had to take the
job of the priest in his parish.

"I didn't have a desire to become a senior priest, but at the church
where I served, a priest, well"—he hesitated—"well, he broke some rules.
He baptized a baby without registering it. People didn't want such events
registered; they didn't want it to be known. But it was found out and he was
dismissed. The authorities persuaded me to take his job and said it would
not be open long if I did not. It all happened against my will; I didn't want
to take the responsibility. Besides reading sermons, I had to take confessions, had to take the responsibility for people's souls. That was very
difficult for me," he said.

It was not an easy time to become a priest. Churches were closing. The
state charged those that remained huge taxes, and the rules became strict
about how a priest could preach only in church, how believers must be
careful not to "corrupt" the young by teaching them the old religions.

"There were usually people watching a priest, following him. Also it
was difficult to do baptizing or a church wedding. They reported on people
and very often they were fired from their jobs for being believers. Very
often I baptized people in my home secretly."

For ten years he stayed in Izmailovo, and then, for reasons that his
friends say probably had to do with his secret baptisms or his refusals to
report to the KGB about the people who worshiped there, he was moved to
a small church in Ivanovskaya near the city of Ivanovo, where he stayed for
eighteen years.

"When I served in Ivanovskaya, it was the most difficult situation—I had to teach, preach, minister, and also sing in the choir. Nina was the choir director," he said.

In some ways, Father Nikolai may have been fortunate to be away from the center during the years when the religious leaders seemed to be growing ever closer to the Soviet apparatchiki. Believing was allowed but watched by authorities who could turn on the churchgoer or his family at any time.

At the height of Soviet stagnation in the 1970s and early 1980s, baptisms like those performed by Otets Nikolai could be overlooked or they could be used to punish believer and priest alike. Still, some surveys showed that about half of the Soviets admitted to being baptized as children, data that many suspected vastly underrated the numbers of people who had connections to the church. One report in *Komsomolskaya Pravda* in 1971 suggested that many children were baptized under a system of "blackmail"—the grandmother refused to take care of the child until the church ceremony was performed.[17] Another Soviet surveyer, finding the huge number of baptized children, reported that 90 percent of the parents "came to the degrading rite under pressure from believing relatives, and by no means for religious motives."[18] Obviously, to be baptized as an adult was a sign of anti-Soviet behavior, and many feared that the state would retaliate if word of their beliefs became public.

"Among those whose baptism was concealed was a famous composer who belonged to the party, many other adults as well," Otets Nikolai said. "It was a risk for them, and, of course, it was a risk for me if I was discovered. I would have been dismissed."

"Why did you do it?" I asked.

"Because he is such a good man," Nina answered smiling.

Nikolai controlled a small grin and put his hand up for her to stop.

"It's very simple. If a person asks a priest for his service, a priest, being a priest, has no right to refuse."

"Many others refused," Nina interrupted. "Many were afraid and would not do it."

"It was a risk of course. But"—he shrugged—"we simply believed that it was right. We also taught children church singing in our apartment."

To teach the young about God was the real sin in the eyes of communism, and for breaking this law, many lost more than their stature in the church. Jobs disappeared; privileges were taken away; and, at worst, the believers could still face prison.

"It was God's miracle that we were not caught," Nina said. "We were doing it in Christ's name, because many, many people wanted to study and sing. But many people also heard us, of course." And, she did not say, they could have turned them over to the authorities.

When I asked the next question, it was one that Otets Nikolai had clearly expected: what about the priests who were in the KGB? It was the period when the first details of those working with the secret police were becoming public. Some in the church had tried to stop these investigations, saying they would be disruptive and would focus too much on human frailty.

"Yes." Otets Nikolai sighed. "We now know that some of the top bishops were associated with the KGB."

"Many couldn't help it," said Nina. "It doesn't mean they are terrible people or traitors. You just have to realize what it was like at that time and that situation."

Otets Nikolai sighed again, as if attempting to forgive them, perhaps thinking of something that he had done or wished he had done himself in those years. Now it was an era when the past still haunted many survivors. Those who had been scoundrels hoped to hide the way they had operated under the old system, and good people like Nikolai berated themselves for not doing more. As an acolyte working for the patriarchy, he may have been high enough in the church to see some of the connections to the Soviet state, but by the time he was a priest, he undoubtedly was too far away from the power to be tainted by it. Some had profited richly from their associations with the Soviet powers, but the Vedernikovs lived not only simply, but in near poverty. They had a small apartment far from the center of the city, and although it had five rooms, for many years it housed six people, including an aging and sick grandfather. Otets Nikolai, however, had forgiven those who profited as long as they kept the church alive.

"They were very much dependent on the government, the church authorities, and if they protested too much, the authorities threatened to close the churches," he continued. "It was not a matter of free will.

"The archbishop would be called and given an assignment, and if he didn't do it, a church closed. He was given a political assignment, and often it was accepted but the priest did not comply. There was one who said [recently], 'Yes, I was cooperating with the KGB but I never reported anybody.' He was using this cooperation to promote his own ideas and our church's desires. Sometimes, he [the archbishop] used it to promote good priests. He managed to promote over one hundred good priests because he had connections with the authorities.

"Of course, it's a sin. But what is the attitude toward him as a sinner? It's human weakness. We believe that a priest, even if he has sinned on a personal level, he is still a priest. We excommunicate him only for false teachings. His personal sin is his personal responsibility; we do not hold that against him and only God can judge him.

"If his higher authorities realize that what he did was for lower purposes, then they may decide such a man is unworthy of being in the church. But I was lucky enough to have good people both above and below me. We knew such priests existed, those who betrayed people and reported people," he said.

Even their confessions?

Otets Nikolai frowned at the possibility. "That's sacrilege," he said softly. "Yes, such cases existed and those people should no longer be priests."

As the young flocked to the churches asking for baptism, Otets Nikolai's problem was explaining how difficult it was to be a Russian Orthodox Christian. The faith, if followed strictly, was hard on a true believer. Church services last for hours, and there are seats only for the very sick and infirm. There are long fasts—periods when many basic foods like milk and meat are forbidden unless one is too ill or too young. (Once I saw Tanya cooking my daughter a cutlet and realized that she had been weeks without meat because of the Lenten fast. She was clearly in some kind of trance— whether because of prayer or hunger, I was uncertain—as she stood over the tiny stove. I interrupted her and began pushing food on her in alarm, and she finally devoured a large bowl of rice to satisfy both of us.)

"By 1983 or at least 1985, we began to feel the first breath of freedom. At first we felt the change in the authorities. There was still registration, but starting with Gorbachev, many were baptized.

"Some say it's fashionable only for the young, and yes, there is some truth there. Religion became a sort of *moda* for some people. In this, the mass media is right. Religion is intimate and should be internal. It is not the ceremonies. God asks for your heart, nothing else.

"Of course, very few people seriously want to do the . . . the work that is the essence of this committment. Ceremonies are meant to facilitate this crucial part of the religion. When one of the bishops asked me what was the most important thing now, I said getting the blessing of the Holy Spirit inside yourself. Everthing else is easy—to be married, baptized, born, and die in the church, it can be nothing more than that, when only the fashion prevails."

I asked Otets Nikolai that evening how the freedom from the old Soviet ways had changed his life as a priest, how it had changed the church. He began with what he called "a little history" about an earlier time of freedom for the church, the fourth century A.D.

"In the first three centuries, Christians were persecuted. Only in the fourth century was it adopted as the state religion of Byzantium, and this gave the church freedom. But if we think that freedom brought a blissful period, with no problems, we are wrong. At that time came many contradictions in the faith. There were all kinds of false teachings. . . . It was a time of troubles within the church, and the period of false teachings continued until the ninth century.

"We can make a comparison with the present here. There are a lot of sects that preach openly a lot of wrong things. Now, there is a lot of advertising for all kinds of preachers. It is everywhere. Then, if you speak of the church itself, the church is being split—the Ukrainian church, the different Russian Orthodoxies from abroad who want to have parishes in Moscow. There is one parish in Moscow that is different from all the rest—innovations, trying to modernize. It may be good, I am not ready to say, but it is looked down upon by others within the church."

By early 1994, the Orthodox were clearly splitting into the reformers and the disciplinarians, the ones who wanted the church to change versus those who wanted it to stand strongly in favor of its old ways—both believing that only their religion could combat the tide of corruption and decadence in the society.[19] The division, Otets Nikolai was saying, simply weakened the church and made it more vulnerable to the invading religions, which day by day were conquering more Russian souls.

"Now there are missionaries who are even spreading the idea that all religions are equal and should be given equal respect. Buddhism, Hinduism, other religions—all equal." He bowed his head to cope with this terrible idea, and Nina patted his hand. She clearly chafed at the possibility that after all the years of work and fear, these alien religious were reaping the rewards. It was like watching a field that you had planted, weeded, and nurtured suddenly being harvested by a gang of thieves. She shook her head; she had no proper word for her feelings about the new crusaders.

"The Russian Orthodox church does not accept this point of view that all religions are equal, and we don't believe this is correct," Otets Nikolai continued, his voice so low that the room became silent as we tried to hear him. "This time equals the other time [the fourth century] when there were so many other religions. If we say all religions are equal, then Christianity does not exist.

"So now the main task of Christianity is to preserve the purity of faith because the church is attacked on all sides by these variations and they are appearing like mushrooms. It is the purity of Christianity that is necessary, and that is why preaching takes such an important role—Sunday schools and other schools. Now we have a great possibility to do it."

As I listened to this speech, spoken softly and without anger, I noticed the people around us that night. Father Nikolai's family; my friend Masha, who had introduced me to Tanya and now to Otets Nikolai; Masha's daughter; and another mutual friend, we were crowded into the small room. All Russian Orthodox believers, they were nodding their heads vigorously in agreement, whispering something, perhaps short prayers. On the tape, I can hear the silence after my next question, a long-winded query about anti-Semitism and about Metropolitan Ioann in St. Petersburg. One of the believers in the room was a Jew who had converted, and I wondered if she and Otets Nikolai had ever talked about this aspect of her newly adopted religion.

Otets Nikolai waved his hand in the air to try to wipe out my concerns.

"We do not have any intolerance toward individuals," he said. "But we cannot tolerate false teachings. It is intolerance toward the teaching, not the individual, because Christ preached love for every human being. We should listen to people whatever they feel, it is part of our duty," he said.

"You know, the Russian Orthodox church has never had an inquisition like the Catholic church," he added. "Still, the purity of the Russian Orthodox church comes first."

There were about 60 million Russian Orthodox Christians in Russia at the end of the Soviet era. For many of them, the church was part of a Slavonic heritage that was becoming a test of Russianness.

Otets Nikolai seemed to sense my thoughts.

"Yes, there is a lot of intolerance on the part of our believers, not only among different nationalities but even between the older generation and the younger. The young come out of curiosity, and the older believers act hostile toward them; they don't show proper love and proper tolerance toward them. They forget that the church is the stronghold of love.

"In every parish, there are some believers who may have been going throughout life without understanding that the church is about love," Nina interjected. "They spoil this idea by being so"—she paused, looking for the right word—"aggressive," she said finally.

Then I asked how the church would look at capitalism, the hardness that was invading the country and making people shed their old concerns for spiritual matters in favor of the push to be rich. Before Lenin, the church seemed to preach that the rich should give to the poor and the poor should accept their status. Would the teachings return to this view?

"I don't know how it will be done, how the church will preach now, but this is a very Christian situation. People who possess wealth can share with those who don't have it now because it is not the time to pass by those in need. Now people do have charity; it was not allowed in the earlier years, not really. Charity is actually a test of people's ability to be Christians. To be happy in giving: this is the essense of Christianity. Your wealth is a good opportunity to share with your neighbor, the poor. If you don't share, it's a spiritual catastrophe, a catastrophe within yourself.

"If you read in the Bible about the rich man's feast, poor Lazarus is simply happy to be there, so patient, so tolerant, with no feelings of jealousy for the rich man. That is why when he died, Lazarus went to heaven and the rich man went to hell.

"Poverty is not either evil or good, though. It's the person's attitude to wealth, not whether you have money or you do not have it. For many people, this might be a period when they can concentrate on their spiritual life."

The priest and his wife were finished with the interview, and as we all began to relax, Otets Nikolai, apparently having something left unsaid, made certain the tape was still running for one last comment.

"Russia, I believe, is having its spiritual resurrection. I have a great deal of hope for the younger generation. The young at confessions especially impress me; they are much more serious, much more responsible than their elders. In Christianity, Russia is considered a source of pure faith." He nodded, and then said it again. "Pure faith."

I saw Otets Nikolai two more times—once in 1993, again in 1995. By then he had begun working in the prisons, converting the prisoners. He started saving souls in Butyrskaya (see Chapter 11), and by 1995 he had become the priest who took confession before prisoners were executed. Tanya said he would come home and sit silently, weighed down by the burden of those confessions.

When I saw him in 1995, he was in better spirits. It was at his home, a small apartment heavy with books and gifts from his parishioners. As I sat around his table with his now frail wife, Nina, his daughters, his granddaughter, Irina, his friends and my friend Kathy Lally, we talked a little about church politics and a little about regular politics. At one point, Otets Nikolai went to a nearby room and brought back one of the toys made for him by a prisoner at Butyrskaya. It had taken the man weeks, maybe longer, to create a little gnome with a head that bobbed up and down and a mosaiclike cloak body made of broom straw and melted food packets. The colors were surprisingly bright, and Otets Nikolai elaborated on the detail and the workmanship as proudly as a parent.

The afternoon was a small celebration, and we sat around a table that Tanya had fixed immaculately with blue-patterned Russian china and elegant old crystal wine glasses. The food was rich and delicious, blinis, sour cream, and caviar, and Tanya had bought champagne, which she poured for each of us. I could not help thinking how much this had taken out of Tanya's lean budget, and the guilt was even more intense when the table was too small for her to squeeze in beside us. She stood behind and over us like one ready to serve. She had said many times that she did not want to be a wife. Perhaps, I thought on this occasion as on others, she would someday be a very good nun.

The meal was full of gentle toasts to Otets, to Russia, to my family, to theirs. At one point, when the priest lifted his glass, it touched against a water goblet near his plate and broke a small chip out of the crystal. The two of us sitting closest to him reached for the glass at once, and the sudden movement surprised Otets Nikolai. Then he saw that part of the crystal was missing. He smiled at us, raised the glass, and to our obvious dismay, drank the rest of the wine. Afterward, in a room that was now deathly silent, he looked at me and whispered *smert* (death). Then he laughed quietly.

Was it a joke? I wondered, laughing along with him nervously. Maybe. Perhaps it was something far more complicated, like a taunt to a non-believer, a sliver of evidence before my questioning eyes of the miracles that were part of his creed. Around us, no one else seemed concerned about Otets Nikolai. His wife was smiling gently from across the table, talking to her daughters beside her. I seemed to be the only one shaken by the possibility that this aging priest might have just swallowed a piece of glass. I went away that day thinking about how an act that would look like madness in America seemed perfectly within bounds in Russia.

The Orthodox church of Otets Nikolai worked for a quiet and internal spirituality among its millions of believers, and it was that Russian concept of the spirit that seemed to be most rudely buffeted by the noisy new religious proclamations around them. Believers in new cults, old orders, exotic faiths, and imported Western evangelism wore their conversions like advertising, and they encouraged belief with a zeal that alarmed and offended many of the Orthodox believers I had come to know. As the flood of unorthodox religions swept onto Russia's streets, Orthodox leaders began to appeal to the state for help in curbing the freedom of religion that they believed had gone too far.

By July 1993, Orthodoxy had convinced friends in the parliament that they should limit the numbers and kinds of outsiders allowed to proselytize on Russian soil. The idea was that the state should protect the innocent Russian believer from the outside pressures. In a letter passed around at the time, Patriarch Aleksy II said: "While firmly supporting the inalienable spiritual freedom of every Russian, the right of a person to choose a religion and a world view, and to change that choice, we, Orthodox Christians, are at the same time convinced that the choice must not be imposed from without, especially by exploiting the difficult economic situation of our people, or through crude pressure that denies a person his God-given freedom."[20]

Another argument was that these outsiders somehow had not earned the right to pluck off Russian souls. As President Yeltsin's advisor Sergei Stankevich told the newspaper *Nezavisimaya Gazeta,* "There can be no comparison between the . . . religion which underwent the hardships of the totalitarian regime and the missionaries loaded with money."[21]

The idea was introduced, with little understanding of the irony, by the Russian parliament's Committee on Freedom of Conscience. The fear of groups like the Moonies and Hare Krishnas or even the more sinister cults was not hard to understand, since parents and priests elsewhere in the world have wrestled with how to combat their influence. Muscovites watched in alarm as the followers of Reverend Sun Myung Moon set up shop, not merely in the streets but in Russia's schools and universities. The Unification church, for example, provided leisure weeks for young people in the Baltics and the Crimea—a vacation that many Russian youths quickly accepted, even though far fewer actually signed up as converts by the end of their tour. Reverend Moon's church also brought Russians to America on "scholarships" and provided other benefits for young people who otherwise had almost no chance to do anything but stand in the streets and sell trinkets. One young woman I talked with after she had returned said that it was an excellent opportunity to see America, and although the propaganda sessions had been irritating, they were worth the trouble. "They were nice people," she said," but if there is anything I know, it is how to recognize propaganda."

Perhaps the strangest of all these high-priced tickets into the centers for Russian youth occured at Moscow State University's journalism school. In early 1992, the once-ragged reading room took on a new coat of paint. The shelves were restored. New chairs and tables arrived, and when the area reopened for business after the *remont,* the library had a new sign on the door, a brass plaque like any of those at Harvard or Stanford that names a room or a building after its benefactor. In this case, the plaque read "L. Ron Hubbard," the father of scientology. As of the spring of 1992, the room was decorated with posters of Hubbard—as an Eagle Scout, pilot, and thinker—and his books had made it to the university's shelves.

The dean of the school's faculty, Yasen Zassoursky, told one correspondent that all this advertising for scientology came at a price—Hubbard's organization had to pay for restoring the reading room.[22] There was no difference between this and the Dana buildings or the Rockefeller cafeterias in American universities, he had suggested. The implication, of course, was that these people's forebears had far worse reputations than someone who was merely ideologically strange, like Hubbard.

In the case of the Moonies and the scientologists, most young Russians seemed to be merely sampling the ideas, figuring their brief appearance at an event was all the price they needed to pay for the food and freebies from a rich outside religion. After twenty thousand Russians attended Moon's summer trips in 1992, only fifty took part in one of the mass marriage ceremony's conducted by Reverend Moon in Seoul.[23] And Hubbard's tomes at the university seemed undisturbed, now gathering dust alongside the works of Marx and Lenin.

The efforts of the Russian Orthodox church to bar such groups quickly disappeared in 1993, as the free world, including many Russians trying to hold on to some remains of democracy, explained the hazards of such protections. This was the first step toward a theocracy, a church-run state, they warned. But the suspicion lingered that Orthodox church leaders would simply wait for another time to try to stop the invasion—not only of Western religions and cults but also of the kinds of Russian spiritualism and mysticism that had operated under the surface atheism of the Soviet years.

Meanwhile, the preachers and healers came in droves, wave after wave, on planes from the West and the East, from villages where they had been perfecting their ancient Slavic voodoos in relative obscurity. At one point, visiting the thrum of humanity at Izmailovo weekend market, a place where most of Moscow's stolen goods could be found at steep Western prices, I saw a group of Russian Baptists wading into the viscous waters of a nearby pond. It was a smart tactic—allowing redemption to nestle closer to the site of sin.[24]

The most surreal of all for me, however, was Billy Graham's first crusade to Moscow in October of 1992. Graham's arrival was trumpeted by a bustling crew of media advisors who set up an advertising blitz like nothing Moscow had ever seen. At first, there were the billboards, almost fifteen hundred of them in dark heavenly blue, carrying only one word:

Pochemoo? (Why?) Radio thumped out the question—"a question asked by children even though the answers are searched for all our lives." The starry night with the huge "Why?" across it appeared on nightly television. Muscovites, of course, found it intriguing and strange. "I know about the 'why', can anybody tell me about the 'because'?" one asked. Or they simply shrugged, a Soviet-era response that combined "I don't know" and "I am not able to know" in one irritating gesture.

A few weeks later the answer appeared, with just as much trumpeting on the new Russian media. This was Billy Graham's third or fourth trip to Moscow (he had once declared in Brezhnev's era that freedom of religion had arrived in Russia, a fact disputed by thousands of religious believers in prisons all over the country), and it had the noisy tone of a conquering hero, or at the very least a head of a state. Besides the billboards and the media, details of his arrival came in the mail. Graham's people were the first ever to ask the Moscow post office to process 3.2 million leaflets to the city's postal customers, and at least half of them apparently made it to their intended locations. Most Muscovites figured that this took more than an earthly payoff. It was clearly a bureaucratic miracle.

Billy Graham's revival that chilly October weekend, like many such events in the new Russia, was held in a sports stadium, in this case, the huge stadium reconstructed for the 1980 Olympics that Graham's born-again president friend, Jimmy Carter, had boycotted to protest the Soviet presence in Afghanistan. The Graham organizers had left nothing to chance. If the billboards and the flyers did not bring in the Russians to fill the stadium that seated forty thousand, they made certain the buses and trains did. They booked twelve trains from cities within riding distance—not only St. Petersburg and Rostov, but also Kiev in Ukraine, Riga in Latvia, and Minsk, capital of Belarus. The trains carried an estimated eighty-five hundred believers to Graham's Rebirth '92.

For the first night, the touring buses rumbled to a halt outside the stadium, depositing load after load of believers into the parking lots. They all had badges; they all had seats. Many carried hymnals and song sheets, and they were ready to celebrate what one of them called "our victory to pray our way into heaven."

From late afternoon into the evening, they slowly filled the stadium, and by the time Graham appeared, following choruses and speakers from churches around the countryside, he was greeted like any superstar at any mega-event in the Western world. His sermon roused the crowd to fever pitch, and even though Graham spoke almost no Russian, he had found an interpreter who was like a Russian echo. The two men, one tall and silver-haired, the other dark and square, preached in a rush of alternating Russian and English, their rhythmic voices booming over the rock microphones, their message rising and falling in counterpoint, finally growing in strength and speed as they reached their spiritual climax about the love of God's only son. "Jeeesuuus," Graham sang out in one long rapturous moment. "*Eeesooos,*" came his Russian echo in precisely the same tone and cadence.

Reverend Graham's Baptists rocked and prayed into the crescendo, but hundreds of Russians who had come for the experience watched from a distance, and they seemed, some of them, like anthropologists who had suddenly happened upon a new and amusing native ritual.

Aleksandr Goretsky was one of the amused observers. He stood on the sidelines with several friends and smiled like a man peeking into some forbidden rite. He seemed to be smirking to his friends when I spotted him, but as I approached, his friends scattered. Goretsky, who said he was sixty-six years old, described himself as an engineer (retired). He listened to my questions and swayed from foot to foot for a moment, eyeing me carefully before he answered.

"I came here for the show," he said cautiously. "And now I see that I didn't hear anything bad."

When I moved away, his friends seemed to reappear, undoubtedly asking what the foreign woman wanted, plugging the international press into the miraculousness of such a strange moment in the new strange Russia.

I crossed the coliseum floor, planning to leave before Graham's next sermon, when I saw a young woman standing near the exit who was transfixed by the activities on stage. An American chorus was singing an old Southern hymn, the crooning sounds and the thumping bass organ all roaring at a decibel level that would satisfy most rock groups. When I asked to talk with her, she pulled me away from the noise and under the bleachers. She was a striking beauty, and I had estimated her to be solidly middle-age, probably thirty-five, but Ira Starova told me she was twenty-three and she worked at a scientific institute in Moscow, which meant that her job was slowly evaporating in the new Russia. About Billy Graham, what did she think? She was disappointed, she said, by the vast gap between the advertising and the reality. It was a new experience for a Russian who expected better than propaganda from a religious man from the West, she said.

"I think he is a good man," she said, "but I wanted to get more answers. His ads said that: 'Why do we love? Why is there so much bad in the world?' I didn't get the answers."

Christened secretly at age three by her babushka, Ira had begun to slip back into the Russian Orthodox church now and then to find "a little relief." Her mother, still a solid believer that religion tainted and softened the mind, had not known of the conversion until recently.

When we stopped talking, Ira pulled her long, fashionable coat with its fur collar around her and slipped toward the exit. I moved back to the music, looking for those who had seen more hope in Graham's message than these two ex–Soviet citizens. I found a cluster of young men under the bleachers, and they seemed to be unpacking song sheets for the crowd. Richard Gagiet was eighteen, a student in Moscow. He listened to my questions and began speaking in almost perfect English while his friends stood nearby smiling.

"This is the awakening of Russia," he beamed. "We can say spiritually that for a long time we were asleep. Jesus has truly come into our hearts. We can feel him now."

Listening to him talk, I suddenly realized what made him seem different from the other Russians I had met: he was intensely happy, happy in a way that I had not seen in Russia very often, certainly not in the cities and seldom in the villages. Russians carried their burdens on their faces almost as a matter of pride, and to watch someone laugh in this country was to see a transformation, as if a raucous spirit had suddenly been let out of an old, crusty bottle. I hurried back into the stadium to determine whether Gagiet was simply being hospitable in his native Georgian manner, whether others looked as openly contented as this young man. In this the sea of believers, now rocking and nodding with the music, I saw waves of smiling Russians, and if this religion was an opiate, somehow I felt they had earned the right to enjoy it. After seventy years of having their spirituality crushed into a hard realism, these people deserved to sample an easy, nice, peaceful religion. The tough belief required by the Orthodox church could eventually lure them back, but this was a kind of spiritual breather.

In many ways Billy Graham and his fellow preachers from the West were the least of the distractions for the newly unleashed Russian soul. In some cases, the spiritual awakening that was being described by the believers had also roused some of the strangest credos or philosophies found on this earth.

For many Russians, this spiritual rebirth of clairvoyants and mystics, whirlers and jumpers, trekkers and flagellants raised the specter of the country's troubled history. As philosopher Nikolai Berdyaev once wrote, "A primordial, unquenchable thirst for the miraculous is hidden in every Russian." Sergei Leskov, a writer for *Izvestia*, added his post-Soviet version: "These days astrologers, sorcerers, psychics and messengers from other worlds are part of Russian reality. . . . History has shown us many times that a mass passion for mysticism is a sign of social crisis. The vacant chair of the Party Secretary has now been occupied in the public consciousness by the sorcerer."[25]

The list of seers and soothsayers became endless. Here are a few examples:

- In 1994, a Russian named Albert Ignatenko, who was president of something called the International Academy of Psychoenergetic Sciences, said he taught his child at age five to use his powers to dissipate clouds. At a press conference in Moscow on September 30, 1994, he and his partner, Valentina Vasilyeva, explained that Russia had a special affinity with the star Sirius, which has an unearthly attachment to the Slavic soul. Any true Russian, defined as someone who has come from the origins of Kievan Rus, would go to Sirius at death, they explained.

- A woman calling herself Maria DelPhano drew over two thousand people to a Moscow stadium in the summer of 1992, where she promised that her tentacles to something called Alpha Centralia would heal cancer, end pain, and fix any uneven limbs in the audience.[26]

- And finally, Anatoly Kashpirovsky was among the most tenacious, his television programs mesmerizing millions of Russians in the earlier days of glasnost. Orthodox church leaders sometimes promised that the old faith could help get rid of obsessions with people like Kashpirovsky, and they became modern exorcists of sorts, ridding the ordinary Russian soul of what one believer called "contaminants."

Of all of them, however, the group that seemed to hold Russians spellbound in fascination and horror was the Great White Brotherhood, whose promise of the apocalypse brought thousands of glassy-eyed people to the streets of Kiev, Ukraine, in late 1993. The brotherhood worshiped a woman who called herself Maria Devi Khristos, a sloe-eyed creature who convinced her followers that she was Jesus Christ returning for the second coming, this time in the body of a woman. Photos of Maria's determined face, with its sad, distant look and Mona Lisa smile, were pasted to metro walls in Moscow, tacked onto street signs in St. Petersburg, and nailed along trees and highways in many towns and villages in western Russia.

In the fall of 1993 several thousand people, mostly single mothers and their children, were drawn to the city of Kiev, following this strange pied piper who promised an end to this sinful world on November 14, 1993. (When nothing happened on November 14, she later amended her prediction for the final coming to November 24.) By the first of November, residents of Kiev were in a frenzy, pressing police and church officials to stop the strange invasion. Ukraine officially protested to Russia about the brotherhood, but it was a problem that both governments seemed at a loss to control. Radio announcers advised parents to keep their children inside, safe from the evil magnetism of Maria Devi Khristos. Some schools closed early so that the young ones could get home before the early winter nightfall. Ukraine's best known Orthodox leader, Metropolitan Filaret, proclaimed: "It is the Antichrist that is described in the Bible."

The strange White Brotherhood, new to Russia, was an old threat to the residents of Rybny Pereulok in a quiet southern section of Kiev. There, in 1990, a man named Yuri Krivonogov, Maria's second husband, moved into an old house with thirty teenagers. Neighbors watched slowly as Krivonogov's crew built a wall around the house—a thirteen-foot-high brick wall with electrified barbed wire that, like walls that people in this country had seen before, were designed not only to keep people out but to lock them in.

Within a few months after the brotherhood built their fortress, the mothers and grandmothers came. They held photos of their children and they showed them to neighbors, begging for news. One neighbor told Stacey Anderson of *The Moscow Times* that occasionally the youngsters would get out and they would rush over to ask him for food. " 'Boris, I am hungry. Please give me something to eat.' It was so cold, and they were working very hard. They had a meal only once a day, and it was only cabbage and apples, he said."[27]

The lore of what was happening behind the walls began to spill into the community. Young people would meet a member of the brotherhood in the metro in Moscow or St. Petersburg, go home and pack a bag, and march off to Kiev. Mothers, often single and unprepared in the non-Soviet world, would drag their bewildered children from cozy dachas to this stern and cold life. The cult, a staple of the disillusioned West, had returned to Russia.

As a few became disenchanted, the stories crept out of the fortress. Inside, obedience was everything, they said. All worldly goods went to Krivonogov. Ceremonies for baptism involved fasting for days, refusing sleep, and drinking a glass of what was supposed to be water from the River Jordan. Mothers were said to hand their virgin daughters for Krivonogov's sex rituals—sacrificing their children for peace of mind. Understandably, the members had to make one crucial promise in order to stay inside the group—absolute secrecy.

By late 1992, the authorities had had enough. Kiev's storm troopers took the house by force, where they found flyers, tools, and boxes full of *valuta,* or U.S. dollars. They called it a labor camp, and when they took the children away to a detention center, they began to find the first examples of what later doctors and youth officials would discover in larger numbers: the brotherhood's young seemed dazed and hypnotized, lost in some dangerous other world that Westerners knew from Jonestown and Waco, Texas.

A year later, on the eve of the well-advertised world's end, police moved in again and arrested Krivonogov for extortion and his wife for hooliganism. About eight hundred followers, many of them children, were also taken into custody as they tried to take over Kiev's famous St. Sophia church. Others were arrested for wearing the white robes with the hoods and crosses on their foreheads. Some were grabbed in the streets for handing out literature. A few began to pose as tourists and visitors, slipping brochures to ordinary people in the secretive manner in which Soviet citizens had once changed money or bought goods on the black market. The ones who were arrested often refused to eat or drink, staging hunger strikes that terrorized the bewildered police agents. Kiev police and medical officials finally decided to send some home; others were simply banished from Ukraine. By the end of 1993, the White Brotherhood seemed to have disappeared.

Perhaps one of the most intriguing clues to the White Brotherhood story, however, was the background of Krivonogov. A crazed man with a shadowy past, he worked, at least for a while, at the Kiev Cybernetics Institute, where the Soviets tinkered with the possibilities of psychological warfare. Did this man, whose picture made him look like a robed Charles Manson, use his expertise to drug or hypnotize his following? For many of those looking for answers to this new hysteria, it was the only way to make sense of it all.[28]

In some ways, however, the answer was simpler than a complex look at the struggles in Kiev. The brotherhood was another notice that Russia had entered the free world of the twentieth century, where religions could sprout strange offshoots and rebellious renderings of the old faiths. If these groups existed elsewhere, they would certainly thrive in this new Russia, a continent inhabited by people with a proud tradition of spirituality.

I wanted to see one of the native religions of Russia that had sprung from the rural past and managed to survive the years of communism. The Molokans, whose name is derived from the Russian word for milk, had appeared as a tiny percentage on the Soviet lists of registered believers in the late 1980s, and their presence in this official toll put them somewhere between a religion and a cult in the eyes of the state. I did not meet Ivan Grigorievich Aleksandrov, the head of the Molokan church in Moscow, until 1993, when his church had become one of many groups that operated in Russian homes and makeshift churches around the country. Aleksandrov first invited me to his apartment to talk about his church and then to a service a few days later.

The flat, two well-organized rooms in one of Moscow's hundreds of grim apartment towers, smelled faintly of spices the day I arrived—cinnamon and nutmeg. They were the first delicious hints of a warm apple cake that would appear a few minutes after Aleksandrov had taken my coat and positioned me in his small living area. He began by explaining that he was a professional baker and that the Molokan faith, which could not provide food for his family, was simply his "true life." I wondered as I stared at this man, with his red hair and warm red cheeks, with his Western-style crew-neck sweater with its alligator logo, how he could fit into Russia's new religious landscape. He did not act strangely. He did not show signs of being a man caught in some deep charismatic trance. In fact, Aleksandrov seemed oddly modern for someone professing a faith with its roots so deeply in a period of spiritual upheaval more than two centuries earlier. It was a time when Russia was flooded with different cults, sects, and schisms—a time of troubles, much like the periods at the beginning of the twentieth century and now again at the end.

The Molokans began their communal brand of worship in the 1760s and 1770s, making it a relatively new sect by the standards of Russian Christianity. The name of their sect, according to most histories of Russia's religions, means "spiritual milk" and comes from the Bible (1 Peter 2:2), "As newborn babes desire the sincere milk of the word, that ye may grow thereby."

The Molokan faith began in a time of spiritual experimentation, as disenchanted churchgoers found solace in the strange movements pursuing religious ecstasy through mortification or simple faith. Flagellants became a staple of the time as some groups practiced the circle procession, whipping themselves into a frenzy of godliness, chanting, "Khlyshchu, khlyshchu, Khrista ishchu" (I whip myself, whip myself, searching for Christ).[29] Soon came other mortifiers—the self burners (who appeared during a particularly violent and cruel time) and the self-castrators (who appeared during Catherine the Great's era of sexual promiscuity).[30]

The Molokans tended to demand far less perverse forms of showing one's dedication to the religion. When I saw a service in 1993—which the participants said was much the same form that caused them to suffer persecutions not only by the communists but earlier by the Russian Orthodox church and the tsars—it was more like evangelical Christianity practiced in the backwoods of Southern America in my youth thirty years earlier. Full of song and scripture, it was designed to bring believers into periods of religious rapture—a brief moment when a mortal human being is supposed to be open to the awesome Spirit of God and to feel his powers to heal, enlighten, and, best of all, obliterate the miserable world outside.

The living room where the service was held, on virtually the opposite side of the city from Aleksandrov's apartment, was large for a Soviet building, even one on the outskirts of Moscow, where the chances of space were exchanged for the distance from the center. The floors were covered with linoleum, all done in a woodenlike pattern. The benches were hardwood, and a few chairs, lined against the wall, seemed perilously frail. A large picture window was covered with a green flowered curtain to block out the winter sun, and the chandelier, a Soviet model much like the type found in any Kmart or Bradlees in America, shed its spare light dimly over the congregation.

As I arrived, six very old women sat rocking silently, their heads covered with shawls or scarves. One middle-aged woman—a newcomer, we would learn later—began crying softly as she sat among the women, holding their hands. By the time the service started later, there were fourteen women and two men, both dressed in their best city suits, both smiling serenely. This was a church for elderly women, it seemed, where there was an odd division of labor. The men seemed in charge of the speaking of words; the women ran the singing. In the beginning, it seemed an equal contest—talk versus song—but by the end, the singers had taken control, especially one particularly forceful woman named Raisa Ignatievna Spitsina. Old and tiny, she weighed no more than eighty-five pounds, I guessed, but she sang with a voice that seemed always to be stronger than the others', no matter how loudly or passionately they sang along. Raisa Ignatievna had a regular job, which she dismissed later with a wave of the hand, but mostly she had the role of head singer. When the group tried to sing along, she sternly corrected them, adjusting the rhythm and the strange melodies in ways incomprehensible to almost everyone but herself.

The music, in fact, would be the key to the Molokans, and I would later learn that the chanting would sometimes continue for hours until the singers, having worked themselves into a cacophonous bliss, were spent and satisfied from their consummation with the Spirit of God.

At a break in the session and long before anybody seemed close to such a moment, I talked with Raisa, a woman named Nadezhda, and Aleksandrov. It was a conversation that reminded me of the music, full of strange detours and interruptions. Raisa had come from Tambov, she said, the city where the Molokan faith started. Tambov (some two hundred fifty miles southeast of Moscow), had been considered a spiritual place for almost three hundred years. It was the fountainhead for many faiths, a Jerusalem for the smaller cults and sects in Russia. The reputation for Tambov's abilities to create spiritual beings is so widespread, in fact, that the city is sometimes called *Tambog*, which means, "God is there."

The songs, which to my ear sounded unstructured, were passed from generation to generation, Raisa said. She knew them by their tunes; the music was simply handed over from one believer with a good ear to another.

Raisa told her story in the way that many Russians did in this period—personal agonies first. She had a difficult life, she said. Her mother died in 1935, when Raisa was fourteen, the oldest of six children. "As she died, she made me sing the sixth psalm," Raisa sighed. They decided to have a meeting in her memory, the way people did then, after forty days. "But the authorities came, and they began shooting," she said. For a fourteen-year-old, it was hard to know exactly why they were shooting, but she knew only that it was a time when such things happened with a cruel regularity.

Just as Raisa was moving into the more recent decades, Nadezhda Petrovna Bolotina, age seventy-four, came over to interrupt and tell her own story, but instead of beginning a personal tale, she began two hundred years earlier, with the Pugachev uprising in 1773. Nadezhda then rambled back and forth in time telling stories of Jesus' crucifixion and the persecutions of Peter the Great as if they were part of some strange bouquet of facts, gathered haphazardly from her memory.

Raisa tried to coax Nadezhda into the twentieth century, and Aleksandrov took a seat nearby to explain how the Molokans had always been quiet and industrious—they do not drink, smoke, or swear, he said. They stick to the "ten commandments of Christ," as Raisa put it, "the way it's written in the Bible." Such industry meant that only a few years into freedom, there were Molokan families in Tambov now who "have already built a house. Two stories." And they had animals, the sign of wealth in the countryside.

"The Molokans have always had a good attitude to animals," Raisa said. "If one's animal is calving, a friend comes to help. We don't eat pork, so we have to have twenty-five sheep. If you eat one per month, it takes twelve sheep, and you keep twelve for the next year. We now grow cereals, potatoes, seeds. We make this year work for the next year," Raisa said.

Nadezhda, perhaps tired of being silenced, finally broke into the twentieth century to tell her part of her story. "My father was in prison," she began. Then she continued a long, elliptical tale that was basically about how he died in prison because he was a quiet Molokan farmer.

Other Molokans survived the communist years, as it turned out, not because they became part of the system or because they worked only underground, but because they did not proselytize, especially among the young.

"We cannot go out and preach to others. They must come to us," Ivan Grigorievich had said when I visited him that day in his apartment. He had shown me a film of a 1993 meeting of Molokans, a historic gathering of people who did not like any formal organization, even their own. What was most striking about the film was that the believers were virtually all elderly. Their children, if there were any, were not in sight.

"Where are the young?" I had asked Raisa.

"They don't like to come," she said. "They aren't interested in these things now."

The Molokans, at least these Molokans, were barely surviving in the new world of the faithful. Perhaps their own faith had allowed them to obey the rules of Soviet life too well by restricting their beliefs to the elderly and refusing to sneak children into their apartments each week to hold Sunday school like the other religions. Perhaps it was the religious version of what was happening in other parts of the society—that this old Russian sect had not kept up with what was happening in the rest of the world, where even in religion some Russian groups were adapting to the high-profile methods of American Pentecostals.

The Pentecostal faith, in fact, was booming in the early 1990s. Tucked into the Baptist category of believers during the Soviet years and often forced to use the same meeting halls, many Pentecostals opted instead to go underground, where they were a quiet but obdurate force of dissent. Vasily Ryakhovsky, an aged bishop from Kiev who served eight years in prison for his refusal to register with the state as a believer, told a writer in the early 1990s that the KGB tormented his circle, spreading the word that Pentecostals like him were child murderers. His son Sergei, who was president of a council of Pentecostal bishops, explained that some made alliances with other persecuted religions like the Jews. "Pentecostals weren't allowed to get together [alone], so many went to Jewish synagogues in Moscow on the Sabbath and prayed in tongues."[31]

The Molokans, who also made some associations with Jews and others who suffered in the Soviet years, did not spring to life so easily once those sufferings ended. Their view seemed to be that converts would arrive automatically once the KGB stopped blocking their way. What they did not count on was how much the huge bazaar that Russia had become would invade their private, religious world. Theirs was a native Russian faith losing ground to the allure of Western missionaries; their potential converts had strayed elsewhere.

I felt that in some ways these Russian Molokans were similar to the Russian entrepreneurs, like Olga Romashko, who found that her home-made face cream would have to compete with something that was called Revlon or Rocher and was produced somewhere, anywhere, outside the country. For all the talk about how Russia was turning inward, in many ways it was also reaching outward, and only a true seer would be able to tell which force would prove to be the stronger.

Indeed, within two years, the curiosity about outside religions appeared to be diminishing, and the Russian government had begun quietly restricting religious groups that had once enjoyed free access, not only to people walking along the streets, but also to public buildings and even schools. Some groups by 1995 were banned from classrooms both in Russia and Ukraine.[32]

Even the big revivals did not have the pull that they once did. When American evangelist Jerry Falwell tried two years later to repeat Graham's 1992 *Pochemoo* campaign—flooding Moscow's streets with almost 3 million books and about eighty thousand flyers—Falwell was far from successful by comparison. The crowd of about eight thousand one September evening at the Olympic stadium had come mostly to hear other speakers and to pay their respects to the memory of Aleksandr Men, the Russian Orthodox priest who was murdered in 1990. Falwell, who spent eighteen months and several hundred thousand dollars advertising his arrival in Moscow, spoke for about ten minutes in front of a screen that said simply "an American evangelist" without saying which one exactly.[33]

11

Murder:
The People's Justice

Where there is a court, there is injustice.
—Old Russian saying[1]

The photograph of Yuri Diomin that his sister would later pass around to observers at the trial was of a young man with dark eyes, a sensuous mouth, and a cruel, hungry look that had been absolutely irresistible to a certain class of young Moscow shop-women. The girl posing with him in the picture, one of many passing through his tumultuous life, looked slightly anxious, and it took a moment to realize the source of her concern. Yuri had his arm over her shoulder, and he had grasped her right hand so that it was twisted in what must have been an uncomfortable, even painful way. People who looked at this picture stared for a moment and then winced when they saw the hand.

Late on the night of September 25, 1990, this same young man, who at age thirty-three had also made a small-time reputation for himself as an antiques dealer in the subterranean black markets of Moscow, wandered home late and uncharacteristically alone. Yuri walked past the skeletons of trees, their leaves shed for the long winter, and into the darkened doorway that led to his new apartment on Third Filyovskaya Street, one of the better sections of Moscow. The two rooms, a palace by the standards of most of his young friends, had once been shared with his wife, Elena, and their infant son. They had been divorced two and a half years earlier, and he had sent them away to her grandmother's. Less than a month ago, Elena had come to ask for money, and, as she would describe it later, Yuri had slammed a large, antique book against her head, a final notice that she and the boy were no longer welcome.

In the months since his wife's departure, Yuri had turned their former apartment into a makeshift vault filled with a treasury of Russian antiques, so rare in the late twentieth century that most Russians could never see them except in a museum. There were gold spoons from the last century, paintings worth thousands of dollars, three-hundred-year-old icons, ancient maps, buttons, clocks, and statues from the tsarist days. The collection, which it would later take a judge almost fifteen minutes to list in court, was hidden in drawers, rolled under the bed, and in a few cases, displayed to impress the girls in their American clothes and heavy French makeup who came to visit him.

Yuri was a *zhulik,* literally a swindler, a guy who moved fast and lived around the edges of Russian society. He had been in jail briefly for having a fight with an official on a train, part of the hotheadedness of youth, his sister had said, even though witnesses had suggested that Yuri had tried to push the man out of a speeding railroad car. By the fall of 1990, Yuri was one of hundreds of young men in the old Soviet state who saw opportunity in the first hints of a changing economy. In the places where antiques were quietly traded, many to be taken out of the country illegally, he would buy and sell each weekend, slowly amassing a small fortune of about twenty thousand rubles, which at that time was about $30,000. He had been told that he would soon get a letter of invitation from America, the ticket West that millions of young Russians craved as the Soviet Union was disintegrating and life was moving swiftly from order into chaos. The letter, which would have meant that Diomin could operate in the rich and free marketplace across the ocean, failed to reach him in time.

As Yuri opened his door that night, two intruders were hiding behind a small screen. When he turned to secure the latch, they hit him on the head with a metal rod. He stumbled and fell, and one of the men grabbed his feet while the other slipped out Yuri's leather belt and jerked it around his neck. The next day, his body was rolled into one of his antique carpets, carried outside the city, and buried in the forest outside Moscow.

After his death, one of Yuri's girlfriends, Lyudmila Voika, began wondering whether he had left the city or even the country without telling her. Finally, she used a key he had given her for emergencies. Inside the apartment, Lyudmila saw the gaping holes where many of Yuri's treasures had been stored. The apartment had been ransacked. Books and papers, clothes and toiletries were scattered across the room. Black patches stained the floor, the blood that had been left untouched in an overheated apartment for several weeks.

Lyudmila recognized that this was the scene of a crime, but like most former Soviet citizens confronted with any act of illegality, from an apple snatched at the corner fruit stand to a friend's unnecessary death, she delayed contacting the authorities. The police themselves were suspect; they still represented all the power, arrogance, and corruption that authority had come to mean at the end of the Soviet era, and an ordinary person knew that they tended to investigate the accusers as much as the accused, to implicate anyone connected with a crime, even someone who reported it.

First, she called to get information from Yuri's ex-wife, Elena—a telephone contact that resulted in an unpleasant meeting with Elena and a policeman named Aleksei Asminin. A short stocky man with blond curls and an air of authority, Aleksei told Lyudmila that Yuri was fine, but that she should not try to pursue him or she would get in trouble with the police. Almost a month after the murder, Lyudmila decided that Yuri was not fine and, after making sure she could talk to some other police official besides Aleksei, she reported to the neighborhood authorities that she suspected her boyfriend had been murdered by his ex-wife.

Within a few weeks three people were arrested—first, the ex-wife, Elena, was taken away on the morning of January 16, 1991, "merely for questioning." After a few days talking to an investigator (without an attorney), she confessed to asking Aleksei Asminin to help her deal with her ex-husband, a man she described as greedy with his money and quick to use his fists against wife and child. Aleksei had been a very sympathetic man when she had come to the police station to complain about the abuse and display the bruises. Aleksei had promised to make her husband "disappear," and she gave the policemen a key to Yuri's apartment. She thought he was going to talk to him, she said later.

Police then picked up Aleksei Asminin, who knew well the system that was turning on him that day. Perhaps for that reason, Aleksei told investigators nothing. Finally, the police arrested Aleksei's younger brother, Aleksandr Asminin, a soldier who worshiped Aleksei and apparently would do anything he asked. Aleksandr, also without attorney, sat in a tiny interrogation cell in Moscow's Butyrskaya prison and confessed.

Almost a year after the three arrests, the trial for the murder of Yuri Diomin was heard in Moscow's central city court.

What was important about the Diomin case for me was that the officals of the day did not see it as a judicial event. The accused were not famous dissidents of the past or notorious mass murderers, like the ones whose terrible stories had begun to sell the new, tabloid newspapers in the big cities. The appearance in Moscow city court of Elena Diomina and the Asminin brothers on murder charges in early 1992 did not serve any higher purpose or make any ideological point. Theirs was the reality of Russian justice as it would be meted out for the ordinary man in the first years of the new Russia.

If this case was a way to see how Russians were treated by their antiquated judicial system, it was also a way to see how intelligent people—prosecutors, lawyers, and judges—worked in a legal structure designed to help prove that whatever the state said was true. As these court officials carried on their drab daily routines, the Russian government was perpetually considering changes in the country's laws and the court's rules. Speeches were made and promises were given to make the system fair and to give judges, lawyers, and jurors their first real independence from the controls of the government. By 1993, the new Russian constitution had revamped the law, giving presumption of innocence to the arrested, the right of an attorney (if the accused could find one), and the choice of a jury trial (if the defendant lived in one of the few areas trying this system as an experiment). The suggestions that judges should be independent, that lawyers for a defendant could do more than argue about the length of the sentence, and that a defendant could be presumed innocent by the law were still newfangled ideas. Some experts on Russian law said that any real reform—which meant taking power away from the prosecutor, or *pro-kuror,* as they are called—was years, perhaps decades, away.

In spite of the talk of reform, the Diomin case was an excellent example of how the legal system really worked in Russia until the mid-1990s. Justice did not bow to the law, as I would learn firsthand in this courtroom; she knelt before the almighty Russian prosecutor. And once the prosecutor had accused the defendant, his chances of being found guilty were over 99 percent. (In the Moscow city court, where the Asminin brothers and Diomina were on trial in January and February of 1992, Chief Judge Zoya Ivanovna Korneva did not remember the precise number of those on trial in her court in 1991—"about four hundred," she said. But what she did remember exactly was how many of those four hundred had been declared innocent in the same period—nine.[2] In 1995, I visited Judge Korneva again. In 1994, four hundred sixty-three were accused of serious crimes. All but sixteen were found guilty and five were sentenced to death.)

Those defendants who later chose jury trials when they became available in a few areas had a better chance of convincing their peers they were innocent. In three hundred jury trials held in Russia by mid-1995, an estimated 15 percent of defendants were acquitted—a rate closer to an American acquittal rate, according to attorney Nicholas Arena, who was working in Moscow for the American Bar Association.[3]

To understand the power of the Russian *prokuratura,* or prosecutor's office, to convict the accused, it is important to know how their army of investigators worked, especially at the beginning of the process. For Elena Diomina and the Asminin brothers, the first days after their arrest were spent in long talks with investigators who could offer or withhold cigarettes, promise water, delay it, flirt, coax, badger, threaten, use any method short of torture to get them to talk about Diomin's murder. Their accuser in this period was still allowed to work without the distraction of a lawyer for the accused, primarily because ordinary people like Elena and Aleksandr Asminin seldom realized that, since 1989,[4] even a person in their precarious position could demand to have someone representing them. Instead, the investigator could make them think he was trying to help, trying to clear up this unfortunate matter, trying to get them out of prison—all of which was a cover for his real purpose, which was to find guilt and to walk out of the tiny investigator's cubicle triumphantly waving a signed confession. Confession not only looked good on the prosecution's record; it also cut short the tedious job of locating witnesses and scouring the crime scene for evidence. Once a person was arrested, taken into prison, he was often separated from everyone except guards, fellow prisoners, and his accuser. A visit to Moscow's most famous prison—Butyrskaya—made it easier to understand why such confessions flowed easily from investigators' offices throughout Russia.

The wall of dusty gray apartment houses on one of the highways going north out of Moscow made it possible to pass without noticing the narrow entrance to the dreaded Butyrskaya prison, a catacomb of eighteenth-century cells that housed three thousand people waiting for trials that would routinely find them guilty. It was here that Elena and the Asminin brothers were sent in January 1991. Almost a year later, I came to see where they had been kept, separated from their family or friends until their trial in January of 1992. Even though I had read about Butyrskaya, which was built in 1787 as a fortress, I was not fully prepared. I was not ready for the way its stale air and gloom descended once we passed through neatly painted doors and down long dark corridors. At one point I caught my breath, as many newcomers must do, when I saw a wall in front of me. It was a heavy wrought-iron gate formed into tiny hearts. The ancient symbol of love and affection stood mocking those entering one of the Russia's most notorious prisons.

The administrator in charge of the prison that day had agreed to let me see Aleksei Asminin and had asked a longtime guard, Nikolai Tikhonov, to escort me to the ancient compound where such prisoners are kept. Tikhonov, like the wrought-iron hearts and an occasional splash of bright color on the walls, was jarringly cheerful as he described a place known through the centuries for punishment and torture. If there was a dark side to his job, it was that felt that the standards of "Moscow's best," as he put it, had begun to slip in the last few decades, especially with the arrival of glasnost and democracy.

"It was better under Stalin," he said without apology or further explanation. "It began to fall apart in 1985," the year that Mikhail Gorbachev took over the Soviet government. Tikhonov's tour was thorough and disturbingly upbeat, and as we walked through dark, forbidding hallways, he chirped about the benefits afforded his "flock," as he once referred to the the faceless army growling behind the rows of rusting metal doors. When we found a trolley of food in one corridor, he held up the oily lid so that I could see inside. It was a large tureen with two inches of grease at the top, and as Tikhonov stirred, a fluttering of tiny vegetables and gristly meat twirled to the surface. Another container had oatmeal, which had already begun to congeal into large lumps. "See, as good as outside," he said, grinning. "The only thing these prisoners don't have is freedom."

Tikhonov's tour, done at a brisk pace that had me breathlessly trying to keep up, brought us to one room that featured black windowless boxes against the walls that looked like telephone booths without the telephones. The booths had small, wooden seats and seemed to have just enough room for one person so that when the door was shut, there would be virtually no light and not much air. "Oh, those," said Tikhonov when we were whisked past the cubicles. "They are the places where prisoners sit when we are walking other prisoners through. One prisoner can't see or meet another unless it is authorized." Prisoners had been known to set up societies behind bars, elaborate systems that became the basis for the *mafiya* in the later years of the Soviet state and the beginnings of the new Russia. The *vory,* or thieves, as these prisoner families were called were run by the *vory v zakone,* the Russian dons who had their own ways of conducting business both inside and outside the prison. But the guards could make their mark on anyone who appeared to be making trouble; a little time stewing in one of these cubicles would give the prison officials a chance to do more than separate prisoners. Even with rules outlawing torture, there could be tortures, I was told. A half hour or more of total darkness and breathing too much of your own air was one of them.

As we wound upstairs, making any idea of our location beyond the understanding of all but those with a keen sense of direction and possibly even a compass, we suddenly walked into a long corridor painted dark green and gold. The rows of doors going into the twenty or so interrogation chambers looked like a classic nightmare, and when we walked past one of the rooms, we could hear people laughing. The guards, Tikhonov explained, were using an interrogation cell for smoking and lunch. When we saw a room where prisoners were brought for questioning by the investigator, I thought it was claustrophobic. Only later did I realize that these rooms brought not only pain and pressure for the prisoners but also relief: there were windows and light, and even someone undergoing a stiff grilling by an investigator could enjoy the brief luxury of seeing outside.

When we finally came to Aleksei's living quarters, I saw why the Helsinki Watch had called the cells "ancient, overcrowded dungeons."[5] For months afterward, I shuddered at the memory of the guard pushing his key into the heavy door and jerking the huge handle a few times to get it open. As the door separated from the jamb, it made a sucking noise, like pulling the top out of a hermetically sealed bottle. Stale air and cigarette smoke rushed over us as we stood in the corridor.

The room, a narrow cavelike area about twelve feet long and eight feet wide, was so dark that we could barely see the faces of Aleksei and his three cellmates. Even on this sunny winter day, the window, covered with dust and bisected with heavy bars, let in almost no light. With a vaulted ceiling like a Victorian jail, the cell was painted a navy blue, which took out even more light, and a naked lightbulb swung from above, spreading the equivalent of a thirty-watt glow barely down to the table underneath. There was a checkerboard on the urinal, and over the basin were four cigarette boxes glued to the wall. In each was a frayed-looking toothbrush, one per prisoner. The cell was very neat and smelled of fresh disinfectant, like most of the rest of the prison.[6] Tikhonov told me to be quick; there was little time for questions; and I tried to be neutral, to ask something that would not get us thrown out before we had finished our tour.

"What do you do with your time here? Do you read?" I asked.

It seemed innocent enough, but Asminin looked at me out of the corners of his eyes to see if this were some kind of trick question. "There is not enough light to read," he said finally, stating what should have been obvious. In earlier times and without the guard watching, he might have answered less politely. He had been known to snarl at friends, family, and other policemen in his days outside.

"What do you do then?"

He shrugged.

One of Asminin's fellow prisoners—they were all policemen, because prison authorities feared they would be murdered in ordinary cells—

handed me something by way of answer to the question. As I turned my hand to look at the gift, Tikhonov snatched it from me, inspected it under the light from the corridor, and then handed it back. It was a crucifix that the prisoner, or *zek,* as they were known in the streets,[7] had made out of a plastic bag and matchsticks. The *zek* told me that the ocher color of the crucifix came from tea, but his colleagues and the guards smiled. Later I learned from someone who had spent time in a Soviet political prison that urine made the best amber tone on these religious amulets. Still, I took it and kept it, thanking the man as we left. The guards then slammed the door loudly and gave it a final kick, not so much to complete the task, it seemed, as to remind the prisoners that they were locked and bolted inside. I tried not to shudder, and Tikhonov turned back toward the outside as he recited, cheerfully, the prisoner's daily routine.

Wake-up is 6 A.M. and bedtime is supposed to be 10 P.M. Some are allowed to watch television, others are occasionally taken for a walk outside. But these were benefits that came with compliance, or perhaps, as elsewhere in the prison world, a little bribe of food or cigarettes. The only real variation in the *zek*'s routine is when he goes to the interrogation halls to be with the prosecuting investigator. If he is among the fortunate, his family has paid a lawyer to be there during all but the first stages of the interrogation. Often, it is not so complicated: the prisoner and the investigator with a guard outside just in case.

One strange variation occured for the Diomin investigation. Midway through the process, Elena Diomina began to feel that she had been mistreated by the legal system and framed by her policeman friend, Aleksei. She started declaring that she was not guilty. The state's prosecutor, unable to budge her with the usual arguments, asked her mother to come "to convince Elena to stop trying to change her story," as her mother explained one day as we waited for the trial to begin. There was no lawyer present when Elena's mother tried to pressure her—not to lie, exactly, but to stick to her original "confession" elicited by investigators shortly after she was arrested.

"I didn't care that our lawyer wasn't there," said Rimma Mikhailovna, Elena's mother. "I was only desperate to see that my daughter was okay."

Most relatives never got past a room near the entrance of the prison where family members came to carry messages or provisions from the outside. They brought food, cigarettes, money, and clothes, all of which was pushed through barred windows where prison officials weighed and sifted through the parcels to make certain they fell within the strict limits of Butyrskaya. Each prisoner was allowed twelve kilograms, or 26.4 pounds, of extra food a month. Alcohol was contraband, and tea was rationed— only one pound per month. The reason was that prisoners brewed tea so strong that it gave the prisoner a rush, like a narcotic.[8] The guards had sophisticated scales and kept families to the microgram. Relatives stripped away any unnecessary packaging to try to stay under the weight limits. Cigarettes were removed from their cartons and even their packs, one hundred or so sent through in a plastic bag. Likewise the tiny boxes and golden foil were removed from Western bouillon cubes, which were a favorite food for those inside Butyrskaya. A large sign from the Soviet days issued its pale order: "Citizen, keep quiet and keep the hall clean." The citizenry was quiet as we passed through on our way out, but the hall was littered with mounds of candy wrappers, cigarette packaging, and bouillon boxes.[9]

As I walked outside the prison into the bright, cold afternoon, I felt a surge of relief that explained why the pressures to confess were so seductive. Investigations were slow and inefficient. Although the courts were beginning to allow more people to go free on personal recognizance during investigations, there was no real bail system, and anyone deemed dangerous or untrustworthy languished in these terrible places without seeing their relatives or the outside world until they went to trial. A confession shortened their stay, and once they were convicted, they could at least see relatives on an occasional basis and hear news about parents or spouses or children. Investigators emphasized this part of the process, not the fact that the same confession brought prison sentences that would taint them for life, remove many of their privileges as citizens, and possibly leave them permanently weakened by tuberculosis and other diseases.[10]

The legal system that processed the Diomin murder case in January 1992 was a leftover Soviet structure that may not have been as corrupt as during the Stalin era, but it was also not yet as advanced as in the decades before communism. Legal scholars after 1991, working to reform the

Russian legal system in such a way that it would be more Russian than Western, were fond of looking for models in the prerevolutionary courts.[11] But some, like Sergei Pashin, who helped create the enlightened legislation promoted by President Yeltsin in this era, feared that concentrating on the distant past would not help Russia in the future.

"We are trying to revive old traditions, but on the other hand, it was never characteristic of these reforms [in the prerevolutionary time] that there was respect for the individual. Respect for power has always been foremost. The chief of police need only send his hat to court sometimes [to have someone convicted], and the legal reforms of 1864 only came about because the tsar allowed it. Seven years later, there were counterreforms, limiting the juries in their rights," Pashin said.[12]

Still, the legal reforms of 1864, which were introduced under Tsar Alexander II shortly after the emancipation of the serfs, established a court system widely regarded as one of the best, if not the best, in Europe. But this system of jury trials and a strong, independent judiciary had its limitations. The tsars who maintained a close watch over these courts, began to take back control, reserving the right to take away political crimes to the military courts, where the royal palace had more say over the process and, presumably, the outcome.[13]

What was left of Tsar Alexander II's legal system survived until 1917, when the new Bolshevik government decided on changes that, in effect, rolled the courts back to prereform days. A group of Russian scholars, working to revise the legal codes in 1991, said that the Soviet state actually turned the department of prosecutors, or *prokuratura,* into a system similar to that established by Peter the Great 270 years earlier. The courts under Peter were known then as "the eye of the tsar," or *oko gosudarevo,* and their job was to do the tsar's bidding.[14]

The Russian court system that existed in the 1990s had been adapted from the French, or continental, system, which emphasizes the investigation before the trial. This investigation is normally carried out by a person who is supposed to seek out the truth about what happened, not the guilt of any particular citizen. In a most basic way, this contrasts with the American system, which has two sides fighting against each other—the prosecution and the defense. This battle between prosecutors and defense lawyers is supposed to ferret out what really happened, with a grand jury to determine whether there should be charges, a judge as a moderator, and the jury giving the final verdict.

The continental system, as practiced in France and Germany, for example, has professional investigators—the French *juge d'instruction* or the German *Untersuchungsrichter*—whose report to the court is considered a weighty and important document. The Soviet investigator, however, had not been independent. He worked for the procuracy, which prosecuted the criminal case for the state and therefore tilted the whole system against the accused.[15] The Soviets turned the continental system, sometimes called the "inquisitorial system" in the West, into a structure with one prime motive: to protect the state and its philosophy. The agents of that system were the members of the procuracy, or prosecutors, whose power was so great that over the years the roles of judge, jury, and defense lawyer had atrophied into a kind of feeble supporting staff.

By 1995, the efforts to reform the old Soviet *prokuratura* had begun, but as Nicholas Arena, a trial lawyer working for the American Bar Association in Moscow, put it, *"Pervy blin komom,"* the first blini is never perfect. The adversarial system became part of the law, but like many such laws, it had not reached most courtrooms. The new juror system, which gave the jury the role of deciding guilt or innocence, had started in nine areas, with four more planned for 1996, but it had stalled in part because of the cost of outfitting the courtroom with so many extra people. These new jurors were paid handsomely for their time, and reformers or consultants like Arena had been trying to spread the word that being a juror should be a privilege and responsibility of citizenship, not a moneymaking proposition.

This experimentation with legal reform in Russia was fragile, and the forces against reform were growing stronger. With the rise in crime, the economic turmoil, and the growing conflict with Chechnya, the Yeltsin government was increasingly focused elsewhere. The adoration of things Western and especially American was waning, and legal reformers feared that when the Russian authorities concentrated once again on the court system, justice would mean more convictions, not more independent jurors, judges, and lawyers, as in the West.

*   *   *

Almost exactly a year after Elena was arrested, she and the Asminin brothers went to trial in a first-floor corner of the old Moscow city courthouse. The courtroom, which I could enter only after knocking on the imposing steel door and explaining to a policeman that I wanted to hear this trial, seemed plain and small, minus the columns and stylistic pomp that comes with most court chambers elsewhere. What stunned me, even though I had seen pictures of it, was that the defendants sat in a large cage set against the right-hand wall of the courtroom. The first time I saw the three accused murderers in this cage, they seemed to be staring out from behind their bars like forlorn creatures in the zoo, and they were guarded by armed policemen who stood glaring at them during the entire trial. The cage gave the proceedings an ominous feel and made it clear that the accused were viewed as guilty and dangerous, even before the trial started.

After a few minutes in the stuffy courtroom, I realized someone had tried to make it cozy, succeeding only, for me at least, to make it more sad and depressing. There were gauzy orange-and-white curtains long in need of cleaning. The brown linoleum floors were chipped but well scrubbed. The walls, even the cage, had been painted a sickly butterscotch color.

A year after this trial, the Moscow city court would move to a grand marble structure in the northeast section of the city. In some ways the new building would be very advanced; for example, over each courtroom door was an electronic notice about the nature of the case inside. The hearing rooms, however, were simply newer versions of the old one I had seen. The same butterscotch color, the same chilling cage.

That first day I walked into the courtroom for the Diomin murder trial, the judge, like everyone else, knew I was a foreigner and that I had no direct relationship with anyone in this case. From his chair, Judge Aleksandr Pavlovich Novikov asked who I was—or, to be precise, "What need do you have to be here?" When I explained that I was a reporter and writer from America, there was a long silence and a short conference with the prosecutor. Then, apparently deciding that the days of locking out the international press were over, they continued the long, exhausting process of essentially ratifying the prosecutor's report.[16]

Judge Novikov for the entire trial wore the same gray crew-neck sweater with a black geometric design and the same gray jacket. There were no black robes like those that would come later, and the effect was of a professor, not a judge, sitting on the dais. Beside the judge sat the two members of the jury required by Soviet and then Russian law. Officially, these two jurors were called lay assessors, but ordinary people with experience in the court system often referred to them as "nodders," because all they were really allowed to do was nod their approval to the dreary spectacle before them. A court reporter took notes by hand—there would be no verbatim court record of this or any other ordinary court case—and the lawyers sat below at a small, rickety-looking table as befit their station as supplicants more than advocates. The prosecutor, a stern-looking woman in a navy power suit that would do nicely in any executive office in the West, sat to one side. She was clearly in control, part of an elite corps of the legal profession whose status and power had been virtually assured within the Soviet legal system.

As in most courtrooms in the West, there were periods of delay and achingly methodical testimony that did not, in the end, make much difference to the case. But each time the trial would be interrupted, the prisoners were taken away, hands held behind their backs as though handcuffed, even though they were not. I learned later that this was the prisoner's walk, enforced with brutality that could quickly include handcuffs if they were deemed necessary.

Citizens in the courthouse were forced to clear the hallways and stand quietly against the walls while prisoners were marched back and forth from the courtroom to their holding area in the courthouse. The guards, who carried submachine guns and led fierce-looking German shepherds that seemed to bark constantly, had no trouble getting people to move out of the way.

In the time I spent in the Moscow city courts, these interruptions seemed almost constant as prisoners were hustled from prison to bus to courthouse cages. It was a strange and hectic period—busy because the crime rate was soaring, unpredictable because the laws kept changing. The Soviet legal system had always been flexible, with laws and even the constitution adaptable to the wishes of the Communist Party apparatchiki and its agents in the procuracy. But after the Soviet system disintegrated there was no fist from above. As elsewhere in Russian society, everything was in flux, and most things, even in the legal system, were up for sale. The rule of law, which most people respect in America, had not established itself in Russia, and laws were often negotiable, at best.

Zoya Ivanovna Korneva, chief judge of the Moscow courts, had granted me interviews throughout this period, and in the first one, on the morning I began observing the Diomin trial, she had tried to explain what was happening to cases in her jurisdiction. A few years earlier, the prosecutor might have asked for the death penalty for Aleksei Asminin, but the parliament had been considering changes in capital punishment, so instead judges were considering death only in extreme cases—multiple murders or killing of innocents such as children. Some laws were clear enough because some crimes—like murder, rape, robbery—would be against any legal code. But economic law was changing as fast as the economy, and judges were stuck either trying to enforce what appeared to be the law, or trying to figure out what seemed right. Judge Korneva said that they often waited for the legislature to give clues about whether today's economic crimes would exist next week.

Some of the crimes for speculation and excessive profitmaking that were punishable by death a few years earlier were suddenly moot. Hundreds of people sat in prisons for engaging in the old Soviet sin of trade, while outside, the streets had turned into an endless bazaar. "The life of a judge is not easy now," Judge Korneva said. "The transition is difficult, and we cannot change the whole system in a snap," she had said in her old courthouse offices.

While many of those involved in the legal system struggled to keep it working, outside the courtrooms people talked openly about how justice was like other services in the new Russia. Once the courts had been run with power and clout; now the difference between a legal and illegal act could be a bundle of rubles, a new car. Each official was different, of course, and it was said that the art was in knowing exactly who could be bought and for how much. The judges who could not be bought needed protection, and in late 1993, Russia provided extra security for its judges, including the right to carry guns.[17]

The lore that justice was negotiable added to the anger and shame of those in prison. If they were not viewed as guilty once they were arrested, they were seen as fools who weren't clever enough to buy or bully their way out of trouble or as unfortunates caught in a capricious legal system. By 1995, it was becoming clear to the ordinary Russian that only small-time criminals went to prison. The big criminals (see chapter 12) lived like kings, not merely of the underworld but in the city streets, the public showplaces.

In the new Russia as in the old one, people saw their laws as lofty documents unconnected to real life. The Soviet legal system had been a sham, a paper courthouse run by the Communist Party apparatchiki. The Soviet constitution promised justice, but Stalin's show trials of the 1930s and the staged legal dramas that resulted in the jailing of hundreds of dissidents in the 1970s made it clear that the communists' laws protected the ruler, not the ruled.[18] Whether the new Russian legal system would continue to serve the powerful, not the weak, was still an open question in the early 1990s.

The first day I saw the Diomin trial, there were three defendants and two lawyers. The third lawyer, a young legal activist named Vladimir Aleksandrovich Bushuyev, was late, delaying the proceedings for about fifteen minutes. When Bushuyev arrived, breathless after rushing from one courtroom to the next to help clients, he would explain later, he apologized to the prosecutor first, then the judge. Bushuyev, who represented Aleksandr Asminin, was a former judge who decided being a lawyer gave him at least a little more power in the Soviet courtroom. At this stage, he was not getting rich in his new profession. His clothes were lumpy and Soviet, the same crew-neck sweater and shiny jacket each day in court. And when I saw him get into his car one afternoon, it was a battered Lada, not the Volvo or Mercedes that his colleagues would favor a few years later. Bushuyev was part of a group of young reformers who wanted to improve conditions in the prisons, and he later took me to a meeting at a Russian Orthodox church where ex-prisoners told their stories about the abuse they had suffered behind bars. One ex-prisoner, who had been a factory manager when he was convicted of stealing government property (which he said was a setup), served his time at a prison in mid-Siberia. Inmates made shoes in underground factories that he said were so damp and claustrophobic that virtually every prisoner was infected with tuberculosis. Ten years for many prisoners was a death sentence.

In the courtroom, Bushuyev labored to protect his client, leaping to the floor like some of his American colleagues whenever it seemed necessary. His fellow advocates were strangely docile by my standards; they had the look of people who expected little change as a result of their role in the trial. Months later, when I went to the supreme court hearing for this case, I arrived ahead of time and was able to witness lawyers from another case making their appeals. One attorney appeared to be either drunk or extremely ill, perhaps even both, as he slurred a perfunctory defense for his client. (Alcoholism, a problem in many other areas of Russian life, was common among the *advokaty,* or lawyers, many of whom started drinking early in the morning.) Another attorney simply failed to appear, and the supreme court decided the client's case without him.

The best lawyers were trained at Moscow State University Law School, in a five-year course that was available only to those with top scores and a heavy folder of recommendations from powerful people. But many more of the nation's lawyers got their degrees in six-year courses at night school, and some, who had started practicing at legal co-ops, received little legal education at all.[19]

Some young lawyers were beginning to fight more for their clients, especially those who were paid well (the equivalent of about $2 a day, an excellent wage at the time), as in the Asminin case. Others were worried about how freeing lawyers might corrupt the system. Elena Bariknovskaya, who organized the Lawyers Committee for Human Rights in St. Petersburg, explained that as a Russian she was worried, not so much how lawyers would operate, but whether they would really help society separate the innocent from the guilty. "I'm not sure I want such wide rights as American lawyers have," she said. "If lawyers have broader rights during investigation, I'm afraid justice will not be served at all. Lawyers will just teach the defendants to lie. I think this is a Russian problem. Here, it is no problem for us to lie, to save our life or to get free."[20]

Bariknovskaya was not the only one who worried that giving lawyers too much independence would skew the process. Moscow's Chief Judge Korneva, who had visited the United States and seen the American courts at work, was concerned that the plight of the victim seemed to get lost in the trial. In Russian courts, victims' families have the status of "aggrieved parties," and they can actually question witnesses or object to certain legal matters in court. "Tell me," Judge Korneva asked sternly one day when I had been questioning her about her legal system. "Where in your courts does one worry about the victims?" When I repeated a few truisms of American jurisprudence, most of which she had heard before, she shook her head. "Not enough," she said somberly. "We think that is wrong."

Lawyers in the Soviet Union had some independence, Pashin told me. But in ordinary cases, their job was more to adjust the sentence than to overturn the prosecutor's case. In an excellent description of the legal process, Robert Rand wrote in his 1991 book *Comrade Lawyer* about an attorney named Silva Abramovna Dubrovskaya, who worked hard to get her clients a deal only slightly better than the one offered by the prosecutor's office:

> Silva, of course, had to measure success in the tiny increments that the system allowed. There was no other yardstick. Defense lawyers, even the very best, rarely achieved outright wins. Success meant obtaining a milder form of punishment for the client, maybe three years of hard labor instead of four. Or less severe prison conditions. A verdict of guilt on reduced charges? Conceivable. Acquittal? Not likely."[21]

By the mid-nineties, some lawyers had the opportunity to speak to the new independent juries, and in those cases, their style quickly changed from the regular obsequiousness in addressing the prosecutor to a wide assortment of seductions for these Russian juries.

Still, their powers were far less than those of an American lawyer—who could interview witnesses in advance of a case and generally do his or her own investigation of the proceedings. Such matters were still the purview of the prosecutor, and for most trials, it was still the prosecutor's show.

In the Diomin murder trial, prosecutor Lyubov Anatolyevna Korshunova clearly had the most clout in the courtroom. When she rose to speak, the courtroom grew silent. A small blond woman, she added to her stature somewhat with a hairdo so stiff and so bouffant that it looked as though it would splinter into small pieces at the lightest touch. Her voice was soft, but she was clearly a tough woman. At the beginning and end of the trial, Korshunova had changed her assessment of the case only in very minor ways.

She recommended that the judge sentence the accused ringleader, Aleksei, to fifteen years in prison plus three years of exile in a city outside Moscow. For his younger brother, Aleksandr, she recommended nine years, and for Elena, eight. The sentence for Aleksei was the maximum prison sentence allowed. The next level of punishment was the death penalty, administered by a prison guard, who shoots a single bullet into the back of the condemned man's neck.

In making her closing arguments, she stood and spoke constantly for four hours and three minutes one afternoon, without a break or even a sip of water. After listening to her it was clear that a murder had been committed and that the group that had been arrested had been somehow involved. But it was not clear who actually committed the murder. Aleksandr accused Aleksei, and Aleksei denied all. The time of the murder was not certain, and there were no fingerprints or laboratory analyses that linked the victim to the defendants.

Boiled down from four hours, her version of the plot was simple: Elena had married the wrong man. She cried on the shoulder of a policeman, who promised to help her. He said he would make him "disappear." She agreed. The policeman asked his brother to help and paid him ten thousand rubles. The policeman also had a number of the husband's antiques in his apartment when he was arrested.

Prosecutor Korshunova, who did not look like the kind of woman who made room in her life for sympathy, nevertheless said she felt some understanding of Elena's plight. Wife abuse was seldom perceived as a crime by police, and most women found that by going to the authorities they got little more than a suggestion to go home and give the old man what he wanted. In Elena's case, she had been wooed by Yuri Diomin when she was an impressionable twenty-year-old, only to learn a few weeks after the ceremony that he had agreed to marry her to get a *propiska*, a pass necessary for anyone to live in Moscow. Yuri quickly turned from a generous beau into a stingy husband. He made her bring receipts home for everything she bought, even tiny items for their newborn son. And when

she disobeyed him—including times when she failed to call him to announce that she was coming home—he beat her, Elena had testified.

When it was her turn to speak, Elena's lawyer, a small round woman who
looked like a kindergarten teacher, stood to plead her client's case—
elaborating on the theme that Elena was the real victim of this murder. She
began by explaining what a violent thug Yuri had been. During their
divorce trial, even with state officials there to oversee the proceedings, Yuri
had thrown a chair at the window in the courtroom. He tried to pummel
Elena with his fists because he said she had failed to tell him that the
divorce would cost him one hundred rubles.

If Elena had a connection to Aleksxei Asminin, it was her husband's
fault, the lawyer said. It had all started one night in 1987, when Yuri came
home drunk, accused her of spying on him and stealing his money, and
then he beat her so badly that she went sobbing to the police station for
help. There she met Aleksei, who consoled her and advised her that he
could help if she would complain only to him. When she came back the
next time, there were fresh bruises, another black eye. Aleksei sympathized
and fumed at such behavior. He was her confidant and friend. If they were
the lovers that many of the neighbors or relatives suspected, neither Aleksei
nor Elena admitted it to the court. Now, behind the bars of her cage, Elena
sat as far away as possible from Aleksei, who brooded in a corner, cursing
to himself and glaring at anyone in the coutroom who caught his eye.

As her lawyer spoke that day, the twenty-six-year-old Elena cried
quietly, her head often leaning against the bars in front of her. It was hard
to imagine her as the beautiful young temptress she apparently had been
only a few years earlier. Her hair was turning a steely brown color, and even
though it had been freshly cut and styled for her appearance, it looked
undernourished, like the rest of her. The eyes were still a bright blue, and
when she unfurled herself enough to sit up straight, which she seldom did,
you could see the high, Slavic cheekbones that give many Russian women
their stunning beauty.

Eventually Elena became almost as afraid of Asminin as she was of her
ex-husband, the lawyer continued. After he asked her if she wanted Diomin
to disappear, she said that her husband did disappear, but that she thought
Asminin, known as a tough character, had convinced him "peacefully" to

leave town. When she finally asked where he was, Asminin told her he was being held at a dacha by his friends.

One of the most difficult moments in the trial for me personally was when Elena's lawyer, bowing to the power of the prosecutor, in effect admitted that her client had participated in the murder even though Elena now said she was not guilty. "Elena didn't wish the murder would happen, but she probably realized that it was possible" when Aleksei said Yuri would "disappear," the lawyer said. In America, whole sections of this trial would be about the meaning of the word "disappear," and her lawyer, if she had a decent one, would have been battling to the last to have this crucial word mean anything but murder. Not here. Even the lawyers were looking for sympathy, not acquittal.

Toward the end of the trial, when it was clear that she was doomed to a prison sentence, Elena was asked for her final words to the court. Dressed in a thin blue sweater and a pleated schoolgirl skirt, she stood slowly and turned her head into the corner of the cage toward the judge and away from Aleksei.

"I ask you not to punish me because I think I am punished enough already. The only thing left in my life is my son. I haven't seen him for a year, and I fear I have lost the meaning of life," she whispered.

The court reporter, taking notes, asked her to speak up.

"If I go to prison," she said slightly louder, "I will have nobody to care for my son because my mother is ill, and my grandmother is almost eighty years old, and I'm not sure about the future for my son if something happens to my grandmother."

As she heard these words, Elena's mother gasped. First, it was clear her daughter did not trust her with the grandson. "She thinks I'm a little crazy," Elena's mother had said earlier, grinning somewhat erratically like a woman with a whole array of private jokes. More than that, Elena's mother had been taking care of the boy for about four months; the grandmother had died and nobody had told Elena while she was waiting in prison for the trial.

For Aleksei, the one accused as the organizer, the prosecutor's evidence came from the other two defendants but also from his former colleagues at the police department. They accused him of being a hothead, a troublemaker. Elena also testified that shortly after the murder, when she had asked Aleksei where her ex-husband was, he said he was at a dacha outside of town and that if she asked any more questions, he would "make her disappear too." His manners in court were less than gentlemanly, but he said repeatedly—during the trial and afterward—that he was part of a complicated plot, possibly by his colleagues at the police department, to get rid of him. It was not an outlandish charge.

The brother, Aleksandr, who spent his time during the trial fingering a circle of worry beads, a crucifix, or sometimes simply a box of matches, was portrayed as a gentle man who adored his older brother, Aleksei. But when the police began questioning him as someone connected to Yuri's murder, he quickly accused Aleksei of the actual killing and said that he had only helped his brother wrap the body in a carpet and bury it in a patch of forest outside Moscow.

When he was asked for his last words, the time when a prisoner is supposed to have his chance to argue with the court, Aleksandr said: "I have nothing to say. I hoped until the last moment that my brother would prove my words true because he is the only witness. But since he holds on to his own life like this, I have nothing to say."

On February 4, 1992, almost a month after the trial had begun, Judge Novikov, who was still wearing his gray crew-neck and sports coat, announced the verdict and the sentence. He began with Aleksei Asminin. The verdict was guilty, and he was given fifteen years—the exact sentence demanded by the prosecutor. The ex-policeman groaned as he heard the judge's decision. He slumped noisily onto the wooden bench at the back of the prisoner's cage. He sat for a few moments with his head in his hands until the judge, who had begun reading the verdicts for the other defendants, suddenly stopped.

"Asminin?" Judge Novikov said loudly in a voice that I had not heard before in the trial. It was an admonition, a stern warning befitting a jurist demanding order in his courtroom.

"Asminin? Will you stand?"

A prisoner must be on his feet when the judge in Russia issues his verdict, but Asminin, like the dozen other listeners in the small overheated courtroom, had already been standing almost two hours listening to the judge's assessment of the case, a rereading almost point by point of the prosecutor's four-hour assessment a few weeks earlier.

Asminin shook his head in answer to Novikov's question and then answered softly but defiantly: "No. I don't agree with anything you have said." The now-convicted murderer's face was gray, and he began pulling off his jacket and sweater. Underneath, his shirt was not damp but wet. "This trial is not lawful. It is not justice."

For a moment Judge Novikov stared at the prisoner, and then, perhaps deciding that there was nothing worse he could do after sending the man to prison, he continued reading, giving the verdict for Aleksandr—eight years in jail—and for Elena—seven years. The verdicts were only slightly less than what the prosecution had wanted for those two, and their lawyers were gratified that the state's recommendation had been cut back by a year for each of them. Their year in Butyrskaya prison would also be subtracted from their sentence.

As Judge Novikov left, the sounds of people sobbing began softly and then quickly overwhelmed the courtroom. Relatives of the accused were crying about the sentences. Those related to the murdered man were crying because no one got the death penalty. For a few minutes, guards allowed the newly convicted to reach out and hug their loved ones. Then they were handcuffed and marched back to Butyrskaya prison, where they would wait for their appeal.[22]

On May 14, 1992, in a small antechamber of the elegant old Moscow building used as the city's high court, three supreme court judges, all in street clothes, listened to a ten-minute digest of the prosecution's charges in the Diomin case. Only two of the lawyers appeared at the hearing; Aleksei's attorney was absent. The chief judge flicked through the pages of the case and yawned as the lawyers for Aleksandr and Elena made their final plea. Then they retired for twelve minutes, and when they returned, they supported the lower court's verdict. The entire public process took thirty-five minutes.

Within a few days, Elena, Aleksei, and Aleksandr were shipped to three different Russian prisons.

Four months later the newspaper *Moskovsky Komsomolets* wrote that in the gulag, or Russian penitentiary system, the tuberculosis rate was seventeen times higher than among the rest of the population, and prison officials themselves acknowledged that every eighth inmate had tuberculosis. The chief physician of the largest tuberculosis clinic in Russia, N. Vezhninz, said that she believed 70 percent of the nation's inmates suffered from tuberculosis and that a tuberculosis epidemic was "raging" in the nation's prisons. The causes were lack of decent food, inadequate medical care, stress, cold in winter, and suffocating heat in summer.[23]

A few days later I told a friend about the terms of prison for those convicted in the Diomin case, especially the one for Aleksei, the gang leader. "It is a death sentence," she said, "just as surely as a bullet to the back of the neck."

When I went to visit her in May 1995, Chief Judge Zoya Ivanovna Korneva of the Moscow city courts had moved to a spacious office that looked down from the top floor of the city's new courthouse. She offered me a seat at the long conference table attached to her desk, introduced me to an assistant, served coffee and tiny round biscuits, and then scolded me gently for being away so long. It had been more than two years since I had visited her and heard her assessment of what was happening in the courts. "There have been many, many changes since you were here last," she said, shaking her head as though I had been tardy at school. Most important, a new constitution had been adopted, she explained, a document that she and others hoped would set the stage for a new code of law.

The law now provided the best of protections, she said proudly. Presumption of innocence was guaranteed. No longer were the arrested and the guilty treated in virtually the same manner. "It is being brought into life, step by step—this criminal code," she added.

The accused can remain silent, she continued, a fact that was not supposed to be used against him. Relatives were no longer required to testify against a defendant. And most important, a prisoner was to be informed immediately of his right to remain silent until he can get a lawyer. This was all in the law now. Moreover, beginning January 1996, Moscow's city court would join nine other regions—including Stavropol, Rostov, and Saratov—using the jury system as an optional choice for the defendant. Legal scholars looking at Russia had said in late 1992 that this kind of change would take ten years. Something had begun to happen in three years; whether it would continue or whether it would ultimately work was still a question in this unpredictable new country. Judge Korneva, although generally optimistic about her emerging legal system, was wise enough to suggest the possibility of failure. As she put it with a weary smile, "How this will all be reflected in human life, we still do not know."

As was leaving her office, I stopped for a moment and stared at a judge's robe hanging near the door. President Yeltsin had decreed that judges should now wear black robes, not crew-neck sweaters.

Judge Korneva smiled. "Zaitsev did this to us," she said.

Russian judicial robes were not ordinary black choir drapes like the ones used by our jurists in America; these were designer fashions, crafted by Russia's most famous couturier, Slava Zaitsev. Hanging there on Judge Korneva's coatrack, it had looked uncommonly elegant with its high neck, puffed sleeves, and embroidered leaves along the yoke. As I murmured my approval, Judge Korneva snorted at the thought that these robes were anything but a nuisance. "Elegant, yes, but they are very hot," she said. "Uncomfortable."

Shortly afterward, as I toured the new courthouse, I saw the robes being worn in a courtroom and realized what the chief judge meant. Like most of Zaitsev's clothes, they were built for his army of inhumanely gaunt models. In a civil courtroom, where the case of a fired employee was being heard by a judge and two nodders, the robes looked as though they had shrunk at the dry cleaner's. The puffed sleeves restricted movement; the collar cut into oversized necks; and the embroidered yoke rode too high on these women's large bosoms. Russian judges and peoples' jurors, as a rule, did not come according to Zaitsev's measure.

The tour of the facility gave me hope that more than the marble floors and burnished wooden walls were new in Russia's legal system. I wandered through the echoing hallways thinking of the progress, the hopes for reform. It did not take long to realize that some of the new ideas had not quite made it down the stairs from Judge Korneva's office.

Judge Tamara Fyodorovna Savina, when I visited her that afternoon, was finishing her day's paperwork in her narrow office while her son sat in the courtroom playing with one of the court's new computers. An attractive forty-year-old with a strong, stern face, Judge Savina had begun earlier that week hearing the case of six young men accused of murdering eleven people for their apartments. The murders had occurred in 1993, and the men—all under thirty years—had been in prison since their arrest.

When I asked her, Judge Savina, who had been working as a Moscow court judge for fourteen years, talked easily about the case. Every year since the rise of capitalism in Russia, there were more murders, she said. "Unfortunately, it is caused by new laws allowing private property, and the arguments over housing. Some are killing for money, professional killers; we see more of that." As her face grew pinched in anger that seemed more personal than official, she added, "When we find them guilty, we show no mercy."

Judge Savina made it clear that she had few doubts that the six young men were not innocent. The trial would be one of the last before Moscow began its own experiment with the new Russian jury system, she said. Those accused of the most serious crimes, the very ones who were often certain that they would be convicted under the old system, would be able to choose a jury of their peers. Now those juries seemed to be more lenient, especially on women, but by the time the new system came, the juries could include many of those people from the streets who were angry about the rising crime rate. These defendants before Judge Savina had no such choice, and the chances of acquittal were minimal.

"These are not *mafiya*, not as the word is understood traditionally," the judge continued, noting that she had seen the more serious gangs in her courtroom, dangerous people who fit the *mafiya* definition more precisely. "But these are simply cruel, cynical people of minimal intelligence. They grew up and no one looked after them. They were raised to go to jail."

Judge Savina shook her head at the idea of turning a child over to the government at kindergarten the way her society had done for decades. "In my opinion, they are neglected children and thus they are of underdeveloped intelligence."

Why would they do it? "Money, I suppose. They were paid in dollars— $5,000 or $6,000 per murder." she shook her head. "They strangled two people, hit one on the head, and shot the rest of them," she explained, pausing again. "Their intelligence is only slightly higher than a chair," she said finally.

As I listened to her, I thought about how presumption of innocence before trial was now part of the law. In this case, I could see that the judge had presumed just the opposite.[24] This was Moscow. This was the sophisticated center of the country, and here was an intelligent city judge who would at least know about the new legal concepts filtering through her profession. Elsewhere these old ideas of trial law would undoubtedly have even a tighter grip on the system. The laws about justice had changed dramatically since the end of the Soviet years; the real workaday system had changed barely at all.

12

The Wild East

A Russian, by whatever name he goes, will get around or violate the law anywhere he can with impunity; and the government will do the same.
—Alexander Herzen, 1850s[1]

Nowadays, it is impossible to work honestly in Russia.
—Stanislav Govorukhin, filmmaker, 1994[2]

The new freedoms that meant liberty for some meant lawlessness for others. Crime rates in Russia soared,[3] and they stunned a nation of former Soviet citizens who were accustomed to feeling safe and protected. It was an old safety that most Westerners and many Soviets found suffocating because its price was a totalitarian government that tried to control every aspect of human life. But when it was gone, evaporating in late 1991, some Russians said they felt like youngsters whose capricious and dictatorial parent had suddenly disappeared. They were trained in the fine art of dodging the rules and tricking the rulers. Suddenly they were in charge of their own lives, forced to find their way in a strange and often hostile new world, to figure out their own forms of survival. Although there were plenty of rules and guidelines and laws on the books—old Soviet laws and new Russian laws scrambled in an incomprehensible legal jumble—Russia in 1991 essentially became a lawless society.

The lawlessness spread steadily to all levels—from the big-time criminals who disregarded the law to get rich to ordinary people who were forced to break the law to stay alive. For many Russians, the "true" criminals were at that top level, either the *mafiya* or the wealthy new businessmen, terms that were often considered synonymous among working people still trying to figure out the difference between legal and illegal capitalism. The ordinary person who disobeyed the law accidentally or as a matter of necessity was not a real criminal, according to these Russians; he was simply a survivor.

For all the separations between rich and poor, the result for society was essentially the same: as a few reformers tried to establish a respect for the laws enacted by a representative government and enforced someday by a fair judicial system, today's citizens could not wait. Many operated around the law, outside it.

There had been lawlessness and corruption in the old days, of course. Many apparatchiki amassed secret bank accounts and unwarranted privileges. Thieves existed in mysterious, complicated prison societies. The black market, the trading "on the left," as it was known, had become the easiest way to buy or sell or get anything done in the last few decades of the U.S.S.R. And pilfering from the state, "borrowing" tires from the industry storehouse or sugar from the cafeteria, was a serious crime that people committed not only to survive but to exact their share from an unfair system.

Now, however, the corruption was open and shameless. From a nation that made the pretense of equality, Russia changed into a country where the haves were waving their money haughtily at the have-nots. Mobsters, whose names became household words, patrolled the city streets with their lights flashing, bullying other drivers out of their way. A new class of rich Russians, whose means of making money fell somewhere between business and grand larceny, built large, expensive fortresses in the suburbs. Casinos, with their garish Las Vegas–style lights blinking into the dark city streets, lured the men who looked like the cartoon-character Kapitalist from the old Soviet propaganda sheets. Fat, oily, covered with diamonds and draped with long-legged women, these men took whatever they could get, with the greediness of people who feared it could all be taken away with the stroke of a pen, a knock at the door.

Crime invaded people's lives, their homes. It came through the door with a drunken crash, bringing a gnarl of young hoods who demanded security money or simply the family treasures. It seeped through the consciousness every night on television, as nightly news in Moscow and St. Petersburg and Vladivostok took on the character of American local broadcasts—body bags, ambulances, patches of blood on the pavement, the gory tales of mass murderers, the pitiful complaints of people who had lost their savings to some bank scam or stock swindle. Every Russian had a story to tell about how law had moved to the streets. One man who bumped a car in Moscow found himself surrounded by thugs with guns. He was given the choice: buy the car for $4,000 or die. (His company paid the money).[4] Worse for the pride of those involved were the hucksters and swindlers who humiliated the innocent Soviet consumer by talking them out of their money, their cars, their apartments.

The Russian people, literate, intelligent, and canny, learned to cope in ways that many of them saw as demeaning, immoral, and necessary. As outsiders, we struggled for analogies. Russia in the 1990s was like America in the robber baron days, the roaring 1880s when money and power could still buy a shady deal and the silence to go with it. It was Al Capone's Chicago or Don Corleone's Little Italy. It was Dodge City, Casablanca, somewhere east of Suez, and how ordinary Russians adapted to their wild new country was the story of this era.

In many ways, the Soviet Union had created the perfect mark. The innocent ex-Soviet who came stumbling into the free marketplace in early 1992 was an easy target. I realized how easy one day when a middle-aged woman I knew asked me to help her. "I don't understand what to do," Elena[5] had said plaintively as she arrived at my door that morning. "You are from the West. My daughter has applied for a job, and you know about how these things work. Please tell me if we are doing the right thing."

As she fluttered nervously, giving bits and pieces of her story and chattering ominously about thieves and robbers, I sat her down on the couch and asked her to start at the beginning. It was, as it turned out, a mistake. It took her forever to reach the point—that her daughter was, at that very minute, being victimized by a gang of sophisticated con artists.

It began with an ad in the paper that offered a job with a Western company for a Western salary. In the rocky summer of 1992, every young person's dream was to earn dollars, more or less legitimately, and to live on rubles. It was a way to be instantly rich, especially as inflation made the dollar worth more rubles every week. Elena's daughter called to inquire and went to the small "office," really a room in a downtown Moscow hotel, to apply. She filled out an application form, attached two photos, and presented her documents verifying that she had graduated from a good Moscow institute.

She was told that they would call her if she got the job, and she and her mother waited and fantasized about living an easier life on a secure currency. A few days later, the call came: "Congratulations," the smooth young man said, "you are employed." Now, he explained in a voice laden with reason and Western savvy, you must do what all modern companies require, you must put up a security deposit so that we can be certain you will remain a trusted and bonded employee. There is so much crime, he explained, that we have to protect ourselves.

Elena's daughter only had one item worth anything. It was her government voucher—the coupon given by the Russian government to all citizens in 1992 so that they could purchase a share of the new society. The voucher at that point was worth about ten thousand rubles (less than $50) and it could be invested in stock, exchanged for rubles in the metros (at a cut rate), or saved in hopes that it would increase in value before it expired in 1994.

A voucher would be fine, the man said, and he arranged to meet Olga at her apartment. I knew how Elena lived; she and her daughter were part of the newly poor, people whose savings had disintegrated almost overnight with the soaring inflation rate. They worked at small jobs, sometimes in shops, for friends, occasionally for Westerners like us. But she could not afford to lose a kopeck, much less a voucher, probably the one thing she had that was worth a little money in the day's marketplace.

"When is this meeting?" I asked as we finally reached this stage of the story.

"Today, this morning," Elena said, wringing a small handkerchief in her hands. "Is this normal?" she asked. I stood up and she stood with me. "Do you have to give away something this expensive to get a job?" she asked.

"No," I said frantically, finding that my Russian phrases in a panic were limited to short barks. "No, this is not right. This man is a thief. He is stealing this voucher. Stop her."

We rushed to the phone, but when she tried to call home, nothing happened. I gave her money for a taxi, and she scrambled to make it back to her apartment in time. Later, she told me that she had thrown open the apartment door to find her daughter standing before her, beaming with pride about her accomplishment. Her "new employer" had just departed, she had said smiling, and he would call to tell her where she would start working the next week.

"Did he take the voucher?" Elena had asked. Her daughter nodded.

Elena and her family never heard from him again, of course, and she did not mention it the next time I saw her. When I asked her about it, she shook her head bitterly. "It showed how we don't understand your capitalism."

"That's not capitalism," I answered, "that's robbery. It's against the law. Why don't you go to the police?" She shook her head again.

I knew better, really. The Russian policeman was not like the cop on the beat, the bobby with his friendly chatter. They were the society's avengers, people whose job it was to find criminals—often among the very people who came to them to report a crime. Elena worried that only informers or people who had lived without breaking one of the nation's many laws could face the *militsia,* or local police.

"That would only make it worse," she said with a depressing finality.

Elena and her daughter were not alone. Russian newspapers were full of similar stories, warnings about how valuables could be stolen, not by pickpockets but by people who quickly learned to outwit the nation's green new consumers. A couple in Moscow who put an ad in the paper saying they wanted to buy an apartment received a call from someone who described the city dweller's dream—two rooms, nice kitchen, quiet building, near metro, good area, unbelievably low price. Bring money, the man on the phone said; there are several other people interested and this could happen very quickly. They brought money and when they arrived at the apartment, the agent very quickly robbed them of their life savings.[6] When apartments could be converted into private residences and then sold, their instant value converted the apartment dweller into a ready target for the new young hucksters. Young men befriended the old and lonely, telling an ancient veteran that his contribution to Russia had not been forgotten, promising an old woman that she would be taken care of in a new private nursing home. Their trust was easy, and those who were not killed by these apartment gangs, were left instantly homeless. By 1995, an estimated seventeen thousand Muscovites had lost their apartments in this manner, and police reported that virtually every work day they had ten to fifteen complaints. Social workers reported old people sharing attics with pigeons and sewers with the rats.[7]

The oldest tricks in the market were being reborn in the new Russia, and many people who had spent their lives perfecting ways to deal with communism were virtually defenseless. The same newspapers that had told them that everything capitalist was bad—filthy, immoral, overindulgent— now trumpeted capitalism as the ultimate good. There seemed to be no concept of a diverse world where some businessmen could be honorable and others crooked, all under the same umbrella of a market economy. Caveat emptor was a new idea, a difficult concept. In the Soviet days, consumers could not beware of the seller. They bought what was available (a choice of raincoats, I remember, meant two styles, two muddy colors, three sizes) and grumbled afterwards. The first time Russian friends brought my child a toy—a Russian doll—she pulled it out of the box, leaving one arm behind. My friends laughed: a Soviet doll, they said, the only ones the toy stores had. Now, there were plenty of dolls, raincoats every price and color and quality. Having a choice about what you did with your money meant the state was no longer to blame if something went wrong.

In St. Petersburg, police uncovered what they were calling the city's "fraud of the century," which involved two private companies that promised investors 250 percent return on their money per month. Peddled at metro stations and in the streets, the tickets sold by the two companies were part of an old-fashioned pyramid operation, so that those who came in first got their money back from those who came in later. Many paid in cash that they had saved in mattresses, but others used their vouchers. By the time police found out and raided the empty offices, 350,000 "investors" had lost at least 1 billion rubles.[8]

A similar scheme in Moscow a year later created one of the most bizarre chapters in Russia's early stages of capitalism. Sergei Mavrodi operated a company called MMM, which lured millions of investors and left most of them ruined by mid-July 1994. Mavrodi was put in jail and charged as a crook. There were plenty of witnesses to Mavrodi's pyramid scheme, but for reasons that bewildered outsiders who had seen the likes of Mavrodi before, many of his investors rallied behind him. They staged protests and hunger strikes in his support and blamed the government for harassing him.

A few weeks after he was arrested, Mavrodi was released, and there are photos of him leaving the Matrosskaya Tishina prison gates in Moscow, waving to his fans and surrounded by flowers as he dips into his bulletproof limousine. No reason was ever given publicly for the release, but at about the same time, Mavrodi registered as a candidate for a midterm election to the Duma, or Russian parliament, from a northwestern district of Moscow called Mytishchi. (He was trying to replace a lawmaker who had been murdered a few months earlier.)

During a visit to Khimki, the part of the district that is closest to Moscow, Mavrodi promised to invest $10 million of his private savings to help build roads and restore dilapidated buildings such as churches and orphanages. When he won the election, Mavrodi won something far more important than a seat in the parliament. He won legislative immunity. As a member of the Duma, he could not be prosecuted for the Ponzi scheme.

Less than a week after the election, Mavrodi caused a massive protest outside the MMM headquarters when he announced that he would not buy up shares of MMM that were still outstanding. He offered shareholders a chance to buy more stock—an offering that some of them took even though they had already lost a good part of their savings—and he announced that MMM would sponsor the Queen of the World beauty show in Moscow a few days later. His wife, a twenty-three-year-old former model, would head the jury.[9]

In a strange postscript, Mavrodi's wife also tried to run for the Duma in 1995 in an area southeast of Moscow. (Being a resident of the area was not required by law, and her whereabouts at that point had been declared a secret.) She was one of eleven candidates (none was a democrat or reformer of any sort), and she was said to have appeared only occasionally to meet the voters. Her white Mercedes-Benz would slide into the area; Elena Mavrodi would wave to the public from underneath layers of the best sable; and then she would be whisked by her team of bodyguards back to safety.[10] Needless to say, this elegance failed to persuade the voters. They elected a local communist instead.

To talk about lawlessness after Soviet communism makes little sense without some understanding of how Russians have traditionally viewed the law. It is a concept that Americans outside the legal system seldom really think about, and even though we have plenty of crime in our country, most people are not criminals and have a strong feeling that laws must be obeyed. We fudge a little, of course. When the speed limit is fifty-five miles per hour, we drive sixty-five. Most of us have made a copy of a video or written a check when the money won't be in the bank until next week. But those are peccadilloes, little transgressions. Mostly we pay our taxes, slow down for schools, don't reprint somebody else's book for profit, don't cheat our bosses or customers—either because we believe the laws are correct or because we are afraid we might be caught.

Those two basic instincts—fear of prosecution and respect for authority—had been perverted over the years by Russian state. Laws in the Soviet Union were a tool of the government—a *kulak* or fist from above. It was not a government or legal system that could engender much respect, but the citizen who obeyed did so primarily out of fear. When the fear was gone, so was the desire to follow the government's rules.

Before he was gunned down in a gangland slaying in April 1994, one of Moscow's most notorious gangsters explained how communism had laid the groundwork for the lawlessness that had allowed him so much sudden wealth and public notoriety. Otari Kvantrishvili, a man who will undoubtedly become a kind of Jesse James in future Russian lore, a man who made millions and then gave interviews to talk about it, told TASS crime reporter Larisa Kislinskaya: "They write that I am the godfather of the *mafiya*. It was V. I. Lenin who was the organizer of the *mafiya*. He triggered this whole criminal state. Whatever the state is, I must serve it."[11]

Russia's legal reformers acknowledged that they had a mountainous task. Their job was to create respect for law in a society that had no real tradition of what Westerners call a rule of law. It was a philosophical quagmire, a chicken-and-egg proposition. The law and the legal system had to be made fair for people to obey it. Because few people could obey the laws and respect the legal system, what good were reforms? What would new laws do in a lawless society?

Some of those hoping for legal reform in these years explained that the new disorder was natural to a nation that never established a respect for law. Before the Soviets took over the law, the tsars had controlled the legal system. There were periods of reform, in 1864 and the early 1900s, but in both cases the reforms had not been allowed to evolve. For the early tsars and then for the Bolsheviks, Russia's legal system had been designed to maintain a powerful state.

After the appearance of Mikhail Gorbachev as Soviet leader in 1985, a group of intellectual Russian reformers had begun trying to establish a rule of law, or *pravovoye gosudarstvo*—a Declaration of the Rights and Freedoms of the Individual and Citizen that was adopted by the Russian Supreme Soviet on November 27, 1991. The document set out a rule of law that charges the state and society with the protection of the individual, not the reverse, as in the past,[12] and in December 1993, Russia's new constitution declared many of those enlightened rights as part of the law. But such documents were founded more on hope than reality.

Russian president Boris Yeltsin acknowledged early in his presidency that it would be difficult to instill the idea of the rule of law in Russian heads. During most of the century, the written law often sounded lofty and enlightened, while in practice, the only law that mattered was the one that came from inside the Kremlin. In Stalin's day, he noted, the constitution was full of proclaimed rights for individuals.

"For many years, the laws in this country played a decorative role," Yeltsin said. "Many of them contradicted both common sense and human nature. They were openly violated or bypassed. Legal and state nihilism are deeply rooted in our minds. An example was provided by those in power, whose life was subordinated to secret orders issued by telephone and mutual cover-up."[13] Often the system was so attuned to the views of the Kremlin that there was no need for those in power to actually make the calls.[14]

Experts on Russian lawlessness were quick to note that the Russian's problems with the law did not start with the communists. A Ukrainian scholar, Bogdan Aleksandrovich Kistiakowsky, wrote an eloquent lament in 1909 about the lack of understanding among the Russian intelligentsia of the rule of law. Here is a key part of his essay:

> The lack of development of legal consciousness of the Russian intel-ligentsia and the absence of interest in legal concepts is the result of an old evil—the absence of any rule of law in the day-to-day life of the Russian people. On this issue Alexander Herzen [a 19th century dissident] wrote in the early 1850's: "the lack of legal security, which has preyed on the people, was in its own way a kind of school. The outrageous injustice of one half of the laws instilled hatred to the other half; the people submitted to them like to force. The total lack of equality before the courts killed any respect for law.
>
> "A Russian, by whatever name he goes, will get around or violate the law anywhere he can with impunity; and the government will do the same."[15]

If there was a way to stop corruption in Russia, it would be to start with those who were supposed to be making and enforcing the laws—i.e., the government. But in the early 1990s, day-to-day corruption seemed to spread from small gifts to the local bureaucrat—a cake or a bottle of cognac that could barely be called a bribe—to huge payoffs that meant the rich could buy any legal commodity. The Russian newspaper *Komsomolskaya Pravda* at one point listed the cost of government approval for business transactions. To open a bank cost $1,200. To open a bank and avoid the banking regulations, which took large percentages of profits, cost $300,000.[16]

The corrupt government official was not new to Russia, to communism, or to post-Soviet democracy, of course. But what seemed to happen in these wild years was that those on the take were more brazen. The fear of being caught seemed to be eased by the knowledge that one could buy his way out of prison.

Every Russian and certainly every visitor had a story about paying his way out of some bureaucratic muddle. When we first arrived, the currency was more often than not a bottle of vodka. My husband, trying to get a wire service machine installed, found a tactic that became well known for a while in Western circles. He called the man in charge and offered him a deal: three bottles of vodka if the machine worked today, two bottles if it worked tomorrow, one if it worked the next day, and after that, well, a letter to the guy's boss. The machine started working that afternoon. By 1995, however, vodka was no longer the favored currency. What worked best was money. Dollars, maybe, or deutsche marks.

The traffic police, the officials that virtually everybody with a car encountered on one occasion or another, were notoriously corrupt. If they stopped your car, too often they were not trying to get you to obey the law, they were trying to get you to give them money. The last time I was stopped, it was shortly after Western businessmen had protested that they were being routinely asked for money by the traffic inspectors. Occasionally, the officer would suggest a blood test to determine alcohol levels in the system, then brandished a worn-looking hypodermic needle as a threat. For a while policemen were on their better behavior, and when I was stopped that time, the official did not ask for money. Instead, he asked if I had any beer. No, I said. What about a ballpoint pen, he suggested. I gave him two, and he beamed. I felt a little sick. It was so pitiful. At about this time, a man from Saratov wrote to *Argumenty i Fakty* magazine that he had been allowed to drive into the closed area near Red Square while the Congress of Peoples' Deputies was engaged in a tumultuous effort to rein in or throw out President Yeltsin. The man had made his way into this inner sanctum by bribing a traffic policeman for one thousand rubles.[17]

In midsummer 1992, an anonymous traffic official explained how it worked: "How much an inspector takes simply depends on what post he occupies. A simple inspector on the road will take small change for running a traffic light or violating a road sign. The higher the GAI's [the letters are pronounced like *Gah-eee* and stand for Government Auto Inspection] position, the more money he will take. For example, the inspector responsible for technical inspection—" He broke off at this point and started laughing. Everybody in Moscow knew that the inspector was really a person who glanced at the dilapidated car, repaired with rope and ingenuity, then collected his dues before filling out the multiple forms saying everything was being done properly. "The technical inspector, he has the power to make a lot of problems for you if he decides your car is not in order, so he is in a position to ask for a lot more money from the drivers."

"Not all of these traffic policemen do this, do they?" he was asked. "Of course, there are GAI who work honestly," he said. "But not many."[18]

The question was not whether the government was involved in crime—it was, as everybody who dealt with it getting driver's licenses or apartment privatization papers knew. The larger concern was whether corruption went to the top. President Yeltsin did not seem to be amassing huge sums of money or living like the Aga Khan, but what about those around him? Were there people keeping him in power with one hand so that they could keep the other palm open for "fees"?

Corruption in the military had become a public affair. In one case, Russian officers in Eastern Germany were found buying supplies for their bases and then reselling them for profit in the civilian marketplaces. Dmitry Kholodov, a young investigative journalist working for *Moskovsky Komsomolets,* was killed while he was investigating such abuses in the military that some said were approved at the very top levels of the Russian Defense Ministry.

By late 1994, some Russian economists were comparing Russia not to the Western economies, but to the tangled corruption in countries like Colombia.[19]

One prosperous Russian businessman, a senior executive in a Russian oil company, said that by early 1995, bribery had become such an accepted part of every transaction with the government and that the question was not whether to bribe but how much. Asking for an export permit, for example, meant going to the appropriate bureaucrat's office, where an official would, at the appropriate moment, hand the businessman a piece of paper with a number written on it. The figure was the amount of the bribe necessary to have the matter settled. If the businessman nodded, the deal was cut without a word spoken. "Why silently?" he was asked. Who exactly was listening in 1995? The KGB, which by then went by new initials FSB? This businessman did not know, but his point was that corruption had gone wildly out of control and that the entire Russian government had the feel of a fifteenth-century Italian city-state, where friends and foes were forever changing positions behind the curtains.

The word "mafia," spelled *mafiya* to mean the operations peculiar to Russia, meant a group of people working together to disobey the law—a conspiracy in U.S. legal terms. There were many Russian *mafiyas*, from small gangs to large, sophisticated organizations, after the end of the Soviet state, and outside Russia, the word became confused with the Italian mob, or La Cosa Nostra. Instead, some of these groups were simply collections of people organizing against the chaos of the day. Others were far more sinister. Some were part of the old prison societies that had begun to surface and carry out their brutal work around the world, sending waves of concern in international crime fighting agencies that the Russian hordes would be even more bloody and unpredictable than their Chinese or Central American brothers.

The members of these Russian groups were called *vory* or thieves and a few leaders had the title *vor v zakone*, or thief within the code, sometimes translated as "thief in law." The details of this code began to surface in the 1990s, and one translation of the thieves' catechism said that a true *vor* refused to get married, even though he might have children, and he could not work for the government, even to join the army. He had to learn the language of the *vory*, teach the young his craft, and fulfill all promises to fellow thieves.[20]

Their methods were also carefully controlled in such a way that the ones who committed the crimes were separated from those who gave the orders. As a result, the "enforcers" were sometimes caught, while someone like Kvantrishvili could appear at every top social event, hugging everybody from Yeltsin to the local television anchor as though they were all close, personal friends. (There was no racketeering law at that time that could make it possible to charge not only the executioner but also the one who gave the orders.)

These new mafiosi became the obsession for many outsiders who watched Russia in this era. The stories of these Russian gangs were bizarre and fascinating, and every city seemed to have its *mafiya* lord—as much a modern Robin Hood in some quarters as he was merely a hoodlum in others. Tsyganov in Yekaterinburg, and Kvantrishvili in Moscow—they were big ugly names. (In Ekaterinburg, the city where the tsar's family was shot after the Bolshevik Revolution, the city's top businessmen were being slaughtered in gangland-style killings, most in broad daylight at one point. Viktor Ternyak, one community leader, was killed one morning in September 1992 as he was leaving his house for work. The city witnessed such

Bonnie-and-Clyde scenes as the day when two cars pulled to a halt at an intersection while men with machine guns began spraying one another with bullets. When they left, two corpses lay on the street.)[21]

By a year after the breakup of the Soviet Union, Russian criminologists had identified twenty-six hundred crime groups across the country—three hundred of which rose to the level of big-time syndicates.[22] By 1995, the number of crime groups seemed to be growing smaller—an indication not that crime was diminishing but that the criminals were becoming more organized. Battles over territories were creating winners, uber-mobsters, who seemed untouchable by any but their own kind.

When Otari was finally murdered, his funeral (and burial at one of Moscow's best cemeteries) brought a stellar cast of mourners. It was a grand event, but in some ways Kvantrishvili's death also brought a new despair to those who watched Russia's *mafiya*. He was, by the low standards of his world, an enlightened man. He contributed to the arts and to various charities. He was known to help young people, and he once said to someone accusing him of being a criminal, "Yes, sure, it is all true. But my children will be honest."[23]

Although it was not clear who killed him—speculation ranged from the government to the business world to the mob—his death undoubtedly left behind a less sophisticated *mafiya* warlord. There are many examples of the brutality of Russia's *mafiya*, but my favorite example of the mentality in this period was an exchange between the novelist John LeCarré and a mobster named Grigori sometime in 1993 at a noisy Moscow nightclub. According to LeCarré, Grigori had indicated that his personal worth was somewhere in the range of $50 million and that Russia was in a state of chaos. "Everything is crooked from the top down," the author quotes an interpreter quoting Grigori. "He has nothing against the law because there isn't any law. It's anarchy here. A man must take whatever he can get."

LeCarré then gave Grigori a little lecture on robber barons, comparing him to America's Carnegie and J. P. Morgan and Rockefeller, who eventually began creating hospitals and art galleries to repay the society they had exploited. "When are you going to start putting something back, Grigori?" LeCarré asked the old thief. The writer had summoned nerve that made anyone familiar with this scene shudder in fear for his life.

The translator apparently repeated LeCarré's views and then listened to a long response from Grigori. One of those infuriating Russians trained by the Soviets to edit as they go along, this interpreter offered only a summation of Grigori's reply: "I regret to tell you, Mr. Grigori says, 'Bug off.' "24

For ordinary Russians, it was seldom clear when a robbery or a shakedown occurred whether it was one of the organized *mafiya* gangs or simply a group of local hoodlums trying to find a little drinking money. Virtually everybody I knew had some brush with the thugs who seemed to be taking over the streets, the economy, the government. A Western journalist was robbed at knifepoint in his darkened apartment courtyard in downtown Moscow; two nervous youths took his watch, his money, and his computer while a drunken associate kept wanting to "have a chance to use the knife" on their quarry. The youths grabbed the goods and ran, carrying their bloodthirsty confederate with them.

The breadwinner in one Russian family we knew was murdered by his envious neighbor; children of another family nearby were sent to an orphanage when their grandmother who took care of them got drunk and killed a former comrade she thought was trying to rob her. In the courtyard of an apartment where I stayed in Moscow, a gangland execution was carried out at three-fifteen one autumn afternoon in 1994, a few hundred yards away from a small kindergarten. When the shooting had ended, two men lay dead, one a Russian, the other a Dagestani.

Dinner conversation—once about the terrors of the state or the poetry of the day—began to focus on what one Russian I knew called "our American-style detective stories." Muscovites told of hearing gunfire from their offices. Residents of elegant St. Petersburg related tales of police noisily searching the streets for mobsters who always seemed to get away. In the summer of 1993, a particularly brutal time, a gang of men with submachine guns sprayed an automobile showroom that had opened in one of the better sections of Moscow, not far from our old apartment and my daughter's old school. In the shoot-out between the gang and the guards, four people died. It was 2 P.M., daylight, an otherwise sleepy Monday afternoon. One shoot-out a few weeks later left four dead; after another, three people were killed in a Moscow office building.25

Some of these victims were from the *mafiya* gangs, rivals losing in the battles for territory. But other targets were businessmen and -women, bankers and government officials. The chairman of the Russian Agricultural Bank,[26] who was described as an honest man even by his enemies, was gunned down as he returned from work to his apartment in early December 1993. At least thirty other bankers were also murdered that year, for reasons that seemed to vary from making a deal with one of the *mafiyas*—and thus knowing too much—or not making a deal—and freezing out people who knew how to take revenge.

Politicians became targets as well. Were they on the take and thus being gunned down by a rival *mafiya*? Or were they refusing bribes and thus being killed for being honest? Or were they being killed for their political views? Andrei Aizderdzis, a banker who was also a deputy, was killed in April 1994 as he came home from work. Valentin Martemyanov, a sixty-two-year-old communist deputy, was beaten to death a few feet away from his home in late 1994.[27] Sergei Skorochkin, a third deputy member, was found dead about eighty miles southeast of Moscow. Skorochkin, who had been shot in the back of the head in the same way prisoners were officially executed in Russia, had killed two people a year earlier.

Skorochkin said the two had tried to extort money, and the Duma had believed him enough that they allowed him to keep his parliamentary immunity from prosecution by the law. However, it was clear that even the Duma could not protect him from someone. A few weeks after the incident, police caught three men trying to break down the door of Skorochkin's apartment. One of those arrested was a policeman.

After he was killed, news reports tried to examine his history and explain what had happened. Said to be one of the young politicians whose career had been launched with the help of a local gang, Skorochkin could have turned his back on his old friends, some conjectured. Others questioned whether the murders were somehow related to the family's liquor business.[28] Whatever the real reason, Skorochkin served as another example of how dangerous it was to do business or politics in the new Russia.

On every level the new Russian worker, especially the one starting out in business, learned how to deal with the local mobster. In a larger sense, these *mafiyas* appeared to control the society—taking on the roles of tax collector and protector that are normally fulfilled by the government. They were not heroes, however, and those who tithed to the *mafiya* never knew when their prices for doing business or staying alive would suddenly drive them out of business or underground.

One young businessman I knew—a very smart man who had taken a few thousand dollars and turned himself into a major importer of European foods—told me that "dues" were simply part of business. Stories about how Westerners managed to thrive in Russia without paying bribes brought looks of skepticism from the new Russian *kapitalisty*—not only the top ones, like the one who sold European foods, but the young hard Russians who were learning business from the street up as managers of Russia's kiosks.

When I arrived in Russia in 1991, there were only a few kiosks allowed. Near our apartment, there were a dilapidated booth for newspapers, an oily-looking hot dog stand, and a small sidewalk booth called Everything for You, which often had almost nothing but shoelaces and used clothing.

By 1992, the first tentative kiosks were being built on virtually every main street in Moscow. The rules for the shape and style of these narrow boxes were established by the city, but many people simply set up shop, learning later that they had to pay either the local policeman or local mafiosi or both to stay in business. By 1995, there were an estimated fifty to seventy thousand kiosks in Russia,[29] and although some cities were trying to ban them (Moscow's mayor managed to get rid of some of the shabbier versions that had crowded around metro stops and favorite city streets), they became an integral part of the commercial structures of cities and towns across the country.

The young owners of a small Moscow kiosk that sold everything from whiskey and cigarettes to cheap lipstick and canned sausage invited a Westerner to spend the night with them during the autumn of 1992 to see why they lived in their booth and never allowed it to go untended. At about 5 A.M., after the long evening in the kiosk, three men came to the front of the shop offering to sell a brand-new Japanese television set. The set was too big to slip through the bulletproof glass, they explained, so they suggested it could go only through the back door. The right response from the owners would have been an invitation for the burly young salesmen to return later in the morning, but the kiosk operators decided to take the chance. "Come around to the back," one said, and when they opened the door, they stared—not at a television set, but at a huge axe and an attacker hissing the word "vodka." The kiosk dwellers, realizing that the man was drunk, sprayed him with a mace pistol, pushed him away, and slammed the door.

"Sometimes during the night, you sit dozing when all of a sudden the glass of the shop window is smashed to pieces, and a couple of guns are facing you. You dive under the counter—but it does not save you from giving up the money you've taken for the day," one owner said.[30]

If such roving freelance criminals caused concern among the nation's new *biznesmeny*, it was even more dangerous not to enjoy the protection of the local mafiosi. When Philip Morris opened a number of Marlboro cigarette kiosks in Moscow, a place where people still enjoy smoking freely and guiltlessly, they were selling a pack of Marlboros for about thirty-three cents, or 145 rubles. At the Russian stands, a pack of Marlboros went for 180 rubles.

Within a few weeks, six of the bright red Marlboro kiosks had been mysteriously firebombed, and shortly afterward, the Marlboros were going for two hundred rubles a pack. Philip Morris said that the increase in price was due to a shift in the dollar rate of exchange in Russia.[31]

Sometimes, the shop was not trashed or burned, but simply stolen. Police said they had reports of about one hundred kiosks disappearing during a six-month period in Moscow in 1993. Official-looking workers would drive up with cranes, lift the kiosk off the sidewalk, and then deposit it into a flatbed truck. The reason for stealing a kiosk was easy to understand. It cost about two hundred thousand rubles (about $2,000 at the time) to buy one, not counting the things that were in it. The joke of the day was that in the West the problem was shoplifting; in Russia, they lifted the whole shop.

Kolya, a young man who ran a kiosk in this period, agreed in late 1992 to talk about how the booths really operated. His protection was that he would not give his whole name.[32] "I decided to open my own *palatka* [kiosk]," he said, using the old term that meant something like a country store. "I came to my friend who was connected with the *mafiya* structure controlling this district [in Moscow], and I got unofficial permission." The "unofficial" permission came from a gang connected to corrupt public officials who are in charge of kiosks.

"If I wanted to do things officially, I would have to pay two or three times as much as I pay the *mafiya*. It's much better to deal with the *mafiya* than with the officials because the government *mafiya* is even more horrible." Kolya, like many other Russians in this period, saw little difference between the street *mafiya* and the government bureaucrat on the take—thus, for him, they were both *mafiyas*. The difference was that bribes to government officials were higher and often didn't work. The street *mafiyas* were more efficient. As a businessman he appreciated that.

"They serve as a substitute for the legal structures, but at a cheaper price. They protect me from the tax inspector, the police, and all the rest," he said. Instead of thirty-six documents needed to license a kiosk officially—i.e., at least thirty-six opportunities for an official to ask for a little "help"—Kolya preferred one-stop shopping.[33]

Russian police repeatedly warned these gangs would eventually take over, either converting the small businessman or -woman into full-fledged criminals or nudging them out of the operation altogether. But most people felt they had no choice. Who could call the police when a criminal arrived on your doorstep?

One Russian family I knew recalled enjoying the last rays of sun one evening at their dacha when a group of thugs with guns burst through their wooden gate and into the garden where they were sitting. The husband—I will call him Igor—had amassed $500 to pay off a bill, and he handed it to the gang in terror. It was not enough, the leader said, and when Igor said he had not a kopeck more, they laughed, and one suggested that he sell his dacha. As they looked over the grounds, one surly young man eyed Igor's teenage daughter hungrily. Then they left, as Igor and his family rushed inside and bolted their feeble door.

At first, as they stood shaking in the kitchen, they were relieved that they had not been killed, that their daughter had not been raped. But as they sat over vodka and tea, Igor's family soon realized they had to find a way to protect themselves. It did not take long to hear about a gang from the Solntsevo (which means roughly Sunny) region who said that they were part of the presidential guard and would begin protection immediately for a modest sum. Igor would not tell how much, per month. The family, however, was left with an uneasy feeling that the first gang and the second were somehow connected.

For many people, these private security services were like a surrogate police force. Not only did businesses pay either security services or the local gangs but they often dealt with a kind of interim police establishment full of ex-policemen who called themselves private detectives. One investigation of this private security business in Moscow uncovered a system that allowed the private detectives to pay the police extra to do their jobs—in these cases to search for lost computer equipment or stolen vehicles. "For half the value [of the equipment]," one investigator said, "you can really get the police moving."[34]

(The stolen car business had become so professional and widespread in Russia that when the car disappeared, it was considered lost, a contribution to the crime world. The car thieves contributed to a massive network of auto body shops or rapid transports over the border that moved far more swiftly than police. Some foreign cars were dismantled into auto parts within hours. In Moscow, where as many as fifty cars were stolen a day, the new car and the stolen car were often just hours apart. Some car dealerships sold the car, then made more money selling local gangs an extra set of keys, spare documents, and the address of the new owner.[35])

On one fresh spring morning in 1992, I walked past the line of people who stood outside the Kievskaya metro selling their wares—the fake Barbie dolls, a handful of narrow sausages, a deck of cards from Delta Air Lines, an eclectic array of stuff that changed from day to day. One old man, his clothes worn, his hands knotted at the joints, was quietly selling tulips. His flowers, an unusual red color with yellow stripes, seemed recently cut, and I bought all that he had, a small armload. When I arrived at work, feeling like a self-appointed beauty queen, I arranged the flowers in glass jars to brighten my desk.

Later that day, when the eternal problems with phones and faxes and editors had becoming overbearing, I took a short walk and found myself in front of a war monument nearby on Kutuzovsky Prospect. In honor of Russia's war dead, flowers had been carefully planted around the monument's base—red tulips with yellow stripes, just like the ones on my desk. At one corner of the flower bed was a large bald spot.

For me, the stolen tulips became a kind of symbol of the way ordinary people had begun looking at the world around them. The state had owned everything and now the people were brazenly taking it back, stem by stem, item by item, to sell or trade or use for themselves. The riches of Russia, once solidly controlled by the Kremlin, were increasingly up for grabs. The smell of cheap talent, unused weapons, vastly underpriced raw materials suddenly lured the world's plundering hordes. Mother Russia was being plucked and stripped by governments, businesses and individuals, both her own and those of the hungry nations that surrounded her. Ores were sold; weapons were hawked; patents and great scientific ideas went West; antiques and art were smuggled to the great art bazaars of Europe and America.[36] Russia was suddenly for sale, and the world was buying.

These losses were hard to track, and sometimes only the holes gave evidence that something of value had once been there. At one point, for example, two thousand Soviet tanks seemed to have disappeared, probably sold to small nations who needed them. A few months later, the Foreign Trade Ministry acknowledged that $2 billion was missing from its bank accounts. Two billion dollars. How much was being drained from the country and poured into more stable economies in the West was anybody's guess. In 1993, one official estimated that $500 million in cash had been lost by midyear, as money poured into banks in Europe and the West.[37] Russians began feverishly buying real estate in the West, investing in a more stable future.

Customs officials began working to stop the flood of art and antiques going over the border, especially out the "Baltic window" into Europe. In 1992, however, they managed to confiscate about five thousand artworks and antiques, almost double the number a year earlier for borders along the entire U.S.S.R.[38] In January 1993, customs officials returned 185 icons to the Orthodox church, but for those they found, they estimated that there were hundreds lost to the international marketplace. (In New York City, at a very expensive antiques shop near my home, there is a small sign in Russian in the window. It says, "We buy icons.")

The feeling that one should take one's fair share of the old Soviet state began to seep into all levels of the new society. In the Lithuanian town of Shiluta, officials were stunned one morning to find a monument missing from the town park. The monument was dedicated to twenty thousand people from the town who were killed during World War II, and its size and nature made it fairly easy for police to track down the thief. The fear was that this was the work of an anti-Semite, since the monument had included Jews massacred in the era, but the arrested man explained that his purpose in committing the crime was financial. He simply wanted to sell a few hundred pounds of bronze across the border.[39]

Lithuania and the other Baltics became conveyor belts for goods and resources rolling into the West. The Baltics, whose governments wisely took their cut of whatever passed through their countries, suddenly became heavy exporters of minerals that were not found naturally within their borders. One traveler in September 1993 reported that during a drive from Russia to Poland, he began noticing the signs. In Russia, of course, the road signs, the billboards, were all in Russian. Then in Ukraine, the signs were in Ukrainian, recently changed from the Russian to reflect Ukraine's independent status. Over the border to Poland, however, the billboards were once again in Russian. Bright, even garish, advertisements proclaimed: "We buy nonferrous metals," "Good prices on nonferrous." The list included about fifteen possibilities, among them aluminum, molybdenum, barium, and zinc.

Communities outside Moscow also found another time-honored method for plucking the riches around them. In what was called the "mini–train robbery," gangs of townspeople in several areas a few hours outside the city would work together to unload freight trains traveling through their territory. One group would cut the electrical current just as a line of railroad cars approached their area. When the train slid to a stop, an army of townspeople would descend on the cars, plucking whatever could be used, traded, or sold. Armed guards, often about four of them per train, were reluctant to fire on their fellow citizens—especially since these gangs were made up of women, old people and children. (In 1993, there were 854 railway thefts in the Moscow region, and police had solved only 119 of them, according to transportation police in the area.)[40]

Get it while you can had become the golden rule.

In early 1995, I sat over a rather depressing dinner in Moscow one evening with a Western diplomat and his wife. It was one of those meals that happened sometimes in this period, when Westerners who generally tried to be hopeful and upbeat about the economic changes in Russia would stop for a moment and speak bluntly about all the problems that went with them. Yes, the markets were starting; the businesses were privatizing, while schools and health care and some welfare services had not fallen apart completely, as the doomsayers had predicted. An optimist could see hope in those facts, but that night, we dwelled on the dark side, the crime, the ugliness, the prejudice that was unleashed with the end of the Soviet state. There were grim stories of the brutality of Russian soldiers fighting in Chechnya, killing women and children like farmers harvesting a field. Too many of those in power viewed the people from the Caucasus in general as part of a lower class of *chornye,* or blacks, the old prejudice against the outsider resurfacing in angry and barbaric ways. One Russian woman, who had a child with a Georgian man, abandoned the baby after he appeared with eyes and hair too dark for a "normal" Russian, the diplomat said. He had helped arrange for its adoption by a Westerner.

It was not such an isolated case. Officials had blamed the merchants from the southern republics for much of the crime and trouble in Russia. President Yeltsin, defensive about world criticism of his assault on the Chechens, had told a press conference in Canada in June 1995 that Chechnya was "the center of world terrorism, of bribery and corruption and *mafiya*.[41] But by 1993, several of Moscow's best markets run by Azeris, Chechens, Dagestanis, and other ethnic groups from the Caucasus region, had been closed or revamped. And the crime continued. Some of the murder, robbery, and extortion that was increasing daily could be blamed on gangs from the Caucasus, but much of it was pure Russian.

In a quiet voice, the diplomat said that for all the changes since the end of the Soviet state, one of the most important was the rise in crime. The rate of crime had grown to the point that it had not only taken over the market, it had taken over the government, and, worse, it had invaded people's psyche. There was a cynicism about the big time criminal that made him seem untouchable. Jails were for the unfortunate, the little guys. A young boy in a juvenile prison in Kolomna, age fourteen, was awaiting trial in a prison built by Catherine the Great. He had stolen less than $4 in potatoes. Meanwhile, the true criminals, the pirates with their gold teeth, were in the clubs like one in the Metropol Hotel that cost $100 to walk through the door. They were riding the streets in Mercedes and BMWs, taking up the old Communist VIP lane down the center of the highway, flashing their lights on the streets the way they flashed their money in the city casinos.

What was better, many people began asking themselves, a layer of communists who may have been as wealthy as these robber barons but who, at least, felt so embarrassed about their illicit wealth that they tried to hide it or these gaudy *nouveau richekies?* More important, how could you convince a Russian, especially a young one, that crime did not pay? Clearly, it paid handsomely, better than any other work around.

What was perhaps most amazing in this era was that there were still millions of Russians who did not steal, who did not murder their neighbors to get what they wanted. They might grumble about paying the doctor extra cash for extra services. They might smile at an official they despised, even offer him a cake, but there was still enough honesty ingrained in enough people that the entire fabric of the nation had not yet disintegrated into a society of looters and inveterate cheats.

A woman shopkeeper makes certain that her customer buys only one lemon. The better ones would come in next week, she says, clearly prepared to lose a few rubles today to maintain her reputation. A writer begins teaching to pay her bills. An artist finds his construction materials in the mounds of garbage outside his apartment. At a bread store, the clerk demands that a customer take the right change, instead of pocketing the extra rubles. An old woman warns me to close my purse on the streets. A customs clerk at the airport demands that I open my suitcase. He is angry at me. I have a cross, he says, frowning. I have forgotten that Otets Nikolai and his daughter Tanya have given me a keepsake. It is new, golden and blue, and as I find it under a knot of dirty clothes, he stares at me a moment realizing it is a religious token, not a stolen treasure. He waves me away. Maybe, I think, this angry young man will catch the old crosses, stop the draining of Russian treasures at least through this one line, at this one airport.

Most Russians clearly did not want this lawlessness. Maybe they didn't want the old communism with its secret corruption and forced equality. Maybe they weren't ready to revive Stalin or bring back Brezhnev, but they wanted order. Like all of us, they wanted some feeling that if certain rules were obeyed, everything would be more or less normal. They wanted the security of knowing they were operating in the right. A young man in the trucking business may have spoken for many of his fellow entrepreneurs when he told me that he operated "like all other businesses in Moscow," with two sets of books—one white, one black. According to the white books, he paid himself about $100 a month in salary. On the black ledger, he had made enough to buy a new car, renovate a house, send a child to "private" extra curricular activities. If he declared the entire income, he said, there would be no money to pay for the business or take a real salary.

"The truth is that I would love to be able to work only on the white ledger," he said. "But if nobody pays taxes on the entire income, why should I? Am I such a fool?" He laughed and shook his head. "But I would love to be at peace with myself."

The taxes were far too high, of course. Russia's new Center for Economic Reform, after surveying businessmen who hinted that most of their transactions were done on the black side of the ledger, decided that "the overwhelming majority of firms (we are primarily considering those in the private sector) would simply collapse if they were to try to pay all the taxes required by law. It seems clear that if a business is functioning, then—to some extent—it must be breaking the law."[42]

When I talked to Moscow's chief city court judge Zoya Korneva about the new lawlessness in society, she had stiffened in her chair and grown noticeably red in the face. "In your country, there are many people who get around the tax law," she had argued. I had not contradicted her, but the IRS did not take kindly to the kind of tax evasion that was going on in Russia. Americans tried to pay the least amount of tax possible. They set up companies and mutual funds and all kind of structures to limit their donations to the government. But the difference was that when these tax systems were successful it was because they were at least arguably legal.

Would Russians ever get to the point that they would be arguing with the tax collectors rather than avoiding them altogether? There were a few hopeful signs. One of my favorite involved Russia's first foreign-run boutique, a shop established in downtown Moscow by Estée Lauder. The store, which opened in 1989 and drew lines of awed Soviet shoppers, who stared at the choices of lipsticks and swooned over the variety of perfumes, was a showplace. It also sold up to $10 million worth of products a year.

Three years after it first appeared on Gorky Street (by then restored to its prerevolutionary name of Tverskaya), the employees of this shop took over the store. It was a mini coup, taking place on a prime bit of Moscow real estate. They threw out Estée Lauder and renamed the shop a perfumery. Estée Lauder representatives, whose company had invested thousands of dollars in redecorating the shop, began by appealing to the government, a route that had taken them well into 1994 with no resolution in sight.

"We put in everything—floors, windows, doors, walls, wiring, plumbing, air conditioning, telephones, furniture," Elizabeth Susskind, director of Estée Lauder's Russian operations, said at one point in the negotiations. "It's as if you were sitting on my couch and suddenly it became yours just because you were Russian and you happened to be sitting there when privatization came along."

Susskind told city authorities that the employees of the shop made up Estée Lauder stationery, created an Estée Lauder stamp, and forged a letter asking for privatization of the company in their names. (Clearly, if true, this was not exactly legal.) Then the director of the former employees group demanded that the company lease the store directly from them, continue renovating it, and resume the flow of goods with the Estée Lauder name. Instead, the company went to court, and Estée Lauder won a court ruling that the takeover was illegal.

But the employees had argued that they had been Estée Lauder representatives, that they had "owned" the store, and that they deserved to keep it. The workers' group had won a lease from the Moscow City Council shortly before it was disbanded. What this meant was that Lauder could wave one document. The Russians could wave another.[43]

Even though this scene horrified potential investors from the West, I found it oddly comforting. This was a Russian trying to figure out how to operate in a hostile new world, and the story helped offset tales like Elena's, who had faced the criminal side of capitalism and lost her daughter's voucher by being too trusting. It helped counter the stories of people who had simply given their lives or their businesses to the criminals, contributing to the disorder by succumbing to it. Waving documents was better than brandishing weapons, and it was far less hazardous to find a solution in the courts than in the back alleys. But like most people watching Russia in this era, I feared this was the exception. One Russian writer had labeled this period, "The era of the big grab," and that whatever they did to survive, most people had little time to make certain it was legal.

Epilogue

Moscow in May 1995 was a different city from the ragged Soviet center I had first seen four years earlier. The chaos that began in 1992 after the end of Communism had now begun to settle into a kind of anxious stability, and Russia had become a new country on its own hard terms. The celebrations and gloating in the West—how the Other Superpower had lost the cold war and converted to democracy and a market economy—slowly disappeared as Russia began to adapt the outside world to its own internal demands. Democracy by 1995 became an unfriendly concept in Russia. It was a word that increasingly meant lack of control or even weakness brought on by meddlers from Washington or Tokyo or the Common Market. Old communists were returning to positions in Parliament, and Russian nationalism was stealing into the open, making the terrible Russian war against the Chechens a matter of Russian pride. The press was still mostly free. People could protest and talk and vote, but the future of many democratic reforms seemed as frail as the ailing president Boris Yeltsin. The turmoil inside the government made many of those outside fear that the Russian conflicts would be resolved the old way—with the return of a dictator, a Russian strongman to bring peace and order and control.

As the democrats began to despair, however, economists saw reasons to celebrate: Russia was establishing the foundations of a Western economy and elbowing its way into the international marketplace.[1] The step from socialist to salesman had been far easier than the leap from communist to democrat.

On a snowy day in February 1992, I had seen the first crude markets in Moscow: Russians stood near the metro stops to sell the plates and auto tires and birth control pills they had been storing in their apartments for barter, for bribes, or for the catastrophes that had been part of their recent past and therefore seemed inevitable in this unpredictable future. A few months later, the first gaudy kiosks had begun to appear on street corners where instant entrepreneurs were selling sausage given as aid from the European market and Chinese down coats and strange cigarettes in bright packets that promised (but did not deliver) American tobacco. By 1995, many of Russia's 70,000 kiosks had turned into walk-in shops that sold not only beer, wine, and cigarettes but also Italian shoes at prices that would have stunned even a tourist in downtown Rome.

The new society set up banks, stock markets, investment funds, and businesses. By late 1994, there were 2,500 banks in Russia, 600 investment funds, 40 million shareholders, 15,779 medium-to-large enterprises producing 62 percent of the officially recorded GDP. Most important of all, about 86 per cent of the industrial workforce was working in privatized enterprises by June 1994. At one in every four shareholder meetings in 1994, shareholders voted to change the management, often so that they could stop producing Soviet goods that no one would buy or perhaps to halt the flow of company assets to the top of the new corporate chain.[2]

As businessmen tried to take control, they vied with powerful vestiges of Soviet culture. Competing for Russia's wealth on every level were the thugs and hooligans and organized criminals who had operated underground or behind bars or even at the top secret levels of government in the Soviet years. They had the advantages of money and access to resources as Russia changed from a control economy to a market economy, and they quickly began to grab Russia's unprotected wealth. A few optimists believed that these crime lords would eventually bring a demand for law—the "gentrification of the *mafiya*" was the favored scenario, a frail hope that the mobster or old apparatchik would want to stop the stealing, now that he was rich, and create a more secure life for his children.

Whatever would happen on a grand scale in the new Russia, on a more human level, the people I saw in 1995 simply looked better. I knew that the old intelligentsia—the writers, the artists, the academicians, the people who defined Russia for many of us—were struggling. Yes, the homeless and the poor stood for many as open refutations that this new experiment worked. The criminals hogged the streets, and even honest people had to break the rules, if not the laws, in order to survive. Still, in the shock of seeing Moscow in the spring, its windows clean, its streets washed, a few people smiling and many looking healthy, I felt that somehow the country had managed to begin its launch toward a more workable society.

One warm spring day in 1995, I walked through the center of Moscow, wandering beyond the walls of apartments into the green interior court-yards where the *pukh*, a fluffy seed that floats from the city's trees like a spring snowstorm, had begun to drift toward the new grass. Apple blos-soms spread their delicious scent over the children's park No. 2 near Novoslobodskaya and as I passed a dog sleeping in the sun, he looked nurtured and sleek. Old men sat on the benches and smoked, lending the scene a Mediterranean look, like some variation of the Greek shore or a small town in Southern Italy. Young women in bright fuchsia coats or fashionable navy blue jogging suits bounded through the pathways in the latest, high-tech running shoes. The children could have been running in an American schoolyard in their blue jeans jackets and sweatpants in bold Western colors. They beamed at each other, their faces pink and whole-some even at the end of the winter. The young provided a stark contrast to the gray children, as I used to call them, of a few years before—the frail little girls who wore organdy bows in their hair and the little boys wearing bulky jackets in dead Soviet colors.

Moscow no longer had the look of a dying city, a cluster of dilapidated buildings where every hinge was beginning to rust, every roof starting to leak. Structures that had been settling into piles of historic rubble now were being restored. These were not haphazard restorations like the fix-it, adapt-it, slap-do work I had seen in the past. These buildings from prerevolution-ary days had been carefully patched and then revived in their original colors—pastel greens and soft shades of apricot, mustard, and seashell pinks—revealing elaborate facades that had gone untended and unnoticed in the gray Soviet years.

Moscow's streets were choked with cars, not merely the battered Ladas and Zhigulis of the past, but now there were Western cars, Mercedes and

BMWs, Fords and Chevrolets, new and used, Volvos by the legion, Hondas and the Russian Agas, minivehicles reminiscent of the old Citroën 2CV in France or the Mini-Minors in England. Near the apartments was evidence that these cars were being guarded fiercely by their owners. Small collapsible garages that fit like a metal shell over most modest-sized automobiles stood in rows along the sidewalks. Former parks and walkways had been taken over by clusters of these tiny Quonset huts whose very presence stood as a hopeful sign that not everybody was either rich or poor in this new Moscow.

I moved around the corner to the grocery store, this one full of delicacies that in earlier years would have been hidden behind guards and heavily curtained windows at foreign stores or apparatchiki shops. There were red oranges from Israel; grapes from Chile. Uncle Ben's rice stood on one shelf, Russian cranberry juice on another. The store was crowded with Russians buying for the evening meal—potatoes and onions, a little sugar, preserved tomatoes. The prices were less than in New York but far more than in the Moscow of a year earlier, and buyers grumbled the way they do everywhere when a lemon costs more than thirty-five cents.

The store, once a state shop, was now owned by a group of women. It was clean. Jars of fruit had been dusted recently. The floor had been swept. The lights were bright enough to see the produce, and a young girl was pulling the rotten onions out of the bin. The director moved around the shop checking the stock and greeting the customers by name. There was no line and no loitering. Customers moved briskly through this store at a pace that had been almost unknown five years earlier.

As I stood staring at the check-out line where the clerk used a cash register instead of a wooden abacus, an older woman asked for a cauliflower. Not the newer ones, she said softly. One from under the counter. The clerk brought out a small cauliflower, its leaves wrinkled, its top faintly brown. She weighed it and announced the price—about thirty cents. The old woman opened her wallet, counted her money and saw that the cauliflower would take it all. She shook her head quietly, apologized for the trouble, and then hurried out of the shop.

The old woman and the millions like her did not refute the progress that Russia had made since shedding the controls of communism, but they tarnished Russia's second revolution this century. Many were prospering in the new Russia, but for others, unbridled liberty or unfettered opportunity were simply more government-inspired slogans that benefited somebody else. The Russians are a patient people who endured seven decades waiting for communism to work. How long they would give this difficult experiment with democracy and capitalism was impossible to say.

Notes

Prologue

1. Obolensky, Dimitri, ed., *The Penguin Book of Russian Verse* (Harmondsworth, England: Penguin Books, 1965). This line is from the prose translation of a poem by Fyodor Tyutchev (1803–73), p. 134.
2. Chelyabinsk local paper reprinted story from *Trud*, October 1, 1992.
3. Nancy Ries, "The Power of Negative Thinking," *The Anthropology of East Europe Review*, 10, no. 2 (1991).
4. *The Moscow Times*, February 22, 1993, p. 8.
5. The government estimate was 123 deaths. The Committee of Assistance to Victims' Families estimated 163. *Izvestia*, October 3, 1995.
6. Adam Tanner, "Moscow's Latest Trend: Rent-a-Bunker," *The Moscow Times*, October 5, 1992, p. 1.
7. Carlotta Gall, "Paychecks Hold Surprises, Not Rubles," *The Moscow Times*, September 6, 1994, p. 3.
8. Douglas Herbert, "In an Age of Despair, Russians Pose an Old Question Anew: What Is to Be Undone?" *The Moscow Tribune*, October 28, 1992, p. 11.

1. Homes for Sale

1. Alexander Gordeyev, "No Room at the Homeless Center," *The Moscow Times*, November 19, 1993, p. 1.
2. Privatization figures, *Russian Economic Trends* 4, no. 1 (1995). Of the almost three

million flats in Moscow, about 40 percent were privatized by late 1994. *The Moscow Times,* October 6, 1994.

3. *The Moscow Times,* March 13, 1992.

4. Fred Hiatt *The Washington Post,* November 13, 1993, p. 1.

5. Steven Erlanger, *The New York Times,* June 7, 1995, p. A10.

6. The couple who bought this Moscow apartment will remain nameless because even though they are nice, respectable people, getting an apartment in 1992 involved breaking or at least bruising the law. In the early 1990s, the laws against speculation, which would seem to cover real estate, were basically advisory, but there was always the chance that the police or the government would suddenly decide to promote law and order, and a reign of enforcement would begin, punishing a few for what many were doing at the time. Just as older correspondents hid the names of their sources for fear of the secret police, I have decided not to give out the names of these people because of the regular police. I have called them Katya and Pavel, not their real names.

7. Figures on Moscow apartments at end of 1992, Russian Information Agency, as reported in *The Moscow Times,* September 11, 1992. By the end of 1992, the official figure was 2.6 million apartments privatized in Moscow, *The Moscow Times,* February 15, 1993.

8. Boris Nemtsov, "Pioneering Land Reform," *The Moscow Times,* September 29, 1995, p. 8.

9. Richard Pipes, *The Russian Revolution,* vol. 2 (New York: Knopf, 1990), p. 191.

10. Dorothy Atkinson, *The End of the Russian Land Commune,* 1905–1930 (Palo Alto: Stanford University Press, 1983), 5.

11. Pipes, vol. 2, 171.

12. John Lawrence, *A History of Russia* (New York: Meridian, the Penguin Group, 1993), 215.

13. Warren Bartlett Walsh, *Russia and the Soviet Union* (Ann Arbor: University of Michigan Press, 1958), 342.

14. Interview, May 1993, David A. J. Macey, professor of history and director of the Center for Russian and East European Studies, Middlebury College, Middlebury, Vt.

15. *The Moscow Times,* September 7, 1994, p. 1.

16. In the first quarter of 1995, private farms produced 2 percent of Russia's meat, 1 percent of milk, 2 percent of eggs. The private farms produced 3.2 percent of all agricultural production. The remainder came from agricultural enterprises and household plots. *Russian Economic Trends* 4, no. 1 (1995).

17. *The Moscow Times,* September 7, 1994, p. 1. By end of first quarter 1995, there were 282,700 private farms in Russia. Private farmland covered 12 million hectares. *Russian Economic Trends* 4, no. 1 (1995).

18. *Sydney Morning Herald,* January 18, 1992, *Good Weekend* magazine, p. 12.

19. Ibid.

20. Ibid.

21. *The Moscow Times*, October 29, 1993, p. 1.

2. Mother Russia

1. Zoya Krylova, interview, at *Rabotnitsa* magazine, 1992.
2. Karen Dukess, "Fighter for Women's Rights," *The Moscow Times*, February 18, 1993.
3. Matt Bivens, "Russian Roulette," *Modern Maturity*, September-October 1994, p. 24.
4. Ibid., 26.
5. Steven Erlanger, "Retired People Are Struggling in the New Russia," *The New York Times*, August 8, 1995, p. A3.
6. Siobhan Darrow report on Russian women for CNN, 1994.
7. The move to keep women at home and, in effect, allow husbands to control many personal decisions for their wives was fermenting through the parliament in this period. At one point a draft law granted the family unit the right to own property. All salaries were to be put into one communal account (by law), and the family was given the right to decide whether a woman should become pregnant. This law was discarded at the time, but many women's experts believed it was a law with strong backing in an increasingly conservative political climate. Report from the Human Rights Watch, Women's Rights Project, "Russia: Neither Jobs nor Justice; State Discrimination Against Women in Russia," 7, no. 5 (March 1995): 12–15.
8. As Olga and I spoke on that first occasion in 1992, research institutions were crumbling all over Russia. In Lenin Hills, the academic section of Moscow, where my family and I had moved in early 1992, news of closings at institute after institute swept the community. Some institutes simply closed as the government ran out of money, but others stayed afloat, drifting while the more intelligent members used the offices, the materials, and the research to create new lives or new companies. One scientist I knew sold his ingenious geological measuring devices to companies in the West, remaining carefully attached as a consultant to the company as part of the deal. Another group began to focus on uses for such Soviet inventions as "blue blood" *(golubaya krov)*, a milky blue blood substitute used on wounded soldiers during the Afghanistan war. One group of scientists and young businessmen, hearing that blue blood made the heart race, converted some of it into a skin cream and sold it in Moscow under such names as Intim Ekstaz or Intim Tonus. The salves were designed to improve the user's sex life—Ekstaz making the woman more sensitive, Tonus giving the male more stamina—and by late 1994, their business was booming as the lore outpaced the modest advertising for their product. Oleg Oksinoyd, the director of research for the company, figured that the years of Soviet research saved his company about $500,000. *The Moscow Times*, October 21, 1994, p. 1.
9. Alix Holt, "The First Soviet Feminists," in *Soviet Sisterhood*, Barbara Holland, ed. (London: Fourth Estate, 1985).
10. Irina Yurna, "Women in Russia: Building a Movement," *From Basic Needs to Basic*

Rights: Women's Claim to Human Rights, Margaret A. Schuler, ed. (Institute for Women, Law and Development, 1995), 477–94.

11. Women's Day, A Special Issue, *The Moscow Times,* March 6, 1994, p. 2.

12. *The Moscow Times,* December 8, 1993, p. 8.

13. Human Rights Watch, Women's Rights Project report, 12–15.

14. Martina Vandenberg, editorial, *The Moscow Times,* March 8, 1995, p. 8.

15. Alessandra Stanley, "Sexual Harassment Thrives in the New Russia," *The New York Times,* April 17, 1994, p. 1.

16. Human Rights Watch, Women's Rights Project report, 12.

17. *The Moscow Times,* November 3, 1994.

18. Igor S. Kon, *The Sexual Revolution in Russia: From the Age of the Czars to Today* (New York: The Free Press, 1995), 189.

19. Human Rights Watch, Women's Rights Project report, 17–18. Also quoted from a 1993 Reuter report on Natasha Belyayeva, an unemployed worker, who during one interview for office secretary at a company was told, " 'Okay, you look good; you're sexy enough. But if you want to work as a secretary, your salary will be very low.' He said I could earn as much in a day as I would in a month as a secretary if I offered clients sexual services." Fiona Fleck, "Russian Women Squeezed Out of Job Market into the Home," *Reuter European Business Report,* February 18, 1993.

20. Human Rights Watch, Women's Rights Project, 19, reported that every fifth person killed in Russia is killed by a spouse, and the majority of those killed by their spouses are women—an estimate from a representative of the Ministry of Social Welfare at a March 22, 1994, meeting on Women's Issues of the Union of Russian Jurists.

21. Martina Vandenberg, interview, Moscow, May 1995.

22. Genine Babakian, "Half Russia's Murders: Husbands Kill Wives," *The Moscow Times,* April 19, 1995, p. 1.

23. *The Moscow Times,* May 27, 1993, p. 3.

24. David Lauter, interview, May 1995.

25. John Erickson, "Soviet Women at War," *World War II and the Soviet People,* John Garrard and Carol Garrard, eds. (New York: St. Martin's Press, 1993), p. 50.

26. Robert Kaiser, *Russia: The People and the Power* (New York: Pocket Books, 1976), 280.

27. *Pravda,* September 2, 1984, p. 6.

28. CNN interviews, Fall 1994, Siobhan Darrow report on women.

29. Artemy Troitsky, *The Moscow Times,* July 3, 1992.

3. Health: Living in Soviet Ruins

1. CNN report, March 1992. This was the response of a Russian heart attack victim to a question by a CNN journalist about whether he will quit smoking now that the doctors have warned him he will die sooner because of it. He said he had no plans to quit smoking or drinking.

2. Murray Feshbach and Alfred Friendly, Jr., *Ecocide in the USSR: Health and Nature Under Siege* (New York: Basic Books, 1992), 2.

3. In November 1993, Vladimir Vladimirovich Kondakov, head of state automobile inspection for Russia, told me in an interview that "Russia has the worst traffic accident rate in the world." At the time, he said there had been 130,507 accidents in the previous nine months, resulting in 26,861 deaths. In 1992, for example, the traffic fatalities listed for the United States were 38,000 for the entire year. Russia's public rate of traffic deaths was 36,471 for the same year. Private estimates were that traffic fatalities in Russia were almost double what the officials said. Kondakov cited as reasons for traffic accidents the lack of good machinery, bad driving habits, and of course, drunkenness. As I left his office, he gave me a packet of souvenirs. One was a bottle opener bearing the insignia of Russia's traffic police.

4. Michael Specter, "Plunging Life Expectancy Puzzles Russia," *The New York Times,* August 2, 1995, p. 1. Other disturbing figures on Russian life include the number of children born in Russia in 1994, 1.4 million—a number believed to be less than half of the number of abortions.

5. Interview with Aleksei Yablokov, *Rossiiskiye Vesti,* September 27, 1992, p. 2.

6. *The Moscow Times,* October 8, 1992.

7. Feshbach and Friendly, 176.

8. Feshbach and Friendly, 1.

9. The estimate on numbers of birth defects came from Dr. Alla Shumilina, a health official from the region that included Chapayevsk. At least one Western medical expert has raised the possibility that the Russians in this period categorized many problems as defects. The systems for collecting data, like the rest of Russia, were in a state of flux. Some numbers were good; some were wild estimates that suited the moment.

10. Kathy Lally, "A Small City Forgotten by God and Man," *Baltimore Sun,* December 31, 1992, p. 1.

11. *The Moscow Times,* September 22, 1992, quoting Oleg Tatarinov, advertising manager for Channel 2 in Moscow.

12. Abstract for Soviet government prepared by Aleksandr V. Telyukov, head of comparative economics at the Soviet National Planning Committee (GOSPLAN), 1991.

13. Feshbach and Friendly, 188.

14. Aleksandr Sergeyev, deputy chief of Moscow's main narcological hospital No. 17. *The Moscow Times,* November 5, 1992.

15. Report for the Brewers Association of Canada, "International Survey; Alcoholic Beverage Taxation and Control Policy," June 1989, 365–70.

16. "Sober Attitude to Soviet Drinking," editorial, *The Guardian,* May 20, 1985.

17. UPI report, October 9, 1992.

18. Fred Hiatt, *The Washington Post,* October 18, 1992, p. 1; *Newsweek,* November 2, 1992, p. 14. Western doctors touring Russia were sometimes told flatly by medical

personnel that vodka protected against radiation. Dr. John Collee said that doctors dealing with the aftermath of the Chernobyl nuclear fire told workers about this remedy.

19. Interviews with Russians about use for children. Journalists began visiting these centers in 1990–91. Slava Zelenin described in detail one of these visits.

20. Michael Hetzer and Alexander Gordeyev, "Treatment of Alcoholics: Still in the Gulag Era," *The Moscow Times*, February 24, 1994, p. 4. Also, interviews at Hospital No. 17 outside ZiL automobile factory in Moscow, October 1992.

21. Dr. Mikhail Zharikov, Moscow psychiatrist, personal interview.

22. *The Moscow Times*, November 5, 1992.

23. Dioxin, a toxic byproduct in the production of many chemicals, "is a carcinogen that causes damage to the reproductive, endocrine, and immune systems in birds, fish, and mammals, including human beings," according to Murray Feshbach. Feshbach writes that in secret Soviet reports during the 1980s, dioxin contamination in Chapayevsk was known to be seventy-five times higher than the levels known to be safe and in some areas two thousand times that level. Western and Russian news reports on Chapayevsk and other areas of the lower Volga were beginning to call attention to the plight of people living in the once-rich agricultural area. Murray Feshbach, *Ecological Disaster: Cleaning Up the Hidden Legacy of the Soviet Regime* (New York: The Twentieth Century Fund Press, 1995), 70–71.

24. *Moscow News*, June 7–14, 1992.

25. Statistically it may be hard to prove whether, after the end of communism, people's health deteriorated or the truth had simply become more available. Soviet data was notoriously and traditionally unreliable. In Moscow in late 1992, Dr. Georgi Komarov, editor of *Meditsinskaya Gazeta*, the chief journal for doctors in the former Soviet states, told me about his days as head of a research institute in Bishkek, the capitol of Kirghizia, when he released data showing a rise in tuberculosis. At first the officials tried to "improve" the data, i.e., to disprove the tuberculosis. When Dr. Komarov resisted, they passed on his report (which was improved at the regional level). Later, they showed Dr. Komarov exactly why he should have lied on data forms himself. They stopped his research and cut back his funds to his clinic because he wasn't doing a good job. The TB level had increased in his area, they explained. The bad data was his fault. Dr. Georgi Komarov, editor of *Meditsinskaya Gazeta*, interview in Moscow office, September 24, 1992.

In some ways, the same thing was happening to the Yeltsin government. As data came out showing the problems that people were facing, Yeltsin's opponents tended to suggest that these new problems were because of the new government.

4. Medicine: Do We Have a Future?

1. G. S. Pondoev, *Notes of a Soviet Doctor* (New York: Consultants Bureau, Inc., 1959), 235.

2. Dr. Zakhar Mikhailovich Simchovich, interview, October 1, 1991.

3. Mark G. Field, *Doctor and Patient in Soviet Russia* (Cambridge, Mass.: Harvard University Press, 1957), 135–141.

4. Dr. Andrei Vorobiev interview, 1992.

5. *The Moscow Times*, November 5, 1994, Insight section.

6. Dr. Mikhail M. Kuzmenko (president, Russian Health Workers' Union), interview, May 8, 1992.

7. *The Moscow Times*, February 27–28, 1993.

8. Murray Feshbach, and Alfred Friendly, Jr., *Ecocide in the USSR* (New York: Basic Books, 1992), 192.

9. *The Moscow Times*, February 27–28, 1993.

10. David K. Shipler, *Russia: Broken Idols, Solemn Dreams* (New York: Times Books, 1983), 221.

11. Dr. Boris I. Dolgushin (leading researcher at All-Union Cancer Research Center, Moscow), interview, October 1991.

12. Anton Chekhov, *Ward Number Six and Other Stories* (New York: Oxford University Press, 1988), 23–69.

13. Western doctors note that hand surgery very often is followed by infection and can be extremely disfiguring without proper antibiotics.

14. Report on Russian medical system for Soviet parliament, submitted in 1991 by Aleksandr V. Telyukov, then head of comparative economics division at the Institute for Economic Studies of the Soviet National Planning Committee (GOS-PLAN), 18.

15. Field, 15.

16. Feshbach and Friendly, 35, quoting from William Horsley Gantt, 141. *A Medical Review of Soviet Russia, Results of the First Five Year Plan* (London: British Medical Association, 1936), 141.

17. *The Cambridge Encyclopedia of Russia and the Soviet Union* (New York: Cambridge University Press, 1982), 256.

18. Nicholas V. Riasonovsky, *A History of Russia* (Oxford: Oxford University Press, 1963), 318–19.

19. *Cambridge Encyclopedia . . . ,* 257.

20. Field, 6.

21. Susan Gross Solomon and John F. Hutchinson, eds., *Health and Society in Revolutionary Russia* (Bloomington: Indiana University Press, 1990), 20–22.

22. Field, 16.

23. Field, 53.

24. Nancy Mandelker Friedan, *Russian Physicians in an Era of Reform and Revolution* (Princeton, N.J.: Princeton University Press, 1981), 150–51.

25. Field, 20.

26. Michael Ryan, *Doctors and the State in the Soviet Union* (London: Macmillan, 1989), 41.

27. Ibid., 20.

28. Ibid., 37. Ryan puts it this way: "Indeed, it seems justifiable to identify multiple interconnections between the high doctor-to-population quotient, low salaries and the high proportion of female doctors [in Soviet life]."

29. William A. Knaus, *Inside Russian Medicine: An American Doctor's First-Hand Report* (New York: Everest House, 1981), 83–84.

30. Field, 20.

31. Ibid., 73.

32. Ibid., 76.

33. Ibid., 73.

34. *Trud,* November 20, 1993.

35. Telyukov report (see note 14), 5, quoting from *Komsomolskaya Pravda,* June 18, 1988.

36. Feshbach and Friendly, 262, from *Komsomolskaya Pravda* interview, July 13, 1990, p. 2.

37. Ryan, 14.

38. *The Moscow Times,* February 27–28, 1993.

39. Telyukov report, 4–5.

40. Dr. Valentina V. Mityaeva, interview, November 13, 1992.

41. Dr. Valentina Lukyanova, interview, Chapayevsk, 1992.

42. Feshbach and Friendly, 226.

43. *Fortune,* May 8, 1989, p. 146.

44. Ibid.

45. *Time,* July 1, 1985, p. 44.

46. Fyodorov was lucky in some ways to have the Soviet government backing him with all the money and equipment he could hope for at a time when he was experimenting with the early techniques, especially in radial keratotomy, the operation for myopia that calls for spokelike incisions in the eye. Although the technique has been refined since the early operations like Fyodorov's, Western eye specialists studied a number of patients in the United States five years after having RK, as it is called, and found that the patients fared relatively well. Approximately 88 percent of those studied had vision of 20/40 after the surgery. "Results of the Prospective Evaluation of Radial Keratotomy (PERK) Study Five Years After Surgery," *Ophthalmology* 98, no. 8 (August 1991). The surgery was begun in the United States in 1978.

   However, some doctors I consulted said that they worried about the side effects of RK. The conveyor belt also has few followers outside Dr. Fyodorov's operation. Many Western doctors want a single surgeon to be accountable for the operation and fear that this mass production increases the possibility of infection spreading among the patients.

47. *Fortune,* May 8, 1989, pp. 145–146.

48. Vladimir Golyakhovsky, *Russian Doctor: A Surgeon's Life in Contemporary Russia and Why He Chose to Leave* (New York: St. Martin's/Marek, 1984), 20.

49. *Argumenty i Fakty* no. 43, November 1991.

50. Feshbach and Friendly, 186.

51. B. Belitskiy, *Trud*, January 27, 1989.

52. *Itar-Tass*, report published by The Social and Political Institute of the Russian Academy of Sciences, April 15, 1994.

53. When I told a British doctor about the inserted pacemaker, he was surprised that any physician would perform such an operation, and it was another reminder that medicine in Russia was still being practiced in a way that would not be tolerated in most hospitals in the West.

54. After the dissolution of the Soviet Union, funding for the Russian health care system changed dramatically. The system was decentralized, and total health care funding dropped by 40 percent in 1991–92. A Compulsory Medical Insurance (CMI) program, patterned on the Dutch and German systems, began in 1992, financed by a payroll tax of 3.6 percent, paid by employers. How well the system worked varied from region to region. By 1994, the CMI was paying for 20 percent to 50 percent of official health care expenditure, depending on the region. However, in total the CMI was only yielding 70 percent of the revenues it was expected to produce. The CMI system appears to work better in regions such as Moscow, St. Petersburg, and Sverdlovsk, where there are a number of competing funds. However, the CMI payroll tax would need to be raised to 5 percent, *or* local health budgets would need to increase by 20 percent, if the new system were to restore health care spending to 1991 levels. [Interview with Linda Bilmes, economist and management consultant who advised the Russian government on health care finance, October 31, 1995].

5. Alternative Medicine: From Herbs to Hocus-Pocus

1. Pokrovsky, interview, *Trud*, October 3, 1991.

2. *The Moscow Times*, August 28, 1992, p. 16.

3. *Trud*, October 3, 1991.

4. British doctor and writer Dr. John Collee, as well as some other medical experts who spent time in the U.S.S.R. and Russia, suggested that part of the failure of science to keep up was because of a loss of scientific objectivity. Without objective reporting and unbiased documentation, two facets of Soviet research that were often missing in such social areas as human medicine, science fails.

5. From press conference, March 21, 1995, attended by Natalia Alexandrova and reported to me on March 31, 1995.

6. In my own interview with Dr. Andrei I. Vorobiev, a few weeks before he was replaced in 1992 for resisting some of the Yeltsin government's changes in medical care, he said, "There are many real charlatans, and they must be jailed. I've written to newspapers, and I've made speeches. But this is an era of lawlessness. I don't think we will realize change in this place while lawlessness reigns."

7. *The Moscow Times*, February 11, 1995, p. 9.

8. Dr. Henry Dolger, clinical professor of medicine emeritus and consultant for diabetes at Mt. Sinai Medical School in New York City, said in an interview August

6, 1993, that the use of urine to treat diabetes may have stemmed from the knowledge from ancient times that a diabetic's urine was sweet with sugar that his body could not properly absorb. It was known as the pissing disease in seventeenth-century England because of the frequency of thirst and urination that characterizes diabetes. The idea of diabetics drinking their own urine was suggested by a French doctor in 1861, who advised that sugar lost from repeated urination could be redigested more easily this way. His theories were quickly dismissed in the West, and the efforts of Russian patients to follow such difficult advice would "all go down the drain," leaving a diabetic to simply grow worse and perhaps die young if not treated with insulin by a doctor.

9. Sir John Maynard, *Russia in Flux* (New York: Macmillan Company, 1951), 171.
10. *The Moscow Times,* February 11, 1995, Insight section.
11. Valentin Pokrovsky, head of the Russian Academy of Medical Sciences, noted that doctors are alarmed about cases such as an AIDS patient who was treated for a month with "charged water" and his immunity fell to zero. *Trud,* October 3, 1991. Also in personal interview, October 1992.
12. Americans also spend almost as much money on unconventional therapies, as the medical profession refers to acupuncture or holistic medicine, as they do in out-of-pocket expenses for their conventional treatments. But studies show that Americans still tend to place their medical faith more firmly in the family doctor, even if they rarely confide in that doctor about their dealings with alternative medicine. *The New England Journal of Medicine,* January 28, 1993, pp. 246–52.
13. My colleague Dr. Collee noted later that lumps in the breast come and go for many women and thus can often be easily "cured."
14. *The Moscow Times,* December 21, 1992, p. 13. From *Pravda.*

6. Sex: Slaking the Oldest Thirst

1. Interview, September 1992. MIR.
2. Masha Gessen *Out* magazine, April/May 1993.
3. *Moskovsky Komsomolets,* May 6, 1995.
4. Igor Kon and James Riordan, eds., article by Kon, "Sexuality and Culture" in *Sex and Russian Society* (Bloomington: Indiana University Press, 1993), 25.
5. Mikhail Stern, "Anonymous Sex," in *Sex in the USSR* (New York: Times Books, 1979), 177–78.
6. Daisy girls, Kon and Riordan, 66.
7. *The Moscow Times,* March 6, 1994. Report on birth control from Russian Association of Family Planning, branch of International Planned Parenthood Federation, p. 5.
8. Ibid.
9. For an interesting version of the Russian sex binge earlier this century see James H. Billington, *The Icon and the Axe: An Interpretive History of Russian Culture* (New York: Vintage Books, 1970), 492–93. There are many books that touch on the sexual upheaval of this complicated era. Another interesting version of the period

after 1905 is Laura Engelstein's *The Keys to Happiness: Sex and the Search for Modernity in Fin-de-Siècle Russia* (Ithaca, N.Y.: Cornell University Press, 1993).

10. The passionate Russian is deeply rooted in myth, much of it undoubtedly based on reality. Ancient Russian folk culture gloried in tales that would have made the Wife of Bath blush, even as the Russian Orthodox church was teaching chastity and fidelity. Mythical heroes—undoubtedly mimicked by ordinary men—had extra wives, a stable of lovers. They seduced virgins, ravaging those who dared refuse to marry them. Sex was basic and savage, and in the villages, areas that no church or bureaucrat could ever fully control, old traditions of trial marriages and seasonal orgies lived on until the late nineteenth century. (Kon and Riordan, 18.)

11. Billington, 494.

12. Ibid., 496–98.

13. Rozanov quote, Kon and Riordan, 21, quoting *Opavshiye Listya* (St. Petersburg, 1913), 322.

14. Billington, 500.

15. Billington, 501.

16. Kon and Riordan, eds. *Sex and Russian Society,* essay by Lynne Attwood, "Sex and the Cinema," p. 66, quoting V. I. Lenin, "On the Emancipation of Women" (Moscow, 1972). Appendix to Clara Zetkin, "My Recollections of Lenin," p. 101.

17. The prudishness of the Soviet society was not simply a Stalinist perversion, it was another effort to control an energetic and unpredictable people. A favorite explanation of Soviet sex policies by those working in the field of sex education in Russia is the description by George Orwell in his *1984:* "It was not merely that the sex instinct created a world of its own that was outside the party's control and which therefore had to be destroyed, if possible. What was more important was that sexual privation induced hysteria which was desirable because it could be transformed into war-fever and leader worship." (London: Penguin Books, 1967), 109. It could also be transformed into neurosis, desperation, sex crimes, and frigidity, but that was not part of the public story, until the Soviet state weakened and then finally disappeared.

18. Boris Estrin quoted in *Megapolis-Express,* no. 44, 1992.

19. Early sex education, *Newsweek,* October 19, 1964, p. 106.

20. Black sea youngsters, Igor S. Kon, *The Sexual Revolution in Russia: From the Age of the Czars to Today* (New York: The Free Press, 1995), 217.

21. Kon's lecture was delivered on October 23, 1992, at High School No. 355, Kapotnia.

22. *Medical Sex Journal of South Africa* 3, no. 1 (1992): 7.

23. Inna L. Alesina, interview, October 27, 1992.

24. *The Moscow Times,* March 6, 1994, p. 5.

25. Sue Bridger (University of Bradford), "Young Women and Perestroika," paper for IV World Congress for Soviet and East European Studies, Harrogate, June 1990.

26. Katrina vanden Heuvel, "Eastward, Christian Soldiers! Right-to-Lifers Hit Russia," *The Nation*, November 1, 1993, p. 489.

27. Inna Alesina, counsel on medical issues, Russian Association of Family Planning, interview, October 27, 1992.

28. Nancy Traver, *KIFE: The Life and Dreams of Soviet Youth* (New York: St. Martin's Press, 1989), 44.

29. Yuri Brokhin, *Hustling on Gorky Street: Sex and Crime in Russia Today* (New York: Dial Press, 1975), 192.

30. Igor Kon, interview, October 3, 1992.

31. Jean MacKenzie, "Russian Men Just Don't Get Valentine's Day," *The Moscow Times*, February 11, 1995, p. 8.

32. Anya Vakhrusheva, interview, September 15, 1992.

33. *The Moscow Times*, April 19, 1995.

34. Surveys on sex, love, and family life in the early 1990s began to document the stress on love and marriage, but it is worth noting that in a wide-ranging survey in 1992, satisfaction with family life remained fairly high with 56 percent of the men and 42 percent of the women saying that they were satisfied at home. Igor S. Kon, *The Sexual Revolution in Russia: From the Age of the Czars to Today* (New York: The Free Press, 1995), 162–77.

35. Press conference in Moscow, October 16, 1992, on American-Russian group starting a women's clinic.

36. Interviews in 1992 with Andrei I. Vorobiev, minister of health for Russia, and Valentin Pokrovsky, deputy health minister, epidemiology.

37. Dr. Nikolai Oleinikov, interview, October 8, 1992.

38. Interview with Dr. Georgi Kavkasside, private women's clinic in Moscow, October 1992.

39. Paul Ferris, *Sex and the British: A Twentieth Century History* (London: Michael Joseph, 1993), 114–15.

7. A Stranger in the Family

1. Igor Kon and James Riordan, eds., *Sex and Russian Society*, chapter on "Sexual Minorities," by Kon, 106.

2. Michael Specter, "Gay Russians Are 'Free' Now But Still Stay in Fearful Closet," *The New York Times*, July 8, 1995, p. 1.

3. Masha Gessen, "The Rights of Lesbians and Gay Men in the Russian Federation," report published by the International Gay and Lesbian Human Rights Commission (1994), San Francisco, 47.

4. *The Moscow Times*, June 15, 1993, p. 1.

5. Igor Kon, interview, October 3, 1992.

6. Kon and Riordan, 100, from *Megapolis-Express*, no. 6 (February 7, 1991), 14.

7. *The Moscow Times*, June 2, 1993, p. 2.

8. Gessen report, 22.

9. About twenty OMON, the paratrooper-style Russian police who have few restric-

tions on their behavior, searched Underground gay bar in Moscow a week after a gay American was murdered. One OMON trooper explained why each person in the bar was searched: "One of *yours* has been killed." Gessen report, 46.

10. Kon and Riordan, 89.
11. Ibid., 89; also Kon, interview, 1992.
12. Kon and Riordan, 89.
13. Ibid., 90.
14. Ibid.
15. Marx and Engels were not especially tolerant of homosexuality. When a German socialist was arrested for homosexual cruising in 1869, neither Marx nor Engels provided support, and their letters made it clear that they thought such activities were abnormal and destructive. Gessen report, 6.
16. Kon and Riordan, 91, quoting from the *Great Soviet Encyclopedia* of 1930, *Bolshaya Sovetskaya Entsiklopediya*, vol. 17, 593–94 (Moscow, 1930).
17. Kon, interview, October 3, 1992.
18. Kon and Riordan, 92.
19. *The Moscow Times*, June 3, 1993, p. 3.
20. Gessen report, 51.
21. Gessen report, 31.
22. Masha Gessen, "Red Army of Lovers," *Out*, April/May 1993, p. 59.
23. Kon, interview, 1992.
24. Kon and Riordan, 108, Kon, "Seks-menshinstva i Mossovet: Lyubov i Soglasie, *Semya*, no. 47 (1990), 2.
25. Ibid., Kon and Riordon, p. 108.
26. Dr. Mikhail Stern, *Sex in the U.S.S.R.* (New York: Times Books, 1979), 219.
27. Western news report of release of a small paperback book in July 1974 by A. M. Svyadoshch called *Zhenskaya Seksopatologia* for about 87 cents each. All one hundred thousand copies were said to be gone within hours. It was one of the few public documents mentioning Freud, Kinsey, or homosexuality. Associated Press, July 26, 1974.
28. Gessen, *Out*, p. 57.
29. Genine Babakian, "Epidemic of Fear," *The Moscow Times*, Insight section, September 3, 1994, pp. i–ii. In 1994, according to this article, some of the posters being used to advertise for safe sex were crude and frightening, including one that became well known in international circles after it was presented by a St. Petersburg physician at an international AIDS conference in 1993. The poster had three sections under the title Sex in Russia. The first drawing labeled "safe sex" showed a man wearing an elaborate condom. The second for "safer sex" showed the man's penis tied in a knot. "Safest sex," however, showed a man standing over a garbage can with an arm raised overhead. In his hand, he had an axe.

By 1995, there were more sophisticated ads in the cities, often a mix of strong warning and suggestive humor.
30. Kon, 1995, from *Ogonyok*, no. 28 (1988).

31. Gessen report, 37.
32. Igor S. Kon, *The Sexual Revolution in Russia, from the Age of the Czars to Today* (New York: The Free Press, 1995), 333.
33. Ibid., 263.

8. Lessons for the Young

1. Personal interview, Arbat, winter 1992.
2. Statistics about youth were increasingly grim in these days. A report from the state statistics department in March 1993 showed an increase of 18 percent in suicides for all ages, while those most inclined to take their lives were teenagers between the ages of fifteen and nineteen. The increase by 1.6 times for this age group was blamed on the stresses of society as well as an increase in use of drugs and alcohol. (Jennifer Gould, "Suicide Among Youths Has Risen Substantially," *The Moscow Times*, March 4, 1993, p. 2.)

   A similar report from *Komsomolskaya Pravda* showing statistics given the UN Committee on Children's Rights showed that up to 20 percent of children in school had chronic diseases and only 10 to 14 percent came to school healthy. More than 100,000 children were in orphanages; 32,000 girls had police records (*Komsomolskaya Pravda*, January 21, 1993, p. 1.)
3. *Rabochaya Tribuna*, January 22, 1992.
4. *The New York Times*, May 22, 1994.
5. *The Moscow Times*, February 5, 1994.
6. *The Moscow Times*, May 8, 1992.
7. *Moscow Guardian*, June 25, 1992.

9. Ballet

1. Personal interviews.
2. Interview with Vadim Gayevsky at his apartment, October 1992.
3. Arnold Haskell, *The Russian Genius in Ballet* (London: Pergamon Press, 1963), 2.
4. Reinout van der Heijen, "Battle for the Bolshoi," *Moscow Magazine*, May 1990, p. 77.
5. Mary Grace Swift, *The Art of the Dance in the USSR* (Notre Dame, Indiana: University of Notre Dame Press, 1968), 92–119.
6. Maya Plisetskaya, interview, *Moscow News* no. 27, reprinted in the *Soviet Culture Guide*, August 1991, p. 42.
7. Swift, *The Art of the Dance in the USSR*, 296.
8. Luke Jennings, "The Czar's Last Dance," *The New Yorker*, March 27, 1995, p. 80.
9. Kathy Berton Murrell, "The Bolshoi's Turbulent Past," *The Moscow Times*, October 23, 1992. Also, Evan and Margaret Mawdsley, *Blue Guide: Moscow and Leningrad* (New York: W.W. Norton & Co., Inc., 1989), 129–30.
10. Horst Koegler, *The Concise Oxford Dictionary of Ballet*, 2d ed. (London: Oxford University Press, 1982), 390.

11. Bolshoi Ballet School Brochure, 1992.
12. Iris Morley, *Soviet Ballet* (London: Collins, 1945), 58.
13. Aleksandr Prokofiev, interview, December 1992.
14. Reinout van der Heijen, *Moscow Magazine*, p. 75.
15. *Literaturnaya Gazeta*, May 27, 1992.

10. The Spiritual Bazaar

1. Dorinda Elliott, "Russia's New Gods," Atlantic edition: *Newsweek International*, August 3, 1992, p. 20.
2. Aleksandr Preobrazhensky, ed., *The Russian Orthodox Church: 10th to 20th Centuries* (Moscow: Progress Publishers, 1988), 169.
3. Ibid., 166.
4. James Billington, *The New Republic*, May 30, 1994.
5. Vladimir Golyankhovsky, *Russian Doctor: A Surgeon's Life In Contemporary Russia and Why He Chose to Leave* (New York: St. Martin's Press, 1984), 78.
6. *The Moscow Times*, January 28, 1994, p. 1.
7. Steven Erlanger, "Moscow Resurrecting Icon of Its Past Glory," *The New York Times*, September 26, 1995.
8. Billington, 27.
9. Michael Hetzer, "Determination, Faith Give New Life to Church," *The Moscow Times*, November 3, 1992, p. 8.
10. *The Moscow Times*, November 5, 1993.
11. Kathy Lally, "Russian Church Struggles over Soul Again," *Baltimore Sun*, November 10, 1994, p. 29A.
12. *Response* magazine, Spring 1993, p. 3.
13. Bulletin (18) of Orthodox Brotherhoods, reprinted in *Inside Russia* magazine, Moscow, July 1992.
14. Reprinted from "De-Zionization" by Valery Emelyanov, written December 1979 in Paris, believed by some to be ideological foundation for Pamyat. *Inside Russa* magazine, Moscow, March 1992, p. 26.
15. "Christians and Pamyat," *Inside Russia* magazine, January 1993, p. 42.
16. The KGB's most valuable agents were described in the secret police files under the code names "Abbot," "Adamant," "Antonov," "Kuznetsov," "Skala" and "Altar." Who were they? The questions were being answered slowly, at least as far as those outside the church knew. By 1992, church activists like Father Gleb Yakunin had looked at least briefly into the KGB archives. Shortly afterwards Yakunin and others began to charge that the KGB had been actively targeting priests that they could not control. In particular, these religious reformers accused the KGB and possibly its agents within the church of slaughtering a renowned outspoken priest, Father Aleksandr Men, who was murdered with an axe in 1990. In November 1994, officials arrested a suspect whose name was not released. The arrest came a week after President Yeltsin demanded publicly that the Interior Ministry focus on several unsolved murders including Men's (*The Moscow Times*, November 17, 1994, p. 2).

17. *Komsomolskaya Pravda*, October 13, 1971.
18. William C. Fletcher, *Soviet Believers: The Religious Sector of the Population* (Regents Press of Kansas, 1981), 189. M. K. Tepliakov, *Problemy ateisticheskogo vospitania v pratike partiionoi raboty* (Voronezh University Press, 1972), p. 170.
19. Billington.
20. Serge Schmemann, "Russia May Curb Foreign Relations," *The New York Times*, July 16, 1993, p. A9.
21. *The Washington Post*, July 3, 1993.
22. Peter Conradi, *The Moscow Times*, April 10, 1992, p. 16.
23. Sander Thoenes, "Moonies Court Russians," *The Moscow Times*, September 25, 1992.
24. Although there appeared to be little data on the number of proselytizers in the new Russia, one American research group, the Institute for East-West Christian Studies at Wheaton College in Wheaton, Illinois, polled twenty agencies they thought would have the largest number of Protestant missionaries in the Former Soviet Union. The poll, released in spring 1995, showed that these agenies had 2,678 missionaries in the former Soviet states. *East-West Church & Ministry Report #3*, no. 2 (Spring 1995): 10.
25. Sergei Leskov, "The Rise of Mysticism," *The Moscow Times*. January 29, 1994, p. 8.
26. *Newsweek*, August 3, 1992.
27. *The Moscow Times*, November 19, 1993, p. 10.
28. *The Moscow Times*. Many of details of this phenomenon came from *The Moscow Times* coverage of activities in Kiev on November 4, 13, 16, 19, 23, 1993.
29. James H. Billington, *The Icon and the Axe: An Interpretive History of Russian Culture* (New York: Vintage Books, 1970), 177.
30. Ibid., 179.
31. Larry Tye, "Witness to Evil Basks in Changes," *The Boston Globe*, November 14, 1994, p. 6. Also, Mark Elliott and Robert Richardson, "Growing Protestant Diversity in the Former Soviet Union," *Russian Pluralism Now Irreversible?* Uri Ra'anan, Keith Armes, and Kate Martin, eds. (New York: St. Martin's Press, 1992). Elliott and Richardson's essay on various Protestant faiths in this period also explains why so many of these evangelicals went underground during the Soviet years. They note that the Soviets tried to force Pentecostals to stop speaking in tongues, an effort which the writers describe as "roughly the equivalent of requiring Catholics to disavow the pope" (p. 193).
32. *East-West Church & Ministry Report*, Spring 1995, p. 10.
33. Anton Zhigulsky, "Falwell Takes a Backseat," *The Moscow Times*, September 13, 1994.

11. Murder: The People's Justice

1. Russian saying is *Gde sud, tam i nepravda*.
2. Judge Zoya Ivanovna Korneva, interview, January 27, 1992.
3. Nicholas Arena, interviews, May and July 1995.

4. Report on courts in Russia by Helsinki Watch, "Prison Conditions in the Soviet Union: A Report of Facilities in Russia and Azerbaidzhan" (New York: December 1991), 105.

5. Ibid., 13.

6. Helsinki Watch had described the Butyrskaya cells as "overcrowded, airless, hot in summer, cold in winter, and usually smelly." Ibid., 14. By 1995, Otets Nikolai had said it was even worse than before. A United Nations report released in December 1994 described conditions in Russian jails and prisons as inhuman and torturous. The report said Moscow prisoners suffered from "the oppressive heat, lack of oxygen, and the odors of sweat, excrement and disease created by gross overcrowding." *The Moscow Times,* January 18, 1995, p. 4.

7. *Zek* comes from documents used by the Soviet Ministry of Internal Affairs to identify prisoners who worked on the White Sea Canal in the 1930's. They were called *"zakliuchionii kanaloarmeietz"* (imprisoned canal army) which had the initials Z/K so that a prisoner became known as a *zek*.

8. In one of the most vivid descriptions of life in a Soviet prison, religious poet Irina Ratushinskaya tells how prisoners used tea to make a well-known prison narcotic called *chifir.* Irina Ratushinskaya, *Grey Is the Color of Hope* (New York: Knopf, 1988).

9. The Helsinki Watch report on prisons, which came out shortly before I visited Butyrskaya, confirmed that "among the worst facilities are the pretrial detention centers, where detainees can be held for years awaiting trial in ancient, overcrowded dungeons, packed into small, hot or cold airless cells, for 23 hours a day, with almost nothing to do but wait." Helsinki Watch report, 13.

10. Under new rules after 1993, such confessions were supposed to be suspect, especially if the accused did not have a lawyer at his side. Judge Korneva at Moscow's main court said that judges often threw out confessions done "the old way," but such diligence in supporting the state's new constitution was criticized by those who saw it as a legal system obstructing even the feeble efforts of police to fight the crime wave.

11. Boris A. Zolotukhin, legal reformer, interview, November 1991.

12. Sergei A. Pashin, advisor to President Yeltsin on legal reform, interview, June 23, 1992.

13. Susan Eva Heuman, "Perspectives on Legal Culture in Pre-Revolutionary Russia," *Revolution in Law,* ed. Piers Beirne (M. E. Sharpe, 1990), 3–4. Heuman cites the proceedings against Vera Zasulich in 1878 as an example of a trial that upset the tsars. Zasulich shot and wounded the St. Petersburg governor general but was acquitted amid cheers in the courtroom.

14. Report from Lawyers Committee for Human Rights, "Human Rights and Legal Reform in the Russian Federation" (New York: March 1993), 38.

15. Harold J. Berman, *Justice in the USSR, An Interpretation of Soviet Law* (Cambridge, Mass.: Harvard University Press, 1963 edition, 1982 printing), 243.

16. Although some Western observers have felt that their time in court changed the

outcome of the Soviet or Russian legal process, I firmly believe that my presence did not alter the trial in any way except that some of the lawyers, knowing a Western reporter was present, gave longer and more flowery speeches than I was told were normal.

17. Stephen Handelman, *Comrade Criminal: Russia's New Mafiya* (New Haven, Conn.: Yale University Press, 1995), 24.

18. Jurors, or lay assessors as they were called, could advise the judge but not overrule him. They were appointed by enterprises—factories, institutes, offices, and, in earlier times, the job was coveted, basically as a way to get off the dreary production line. By mid-1992, however, Russians were refusing to appear for jury duty because they had no confidence their jobs would still be there when they returned, and there were so few jurors that many civil cases were being delayed for months. During the spring of 1992, Moscow was known by many couples as the time when two jurors suddenly became the most important people in their world. Without them they could not get a divorce, according to Judge Irina Nikolayevna Kuprianova, in an interview in June 1992.

Jurors in the new experimental jury trials were well paid—their salary was about half the judge's pay. It was a cost that many areas decided was too high for a Western-style idea that many were against for other reasons as well, Nicholas Arena said in interviews in May and July 1995.

Judges were soon protected by a new law designed to enhance their status and enforce their independence. By 1995, they earned between $170 and $180 a month, which would be negligible except that it included housing, medical care, retirement benefits, and protection. Still, judges could earn far more as lawyers. In 1992, there were twelve thousand judges' positions in Russia, and twelve hundred were vacant. By 1995, Moscow courts were missing almost a third of the judges they needed, according to Chief Judge Korneva.

Still, there were twenty-two thousand lawyers in Russia in 1991, and most reformers said they needed two hundred thousand by the end of the century. Although the 1993 constitution gave the accused the right of counsel, the system had almost no way to keep up. A lawyer assigned to an indigent defendant might end up earning a dollar a day for his effort, after he had turned over the necessary fees to his office, according to Arena.

19. Robert Rand, *Comrade Lawyer: Inside Soviet Justice in an Era of Reform* (Boulder, Colo.: Westview Press, 1991), 141.

20. Elena Bariknovskaya, interview, February 1992.

21. Rand, 2. Also, Eugene Huskey, "The Politics of the Soviet Criminal Process: Expanding the Right to Counsel in Pre-Trial Proceedings," *The American Journal of Comparative Law* XXXIV, no. 1 (Winter 1986): 93–112.

22. Under Russian law either party could appeal the verdict—not only the convicted criminal but the prosecutor who questions the sentence or the acquittal. Nicholas Arena, interview, July 1995.

23. V. Abramkin, *Moskovsky Komsomolets*, September 16, 1992, p. 2.

24. Accusatory bias in the legal trade was not unusual in the Soviet days. As Boris Zolotukhin told me in late 1991, "The court of today is not interested in human rights. There are one judge and two jurors, and they are always purely decorative. The old judges, many of them, are motivated not to support human rights but to support the prosecution. . . . The Soviet court system was a rather perfect product of a totalitarian system. It was formed so that the party apparatus could have complete and unlimited power."

(One telling example of *obvinitelnyi uklon,* or accusatory bias, in the legal trade came a few years earlier when a judge named L. V. Borisenko of Moscow's Timiryazevsky district was hearing a case against a man charged with drunk driving. The judge refused to call a witness for the defense saying, "He will only repeat the story that the defendant made up." Rand, 42.)

12. The Wild East

1. Report from the Lawyers Committee for Human Rights, "Human Rights and Legal Reform in the Russian Federation" (New York: March 1993), p. 19.
2. Stanislav Govorukhin, *The Moscow Times,* May 5, 1994, from *Press Center News* 2, no. 18.
3. The Russian Ministry of Internal Affairs said the rate of murder per 100,000 people went from 15.5 in 1992 to 21 in 1994. Briberies went from 2.2 per 100,000 in 1992 to 3.2 two years later. *The Washington Post,* February 26, 1995, p. A23.
4. Personal interview.
5. Personal interview, not her real name.
6. *Moskovsky Komsomolets,* November 28, 1992.
7. Yuri Belkin, *The Moscow Times,* April 15, 1995, from *Pravda Rosii.*
8. Igor Zakharov, "Swindlers Embezzle a Billion," *The Moscow Times,* February 16, 1993, p. 1.
9. *The Moscow Times,* October 14, 1994, and November 2, 1994.
10. Lee Hockstader, *The Washington Post,* May 15, 1995, p. 1.
11. Lee Hockstader, *The Washington Post,* April 15, 1994, p. 22.
12. Lawyers' Committee for Human Rights report, p. 19.
13. Steven Erlanger, *The New York Times,* May 11, 1992, p. 1.
14. Ibid.
15. Lawyers' Committee for Human Rights report, p. 17.
16. *The Washington Post,* November 13, 1994, p. A36.
17. Adam Tanner, "So Crime Doesn't Pay? Tell That to the GAI," *The Moscow Times,* December 23, 1992, p. 9.
18. *The Moscow Times,* June 13, 1992, p. 7.
19. *The Washington Post,* November 13, 1994, p. A37.
20. *The Washington Post,* February 26, 1995, p. A23. From an unpublished paper, "Thieves Professing the Code," by Joseph Serio and Vyacheslav Razinkin.
21. Stephen Handelman, *The New York Times Magazine,* January 24, 1993, p. 75.
22. Ibid., p. 15.

23. Yuri Shchekochikhin, "Death of a Mystery Man," *The Moscow Times*, April 9, 1994, p. 8.
24. John LeCarré, *The New York Times Book Review*,. February 19, 1995, p. 32.
25. Celestine Bohlen, *The New York Times*, August 15, 1993, p. 1.
26. Fred Hiatt, *The Washington Post*, December 7, 1993.
27. *The Moscow Times*, November 9, 1994, p. 1.
28. Stephen Handelman, *Comrade Criminal: Russia's New Mafiya*, (New Haven, Conn.: Yale University Press, 1995), 312.
29. *The Economist*, April 8, 1995, p. 14.
30. *The Moscow Tribune*, November 6, 1992.
31. Associated Press, October 7, 1992.
32. Interview given to Brooke Gladstone of National Public Radio in the autumn of 1992.
33. Ibid.
34. Dmitry Ukhov, *The Moscow Times*, from *Moskovskiye Novosti*, September 3, 1994, p. 8.
35. Vladimir Gubarev, *The Moscow Times*, October 22, 1994, from RIA Novosti news service.
36. Michael Dobbs and Steve Coll, "The Profits of Chaos," *The Washington Post*, January 31–February 2, 1993. Also, Suzanne Possehl, *The New York Times*, March 17, 1993, p. B3.
37. Celestine Bohlen, *The New York Times*, August 16, 1993, p. 1.
38. *The New York Times*, March 17, 1993, p. B3.
39. *Inside Russia* magazine, Moscow, September 1992.
40. *The Moscow Times*, February 18, 1994, p. 5.
41. *The New York Times*, June 18, 1995, p. 1.
42. Vladimir Buyev, *The Moscow Times*, September 8, 1994, p. 8.
43. *The Moscow Times*, November 4, 1994, p. 1.

Epilogue

1. Anders Aslund, *How Russia Became a Market Economy* (Washington, D.C.: The Brookings Institution, 1995).
2. *The Economist*, April 8, 1995, pp. 3, 6, 10.

Notes on Transliteration

Although there has been considerable effort by several skilled Russian speakers and editors to make the transliteration of the Russian consistent in this document, experts may find some differences in the changes from Russian to English in various names and words. One reason for these differences is that we have tried to use the journalistic transliterations adapted by the Associated Press and Reuters which are done, not for scholars, but for ordinary readers. These frontline adaptations of the Russian language change more frequently, however, and there are some words that can be confusing. For example, in 1991 we used the word Mafia or mafia as the equivalent of the Russian term for gangs of criminals—be they on the streets or in various divisions of the government. As the criminal element adapted, so did the language, and we are now using the term *mafiya* to mean criminal gangs organized or disorganized in Russia.

I have also tried to use the English spellings as given to me by Russians—such as that of former Yeltsin health minister Andrei Vorobiev, whose name has been spelled a number of different ways in print. His card, with Russian on one side and English on the other, spelled it Vorobiev and I have kept it that way. Similarly, Natalia Alexandrova prefers her name spelled with an "i," not a "y," and I have left it her way.

Acknowledgments

This book could not have been written without the cooperation and patience of my family, my friends in Russia, and my colleagues at *The Washington Post*. Slava Zelenin and his wife, Natalia Alexandrova, helped guide me through many interviews and adventures, all with a patience that is still astonishing. Olga Podolskaya was particularly helpful when Russia seemed overwhelmingly mysterious. Lyuba Aratieva, Katya Parkamenko, and Irina Makarova, who worked for *The Washington Post* bureau, all took me behind Russia's daunting exteriors, providing wise counsel and much information about Russian life. Masha Lipman, a learned Muscovite who generously shared her wisdom and counsel with the Americans that she knew, read the manuscript for errors large and small. An editor, translator, interpreter, and friend, she argued me out of arguable theories and scolded me for inconsistencies. What's more, Masha caught mistakes not only in her native Russian but in my native English.

Special thanks go to Svetlana Makurenkova, who constantly reminded me of the loftier side of Russian existence; to Masha and Boris Ryzhak, who welcomed us from the first like family; to Tanya Vedernikova, who brought serenity and a joyous side of Russia to my daughter, Victoria; to Irina Akimushkina, who endured many of my questions about women and family life, and to Fanny Barrientos, who explored Moscow with me in the early days.

My colleagues in Moscow included David Remnick, who provided sage advice and humor at critical moments, and his wife, Esther Fein, who shared some of Moscow's secret places with me. Michael and Lisa Dobbs endured my pestering about how Russia worked, and Margaret Shapiro and Fred Hiatt became close friends as we explored this strange land.

At *The Washington Post*, my thanks go to my editors and friends. Russian expert Robert G. Kaiser, now the paper's managing editor, helped steer me into this project and suggested many of its possibilities. Editors David Ignatius, Michael Getler, and Karen DeYoung provided patience and support during my time in Russia and while I was writing this book in New York City. And finally, during my time at *The Post*, I was lucky enough to work for one of the most inspiring editors in the history of American journalism, Benjamin C. Bradlee.

Experts in various fields generously read and provided advice on the manuscript—Nicholas Arena, the American Bar Association's Moscow consultant, counseled me on trial law; longtime women's advocate and Russian expert Colette Shulman made suggestions on the women's section; Stephen Handelman, author of *Comrade Criminal: Russia's New Mafiya* (Yale University Press, 1995), gave advice on crime; *Moscow Times* ballet critic Margaret Henry made suggestions in the field of ballet; Alex Papachristou, who practiced law in Moscow and continues as a legal consultant, on real estate law; Strobe Talbott, on poet Fyodor Tyutchev; and Dr. John Collee, a British physician who has written extensively on Russian health care, on health and medicine. Historian and longtime Russian expert Susan Heuman allowed me to air ideas and was especially helpful on property and legal issues.

My appreciation also goes to the Harriman Institute at Columbia University in New York City, where I was a visiting scholar in 1993, as well as to the staff of *The Moscow Times*, which has become the Westerners' paper of record in Moscow.

Robert Haupt generously gave me access to his Moscow apartment, introduced me to some of the most interesting Russians I knew, and provided editorial help and humor when both were desperately needed. Lindy Sinclair, a friend who also read the manuscript, shared advice, cheer, food, and recreational novels during our days together in Moscow. My literary agent, David Black, has helped nurture this book through many years and trials.

At Simon & Schuster, editor Alice Mayhew gave expert guidance and friendship, pushing always toward clarity and excellence. Sarah Baker and Elizabeth Stein also greatly helped me with the final manuscript as well as negotiating me through several computer disasters. Thanks also to copy editor Isolde Sauer.

My husband, Peter Pringle, has been a loving nudge throughout the writing of this book. In the name of adventure, he took us to the Soviet Union and, in the process, introduced us to the new Russia, a place and a people who have changed our lives forever.

Those who graciously agreed to spend time correcting me and helping me understand how Russians endured this era contributed greatly to the strengths in this work. The weaknesses, of course, are my own.

Index

abortion, 71, 130, 133, 151, 152, 193, 198, 199–201, 202, 210–11
Academy of Sciences of the U.S.S.R., 32
acupuncture, 138
Afghanistan War, 48, 319, 393*n*
AIDS, 125, 136–37, 156, 182, 187, 189, 196, 202, 203, 217, 225, 231–33, 256, 403*n*
Aizderdzis, Andrei, 373
Aizenshtadt, Yakov, 218–19
Akimushkina, Irina, 68–69
alcoholism, 49, 83, 108, 119, 120–24, 154, 241, 250, 347
Aleksandr Prokofiev Ballet Company, 283
Alesina, Inna L., 199, 201
Aleksandrov, Ivan Grigorievich, 325–27, 328, 329
Aleksy II, Patriarch, 299, 300, 302, 307, 308, 316–17
Alexandrova, Natalia, 22, 24, 28–29
Alex (street merchant), 256
Alexander II, Tsar of Russia, 341
Alexandra, Tsarina, 47, 175
Alliance, 224
Alliance bridal agency, 86–93
All-Union Public Opinion Center, 216–17
Almanac: Women and Russia, The, 70
Amirdzhanov, Sergei, 196–97
analgesics, 135, 140, 199, 200
Ananiashvili, Nina, 262
Anderson, Stacey, 324
Andrei (business student), 249–50

Andrei (masseur), 176
Andropov, Yuri, 273, 278
Angelyuk, Yaroslav, 71
Antabuse, 123
antibiotics, 131–32, 133, 138, 167, 203
antihistamines, 184
antiques, 332–33, 349, 378
anti-Semitism, 301, 302–3, 313–14
Anton (street merchant), 255–56
apartments:
  communal areas of, 30–31, 98, 103
  cooperative, 37
  documents for, 29–30, 40–46
  hoarding of, 38
  for homosexuals, 216, 221
  leases of, 37
  murders committed for, 40, 356–57, 363
  ownership of, 12, 29–30, 36–46, 271
  prerevolutionary, 46
  privatization of, 38–40, 42, 46
  purchase of, 37, 40–46, 392*n*
  renting of, 38, 46, 55
  sale of, 12, 36, 37
  scams on, 362–63
  taxation on, 39, 46
  utility bills for, 39–40
apparatchiki, *see* bureaucrats
Aratieva, Lyuba, 255
Arena, Nicholas, 335, 342, 408*n*
Argumenty i Fakty, 30, 61, 155, 368
Arkhangel'sk, 18, 20, 31

Artanov, Vladislav, 218, 219–21, 228
Article 121, 215
Artsybashev, Mikhail, 194
artsybashevshchina, 194
Asminin, Aleksandr, 334, 335, 343, 346,
    349, 352, 353
Asminin, Aleksei, 333–39, 343, 345, 349,
    350–53, 354
asthma, 112, 119, 181–82
astrologers, 171, 322
atheism, 295, 296, 298
atomic energy, 75, 118, 122
automobiles, 250, 258, 368–69, 377, 387–
    388, 395*n*

babushkas, 56–64
    as beggars, 64, 157
    folk medicine of, 168
    religiosity of, 309, 321
    resourcefulness of, 58, 62, 67, 281
    scolding by, 57–58, 254
    shopping by, 56–64
    survival of, 56–57, 61
Babylon, 41, 42
Baha'is, 294
Balanchine, George, 281
ballet, 260–92
    choreography for, 267
    critical appreciation of, 264, 265
    expatriate stars of, 264, 267, 272
    favoritism in, 264, 272–73, 274, 278–
        279, 283–84
    foreign students of, 277–78, 280
    form in, 263, 274, 276, 279–80, 285–
        286
    funding of, 260, 269–72, 277
    girls in, 274, 279–80, 285–86
    mafiya and, 289–90
    principals in, 260, 263–64, 274
    provincial, 270, 274, 280, 287
    Russian tradition in, 264, 265–67, 272,
        275, 276–77, 281, 284, 288
    salaries in, 269–70, 286, 291–92
    slippers for, 266, 267–68, 276
    Soviet period of, 265, 266–67, 277, 278,
        290
    standards for, 277–78, 286
    teachers of, 282–85, 292
    training for, 261, 262–63, 264, 268–69,
        272–90
"Baltic window," 378–79

banking, banks:
    danger of, 26–27, 251, 373
    foreign, 15, 41–42
    income, 26
    interest rates of, 26
    loans by, 24, 75, 78
    mortgages from, 24
    number of, 386
Baptists, 294, 318–22, 329
Bariknovskaya, Elena, 347
Baryshnikov, Mikhail, 267, 281
Belyayeva, Natasha, 394*n*
Berdyaev, Nikolai, 322
Bespakhotny, Aleksei, 54
Bessmertnova, Natalya, 279, 282
bezdomniye (homeless), 21–22, 34–35, 387
Bibirevo, 103
Bilmes, Linda, 399*n*
birth control pills, 71, 192–93, 201
birth defects, 112, 155–56, 395*n*
birth rate, 111–12, 128, 157, 200
blat (clout), 132–33
Bolotina, Nadezhda Petrovna, 328, 329
Bolsheviks, 19, 47–48, 194–95, 221–22
Bolshoi Theatre, 272–90
    ballet school of, 261, 262–63, 264, 272–
        290
    buildings of, 259, 265, 275–76
    competition of, 275, 286–90
    corps de ballet of, 263, 287
    history of, 275
    touring by, 270
Bonner, Elena, 185
Borisenko, L. V., 409*n*
Botkin Hospital, 297–98
Boy George, 294
bread, 13, 58, 59, 60, 61, 62, 64, 117
breast cancer, 192, 214
breast milk, 112
breathing cure, 181–82
Brezhnev, Leonid:
    culture under, 262, 267, 273
    domestic conditions under, 63, 118, 381
    drinking by, 121
    health care policies of, 136
    religious freedom and, 319
    spiritualist of, 168–69
bronchitis, 112, 167
Bulanova, Tatyana, 183
Buranov, Shamil, 254
Burdenko Institute, 136

bureaucrats:
  bribery of, 25, 37, 76, 132–33, 359–60,
    367–69, 373–76, 381, 386
  entrepreneurs and, 74, 76
  as former communist functionaries, 13,
    18, 23
  for housing, 29–30, 37, 40–46
  salary of, 27
Burnt by the Sun, 106
Burova, Ekaterina, 136–37
Bush, George, 16
Bushuyev, Vladimir Aleksandrovich, 346,
  347
Buteiko, Konstantin, 181–82
Butyrskaya prison, 315, 336–40, 353, 407*n*
Buyanov, Mikhail, 235

cancer, 112, 118, 126, 130, 149, 173, 192,
  214
capitalism:
  as bazaar, 12
  communism vs., 18–19, 21, 61, 81, 181,
    258, 264, 389
  illegal vs. legal, 359, 362, 363–64, 383–
    384
  inhumanity of, 15, 41, 73, 106, 247–48,
    314
  wild, 19, 27, 67, 123
  see also free market
capital punishment, 345, 349, 353, 354
Carter, Jimmy, 319
casinos, gambling, 359–60
Cathedral of Christ the Savior, 298–99
Catherine the Great, Empress of Russia,
  68, 77, 138, 139, 326, 380
Catholic church, 314
cats, 65, 93, 94, 96, 97–101
censorship, 89, 90, 188, 266
Center for Economic Reform, 382
Central House of Literary Writers, 228,
  259
Chapayev, 110–11
Chapayev, Vasily Ivanovich, 110–11
Chapayevsk, 20, 110–18, 119, 124–28,
  396*n*
Chazov, Yevgeni, 148
cheating, 245–46
Chechnya, 38, 342, 380
Chekhov, Anton, 137–38
Chelyabinsk, 12, 110
Chernobyl nuclear plant, 69, 110, 180, 396*n*

Chernomyrdin, Viktor, 37
chifir (narcotic tea), 407*n*
childbirth, 71–72, 140, 152, 154, 201,
  210–11
children:
  abuse of, 154
  AIDS in, 232–33
  camps for, 104, 191, 197–98
  in cults, 323–24
  education of, 20, 96, 105, 114, 237–52
  "gray," 387
  health care for, 110–12, 116, 149, 151–
    156, 167, 404*n*
  importance of, 104, 105–6
  neglect of, 356
  playgrounds for, 30
  punishment of, 123
  toys for, 104, 282, 315, 363
chloracne, 125–26
cholera, 145–46
chornye (blacks), 380
Chumak, Alan, 178–79
Church of Christ of Nativity, 308
Classical Ballet Theatre, 288–89
Club Fauna, 97–101
Collee, John, 179, 181, 396*n*, 399*n*
Committee on Freedom of Conscience,
  317
communism:
  capitalism vs., 18–19, 21, 61, 81, 181,
    258, 264, 389
  collectivism of, 113–14
  ideology of, 242, 248, 266, 267, 277,
    278, 290
  indoctrination in, 242, 248
community activists, 114–15, 127
Compulsory Medical Insurance (CMI),
  399*n*
computers, 14, 251
Comrade Lawyer (Rand), 348
con aratists, 360–65, 383
"Concept of Friendship in Ancient Greece,
  The" (Kon), 223
condoms, 187, 192, 196, 201, 202, 211,
  225, 233
consumers, 67, 362, 388–89
contraception, 71, 187, 189, 192–93, 196,
  198, 199, 200, 201, 202, 211, 225, 233
cosmetics of, 65, 66–79
Cosmopolitan, 186, 210
crime rate, 72, 342, 344, 360, 361, 369–82

culture, 259–92
  commerce vs., 260, 261, 264, 271, 278, 290
  popular, 264, 267, 296
  "purgatory" in, 264–65
  Soviet, 259–60, 262, 265, 267, 273

dachas, 31–35, 36, 37, 55, 111
Danilyan, Viktor Danilov, 109
Davitashvili, Djuna, 168–69
DDT, 108
death rate, 111–12, 128, 136, 149
Debryanskaya, Yevgeniya, 228–30
Declaration of the Rights and Freedoms of the Individual and Citizen, 366
DelPhano, Maria, 322
democracy:
  dissent in, 114–15, 300, 329, 334
  establishment of, 385–89
  middle-class basis of, 24
  opposition to, 243
  religious freedom and, 318
  Russian style of, 14–15
detsky sad (state kindergarten), 96, 237–40
Detsky Sad No. 1179, 237–40
Devi Khristos, Maria, 323
Dezikova, Irina, 286
diabetes, 173, 399n–400n
Diaghilev, Sergei, 221, 281
diky kapitalizm (wild capitalism), 19, 27, 67, 123
Diomin, Yuri, 331–40, 343–54
Diomina, Elena, 332, 333–35, 339, 343, 349–51, 352, 353
dioxin, 112, 114, 116–17, 125–26, 396n
diphtheria, 144, 156, 276
dissidents, 114–15, 300, 329, 334
disulfiram, 123
divorce, 95, 256, 291, 292, 350
Doctor and Patient in Soviet Russia (Field), 147
doctors:
  diagnosis by, 131, 181
  emigration of, 134
  persecution of, 144, 145–46
  political views of, 147
  rotation system for, 131
  salaries of, 133, 134, 146, 151, 152, 158
  smoking by, 119
  specialization by, 131
  training of, 131, 139, 144–49

women, 146, 149, 150, 151–56, 202–6, 304
  zemstvo (government), 144–45
dogs, 98–99
Dolger, Henry, 399n–400n
dollars, U.S., 12, 25–26, 42, 260, 324, 361, 368, 375
Dostoyevsky, Fyodor, 114
DPT vaccine, 156
drug abuse, 241, 250, 256–57, 258
drugs, prescription, 131–32, 133, 135, 138, 140, 143, 156
Dubrovskaya, Silva Abramovna, 348
duma (parliament), 22, 299, 316, 317, 364, 373
Dzerzhinski, Felix, 17

Ecocide in the USSR: Health and Nature Under Siege (Feshbach and Friendly), 110
economy:
  barter, 17, 18
  capital flight in, 15
  competition in, 17–18, 330
  free-market, see free market
  reform of, 11–15, 50, 60–61
education, 237–52
  business, 248–49
  of children, 20, 96, 105, 114, 237–52
  discipline in, 240, 241–42
  examinations in, 245–47, 248
  government support for, 105, 244
  initiative and, 95–96, 240
  jobs vs., 240, 248–49
  parents and, 240–42
  private, 239, 243–45
  public, 105, 237–39, 244, 245
  sex, 190–202, 212–14, 217, 233, 401n
  Soviet, 13, 114, 241–42
  spiritual, 114, 246–47
  standards in, 242, 243–47
Ekaterinburg, 370
elderly, 13, 40, 58, 62–63, 160–61, 299, 363
electricity, 33, 34, 39–40, 49
Elena (con artist victim), 360–62, 383
Elenova, Marina, 141
Elista, 232–33
émigrés, 46, 264, 267, 272
"energized water," 172
Engels, Friedrich, 403n

entrepreneurs:
  bureaucracy for, 74, 76
  competition of, 330
  loans for, 75, 78
  markets created by, 11–12, 14–15, 17,
    25
  production facilities of, 75–77
  resentment of, 68–69, 78, 117
  Russo-American joint ventures of, 73
  taxation of, 74, 382
  wealth of, 161, 359
  women as, 15, 65, 66–79
epidemics, 144, 145–46
Estonia, 16
Estrin, Boris, 196
evangelicals, 201, 294, 316, 326–27, 330,
  406n
"evil eye," 177

face-lifts, 77, 158
factories, 75–77, 112–13, 117–18, 119,
  121, 123, 124–28, 143, 150–51
Falwell, Jerry, 330
families, 62, 63, 83–84, 225–26, 230
farms:
  collective (kolkhozes), 48–50, 54, 126–
    127
  dairy, 49, 50–54
  Molokan, 328–29
  pollution of, 108
  private, 36, 46–47, 392n
  women on, 79–81
fat, 124–25
Felgenhauer, Pavel, 242
feminism, 65, 69–70, 84
Feshbach, Murray, 110, 396n
Field, Mark, 147
Filaret, Metropolitan, 323
Filchenkov, Grigori, 154
First Leningrad Medical Institute, 146
fish, 58–59, 117
Fokine, Isabelle, 283
Fokine, Mikhail, 283
food:
  distribution of, 58
  price of, 59, 60–61, 62, 67, 117, 388
  in prisons, 337, 340, 354
  shopping for, 11, 56–64, 117, 118
  storage of, 108
Forbidden Fruit (Kon), 213–14
Ford, Henry, 151

Foreign Political Association, 70
free market:
  "addiction" of, 78–79, 250
  economic impact of, 11–12, 14–15
  establishment of, 11–12, 14–15, 16, 17,
    21, 25, 61, 363, 385–89
  for medicine, 161–64, 180–81, 184
  opposition to, 247–48
  unregulated, 17, 27, 60–61
Freud, Sigmund, 195, 207, 234, 242, 403n
Friendly, Alfred, Jr., 110
FSB, see KGB
Furtseva, Ekaterina, 273
Fyodorov, Svyatoslav, 150–51, 398n

Gagiet, Richard, 321
Gaidarenko, Natalya, 209
Gaidash, Maria, 72
Galperin, Yakov Grigorievich, 170–74
Gayevsky, Vadim, 276–77, 278, 287, 288,
  289–90
Genghis Khan, 207
Georgia, 16, 38
Gessen, Masha, 223, 225
Giselle, 261, 263–64, 266, 286
Gladkova, Klara, 117–18
glasnost, 16, 70, 83, 129, 147, 156, 195,
  223, 275, 297, 323, 336
Glazshneyder, Andrei, 267, 269, 270, 271,
  273, 274, 291
Going For It: How to Succeed as an
  Entrepreneur (Kiam), 79
Golovkina, Sofya Nikolayevna, 273–89
golubaya krov ("blue blood"), 393n
Golyakhovsky, Vladimir, 152, 297–98
gonorrhea, 202, 203, 204, 206, 232
goods:
  distribution of, 57, 66–67, 73, 74, 77,
    252
  foreign, 16
  hoarding of, 17, 238
  prices of, 17, 59, 60–61, 62, 67, 117,
    270, 318, 388
  shopping for, 11, 17, 25, 56–64, 66–67,
    117, 118, 318, 362, 388–89
Gorbachev, Mikhail:
  agricultural policies of, 47, 50, 51
  attempted coup against, 16, 68, 79
  baptism of, 311
  granddaughter of, 273, 278
  health care policies of, 148

Gorbachev, Mikhail: (*cont.*)
  leadership of, 23
  prison system under, 336–37
  reforms by, 16, 19, 47, 70, 83, 89, 109,
    118, 129, 147, 148, 156, 195, 212,
    223, 267, 275, 297, 323, 336–37
  vodka production limited by, 121
gorchichniki (mustard plasters), 167
gorchitsa (mustard), 167
Goretsky, Aleksandr, 320
Gorky, Maxim, 86
Government Auto Inspection (GAI), 368–
  369
Govorukhin, Stanislav, 358
Graham, Billy, 318–22, 330
grain supplies, 48, 49–50, 64
Gray Is the Color of Hope (Ratushinskaya),
  226
Great White Brotherhood, 323–25
Grebesheva, Inga, 210
Grigori (mobster), 371–72
Grigorovich, Yuri, 262–63, 286, 287, 291
Gritsenko, Anatoly, 179–81
Gromyko, Andrei, 273
Gurevich, Pavel, 293

Hare Krishna sect, 293–94, 317
Haskell, Arnold, 265–66
Haupt, Robert, 53
healers, 165–66, 171, 174–79
health, 107–28
  of children, 110–12, 116, 149, 151–56,
    167, 404*n*
  diet and, 124–25
  exercise and, 107, 108
  hazards to, 107–28
  standards of, 109–10, 148, 156–57,
    396*n*,–399*n*
  of women, 108, 130–32, 140, 181, 183,
    203–5
  see also medicine
health insurance, 133, 160, 161, 164, 399*n*
heart conditions, 112, 119, 126, 160–61,
  394*n*
Helsinki Watch, 338, 407*n*
herbicides, 112, 116
Herzen, Alexander, 358, 367
homeless *(bezdomniye)*, 21–22, 34–35, 387
homosexuals, 187, 192, 195, 202, 215–36
  activists for, 216, 223–26, 230, 234–36
  as "blues," 215, 235

in families, 225–26, 230
  laws on, 215, 216, 217, 219–20, 222, 229
  in marriages, 216, 220, 221
  minors and, 221, 222, 224, 234
  pathology of, 223–24, 225, 227, 235
  as prisoners, 215, 216, 217, 222–23,
    226–27, 230
  publications of, 218, 233–34
  public disapproval of, 216–18, 223–25,
    230–31, 234, 235, 236, 245
  Soviet attitude toward, 215–16, 221–23,
    403*n*
  tolerance of, 215–18, 221, 225–26, 234
  violence against, 218–20, 234
Hospital No. 4 (Moscow), 137–44, 150,
  157–64
hospitals:
  bribery in, 132–33
  children's, 149, 151–52
  conditions in, 130–32
  costs of, 131, 132, 158, 160
  deterioration of, 129–30, 139–40, 150
  equipment for, 137, 141, 142, 160
  patients in, 130, 132, 140–42, 143, 158
  personnel of, 139–40
  private vs. public, 142, 143, 158, 161–64
  see also surgery
housing, 21–55
  agents for, 23–24, 27–29, 39, 40, 41
  bureaucracy for, 29–30, 37, 40–46
  communal, 28, 41, 96–97, 115–16
  construction of, 23, 29
  criminal activities in, 40, 356–57, 362–
    363
  fees for, 24–25, 27, 28, 41, 46
  laws for, 36–39
  market for, 21–28, 36, 39, 41
  middle-class, 27–28
  price of, 24–26
  for privileged, 32, 74–75
  rental of, 31–36, 38, 46, 55
  sale of, 12, 22–29, 36, 37, 38
  title in, 38
  see also apartments
Hubbard, L. Ron, 293, 317–18
hydrochloric apomorphine, 227
hysterectomies, 131, 183

Ignatenko, Albert, 322
Imperial Ballet School, 275
impotence, 207, 210

Independent, The, (of London), 53
individualism, 21–22, 240
infant mortality rate, 109, 111–12, 128, 144
infertility, 210–11
inflation, 13, 25–26, 40, 60–61, 62, 133, 160, 361
intelligentsia, 244, 367
International Academy of Psychoenergetic Sciences, 322
International Conference on Women and the Free Market, 65–66
International Planned Parenthood Federation, 193
Intim sex shop, 211
Intourist Hotel, 86, 87, 257
investors, 14, 26, 29, 363–64, 383, 386
"invisible ones," 56–57
Ioann, Metropolitan, 301, 313
Irina (farmer's wife), 79–81
Itar-Tass, 157
IUDs, 71, 192, 201
Ivanova, Irina Mikhailovna, 260–63, 290, 291
Ivanova, Masha, 261–65, 267–75, 278, 284, 286, 287, 288, 290–92
Ivanova, Tatyana, 70–71
Ivanovna, Nina, 151–56
Ivanovskaya, 308–9
Izmailovo, 308, 318
Izvestia, 74, 128, 241

Jews, 295, 298, 301, 302–3, 313–14, 330
jobs:
    education vs., 240, 248–49
    experience and, 258
    loss of, 18, 66, 70–71, 113, 117, 216
    scams on, 360–62
Johnson, Magic, 182

Kalinin, Mikhail, 293
Kalinin, Roman, 223–25
Kasatkina, Natalia, 288–89
Kashpirovsky, Anatoly, 322–23
Katya and Pavel (apartment hunters), 40–46, 392*n*
Kaurov, Georgy, 122
KGB:
    agents of, 300, 405
    files of, 79

headquarters of, 17
religion suppressed by, 300, 303, 308, 310–11, 329, 330, 405*n*
Russian Orthodox church and, 300, 303, 308, 310–11, 405*n*
surveillance by, 16, 31, 60, 153, 171, 216, 369
Kheta, 153
Khimki, 364
Kholina, Natalia, 247–48
Kholodov, Dmitry, 135, 369
Khrushchev, Nikita, 121, 294
Kiam, Victor, 79
kidney problems, 112, 172–73, 399*n*–400*n*
Kiev, 323, 324–25
Kiev Cybernetics Institute, 325
Kim, Lyudmila, 167–68
kiosks, 249, 253–54, 255, 374–76, 386
Kirov Theatre, 275
Kislinskaya, Larisa, 365
Kistiakowsky, Bogdan Aleksandrovich, 367
Kobakhidze, Amiran, 25–26
Kochetkov, Georgi, 300–301
Kollontai, Aleksandra, 194–96
Kolya (kiosk manager), 375–76
Komarov, Georgi, 181, 396*n*
Komsomol, 147, 306
Komsomolskaya Pravda, 72, 309, 367, 404*n*
Kon, Igor, 195–98, 208, 213–14, 222, 223, 225, 232
Kondakov, Vladimir Vladimirovich, 395*n*
Korneva, Zoya Ivanovna, 335, 345, 347–348, 354–55, 382, 407*n*, 408*n*
Korotkov, Aleksandr, 215
Korshunov, Vyacheslav Fedorovich, 161, 163
Korshunova, Lyubov Anatolyevna, 344, 348–50
kottedzh (cottage), 24, 31
Kovalevsky, L. P., 51
Krasin, Aleksandr, 146–47
Kristina (prostitute), 84–85
Krivonogov, Yuri, 323–24, 325
Kruchin, Vladimir, 111
krupniye khozyaistva (larger-scale farms), 50
Krylova, Zoya, 56
Krymova, Valentina, 93–102
Kuprianova, Irina Nikolayevna, 408*n*
Kuzmenko, Mikhail M., 134–36

Kuznetsk, 299
Kuznetsova, Tatyana, 40
Kvantrishvili, Otari, 365, 370, 371

Lake Karachay, 110
Lally, Kathy, 20, 111, 116, 118, 315
land:
    acquisition of, 50–54
    ownership of, 23, 36, 38–39, 46–47,
        392n
    reform for, 46–49, 51
    see also farms
landlords, 23, 30
Lauder, Estée, 66, 79, 382–83
laws, 358–84
    breaking of, 241, 247, 345–46, 358–84,
        387
    corruption vs., 359–60, 367–69, 375–
        376, 381
    economic, 345
    on homosexuality, 215, 216, 217, 219–
        220, 222, 229
    housing, 36–39
    property, 23, 36–39
    reform of, 366–67
    Russian attitude toward, 19, 36, 358–59,
        365, 366–67, 377–79, 381–84
    Soviet, 358–59, 365–67
    tsarist, 366
Lawyers Committee for Human Rights,
    347
lay assessors, 344, 408n, 409n
LeCarré, John, 371–72
legal system, 331–57
    acquital rate in, 335, 356
    advokaty (lawyers) in, 253, 334–35, 339,
        344, 346–48, 350–51, 354, 407n,
        408n
    bail in, 340
    constitution on, 334, 354–55
    criminal code in, 354–55
    defense in, 334–35, 342–43, 344, 346–
        348, 350–51, 354–55
    as "inquisitorial system," 342
    judiciary in, 209, 334–35, 343–44, 345,
        347–48, 352–57, 407n, 408n, 409n
    jury trials in, 335, 341, 342, 344, 348,
        354–55, 356, 408n, 409n
    press coverage of, 343
    presumption of innocence in, 334–35,
        356–57

prokuratura (prosecutor's office) in, 209,
        335–36, 339, 341–42, 343, 344, 348–
        350, 351–52, 353
    reform of, 340–42, 346–48, 354–57,
        407n–8n
    sentencing in, 334, 349, 352–53, 354
    Soviet, 335–36, 340–41, 344–45, 346,
        409n
    tsarist, 341, 407n
    U.S. system vs., 335, 347–48
    victims represented in, 347–48
    see also laws; prisoners
Lena (lab technician), 76–77
Lenin, V. I.:
    agricultural policies of, 48
    culture as viewed by, 267
    economic policies of, 48–49
    ideas of, 147, 242, 318, 365
    medical reforms of, 144, 145, 146
    portraits of, 157, 279
    religion attacked by, 295, 296–98
    sexuality as viewed by, 195, 196,
        222
    Soviet state created by, 16
    tomb of, 294
    vodka production opposed by, 121
lesbians, 69, 187, 192, 215, 217, 225,
    226–230, 234
Leskov, Sergei, 322
Lidiya (mail-order bride), 92–93
life expectancy, 109, 112
Lipchenko, Yuri, 112–13, 116
Lipman, Masha, 246–47
literature, 107, 228, 259, 260, 278
Literaturnaya Gazeta, 288–89
Lithuania, 16, 79–80, 378–79
Little Vera, 192
Loseva, Olga, 202–6
Lukyanova, Valentina, 125, 126, 150
lung cancer, 118
Lyuba (patient), 203–4

Macey, David A. J., 50
MacKenzie, Jean, 208
mafiya (mafia), 369–77
    ballet and, 289–90
    bankers killed by, 26, 373
    businesses controlled by, 370, 372–76,
        386
    code of, 370
    as conspiracy, 369–70

mafiya (mafia) (*cont.*)
  as criminals, 356, 359, 365, 370, 371, 380–81
  "gentrification" of, 386
  junior, 250
  kiosks controlled by, 253–54, 255, 374–376
  leaders of, 337, 346, 370, 371–72
  local gangs of, 191, 218–19, 254, 376–377
  markets controlled by, 13, 18, 42
  for medicine, 179–81
  in prisons, 337, 370
  protection by, 19, 25, 76, 254, 370–74, 376–77
mail-order brides, 85–97
Makeyev, A. M., 183–84
Makurenkova, Svetlana, 261, 263
Maltsev, Nikolai Sergeyevich, 127
Maltsev, Sergei, 122
Maria (women's group), 70
Marlboro cigarettes, 120, 375
marriage, 43, 85–97, 216, 220, 221, 256, 271, 295, 308
marriage brokers, 85–97
Martemyanov, Valentin, 373
Marx, Karl, 147, 196, 242, 318, 403*n*
Masalsky, Pavel, 222
massage, 138, 173, 183–84
masturbation, 212–13
matrioshka (nesting dolls), 241, 252, 253
Mavrodi, Elena, 364–65
Mavrodi, Sergei, 364
Maxim (street merchant), 202, 237, 256–257
Maximova, 280, 282
Medical Engineering Center for the Restoration of Segmentary Innervation of Organs and Tissues, 179
medicine, 129–84
  alternative, 107, 165–85, 400*n*
  corruption in, 132–33
  doctor-patient relationship in, 125, 126, 130, 132, 140, 147, 149, 159–60, 182
  free market for, 161–64, 180–81, 184
  government support for, 134, 140, 142, 143, 144–45, 161, 168, 399*n*
  herbal, 107, 166–68, 171
  mafiya for, 179–81
  for poor, 138, 140–42
  quack, 165–66, 168–69, 178–82
  Soviet, 129–30, 134–35, 144–49, 151–152, 165, 174, 175
  supplies for, 134, 135, 136–37, 138
  tsarist, 138, 144–46
  see also doctors; hospitals
Meditsina i Reproduktsiya (MIR) clinic, 211–13
Meditsinskaya Gazeta, 181, 396*n*
Melekhova, Lyudmila, 259
Melikyan, Anatoly, 65
Men, Aleksandr, 330, 405*n*
META cooperative, 162
Mikhalkov, Nikita, 106
military, 14, 246, 249–50, 369, 378
milk, 59, 62, 108, 112
Mironov, Andrei, 119
Mishina, Elena, 125–26
Mityaeva, Valentina V., 149
MMM, 364
Mocha River, 110
Molokans, 325–30
Molokhov, Vladimir, 289
monuments, 378–79
Moon, Sun Myung, 317, 318
Mormons, 294
Morozova, Elizaveta, 60, 61, 64
Moscow:
  Arbat in, 252–58
  black market in, 12, 214, 359
  churches of, 297–99
  City Council of, 383
  city courts of, 343–45, 353, 408*n*
  city metro of, 269, 386
  foreigners in, 15–16
  housing in, *see* housing
  Lenin Hills section of, 393*n*
  metro of, 269, 386
  modern architecture in, 293–94
  pollution in, 13
  post-Soviet conditions in, 11–17, 386–389
  street names in, 98
Moscow Academic and Choreographic School (MAKHU), 261, 262–63, 264, 272–90
Moscow Conservatory, 259
Moscow Institute of Biophysics, 67
Moscow Law Institute, 252–53
Moscow News, 128

Moscow Research Institute of Eye Micro-
surgery, 150–51, 398n
Moscow State Conservatory, 306
Moscow State University, 13, 317–18,
347
Moscow Times, The, 208
Moscow Women's Bank, 71
Mosfilm industry, 259
Moskovsky Komsomolets (MK), 135, 234,
353–54, 369
Mukhamedov, Irek, 274, 281, 287
murders, 26, 40, 72, 331–40, 343–54,
356–57, 360, 363, 373
music, 226–27, 260, 306, 307, 327, 328
Muzurov, Igor, 113–14, 116, 117, 123, 125,
127

Nakhodka bridal agency, 89, 92
Nasedkina, Lidiya Mikhailovna, 99, 100
Natasha (patient), 204–5
Natasha (street merchant), 254–55
Natasha cooperative, 162–64
necrophilia, 224
nedvizhimost (immovable property), 22
needles, hypodermic, 142, 156, 160, 232–
233, 368
Neparade, Nikolai, 231, 234
New Economic Policy (NEP), 48–49
Nicholas II, Tsar of Russia, 99
Nikolina Gora, 32
1984 (Orwell), 401n
nishchiye (beggars), 22, 64
Notes of a Soviet Doctor (Pondoev), 129
Novaya Zemlya test site, 118, 122
Novikov, Aleksandr Pavlovich, 343–44,
352
Novodevichy Convent, 13–14
Novosibirsk Ballet Theatre, 282
Nureyev, Rudolf, 267
nurses, 139, 140, 142–43, 199–200

obshchezhitiya (dormitories), 22
obvinitelnyi uklon (accusatory bias), 409n
oko gosudarevo ("eye of the tsar"), 341
Oksinoyd, Oleg, 393n
Oktyabrskaya metro stop, 261
Old Believers, 295
Oleg (computer consultant), 14
Oleinikov, Nikolai, 185, 211–13, 226, 230–
231, 232, 234, 235–36
Olga face cream, 65, 66–79, 330

Onania, or the Heinous Sin of Self-Pollution
and All Its Frightful Consequences,
212–13
Orwell, George, 401n
outhouses, 33, 115–16

pacemakers, 160–61, 399n
Pakhra River, 29
palatka, see kiosks
Pamyat, 234, 302–3
Papachristou, Alex, 36, 37, 38
Pappe family, 39
Pashin, Sergei, 341, 348
Pavel (street merchant), 252–54
pederasty, 221, 222, 224, 234
pensioners, 13, 58, 62–63, 299
Pentecostals, 329–30, 406n
Peredelkino, 32
perestroika, 16, 83, 212
Perm, 287
Perov, Vasily, 297
pesticides, 116
Peter the Great, 144, 221, 341
Petrovsky Theatre, 275
Philip Morris, 120, 375
Pioneer Corps, 104, 306
Pirogov Society, 145
Playboy, 186, 214
Plisetskaya, Maya, 266–67, 280–81, 282
Poddubny, Fyodor, 15
Podolskaya, Olga, 15, 57, 59–61, 63–64
Pokrovsky, Valentin Pavlovich, 165, 168,
217, 232
police, 219–20, 234, 253, 255, 258, 333,
338, 341, 362, 363, 368, 372–77,
395n
poliklinika (polyclinics), 137, 214, 232
pollution, 107–18
air, 107, 109, 118, 184
industrial, 108, 110–18, 124–28
water, 107–8, 116–17, 118
pomoika (garbage dump), 273
Pondoev, G. S., 129
Popova, Valentina Stepanova, 238–40
pornography, 90, 165, 186–87, 188, 191,
202, 207, 213, 217, 234, 267, 278
Pravda, 83
pravovoye gosudarstvo (rule of law), 366
pregnancies, 84, 189, 190, 192, 193, 199,
200, 202, 210, 233, 256, 393n
Pringle, Peter, 15, 53, 131, 187–88, 367–68

Pringle, Victoria, 15, 55, 130, 167, 265, 267, 303
prisoners:
  conditions for, 336–40, 346–47, 353–354, 407n
  confessions of, 336, 340, 407n
  food for, 337, 340, 354
  guilt of, 334–35, 345–46, 352–53, 356–357
  homosexuals as, 215, 216, 217, 222–23, 226–27, 230
  interrogation of, 336, 337–38, 339, 340
  in *mafiya*, 337, 370
  relatives of, 339–40, 353
  religious conversion of, 315
  rights of, 334–35, 354
  torture of, 337
private property, 22, 23, 29–30, 35–39, 46–47, 392n
privatizatsiya (privatization), 18, 29, 38–40, 42, 46, 382–83
profilaktory (health center), 119, 124–125
Progress kilkhoz, 49–50
Prokofiev, Aleksandr A., 282–85
propiska (residence pass), 42–45, 90, 349
prostitutes, 84–85, 87, 92, 165, 186, 217, 241
Protocols of the Elders of Zion, 301, 302
psychics, 322–23
psychotronics, 171–72
publishing, 107, 259, 260
Pugachev uprising (1773), 328
pukh (fluffy seed), 387
pyramid schemes, 363–64

Rabochaya Tribuna, 241
Rabotnitsa, 106
radial keratotomy (RK), 150–51, 398n
radiation poisoning, 122, 180, 395n–96n
Raduga (Rainbow), 225–26, 230, 235
Ralo, Viktor, 49
Rand, Robert, 348
rape, 65, 72, 207, 209, 221, 234, 345
Rasputin, Grigory, 174–75
Ratushinskaya, Irina, 226, 407n
religion, 293–330
  cults in, 322–30
  equality of, 313
  freedom of, 293–95, 316–17, 318, 319, 323, 326

Soviet repression of, 295, 296–98, 300, 303, 308, 309–11, 325, 329, 330, 405n
  teaching of, 114, 246–47
  Western, 201, 294, 316–22, 330, 406n
  youth's attitude toward, 311–12, 315, 317, 318, 323–25, 329
  see also Russian Orthodox church
remont (renovate), 94, 218–19, 291–92, 317–18
Repentance, 299
Reznichenko, Katya, 247
RISK, 218
R. J. Reynolds, 120
rodilnye doma (birthing houses), 152
Rodion (computer student), 251
Rollband, Ron, 92–93
Romashko, Olga Olegovna, 65, 66–79, 330, 393n
Romashko, Tatyana, 77, 78, 79
"roosters," 215, 222, 223
Rozanov, Vasily, 194
ruble:
  exchange rate for, 12, 25–26, 42, 260, 324, 361, 368, 375
  inflation of, 13, 25–26, 40, 60–61, 62, 133, 160, 361
Russia:
  change in, 15, 61, 78, 210, 246, 380, 386–89
  chaotic conditions in, 12–13, 18–19, 240–41, 260, 371, 377–82
  communal society in, 28, 41, 47, 48, 96–97, 113–16, 240, 247
  constitution of, 36, 334, 354–55, 366
  dictatorship in, 106, 381, 385
  duma (parliament) of, 22, 299, 316, 317, 364, 373
  émigrés from, 46, 264, 267, 272
  ethnic groups in, 157, 380
  freedom in, 11, 16–17, 20, 62, 109, 113, 388–89
  GDP of, 386
  GNP of, 134
  as "Mother Russia," 81, 378
  poor vs. rich in, 25, 115, 116, 117, 151, 243, 297, 314, 388
  population of, 43, 157
  rural areas of, 46–47
  territorial conflicts of, 38–39, 342, 380
  tsarist period of, 12, 111–12, 138, 144–146, 326, 341, 366, 407n

Russia: (*cont.*)
  urban areas of, 43, 46
  U.S. compared with, 23, 27, 108, 109,
    124, 185
  Western ambivalence about, 13–15,
    379–81
  see also Moscow
Russian Academy of Sciences, 157
Russian Association of Family Planning,
  193
Russian Association of University Women,
  69
Russian Orthodox church, 296–317
  baptism in, 308, 309, 311, 321
  confession in, 311, 315
  fasting in, 311
  hierarchy of, 300–301, 312–13
  homosexuality opposed by, 221
  KGB and, 300, 303, 308, 310–11, 405n
  membership of, 73, 295–96, 297, 311–
    312, 321, 322
  priests of, 297, 299–301, 306–16
  property of, 296
  reform of, 300, 312–13
  religious freedom and, 316–17, 318,
    323, 326
  rituals of, 300–301, 307, 308, 309, 311–
    312, 315
  Soviet persecution of, 296–98, 309–11
  status quo supported by, 297
  taxation of, 308
Russians:
  cold endured by, 139, 141, 252
  foreigners as viewed by, 14, 15–16, 19–
    20, 28, 31, 34–35, 80–81, 118, 125,
    131, 174, 177, 178, 189–90, 230–31,
    343, 380
  in middle class, 24, 27–28
  moral superiority of, 73
  resentment felt by, 36, 51, 68–69, 78,
    117
  survival of, 14, 18, 19, 56–57, 61, 81,
    102, 383–84
Russian State Humanities University, 248–
  251
Russian Statistics Agency, 128
Ryakhovsky, Sergei, 329–30
Ryakhovsky, Vasily, 329
Rybny Pereulok, 323–24
Ryzhak, Boris, 55
Ryzhak, Masha, 55, 239, 313

St. Seraphim of Sarov, 301–2
St. Sofiol Cathedral, 324
Sasha (patient), 140
Savina, Tamara Fyodorovna, 355–57
Savitskaya, Regina, 207
scientific research:
  on atomic bomb, 75
  funding of, 68–69, 320–21, 393n
  privileged status of, 32, 74–75, 393n
scientology, 293, 317–18
Semenov, Nikolai Nikolayevich, 32
Semyonova, Marina, 266
Serdyukovsky, Georgi, 154
Sereisky, Mark, 222
serfs, 36, 47, 48, 113, 144, 145, 221, 341
Sergeyev, Aleksandr, 124
sewage, 107–8
sex, 185–214
  anonymous, 191
  diseases transmitted by, 191, 192, 198,
    202–6
  education on, 190–202, 212–14, 217,
    233, 401n
  enjoyment of, 119, 209–10, 393n, 402n
  experience in, 104, 191, 197–98, 200,
    201–2, 255–56
  folklore on, 194, 401n
  free, 194–95, 196
  group, 191
  parental guidance on, 191, 199, 201,
    205–6
  premarital, 104, 191, 197–98, 200, 201–
    202
  problems of, 206, 207, 210–14
  prudishness about, 89, 185–90, 207,
    401n
  romance and, 208–9
  safe, 198, 233, 403n
  Soviet attitude toward, 185–89, 191,
    193–97, 198, 208, 401n
  stress and, 210, 212
  techniques for, 185, 192
Sex in the Soviet Union (Stern), 227
sexopathologists, 212, 226
sexual harassment, 72, 84, 209
sexual transcendentalism, 194
Shadrova, Lidiya, 60–61, 64
Shiluta, 378–79
Shkunova, Tamara, 88–92, 93, 95
shop clerks, 66–67
Shumilina, Alla, 112, 395n

Siberia, 41, 47, 49, 153
Siemens, 160
Sigov, Yuri, 30, 61–62
Silent Scream, The, 201
Simchovich, Zakhar Mikhailovich, 129, 136
Simonov Monastery, 298
600 Seconds, 224
Skorochkin, Sergei, 373
smoking, 12, 17, 108, 109, 119–20, 125, 268, 375, 386, 394*n*
Sobor, 196
sobstvennost (ownership), 37
sodomy, 221
Solzhenitsyn, Alexander, 223
Sorokin, Aleksandr, 125, 126–27
Southwestern Conference Center, 65–66
Soviet-Anglo-American School (SAAS), 244
Soviet National Planning Committee (GOSPLAN), 148
Soviet of Medical Collegia, 145
Soviet Union:
    ballet in, 265, 266–67, 277, 278, 290
    collapse of, 15–16, 18–19, 37, 79, 275, 277, 344–45
    constitution of, 346
    culture in, 259–60, 262, 265, 267, 273
    education in, 13, 114, 241–42
    founding of, 16, 19
    homosexuals in, 215–16, 221–23, 403*n*
    industrialism in, 108, 110–18, 123
    laws of, 358–59, 365–67
    legal system of, 335–36, 340–41, 344–345, 346, 409*n*
    medicine in, 129–30, 134–35, 144–49, 151–52, 165, 174, 175
    propaganda of, 82, 110–11, 129, 200, 317, 359
    religious persecution in, 295, 296–98, 300, 303, 308, 309–11, 325, 329, 330, 405*n*
    sexual attitudes in, 185–89, 191, 193–197, 198, 208, 401*n*
    stagnation in, 19, 160, 196, 262, 309
    women's role in, 56, 64, 70
spekulyanty (speculators), *see* entrepreneurs
Spitsina, Raisa Ignatievna, 327, 328–29
Squad 6, 223
squatters, 39, 41

Sretensky Monastery Cathedral, 301
Stalin, Joseph:
    agricultural policies of, 48–49
    economic policies of, 48–49
    education policies of, 13
    homosexuality opposed by, 215, 222
    legal system under, 336, 340, 346
    propaganda by, 110–11
    puritanism of, 195, 196
    religion attacked by, 298
    repression by, 16, 41, 48–49, 63, 82, 150, 183, 266, 381
    show trials of, 346
    vodka production supported by, 121
Stanislavsky and Nemirovich Danchenko Musical Theatre, 260, 263, 267, 268, 269–70, 280, 286, 291–92
Stankevich, Sergei, 317
Starova, Ira, 320–21
State Committee for Sanitary-Epidemiological Surveillance, 232
State Institute of Theatrical Arts, 282
Stekolnikov, Oleg, 50–54
Stekolnikova, Valya, 51, 53
Stepanov, Aleksandr, 138–44, 150, 157–61
Stepanov, Aleksei, 174
Stern, Mikhail, 227
stock market, 14, 29
Stolypin, Pyotr Arkadievich, 47–48, 50
sugar, 63, 117, 238
superstition, 144, 176–77
surgery:
    brain, 136
    cosmetic, 77, 158, 161, 162–64
    eye, 150–51, 398*n*
    hand, 161–62
    supplies for, 137
Susskind, Elizabeth, 383
Svetlana cooperative, 162–64
Svyadoshch, A. M., 227, 403*n*
Swan Lake, 259, 264, 265, 266, 278, 281
Sychkova, Aleksandra, 175
Sydney Morning Herald, 53
synagogues, 298
syphilis, 198, 202, 203, 204, 206, 232

Tambov, 328
tapochki (bedroom slippers), 55, 238
Tarasova, Tamara, 99
TASS, 224–25
taxation, 39, 46, 74, 308, 382

Tchaikovsky, Pyotr Ilich, 221
teachers, 104, 190–98, 242, 243, 245–47
Tea Drinking in Mytishchi (Perov), 297
telephones, 23, 42–45
television, 199–201, 296, 360
Telyukov, Aleksandr V., 148–49
Ternyak, Viktor, 370
Tikhonov, Nikolai, 336–37, 338, 339
Tolstoy, Leo, 306
torpedo (antialcohol medicine), 123–24
Torpedo Soccer Stadium and the Palace of
    Culture, 298
toxic waste, 110–18, 128
toys, 104, 282, 315, 363
Traditional People's Medical Center, 169–
    174
traffic deaths, 108, 109
Transtrade Trading House, 22–29
travel:
    by airplane, 16, 108
    by rail, 31–32, 79–81, 319, 379
    restricted, 16
    unrestricted, 19–20
travka (marijuana), 256
Triangle, 216
Trud, 148, 156
TSUM department store, 74
Tsvetayeva, Marina, 217
tuberculosis, 112, 340, 346–47, 353–54,
    396n
250 Folk Medicine Prescriptions (Kim),
    167
typhoid, 107, 144
Tyutchev, Fyodor, 11

Ukraine, 16, 323
Umnov, Vladimir, 156
unemployment, 18, 66, 70–71, 113, 117,
    216
Unification church, 317, 318
Union of Orthodox Brotherhoods, 302
urine therapy, 172–73, 399n–400n

vaccinations, 156, 232–33
Vakhrusheva, Anya, 208
valuta (dollars), *see* dollar
Vandenberg, Martina, 72, 73
Vasiliev, Vladimir, 282, 287, 291
Vasyukhin, Piotr Mikhailovich, 114–15
VDNKha park, 182–83, 184
Vechernyaya Moskva, 178

Vedernikov, Otets Nikolai Anatolievich,
    303, 304, 305–16, 381, 407n
Vedernikova, Nina, 305, 309, 310, 313,
    314, 316
Vedernikova, Tanya, 303, 304, 311, 313,
    381
venereal diseases, 191, 192, 198, 202–6
Verbitsky, Igor, 173
Vezhninz, N., 354
Vilnius, 80
Vlasova, Tanya, 89–90
vodka, 11, 55, 108, 119, 120–24, 146, 166,
    188, 189, 367–68, 395n–96n
Voika, Lyudmila, 333
Vorobiev, Andrei I., 134, 155, 168, 232,
    399n
vory (thieves), 241, 359, 360–65, 370
vouchers, government, 11, 29, 361–62,
    383

"Ward Number Six" (Chekhov), 137–38
Washington Post, The, 11, 15, 255, 277
Wieben, Sarah, 245–46, 247
women:
    abuse of, 72, 207–9, 349–50
    Americanization of, 90–91
    arranged marriages for, 85–97
    as doctors, 146, 149, 150, 151–56, 202–
        206, 304
    domestic role of, 71, 83–84, 105–6, 146,
        287, 393n
    as entrepreneurs, 15, 65, 66–79
    equality of, 65, 70, 83, 84, 90, 106
    on farms, 79–81
    femininity of, 70, 83, 84, 90–91
    foreign citizenship sought by, 87, 102
    health of, 108, 130–32, 140, 181, 183,
        203–5
    as judges, 209, 335, 345, 347–48, 354–
        357
    men vs., 81–84
    as mothers, 18, 71–72, 83, 95, 255
    movement for, 65, 69–70, 71, 73, 74, 84
    old (babushkas), 56–64
    power of, 81–82, 101
    propaganda against, 69–70
    as prosecutors, 209, 344, 348–50
    as prostitutes, 84–85, 87, 92, 165, 186,
        217, 241
    rights of, 56, 64–65, 73, 84
    salaries of, 70, 77, 394n

in Soviet Union, 56, 64, 70
as survivors, 56–57, 61, 81, 102
unemployed, 66, 70–71
in workforce, 18, 64–65, 66, 70, 71, 72, 77, 83–84, 159, 394*n*
Women's Alliance, 70
Women's Day, 121
"worker-peasant position," 185
World Health Organization, 232
World War I, 82, 111, 121
World War II, 82, 153, 161, 306

X-rated films, 186–87, 191, 202

Yablokov, Aleksei, 109
Yablonevka prison, 223
Yakunin, Gleb, 300, 405*n*
Yalta, 108
Yamburg, Evgeny, 242
Yanvariov, Valerii, 71
Yelokhovsky Cathedral, 301–2
Yeltsin, Boris:
    agricultural policies of, 47, 51, 54
    astrologers for, 171
    attempted coup against, 79, 299
    Chechnyan conflict and, 380
    decrees of, 15, 36
    drinking by, 121
    educational policies of, 244
    health of, 385
    as president, 15, 16, 22, 36, 79, 114, 279, 299, 341, 342, 368
    reforms by, 127, 355
    rule of law supported by, 366, 369, 405*n*
Yeremin, Aleksandr, 172
Yereyev, Yuri, 216
Yermolino farm, 54
Yershova, Yelena, 56

Yesekhin, Sergei Nikolaevich, 162
You Can Go Mad, 199–201
youths:
    drug abuse by, 241, 250, 256–57, 258
    entertainment of, 119
    military duty for, 246, 249–50
    parents and, 240–42, 258
    religion and, 311–12, 315, 317, 318, 323–25, 329
    sex education for, 190–202
    sexual experience of, 104, 191, 197–98, 200, 201–2, 255–56
    in street trade, 12, 249, 251–58
    suicide rate for, 241, 404*n*
Yurna, Irina, 70

Zagorsk (Sergiev Posad), 43
Zaitsev, Slava, 355
Zastavenko, Andrei, 23–25, 27
Zassoursky, Yasen, 318
Zasulich, Vera, 407*n*
zek (prisoner), 407*n*
    see also prisoners
Zelenin, Slava, 94, 96, 97–98, 170, 172–173, 238, 276
Zelenogradskaya, 31–36
Zemshchina, 302
Zhdanov, Andrei, 266
Zhenskaya Seksopatologiya (Svyadoshch), 227, 403*n*
Zhurakovskaya, Natasha, 90
znakharstvo (spiritual healing), 175
Zolina, Lena, 101
Zolotova, N. V., 282
Zolotukhin, Boris, 409*n*
Zubkova, Tatyana, 190–94
Zvonarev, Andrei, 103
Zvonareva, Natasha, 102–6